CONSTRUCTION VERSUS CHOICE IN COGNITIVE MEASUREMENT:
Issues in Constructed Response, Performance Testing, and Portfolio Assessment

CONSTRUCTION VERSUS CHOICE IN COGNITIVE MEASUREMENT:
Issues in Constructed Response, Performance Testing, and Portfolio Assessment

Edited by
Randy Elliot Bennett
William C. Ward
Educational Testing Service

IEA LAWRENCE ERLBAUM ASSOCIATES, PUBLISHERS
1993   Hillsdale, New Jersey   Hove and London

Lawrence Erlbaum Associates, Inc., Publishers
365 Broadway
Hillsdale, New Jersey 07642

Library of Congress Cataloging-in-Publication Data

Construction versus choice in cognitive measurement: issues in
  constructed response, performance testing, and portfolio assessment
  / edited by Randy Elliot Bennett, William C. Ward.
      p. cm.
    Includes bibliographical references and indexes.
    ISBN 0-8058-0964-3
    1. Educational tests and measurements – United States – Evaluation –
  Congresses. 2. Examinations – United States – Design and
  construction – Congresses. 3. Examinations – United States – Validity –
  Congresses. I. Bennett, Randy Elliot, 1952–   II. Ward,
  William C., 1939–
  LB3050.5.C66   1993
  371.2'6'013 – dc20   92-31274
                                                            CIP

Books published by Lawrence Erlbaum Associates are printed on acid-free
paper, and their bindings are chosen for strength and durability.

Printed in the United States of America
10 9 8 7 6 5 4 3 2 1

For
Norman Frederiksen
in recognition of more than 40 years of contributions
to what are today's innovative methods of assessment.

CONTENTS

PREFACE

The multiple-choice question is the mainstay of standardized testing programs in the United States. The format has achieved this position because it permits inexpensive and apparently objective scoring; because such questions can be answered quickly, allowing broad content coverage within a testing session; and because a sophisticated statistical technology has evolved to support the analysis and interpretation of test results.

The reliance on multiple-choice questions, however, is increasingly criticized. Many have argued that tests and, in particular, test formats significantly influence education. Multiple-choice assessments are said to encourage the teaching and learning of isolated facts and rote procedures at the expense of conceptual understanding and the development of problem-solving skills. It is believed that, for education reform to occur, the methods used to measure attainment must themselves be transformed.

To address the limitations of the multiple-choice format, many educators and psychologists have advocated increased use of constructed-response tasks. These tasks may be as simple as producing a numerical answer to an arithmetic question or as extensive as producing the numerous drafts that culminate in a finely honed essay or planning and conducting a series of scientific experiments. Proponents argue that constructed-response assessments, especially those that require extended problem solving and yield complex productions, measure different skills and promote deeper learning than do multiple-choice measures.

The use of such tasks, however, raises several critical concerns. If the answer to a question is an extended problem solution, fewer questions can be asked in a fixed testing period, reducing the breadth of content coverage possible. The less constrained the task and the solution, the greater is the possibility that lack of standardization in test administration, and lack of objective criteria for evaluation, may adversely affect the comparability of results across persons and situations. These conditions can threaten the representativeness of the test results as a sample of the individual's capabilities, and thus the validity and fairness of the test.

Growing attention to these and related issues has suggested that it would be timely to bring together persons who could contribute to an understanding of problems and possibilities associated with the various assessment formats. First a conference, and then this volume, resulted.

The conference, sponsored by Educational Testing Service, was held in Princeton, New Jersey, in November, 1990. Speakers and attendees represented a variety of viewpoints in educational research and policymaking. The presentations and discussions were informative, provocative, and notably lacking in polemics.

This book, comprising nine chapters based on the major conference presentations plus five newly invited contributions, maintains the same tone. Rhetoric calling for the abolition of traditional testing methods as useless or pernicious, or on the other hand for dismissal of new approaches as impractical, is lacking. Rather, the authors seek to provide perspectives and build frameworks that will contribute to future research agendas and policy debates. Such statements are not as dramatic as the more extreme positions that can be found in the press and even in journals, but they are, we believe, more useful.

The first chapter in the volume, that by Bennett, explores the meanings of "constructed response" within a framework provided by validity theory. The next three chapters discuss the construct validity of constructed-response measures. Traub provides a psychometric perspective; Snow, a psychological one; and Messick, an integration of the two.

The chapters in the following group address measurement techniques that will contribute to the incorporation of constructed-response measures into standardized assessments. Mislevy outlines the use of "inference networks" in evaluating the contributions of different types of test questions. Tatsuoka discusses a model for item design to elucidate the skills and knowledge underlying observable performance. Dorans and Schmitt describe techniques for the analysis of group differences in item performance. Finally, Braswell and Kupin examine alternative formats for assessment in mathematics.

With the next group of chapters, attention turns to discussions of more extended assessment exercises. Camp explores the role of portfolios in the assessment of writing. Wolf draws from both the classroom and the reflections of practicing artists to view assessments as occasions of learning. Gitomer provides a framework for the design of performance assessments in educational measurement.

Dwyer's chapter uses the assessment of teachers to illustrate issues in the reform of educational measurement. It provides a transition to the final chapters in the volume, which focus on questions of policy—Hartle and Battaglia from the perspective of the federal government's role, and Robinson exploring the conflicting perspectives that influence decision making.

Important contrasts between the more narrowly psychometric and the social policy perspectives are evident in these chapters. The two viewpoints are in agreement in seeking means of improving educational measurement; but they differ, at least implicitly, in what is meant by "better." From the policy perspective, better measurement involves tasks that have verisimilitude, that send the right messages to those concerned with education, and that help directly and indirectly to cause increased success for learners. From the psychometric, "better" means more reliable or more representative of cognitive skills underlying an achievement, or perhaps less susceptible to contamination by construct-irrelevant group differences. From the first of these perspectives, it may make good sense to trade some accuracy of measurement for a superior assessment; from the second, that proposition is almost a contradiction in terms.

Another aspect of the contrast in perspectives is that there are significant differences in how the line is drawn to distinguish variations in measurement methodology that make a difference. From the psychometric viewpoint, the step from a multiple-choice mathematics question to one in which the examinee is asked to grid an answer in is a very big change; one has to be concerned about the consequences of this change for test reliability, difficulty, speededness, and so on. Any variation in format and scoring rubric must be studied exhaustively. From the policy perspective, however, such changes are minor. The constructed-response measures that are seen as likely to make a difference are far more complex and real-worldly, barely on the same continuum with the array of measures likely to be considered by those for whom such factors are the critical concerns.

Just as evident as the differences should be the indication of ways in which these contrasts might be bridged. Several of the chapters offer organizing schemes and discussions that can begin the synthesis needed to promote the objective shared by all of the contributors: achieving more socially useful, socially responsible measurement. We hope this volume contributes, if only in a small way, to that important goal.

Randy Elliot Bennett
William C. Ward

1

ON THE MEANINGS
OF CONSTRUCTED RESPONSE

Randy Elliot Bennett
Educational Testing Service

Large-scale testing programs are devoting more attention to constructed-response items than at any time in recent memory. Witness the planned introduction of open-ended mathematical items in the revised Scholastic Aptitude Test (SAT) (Braswell & Kupin, this volume), the inclusion of the observation of teachers' classroom performances in Praxis: Beginning Assessments for Professional Teachers™, the use of hands-on tasks in state testing programs (Baron, 1991; DeWitt, 1991), and the President's call to go beyond multiple choice in the proposed American Achievement Tests (Bush, 1991). Discussion of the motivations, implications, and results of this increased use presupposes an understanding of what *constructed response* means. This chapter explores the term, with attention to its descriptive, applied, evaluative, and consequential meanings.

CONSTRUCTED RESPONSE
AS A SUPERORDINATE CLASSIFICATION

Even a cursory review of the literature makes clear that *constructed response* implies a broad range of tasks from relatively minor variations of multiple choice to extended projects and complex performances. For example, as a measure of science achievement the term includes such tasks as inserting the missing word in a sentence about the scientific method, writing an essay describing an experiment, or actually conducting an investigation. A general definition that reflects this diversity is that a constructed response is any question requiring the examinee to generate an answer rather than select from a small set of options. Although it may capture the essence of constructed response, this definition is too broad to guide discussion of research very effectively. As a consequence, several investigators have attempted to impose greater structure by developing provisional organizational schemes. Among these are schemes by Bennett, Ward, Rock, and LaHart (1990), and by Snow (this volume).

Generally similar to the Snow (this volume) framework, the Bennett et al. (1990) organization reflects a hypothetical gradation in the constraint exerted on the nature and extent of the response (but not necessarily on the complexity of the problem-solving underlying it) (see Table 1.1). *Multiple choice* and *presentation* represent opposite ends of the continuum, with the latter permitting a much wider range of response possibilities. Note, however, that a high degree of constraint does not preclude construction (nor does it eliminate complex problem solving), which may be required by many multiple-choice tasks (Snow, this volume). Also, consider that the effects of format on responding may extend to conative, motivational, volitional, and affective domains (Snow, this volume).

These schemes permit constructed response to be linked with such common associated terms as *performance, authentic*, and *portfolio* assessment. The linkages are necessarily loose because these terms also have multiple meanings. Baron (1991) regards performance assessment as a constructed response in which students are actively engaged in solving a realistic problem that demands more than simply recalling memorized knowledge. The problem may be relatively limited (requiring 5 or so minutes) or it may be "enriched," extending over many days and encompassing a broad, sustained, loosely structured project dealing with the central ideas in a discipline. Baron's notion of performance assessment would appear to include the lower portions of the Bennett et al. (1990) and Snow (this volume) organizations (e.g., *construction* or *presentation* in the former scheme).

Authentic assessment appears to be a subset of performance assessment akin to Baron's (1991) notion of enriched performance tasks.[1] Among other things, "authentic" tasks are intended to replicate the challenges and standards of performance that typically face members of a professional discipline (Wiggins, 1989a). These tasks are administered repeatedly, tend to be highly contextualized, often require collaboration, presuppose an audience (e.g., a panel of judges), and facilitate learning. The evaluation of responses requires human judgment, emphasizes both process and product, and uses multifaceted

---

[1]We enclose the term *authentic* in quotes to indicate that proponents' rhetorical claims to goodness should not be accepted without further examination. As quoted in Reynolds (1982), concerning a related problem, "In God We Trust: All Others Must Have Data."

TABLE 1.1
A Scheme for Categorizing Item Types

---

0. *Multiple choice:* Items in this class require the examinee to choose an answer from a small set of response options.

> *Example.* Choose the word which, when inserted in the sentence, best fits the meaning of the sentence as a whole.
>
> Unable to focus on specific points, he could talk only about _____; indeed, his entire lecture was built around vague ideas.
>
> (A) personalities
> (B) statistics
> (C) vulgarities
> (D) particulars
> (E) abstractions

---

1. *Selection/identification:* This category is characterized by choosing one or more responses from a stimulus array. In contrast to multiple choice, the number of possible choices is typically large enough to limit drastically the chances of guessing the correct answer. In addition, in its ideal form, the response to this item type is probably mentally constructed and not simply recognized. Examples include keylists, cloze elide (i.e., deleting extraneous text from a paragraph), and, via touch screen, tracing orally presented directions on a computer generated map.

> *Example.* Delete the unnecessary or redundant words from the following paragraph:
>
> Andy Razaf is not a quickly recognizable name that is familiar to most people. Yet Razaf wrote the lyrics to at least 500 or more songs, including the words to the popular "Ain't Misbehavin'," "Honeysuckle Rose," and "Stompin' at the Savoy" as well. The American-born son of an upper class African nobleman, he still continues to be overshadowed by his composer–collaborators who worked with him, Fats Waller and Eubie Blake.

---

2. *Reordering/rearrangement:* Here, too, responses are chosen from a stimulus array. However, the task in this case is to place items in a correct sequence or alternative correct sequence. Examples include constructing anagrams, ordering a list of sentences to make them reflect a logical sequence, categorizing elements in a list, arranging a series of mathematical expressions to form a correct proof, arranging a series of pictures in sequence, and putting together a puzzle.

> *Example.* Rearrange the following group of words into a complete and meaningful sentence. Capitalize the first word and end with a period. No other marks of punctuation should be needed.
>
> a and be both can comedy enlightening entertaining good

---

3. *Substitution/correction:* This item type requires the examinee to replace (as opposed to reorder or rearrange) what is presented with a correct alternative. Examples include correcting misspellings, correcting grammatical errors, substituting more appropriate words in a sentence, replacing several sentences with a single one that combines the meanings of each, correcting faulty computer programs, and substituting operators to create a true mathematical expression.

> *Example.* Combine the two sentences below into one grammatically correct sentence that conveys the same information as the original pair.
>
> 1. Stephen King is the author of numerous horror novels.
> 2. Many fans of Stephen King assume that he is as crazy as some of his characters.

(Continued)

3

TABLE 1.1
(Continued)

---

4. *Completion:* In this item type, the task is to respond correctly to an incomplete stimulus. Cloze, sentence completion, mathematical problems requiring a single numerical response, progressive matrices, and items that require adding a data point to a graph when given appropriate numerical data are examples.

> *Example.* Fill the blank in the following sentence with *one* word that makes the sentence grammatically and logically complete.
>
> Melodramas, _____ present stark contrasts between good and evil, are popular forms of entertainment because they offer audiences a world where there is moral certainty.

---

5. *Construction:* Whereas the *Completion* type requires that a stimulus be completed, here construction of a total unit is required. Examples are drawing a complete graph from given data, listing a country's exports, stating why condensation forms on windows, writing a geometric proof, producing an architectural drawing, and writing a computer program or essay.

> *Example.* Describe some event or phenomenon in the natural world, (e.g., earthquakes, thunderstorms, rainbows) that has always interested you and that you would like to know more about. What in particular would you like to know about this subject, and why? (You will have ½ hour in which to write this essay.)

---

6. *Presentation:* This item type requires a physical presentation or performance delivered under real or simulated conditions in which the object of assessment is in some substantial part the manner of performance and not simply its result. Examples include repairing part of an automobile engine, playing an instrument, diagnosing a patient's illness, teaching a demonstration lesson, conducting a science experiment, giving a theatrical audition.

> *Example.* Perform two contrasting solo pieces not to exceed two minutes each. Timing begins with an introduction in which you announce the audition in the following manner: "My name is (given name). My first piece is from (title of play) by (author). I play the part of (character). My second piece is from (title of play) by (author). I play the part of (character)." Props are limited to one stool, two chairs, and one table. To allow you to show your versatility, it is to your advantage to have the greatest possible contrast between your pieces. You will be judged on your ability to demonstrate control of material; flexibility of voice, movement, and expression; and vocal and physical articulation.

Note. From *Toward a framework for constructed-response items* (RR-90-7) by R. E. Bennett, W. C. Ward, D. A. Rock, and C. LaHart, 1990, Princeton, NJ: Educational Testing Service. Copyright 1990 by Educational Testing Service. Adapted by permission.

scoring systems that disaggregate the components of complex performance (Wiggins, 1989a, 1989b). This conception is at least partially reflected in the Bennett et al. (1990) *presentation* category and in Snow's (this volume) *long essay/demonstration*. Finally, *portfolio* assessment (Camp, this volume; Wolf, this volume) can be seen as the collection over time of a selected class of constructed responses, in particular, those task categories associated most closely with performance and "authentic" assessment.[2]

---

[2]Other conceptions of these terms are possible. For example, it is not uncommon in the education literature to use "performance" assessment to indicate non-multiple-choice tasks in general. The Office of Technology Assessment (OTA) employs the term this way, with *constructed response*

Although these organizational schemes emphasize a single dimension along which item formats vary, other test design facets clearly need to be considered, including assessment purpose and content domain (Snow, this volume). This consideration is necessary because a response format may take on a new psychological meaning when crossed with a given facet. For example, in the National Assessment of Educational Progress, constructed-response tasks are omitted far more often than multiple-choice questions, suggesting that motivation may be a larger component of what the former response type measures when the testing purpose emphasizes institutional accountability and ignores individual results (D. Rock, personal communication, December 9, 1991).

That format might psychologically influence responding raises questions of validity, of what specifically is being measured when constructed-response formats are used (Snow, this volume). However, as links with such terms as *performance* and *"authentic" assessment* suggest, constructed response has broader connotations. For many proponents the main implication is the putative influence on school curricula and on teachers and students (e.g., J. R. Frederiksen & Collins, 1989; N. Frederiksen, 1984). Strong value implications—related to enabling students and to school reform—also attend.

VIEWING CONSTRUCTED RESPONSE THROUGH A UNIFIED CONCEPTION OF VALIDITY

Constructed response, then, has important meanings beyond traditional psychometrics. That they are beyond psychometrics is not to say they are incidental to it. On the contrary, accounting for these meanings is essential, not only because they are driving large testing programs to incorporate response formats other than multiple choice, but because these meanings must be part of any comprehensive rationale for educational assessment.

A formulation that encompasses the range of meanings connoted by constructed response is Messick's (1989, 1992) validity framework (see Table 1.2). This multifaceted conception integrates construct validity, relevance and utility, value implications, and social consequences as underlying justification for test interpretation and use. Thus, the meaning of constructed response in any instantiation—from a sentence-correction keylist to a writing portfolio—can be viewed through each of these facets.

Several comments about Messick's framework may help in understanding its application to constructed response. First, the framework distinguishes test interpretation and use because the underlying bases for the activities

a subcategory denoting paper-and-pencil "performance" tasks (Congress of the United States, 1992). The point we wish to stress, however, is not so much how these terms should be defined as that some meaningful organization of task types is necessary to guide research and communication.

TABLE 1.2
Facets of Validity

	Test Interpretation	Test Use
Evidential Basis	Construct validity	Construct validity Relevance/utility
Consequential Basis	Construct validity Value implications	Construct validity Relevance/utility Value implications Social consequences

Note. From "Validity of Test Interpretation and Use" by Samuel Messick. Reprinted with permission of Macmillan Publishing Company from *Encyclopedia of Educational Research* (6th ed., Vol. 4), Marvin C. Alkin, Editor in Chief. Copyright © 1992 by American Educational Research Association.

are not identical. Interpretation derives meaning from both construct validity evidence and an appraisal of value implications. Use requires additional foundation, including evidence of relevance/utility in a particular applied setting and an examination of potential social consequences. The same interpretation (e.g., of scores as indicators of quantitative ability) may have varied uses (e.g., college admissions vs. course placement), each of which necessitates somewhat different evidential and consequential support. Second, two sources of justification, appraisals of evidence and consequence, are distinguished. The former refers to construct validity and relevance/utility, whereas the latter adds an examination of value implications and social consequences. Third, *test* is used in its generic sense to mean any *mode of assessment*. Finally, the framework subsumes an abundance of issues related to the meaning of constructed response, the more salient of which we now discuss.

Constructed Response as Construct Validity

Skill Differences. *Construct validity* is "an integration of any evidence [including theoretical rationales] that bears on the interpretation or meaning of the test scores" (Messick, 1989, p. 17). A key claim in the constructed-response/multiple-choice debate is that format affects the meaning of test scores by restricting the nature of the content and processes that can be measured (N. Frederiksen, 1984). Even minor format differences, such as those between multiple-choice and completion items, are asserted to change the nature of the construct assessed from, for example, test-taking skills to content knowledge, recognition to recall, or factual knowledge to higher order thinking skills (e.g., Guthrie, 1984). More substantial construct differences have been claimed as tasks diverge from multiple choice (e.g., N. Frederiksen, 1984; Wiggins, 1989a, 1989b).

As Messick (1989) suggested, these arguments can be evaluated on both theoretical and empirical grounds. From a theoretical perspective, testing critics—as well as some respected psychometricians—claim the underlying rationale for conventional tests is seriously outmoded (Masters & Mislevy, 1991; Mislevy, in press; Resnick & Resnick, 1990; Shepard, 1991a, 1991b). Among other things, they argued that the multiple-choice format (a) presumes complex skills can be decomposed and isolated from their applied contexts (Resnick & Resnick, 1990); (b) encourages posing a limited range of well-structured, algorithmic problems (Gitomer, this volume); and (c) has engendered a scoring scheme based on a view of learning in which skills and knowledge are incrementally added (Masters & Mislevy, 1991). These characterizations conflict with current cognitive theory, which depicts "real-world" problem solving as calling upon skills that are highly integrated and tied to conditions of application (Glaser, 1988, 1991), and real-world problems as frequently *ill*-structured (N. Frederiksen, 1984). Learning is conceptualized as a constructive process in which new knowledge is not simply added but is integrated into existing structures or causes those structures to be reconfigured. These learning conceptions form much of the theoretical basis for "authentic" assessment (Gitomer, this volume; Wiggins, 1989a; Wolf, this volume).

That conventional tests are totally out of step with cognitive theory is not universally accepted, especially as regards ability tests. For example, Bejar, Embretson, and Mayer (1987) argued that the Scholastic Aptitude Test (SAT) is "cognitively sound" because its items tap dimensions that are considered important by cognitive psychologists. This assertion is based on the fact that substantial research has been conducted on test-like tasks (particularly verbal analogies), with the finding that such tasks call upon an aggregation of problem-solving skills (e.g., translation, representation, planning, execution, monitoring). The authors described how cognitive theory might play a more explicit role in test construction by guiding the development of multiple-choice items that tap *specific* processes, though they believe that such items are more appropriate for diagnosing processing components than for ranking examinees.

There is also disagreement about the theoretical role of context in learning and assessment. Conventional multiple-choice tests present many items with minimal, but varied, contexts intended in the aggregate to measure an ability (e.g., verbal reasoning) evinced across multiple learning situations. Research on the domain-specific nature of expertise has helped to shift interest in cognitive psychology from general abilities to "situated" cognition (Brown, Collins, & Duguid, 1989). Perkins and Salomon (1989), however, proposed a balance between general and context-specific views, arguing that general and specialized knowledge work together. Whereas general skills in the absence of a rich domain-specific knowledge base are ineffectual, a domain-specific knowledge base without general skills may only function effectively with formulaic problems. Thus, from a theoretical perspective, conventional multiple-choice tests—which are often built to measure a single underlying dimension—might be viewed as contributing information on the more general, cross-contextual components of cognitive skill.

Despite the strong assertions by cognitive theorists, the empirical research has afforded only equivocal evidence that constructed-response tasks necessarily measure skills fundamentally different from the ones tapped by multiple-choice questions. Numerous investigations have been conducted using constructed-response formats with content from many domains. Several reviews of this literature have been made. Hogan (1981) concluded that the formats measured the same abilities. Traub and MacRury (1990), considering more recent studies, determined that somewhat different characteristics were being tested but that the nature of those differences was not evident. In an even more recent examination, Traub (this volume) concentrated on the few studies that attempted to explain the observed differences and concluded that the evidence was too spotty to support a firm conclusion. The studies did appear, however, to support the importance of domain as a mediating variable, with format effects found less frequently for reading comprehension and quantitative content than for writing and word knowledge.

Several reasons might account for the failure to detect consistent evidence of construct differences. One reason is that the tasks most likely to show such differences (e.g., presentation tasks) have not been widely studied. N. Frederiksen (1984, 1990) noted that many investigators compose their constructed-response items to be direct counterparts of existing multiple-choice questions. If the multiple-choice format is, in fact, best suited to problems that tend to tap lower order skills, transforming these problems to constructed response may make little difference in what is measured. Consequently, it would seem desirable to begin with constructed-response problems designed to measure complex skills and transform *them* into multiple-choice items. N. Frederiksen's work with ill-structured problems, as represented by the Formulating-Hypotheses (F-H) item type, followed this logic, detecting evidence that the F-H format measured a construct different from multiple choice and that this construct was more related to ideational fluency (an ability to generate ideas), and to documented accomplishments (N. Frederiksen & Ward, 1978; Ward, N. Frederiksen, & Carlson, 1980).

A second reason for not regularly detecting construct differences (even when more complex items have been used) is overreliance on correlational and covariance-structure methods. Analysis of cognitive processes has been largely ignored.[3] This oversight is potentially significant as different item

---

[3]However, see van den Bergh (1990); Ward, Dupree, and Carlson (1987); and Ward et al. (1980) for psychometric investigations that have employed cognitive markers to explain differences between item formats.

formats may produce highly correlated scores even when distinct processes are involved (e.g., one process might cause another or both might be caused by a third variable, such as having been learned contiguously). Although such highly correlated scores might be treated equivalently for some purposes, they are not measures of the same attribute.

Finally, differences might not have been more widely detected because most studies used scoring schemes designed to capture the same proficiency dimensions that multiple-choice contrasts tapped. This design strategy successfully identified whether different formats *could* measure the same dimension but said little about what new information constructed responses might add. Consequently, there may be cases where scoring the same items according to different response characteristics (e.g., insightfulness, efficiency) produces attributes distinct from multiple choice.

Reliability.   Whereas it may be true that fundamental differences will more likely be found for formats that significantly diverge from multiple choice (e.g., *construction* and *presentation*), these tasks by their very nature will produce less reliable scores. Lower reliability will make the measurement of new constructs relatively inaccurate, limiting the ability to generalize performance beyond the administered tasks and the specific raters grading them. Underlying this lower reliability is the larger constellation of skills that these tasks appear to assess.

In many instances, performance on such tasks is summarized as a single index. Establishing scoring rubrics, training judges, and monitoring the scoring process are all intended to help judges grade on a common scale. For some item formats and some domains, these efforts are only moderately successful. For example, in a large-scale study of writing assessment (Breland, Camp, Jones, Morris, & Rock, 1987), the average rater reliabilities for a single essay holistically scored by a single rater on a 6-point scale ranged from .52 to .65, values generally consistent with studies previously reviewed by Breland (1983).

Not only do *construction* and *presentation* tasks appear to require multiple skills, but the *particular* constellations seem to vary considerably across tasks. Success is dependent, in part, on context-bound skills, as well as on knowledge of the context itself. For example, both topic and writing genre (e.g., narrative, persuasive, expository) determine what essay tasks measure (Breland et al., 1987; Quellmalz, Capell, & Chou, 1982); that is, individuals who write well on one topic or for one purpose often do not do so for another. The extent of variation can be seen in the average *score* reliabilities for a single essay scored by a single reader (which account for variation across both tasks and raters). In Breland et al.'s (1987) analysis, these values ranged from .36 to .46, again generally consistent with previous estimates (Breland, 1983), and considerably lower than the values for variation over raters alone.

Thus, although such tasks engender a "rich" response, that richness may be so narrowly situated as to limit generalizability severely.

Task and rater generalizability can be increased by aggregating the ratings from multiple essays, multiple independent scorings, or both, thereby washing out context and rater dependencies (though at theoretical cost to those who value the role of context and its meaning for construct interpretation). The amount of time required to administer and score such items puts limits on the breadth of content and rater sampling that can occur in applied settings, to which we now turn.

Constructed Response as Relevance/Utility (and Construct Validity)

Construct validity evidence provides general testimony to the meaning of scores (Messick, 1989). In applied settings, this evidence plays an important role because it explains why a test works. This knowledge is useful in avoiding circumstances in which the test is unlikely to be effective, explaining variation in its effectiveness across settings, and evaluating the appropriateness of test use when adverse consequences result.

Construct evidence, however, needs to be complemented by specific proof of relevance to the applied purpose and utility in the applied setting. Relevance derives from, among other things, professional judgments of the test in relation to the applied domain, evidence that the test reflects processes or constructs judged important in domain performance, or significant test correlations with criterion measures of domain performance. Utility refers to usefulness for a specific decision-making purpose and has generally been based on test–criterion correlations in relation to the benefits and costs of testing in a given context. Although central to building a case for test *use*, evidence of relevance and utility also contribute to understanding the meaning of scores and, therefore, feed back to construct validity.

Postsecondary Admissions. College and graduate admissions tests are intended to help institutions select qualified applicants. In this context, the major determinant of relevance has been test correlations with criterion measures of subsequent performance, usually grade point average (GPA), but also scholarship, leadership, accomplishment, and graduation (e.g., Willingham, 1985). From the institutional point of view, predictive validity is a sensible standard: The institution wants to choose students with the greatest chances of succeeding; success is indicated by various observable criteria; being able to predict these criteria informs whom to select.

One means of evaluating the relevance of constructed response in this setting is to examine its *incremental* predictive validity over multiple-choice examinations. Bridgeman (1991) studied the incremental validity of a short, holistically scored, expository essay for predicting freshman grade point average in large examinee samples drawn from multiple institutions. He found that the essay added essentially nothing after high school average, SAT score, and the score from a multiple-choice writing test had been taken into account. In a similar multi-institutional study, Bridgeman and Lewis (1991) examined the predictive validity of a multiple-choice test section versus a two- to three-question essay section for four Advanced Placement tests: American History, European History, Biology, and English Language and Composition. Zero-order correlations showed the multiple-choice sections to correlate as highly or more highly with freshman GPA than the essay sections; further, in each case a composite score based on a weighted sum of the essay and multiple-choice tests was no better, for practical purposes, than the multiple-choice score alone. Finally, Willingham (1985), also using a sample from several institutions, examined the relation of achievement and other personal qualities to measures of college scholarship, leadership, accomplishment, and faculty nominations. The predictor most similar to a constructed-response task was an unstandardized personal statement scored for both content and writing quality. Beyond SAT and high school rank, this measure significantly contributed to predicting only one of the four criteria, scholarship. Adding the personal statement along with three other measures (one of which was statistically significant and had a regression weight equivalent to the personal statement), increased the relation between actual and predicted criterion scores from .57 to .61.

Utility in the admissions context is typically viewed narrowly as a comparison of the predictive validities and operational costs of one versus another method. The costs of adding a single essay to a large-scale admissions testing program are substantial, about three to five times the cost of a 150- to 200-question multiple-choice test (P. Engel, personal communication, June 10, 1991). Given the existing data, a standardized essay would appear to have little utility by this definition. A personal statement would also seem to have only slight predictive benefit but, in contrast with the standardized essay, much lower costs and consequently somewhat greater utility.

College Placement. Colleges use placement tests to route entering students to different steps in a course sequence (e.g., developmental, introductory, advanced), as well as to award credit for college-level courses taken in secondary school. In this setting, incremental predictive validity also is a common indicator of relevance but the criterion is individual course performance instead of GPA. Here, the increments are generally somewhat higher than in admissions, perhaps because, vis-à-vis multiple choice, the requirements of constructed response overlap more with the skills emphasized in specific courses than with the more general abilities reflected in grade point average. In Breland et al.'s (1987) large-scale study, multiple-choice and essay tests were used to predict writing performance as indicated by other assessments, instructors' judgments of writing skill, and freshman English composition course grades. Multiple correlations for two multiple-choice tests (the Test of Standard Written English and the English Composition Test) and a single essay scored once ranged from .57 to .62, depending on the essay genre and topic. The incremental validity of the essay ranged from .03 to .07, remarkably consistent with results from previous studies reviewed by Breland (1983). When the essay was scored three times, the multiple correlations ranged from .59 to .65 and the increments ran from .05 to .09.[4]

Little work on the utility of item formats has been done in the placement setting. Wainer and Thissen (1992) gave an indirect indication in illustrating two utility measures designed for situations where test–criterion correlations are not readily available and where different formats measure the same construct. The measures are ReliaMin, reliability as a function of testing time, and ReliaBuck, reliability as a function of scoring costs. These authors report that the multiple-choice section of the Advanced Placement (AP) Chemistry examination, which requires 75 minutes of testing time and $.01 per examinee to score, has a reliability of .91. To achieve the same reliability, the examination's constructed-response section would need to be 185 minutes and would cost $30 per examinee to score. According to Wainer and Thissen, these figures are representative of AP exams in the sciences and mathematics. For AP Music: Listening and Literature, a .91 reliability would require 26 hours of testing time and $100 in scoring cost! Because Wainer and Thissen's costs consider only scoring, they present a somewhat extreme view; differences in the *overall* costs of multiple-choice versus essay tests are less dramatic because the latter are cheaper to develop (P. Engel, personal communication, June 10, 1991). However, the basic point is well taken: For equal levels of reliability, a conventional multiple-choice test will generally cost far less overall than an essay assessment.

Accountability. A third context for educational testing is assessing the status of an education system and its components. Here, prediction is less relevant, for the objective is to summarize past performance rather than project future accomplishment. Reliability also becomes less critical when only group scores are reported (e.g., as in the National Assessment of Educational Progress) because the reliability of the mean is generally higher than that for individual scores. More significant is the test's congruence with the curriculum. For tests intended to assess the status of an education system, it is

---

[4]Breland et al. (1987) also examined the incremental validity of the multiple-choice tests over the essay. Here, the largest increments (.10 to .16) were over one essay scored by a single reader. As the essay score became more reliable through multiple readings, the multiple-choice exam contributed less, though the choice exam's addition was still notable (e.g., .05 to .10 over an essay scored three times).

consonance with the ultimate objectives of domain coverage—rather than agreement with any specific curriculum—that is of interest. Most standardized school accountability tests attempt to capture these ultimate objectives by reflecting the generality of extant curricula in a subject matter domain, as defined through reviews of curricula and commonly used textbooks, and the judgments of experts (Messick, 1989). In practice, this generality does not necessarily represent an organized, current conceptualization of what students must know and be able to do in a discipline, but what schools are teaching.

As individuals become more mobile, society more dynamic, and the world's economies more intertwined, the need for coherence and currency increases: A generality taken across many sets of locally determined objectives produces a diffuse patchwork of curricular priorities that goes against building the core competencies needed by individuals and society. In response to this need, President Bush (1991) called for national standards in five core subjects, and professional communities are reconceptualizing their subject matter domains (e.g., see *Curriculum and Evaluation Standards for School Mathematics*, Working Groups for the Commission on Standards for School Mathematics of the National Council of Teachers of Mathematics, 1989).

The implications of these attempts for accountability tests, as well as for local curricula, are profound. The National Council of Teachers of Mathematics (NCTM) *Standards* denotes a significant shift in the underlying principles of mathematics instruction, emphasizing the development of mathematical "power."

> This term denotes an individual's abilities to explore, conjecture, and reason logically, as well as the ability to use a variety of mathematical methods effectively to solve nonroutine problems. This notion is based on the recognition of mathematics as more than a collection of concepts and skills to be mastered; it includes methods of investigating and reasoning, means of communication, and notions of context. In addition, for each individual, mathematical power involves the development of personal self-confidence. (Working Groups for the Commission on Standards for School Mathematics of the National Council of Teachers of Mathematics, 1989, p. 5)

Not surprisingly, the *Standards* also denotes a shift in what constitutes relevance in assessment: "In an instructional environment that demands a deeper understanding of mathematics, testing instruments that call for only the identification of single correct responses no longer suffice. Instead, our instruments must reflect the scope and intent of our instructional program to have students solve problems, reason, and communicate" (p. 192). Thus, mathematical achievement according to the *Standards* cannot be comprehensively measured by the conventional multiple-choice test alone, making format a central concern: ". . . areas that might require particular formats for assessment include communication (which may involve talking, listening, or writing), reasoning (which might involve justifying or explaining responses), problem solving (which might involve recording processes as well as results), and estimation" (p. 194).

As might be imagined, the costs of operating a testing program aligned with such a domain conception are substantial. To increase utility, several state assessment programs are attempting to make accountability testing simultaneously serve instructional purposes (e.g., see Baron, 1991).

Instruction.   Assessment can be used to guide instruction or to deliver it. With respect to guidance, it is difficult to ascertain from conventional multiple-choice items how well students perform tasks requiring the integration of many skills or where in the problem-solving process they are encountering difficulty. As noted, some value might be had by writing multiple-choice items to tap important problem-solving components (Bejar, Embretson, & Mayer, 1987). Changing multiple-choice items to *completion* formats requiring generation of a response or to *construction* tasks involving the specification of the solution process also might aid diagnosis (Bennett, in press; Bennett, Sebrechts, & Yamamoto, 1991; Birenbaum & Tatsuoka, 1987). To guide instruction most effectively, however, assessment will need to track closely changes in curricula presaged by new domain conceptions like the NCTM *Standards*. If that document is any guidepost, instructional assessment will have to rely more heavily on the kinds of *construction* and *presentation* tasks that appear to reflect the complex understandings educators wish to impart (Working Groups for the Commission on Standards for School Mathematics of the National Council of Teachers of Mathematics, 1989).

Domain relevance is also central to using assessment for delivering instruction. As illustrated in the ARTS Propel portfolio model (Camp, this volume; Wolf, this volume), assessment tasks are generally extended projects similar to the problems faced by practitioners of a given discipline. The tasks are intended to generate an ongoing record of learner progress but, more importantly, to help students internalize standards of excellence, encourage them to reflect on their work, and make them knowledgeable critics and beneficiaries of criticism (Gitomer, this volume).

The costs of creating programs like ARTS Propel are high: Teachers must develop a deep understanding of the domain, come to agreement on performance standards, and learn to apply those standards uniformly in evaluating student productions. These costs are balanced by substantial expected instructional, assessment, and staff development returns, arguably making utility more competitive with conventional approaches that strictly demarcate testing and instruction.

Constructed Response as Value Implications (and Construct Validity)

Values influence the development of theories, the definition of constructs, and the interpretation of test scores. These influences can become destructive biases when undetected. Consequently, values need to be made explicit if their implications are to be properly accounted for in the interpretation of assessment results.

Messick (1989) stated that value connotations in score interpretation stem from the evaluative overtones of construct labels, the value connotations of the broader theories in which constructs are embedded, and the value implications of still broader ideologies about the nature of humankind, society, and science. Although evaluative overtones are evident in the language of some segments of the constructed-response movement (e.g., Wiggins' [1989a] use of "true" test), it is not so much the labels but the broader theories and ideologies that pose the starkest contrast with traditional assessment perspectives. This contrast is best illustrated with respect to "authentic" assessment. Value conflicts are evident in the conception of assessment, in its tasks, and in their administration and scoring.

Conception. First, "authentic" assessment is conceptualized as a mechanism for directly facilitating student growth (Wiggins, 1989a; Wolf, this volume)—even when the test is intended to serve other potentially competing ends (e.g., statewide accountability). For example, Wiggins stated: "Tests should be central experiences in learning. The problems of administration, scoring, and between-school comparisons should come only after an authentic test has been devised—a reversal of the current practice of test design" (p. 705). Second, assessment is seen as a means of achieving educational reform by driving instruction toward valued educational goals (Wiggins, 1989a). In contrast, traditional approaches have tended to emphasize institutional purposes (e.g., accountability, admissions, certification). Through the principle of content validity (i.e., developing a test to match accepted instructional goals), they also have attempted to follow instruction rather than lead it.

Tasks. The tasks of "authentic" assessment are, among other things, contextualized, ill-structured, and often collaborative. Problems are contextualized to engage students with varied backgrounds and interests, and to give practice applying skills in realistic situations (Wiggins, 1989b). Problem contexts illustrated in the NCTM *Standards* (Working Groups for the Commission on Standards for School Mathematics of the National Council of Teachers of Mathematics, 1989) include baseball, basketball, motorcycle racing, construction, and grocery shopping. These contexts are almost surely differentially appealing to population subgroups—boys and girls in the mentioned cases—but differential appeal is, in part, what drives engagement. In contrast, traditional assessment programs have never been very concerned about engagement, possibly because their "high stakes" purposes provided enough motivation. Additionally, contexts that might be differentially appealing to population subgroups are assiduously avoided because of their potential for causing test bias.

Besides context, "authentic" assessment values problems that are "ill-structured" (Wiggins, 1989a). Such problems are different from well-structured ones more in degree than in kind (Simon, 1978). Ill-structured problems (a) have more complex and less definite criteria for knowing when a solution is reached; (b) do not include in the instructions all the information needed to solve the problem and offer only a vague sense as to what information is relevant; and (c) have no simple "legal move generator" for finding all of the alternative possibilities at each solution step.

Ill-structured problems are valued because tasks encountered in practical settings are often loosely formulated. Wiggins (1989a) stated: "Authentic challenges—be they essays, original research, or artistic performances—are inherently ambiguous and open ended" (p. 706). N. Frederiksen (1984) argued more generally: "Most of the problems one faces in real life are ill-structured, as are all the really important social, political, and scientific problems in the world today" (p. 199). In ill-structured situations, the problem-solving process takes on obvious importance. In the extreme case where there is *no* unambiguously correct answer, a solution is lent meaning only by the reasoning or justification that underlies it.

In contrast, conventional assessment approaches have valued *well*-structured problems that emphasize an end-product. This preference is consistent with a conception of both disciplinary and real world knowledge that believes there frequently *are* "right"—or at least "best"—answers. For example, when balancing a checkbook or consulting a doctor for a differential diagnosis, one wants an *un*ambiguously correct result. This preference is also consistent with the institutional purposes these testing programs serve. For these purposes, evaluation of the end-product provides sufficient information for decision making; analyzing the response process is unnecessary.

A third, sometime characteristic of performance tasks is their collaborative nature (Baron, 1991; Wiggins, 1989a). Collaboration is valued because it is commonly required in employment settings, is obviously key to successful social relations, and may play an important role in learning. Assessment programs have traditionally valued demonstrations of competence in isolation and competition among individuals. These values arguably stem from—

and are maintained by—an economic, social, and constitutional tradition that emphasizes individual rights and rewards individual accomplishments.

Administration and Scoring. "Authentic" assessment values examinee choice (Camp, this volume). Choice is consistent with cognitive engagement as examinees are more likely to become engrossed in problems that they choose. In keeping with institutional purposes, conventional assessment has traditionally valued stricter control to allow the comparability of results across individuals (although some programs, like Advanced Placement, permit limited choice in some subject areas). Without such control, individuals may choose tasks based on personality characteristics like risk taking and interest, or on perceptions of task difficulty, making the resulting performance an indicator of characteristics tangential to the target skills. How to correct for these questionable influences is not clear (Wainer, Wang, & Thissen, 1991).

The conflict in scoring rests in the value placed on human judgment. In "authentic" assessment, judgment—especially teacher judgment—is highly respected. Again, we cite Wiggins (1989a): "In the context of testing, equity requires us to insure that human judgment is not overrun or made obsolete by an efficient, mechanical scoring system" (p. 708). Consequently, performance standards and rubrics are developed through a consensual process. Usually, this process is a local one intended to (a) give prominence to the judgments of those who will be affected by the assessment; (b) serve as a learning experience by improving understanding of valued performance and how to assess it; and (c) develop a sense of ownership in the process. Differences in judgments, or between judgments and the results of standardized measures, are "socially moderated," with deference often given to the perceptions of the student's classroom teacher, who knows the examinee best (Department of Education and Science, 1987; Wiggins, 1989a). Even the terminology—*judge*—evokes images of wisdom and respect.

Conventional testing programs have traditionally distrusted human judgment in scoring, *particularly* that of the examinee's teacher. This distrust appears to stem partly from accountability concerns; the American public will not accept the judgments of those it is attempting to hold accountable as evidence that education monies are being well spent (Hartle & Battaglia, this volume). Human judgment also seems to be distrusted because it has so often been historical companion to bias. True, objective tests have been used to achieve prejudicial ends and bias has been found in objective tests; but at least in this country, bias attributable to human judgment—from segregation to unfair employment practices—long preceded that alleged for tests. Thus, conventional testing programs consider differences in judgment to be error and, as in Advanced Placement (AP), use *readers*, not judges. In AP, readers are carefully trained and their ratings monitored. Papers are assigned and identities concealed so readers will *not* know the student or school; responses made by the same student to different questions are given to separate readers; and ratings awarded to the same paper by multiple readers are independently rendered and equally weighted (College Entrance Examination Board, 1988).

Constructed Response as Social Consequences (and Value Implications, Relevance/Utility, and Construct Validity)

In addition to the construct validity, relevance/utility, and value implications of assessment results, functional worth in terms of the social consequences of use must be considered (Messick, 1989). This appraisal should take into account all the intended and unintended ends of assessment, including institutional and individual outcomes as well as societal and systemic ones. From this perspective, the value of assessment depends on its total set of effects, with construct meaning used to pinpoint potential unintended consequences and to help discern whether any known effects stem from test *in*validity.

Learning and Instruction.   One of the most commonly cited social consequences of testing is its reputed negative effect on learning and instruction. This effect is said to stem from the enormously increased use of tests for accountability over the past 25 years: As pressure for high performance grew, teachers reoriented instruction to mirror the content and format of assessment (N. Frederiksen, 1984). What does the evidence suggest?

Shepard (1991a) argued that multiple choice tests encourage poor attitudes toward learning and incorrect inferences about its purposes (e.g., that there is only one right answer, that the right answer resides in the head of the teacher or test maker, and that the job of the student is to get that answer by guessing, if necessary). Research supports Shepard's assertion in that studies have consistently found students to prefer taking multiple-choice measures even though they regard constructed response as a more accurate indicator (Braswell & Kupin, this volume; Bridgeman, in press; also Anderson, 1987, and Zeidner, 1987, cited in Traub & MacRury, 1990). Students' preferences for multiple choice appear to derive from the perception that it requires less preparation and instills greater self-confidence (Traub & MacRury, 1990).

These attitudes suggest that constructed-response measures should cause students to work harder, prepare more broadly, and, hence, learn more. Much research has been conducted on this "expectancy" effect. In a meta-analytical review of 107 studies, Lundeberg and Fox (1991) concluded that the effect differed as a function of setting. In laboratory settings, where simple recognition and recall tasks were used, students who expected a recall test did better—on both task types—than those anticipating the recognition test, upholding the expectancy hypothesis. However, in classroom studies, where more conventional multiple-choice, completion, and essay tasks were employed, students performed more adequately on the format they expected, detracting from the argument that studying for constructed response necessarily facilitates deeper, more complete learning than does preparing for multiple choice. The authors noted, though, that the small number of available classroom studies provides an inadequate basis for firm conclusions about that setting. Lundeberg and Fox's caution is shared by Traub and MacRury (1990), who reviewed seven expectancy investigations, several of which had been surreptitiously conducted as part of ongoing courses. These reviewers concluded that the evidence was mixed, in part because of the confounds introduced by those classroom studies that counted test results toward course grades: Aside from the obvious ethical issues, the anxiety created by confronting an unexpected format might have affected student performance on the response types differentially.

What are the effects on teachers and classroom processes? Smith (Smith, 1991; Smith & Rottenberg, 1991) conducted an extensive, 2-year qualitative study of conventional accountability testing in two elementary schools. She concluded that testing had several detrimental effects. First, preparation and recovery activities reduced the time available for instruction by 3 to 4 *weeks* each year.[5] Second, tests exerted a strong gravitational pull: As the administration date approached, instructional content and methods dramatically shifted course. Some subjects, such as science, social studies, and health, disappeared altogether, whereas in others, like writing, activities changed from producing essays to completing worksheets. Finally, because teachers abandoned more creative methods, they permanently lost valuable instructional skills: "Multiple-choice testing [led] to multiple-choice teaching" (Smith, 1991, p. 10).

Adverse Impact. A second potential social consequence of item format is adverse impact on population subgroups. Commonly defined as a difference in score means disfavoring a subgroup, impact does not necessarily imply psychometric bias (Dorans & Schmitt, this volume). Tests without mean differences can be biased, just as tests with large disparities may truthfully represent essential distinctions in group performance. All the same, impact can have very visible effects on a group's life chances, such that greater impact will be quickly noted and vigorously challenged. From this viewpoint, impact demands careful investigation.

There are few published data on the performance of racial/ethnic groups on multiple-choice versus constructed-response items. All the same, there is

---

[5]These estimates are similar to ones reported by the Office of Technology Assessment (Congress of the United States, 1992), which found that for each of two test administrations, teachers in a large, urban school district spent 4 days on test administration and from 0 to 3 weeks on test preparation.

concern that impact may remain unchanged—or even increase with greater use of the more complex constructed-response tasks—because of group differences in task familiarity and motivation (e.g., Linn, Baker, & Dunbar, 1991).

For the case of females, the data base is larger and the consequences appear more positive. Several studies have found that relative to males, females perform better on constructed-response than on multiple-choice items (Bolger & Kellaghan, 1990; Breland & Griswold, 1981; Mazzeo, Schmitt, & Bleistein, 1991; Petersen & Livingston, 1982). (Studies reviewed by Traub & MacRury, 1990, also support this finding.) The large-sample study by Mazzeo et al. (1991), which centered on the Advanced Placement (AP) examinations, is particularly notable because this effect held over subject matter areas (sciences, social sciences, and humanities), constructed-response formats (essays and short answers), scoring schemes (analytical and holistic), and racial/ethnic groups (White Americans, Black Americans, Asian Americans). Further, the effect persisted after differences in the reliability of the formats were accounted for.

Using the same AP data, Schmitt, Mazzeo, and Bleistein (1991) investigated the hypothesis that gender differences appear larger on the multiple-choice section due to a few items affected by performance factors related to gender but unrelated to the focal construct (e.g., comfort and skill in guessing, familiarity with stereotypically male activities). Their results showed little consistent evidence of gender-related differential item functioning, and when differentially functioning items were removed, gender differences on the multiple-choice section were reduced only slightly. Again, these findings held over subject matter areas, constructed-response formats, scoring schemes, and racial/ethnic groups.

Bridgeman and Lewis (1991) examined the correlational pattern of AP multiple-choice and constructed-response scores with college course grades averaged within a subject matter area. This multi-institutional study detected only negligible differences in prediction across gender groups for the three subject matter tests evaluated: English Language and Composition, American History, and Biology. For American History, however, level differences were apparent in the test–criterion relationship: Even though there were no significant gender disparities in mean course grades, mean gender differences on the multiple-choice AP section were substantially larger than on the essay section. Analyses at the individual course level revealed the same pattern, indicating that the result was not due to the relative difficulty of the courses being taken by the two groups. Finally, a telephone survey of the largest colleges found that essay tests were always the primary grading criterion in history courses whereas other courses frequently relied on multiple-choice examinations.

Breland (1991) further explored the causes of AP gender-related format differences, choosing the American and European History examinations because they showed no gender differences on the essay sections but large ones on the multiple-choice portions. Breland re-scored the essay items according to English composition quality, historical content, responsiveness to the question, factual errors, handwriting quality, neatness, and words written. These variables were then used (along with the AP multiple-choice score) to predict the free-response scores assigned during the original reading. The significant predictors were AP multiple-choice score, historical content, English composition quality, and the number of words written. Using the total-group regression equation, essay scores were then predicted from multiple-choice performance for each gender group, producing underprediction for females and overprediction for males. These effects diminished when English composition quality was added, suggesting one factor in reducing format-related gender differences. Finally, Breland used multiple-choice verbal ability and writing tests (in addition to AP multiple-choice scores) to predict essay performance, finding verbal ability to be a significant factor.

The search for causes of gender-related format differences can be conceptualized in terms of two major threats to validity, construct-irrelevant variance and construct underrepresentation (Messick, 1989). Breland (1991) hypothesized that females performed better on history essays than on multiple-choice items because the former tasks required attributes in which females were strong (i.e., English composition skill and verbal ability), whereas the multiple-choice items called upon knowledge they had not developed as completely (i.e., of history). If we accept this interpretation, the key issue becomes relevance to the focal construct, college-level introductory subject matter proficiency. Narrowly defining this proficiency as historical knowledge consigns composition skill and verbal ability to construct-irrelevant variance, and questions the role of essays. A broader conception consistent with the AP course description (College Entrance Examination Board, 1991) might assert that historical analysis requires the formulation and written presentation of verbal arguments, thus suggesting that multiple choice underrepresents the focal construct and should be complemented by essay results. That these alternative conceptions have opposing action implications only highlights the need to base evaluations of social consequences not just on a more thorough understanding of what different formats measure, but on a well-formulated description of domain proficiency.

CONCLUSION

This chapter has described constructed response as a superordinate classification encompassing a broad array of non-multiple-choice formats. The meaning of these formats derives from a unified conception of validity composed of four facets: construct validity, relevance/utility, value implications, and social consequences. Other considerations also may affect meaning, including content domain, population, and assessment purpose.

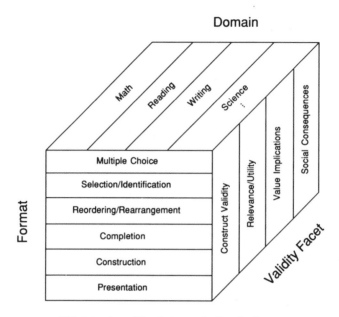

FIG. 1.1.   A multifaceted organizational scheme.

Figure 1.1 is an extension of the preliminary organizational scheme posed by Bennett et al. (1990) and presented earlier as Table 1.1. The extended structure explicitly integrates format, content, and validity facet. For simplicity, assessment purpose and population are implicitly represented. This representation occurs along the validity dimension at two levels. A general distinction is made between test interpretation and use, which call upon different combinations of validity facets and presume particular target populations. Within facets, target population is an important factor throughout, whereas specific applied purposes become salient in discussions of relevance/utility and social consequences. Also for simplicity, the dimensions of Fig. 1.1 are generally specified. In practice, further detail is needed to capture important format distinctions: Individual format categories are not necessarily homogeneous (Bennett et al., 1990), each validity facet subsumes multiple issues, and the content domains are both too expansive and undefined as to the nature of their representation.

Although simplified, this organizational structure helps frame several closing observations about the meaning of constructed response. First, we have argued that the connotative significance of constructed response is broad. Participants in the constructed-response/multiple-choice debate often appear to be arguing from narrower perspectives. It is not uncommon to find psychometricians and educators disagreeing on whether essay tasks are worth their operational cost for large-scale assessment (e.g., see Wainer & Thissen,

1991, and Wiggins, 1989a). The traditional psychometrician, schooled in technical concerns, sees low reliability and marginal increments in predictive validity, or a paltry result at a nontrivial cost. The reform-minded educator envisions closer ties to domain conceptions and more positive instructional effects that, together, make the increased expense well worthwhile. Arguing from perspectives that the other knows little and values less, the two inevitably talk past one another. Reformulating the debate to encourage discussing the full array of validity concerns might help participants confront opposing perspectives directly and, perhaps, appreciate the legitimacy of the other's view. Thereby, the chances for productive dialogue increase, as do the possibilities for improving educational assessment.

A second observation is that format and content are deeply intertwined. Domain considerations should drive the choice of format for any given purpose in that a principled description of what constitutes key domain proficiencies suggests task types needed to mark skill development. To the extent that formats recapitulate conceptions of what learners must know and be able to do, the argument for construct validity is strengthened. Other validity or practical considerations may dictate that task formats be modified. However, to preserve the link to domain proficiency, these deviations should be theoretically guided and the results empirically checked. Otherwise, measurement of the intended proficiency may be distorted.

A third observation, motivated by the cellular structure of Fig. 1.1, is the considerable potential for interaction effects. So, for example, a format might have instructional effects that vary by domain. Advocates of performance and "authentic" assessment assert that complex tasks have positive instructional consequences. Less complicated tasks are of little interest (e.g., Robinson, this volume). In computer science, however, substitution/correction tasks, which ask the student to debug someone else's faulty computer program, provide practice in code simulation and replicate what professional programmers must often do. Whereas using this format for large-scale assessment might not encourage desired instructional practice in other domains, it arguably should do so in this content area.

Fourth, the knowledge base represented by Fig. 1.1 is sparsely filled, suggesting that meaning will evolve. Major gaps include the construct differences associated with multiple-choice versus presentation tasks, the cognitive processing requirements of the different formats, and the impact of different formats on population subgroups, minority students in particular. Other topics wanting theoretical and empirical attention include differential item functioning, equating, and differences among approaches to scoring essay tasks, to name a few. As these gaps are filled, the meaning of constructed response in particular instantiations, and in general, will deepen.

Whereas there is much we do not know, some provisional generalizations appear tenable. With respect to construct validity, research has failed to show that the most studied constructed-response tasks (i.e., *completion* and *construction*) necessarily measure attributes fundamentally different from multiple choice (although in some contexts, such as AP, construct differences may well exist). Further, there is good evidence that per unit of testing time, essay tasks are less reliable than forced-choice items. Even so, some of the precepts underlying multiple-choice testing conflict with prevailing cognitive and domain conceptions. As to relevance and utility, essay tasks appear to add little predictive value over multiple choice in admissions; the incremental value of essays in placement contexts is more palpable, although the high cost of scoring lowers usefulness. When the context changes to accountability and classroom instruction, the match with domain conceptions becomes key, increasing the relevance and utility of the more complex tasks. Regarding value implications, it is clear that conventional multiple-choice tests and "authentic" assessment represent world views that differ radically in conception, tasks, and scoring and administration. Lastly, the available evidence suggests that conventional tests have had at least some negative social consequences for teaching and learning, and, though the cause is unclear, greater adverse impact for female examinees than essay items have had.

The current rhetoric often depicts constructed response as an alternative to multiple choice (e.g., Wiggins, 1989a, 1989b). The categorical nature of the rhetoric derives in part from extensive reliance on the latter format by conventional testing programs. But just as an exclusive concentration on the products of well-structured, decontextualized tasks is limiting, so too is a focus on the processes involved in solving deeply situated, ill-structured problems. This position argues for a prudent balance of openness versus constraint, process versus product, and contextualization versus abstraction—in other words, for the complementary use of conventional and novel approaches. Balance is also recommended by our knowledge state. We know enough to realize that there are serious limitations to both multiple choice and constructed response (whatever the specific form), and that additional difficulties are sure to arise as our knowledge accrues. In reasoned complementarity there is some protection against methodological idiosyncrasy: Ideally, the irrelevant variance associated with different methods cancels out and the scope of valid measurement extends to represent the intended construct more thoroughly (Messick, this volume). It is in this sense that the ultimate meaning of constructed response may be a broadening and balancing of educational assessment.

ACKNOWLEDGMENTS

Appreciation is expressed to Hunter Breland, Brent Bridgeman, Kalle Gerritz, Drew Gitomer, William Ward, and Howard Wainer for their helpful comments on an earlier draft of this chapter.

REFERENCES

Baron, J. B. (1991). Performance assessment: Blurring the edges of assessment, curriculum, and instruction. In G. Kulm & S. M. Malcolm (Eds.), *Science assessment in the service of reform* (pp. 247–266). Washington, DC: American Association for the Advancement of Science.

Bejar, I. I., Embretson, S., & Mayer, R. E. (1987). *Cognitive psychology and the SAT: A review of some implications* (RR-87-28). Princeton, NJ: Educational Testing Service.

Bennett, R. E. (in press). Intelligent assessment: Toward an integration of constructed-response testing, artificial intelligence, and model-based measurement. In N. Frederiksen, R. J. Mislevy, & I. I. Bejar (Eds.), *Test theory for a new generation of tests*. Hillsdale, NJ: Lawrence Erlbaum Associates.

Bennett, R. E., Sebrechts, M. M., & Yamamoto, K. (1991). *Fitting new measurement models to GRE General Test constructed-response item data* (RR-91-60). Princeton, NJ: Educational Testing Service.

Bennett, R. E., Ward, W. C., Rock, D. A., & LaHart, C. (1990). *Toward a framework for constructed-response items* (RR-90-7). Princeton, NJ: Educational Testing Service.

Birenbaum, M., & Tatsuoka, K. K. (1987). Open-ended versus multiple-choice response formats—It does make a difference for diagnostic purposes. *Applied Psychological Measurement, 11,* 385–395.

Bolger, N., & Kellaghan, T. (1990). Method of measurement and gender differences in scholastic achievement. *Journal of Educational Measurement, 27,* 165–174.

Breland, H. M. (1983). *The direct assessment of writing skill: A measurement review* (College Board Report No. 83-6). New York: College Entrance Examination Board.

Breland, H. M. (1991). *A study of sex differences in Advanced Placement history tests* (RR-91-61). Princeton, NJ: Educational Testing Service.

Breland, H. M., Camp, R., Jones, R. J., Morris, M. M., & Rock, D. A. (1987). *Assessing writing skill*. New York: The College Board.

Breland, H. M., & Griswold, P. A. (1981). Group comparisons for basic skills measures (College Board Report No. 81-6). New York: College Entrance Examination Board.

Bridgeman, B. (1991). Essays and multiple choice tests as predictors of college freshman GPA. *Research in Higher Education, 32,* 319–332.

Bridgeman, B. (in press). *A comparison of open-ended and multiple-choice question formats for the quantitative section of the Graduate Record Examination*. Princeton, NJ: Educational Testing Service.

Bridgeman, B., & Lewis, C. (1991). *Sex differences in the relationship of Advanced Placement essay and multiple-choice scores to grades in college courses* (RR-91-48). Princeton, NJ: Educational Testing Service.

Brown, J. S., Collins, A., & Duguid, P. (1989). Situated cognition and the culture of learning. *Educational Researcher, 18*(1), 32–42.

Bush, G. (1991). *America 2000: An education strategy*. Washington, DC: U.S. Department of Education.

College Entrance Examination Board. (1988). *The College Board technical manual for the Advanced Placement Program*. New York: College Entrance Examination Board.

College Entrance Examination Board. (1991). *Advanced Placement course description: History*. New York: Author.

Congress of the United States, Office of Technology Assessment. (1992). *Testing in American schools: Asking the right questions* (Summary). Washington, DC: Author.

Department of Education and Science. (1987). *National curriculum: Task group on assessment and testing*. London, England: Author.

DeWitt, K. (1991, September 1). In Vermont schools, test on how well students think draws new interest. *The New York Times*, Section 1, p. 18.

Frederiksen, J. R., & Collins, A. (1989). A systems approach to educational testing. *Educational Researcher, 18*(9), 27–32.

Frederiksen, N. (1984). The real test bias: Influences of testing on teaching and learning. *American Psychologist, 39,* 193–202.

Frederiksen, N. (1990). Introduction. In N. Frederiksen, R. Glaser, A. Lesgold, & M. G. Shafto (Eds.), *Diagnostic monitoring of skill and knowledge acquisition* (pp. ix–xvii). Hillsdale, NJ: Lawrence Erlbaum Associates.

Frederiksen, N., & Ward, W. C. (1978). Measures for the study of creativity in scientific problem solving. *Applied Psychological Measurement, 2,* 1–24.

Glaser, R. (1988). Cognitive and environmental perspectives on assessing achievement. In Educational Testing Service (Ed.), *Assessment in the service of learning* (Proceedings of the 1987 ETS Invitational Conference) (pp. 37–43). Princeton, NJ: Educational Testing Service.

Glaser, R. (1991). Expertise and assessment. In M. C. Wittrock & E. L. Baker (Eds.), *Testing and cognition* (pp. 37–43). Englewood Cliffs, NJ: Prentice-Hall.

Guthrie, J. T. (1984). Testing higher level skills. *Journal of Reading, 28,* 188–190.

Hogan, T. P. (1981). *Relationship between free-response and choice-type tests of achievement: A review of the literature.* Green Bay, WI: University of Wisconsin. (ERIC Document No. ED 224 81)

Linn, R. L., Baker, E. L., & Dunbar, S. B. (1991). Complex, performance-based assessment: Expectations and validation criteria. *Educational Researcher, 20*(8), 15–21.

Lundeberg, M. A., & Fox, P. W. (1991). Do laboratory findings on test expectancy generalize to classroom outcomes? *Review of Educational Research, 61,* 94–106.

Masters, G. N., & Mislevy, R. J. (1991). *New views of student learning: Implications for educational measurement* (RR-91-24-ONR). Princeton, NJ: Educational Testing Service.

Mazzeo, J., Schmitt, A. P., & Bleistein, C. A. (1991, April). *Do women perform better, relative to men, on constructed-response tests or multiple-choice tests? Evidence from the Advanced Placement examinations.* Paper presented at the annual meeting of the American Educational Research Association, Chicago.

Messick, S. (1989). Validity. In R. L. Linn (Ed.), *Educational measurement* (3rd ed.) (pp. 13–103). New York: Macmillan.

Messick, S. (1992). Validity of test interpretation and use. In M. C. Alkin (Ed.), *Encyclopedia of educational research* (6th ed.). New York: Macmillan.

Mislevy, R. J. (in press). Foundations of a new test theory. In N. Frederiksen, R. J. Mislevy, & I. I. Bejar (Eds.), *Test theory for a new generation of tests.* Hillsdale, NJ: Lawrence Erlbaum Associates.

Perkins, D. N., & Salomon, G. (1989). Are cognitive skills context bound? *Educational Researcher, 18*(1), 16–25.

Petersen, N. S., & Livingston, S. A. (1982). *English composition test with essay: A descriptive study of the relationship between essay and objective scores by ethnic group and sex* (SR-82-96). Princeton, NJ: Educational Testing Service.

Quellmalz, E. S., Capell, F. J., & Chou, C. P. (1982). Effects of discourse and response mode on the measurement of writing competence. *Journal of Educational Measurement, 19,* 241–258.

Resnick, L. B., & Resnick, D. P. (1990). Tests as standards of achievement in schools. In J. Pfleiderer (Ed.), *Proceedings of the 1989 ETS Invitational Conference: The uses of standardized tests in American education* (pp. 63–80). Princeton, NJ: Educational Testing Service.

Reynolds, C. R. (1982). The problem of bias in psychological assessment. In C. R. Reynolds & T. B. Gutkin (Eds.), *The handbook of school psychology* (pp. 178–208). New York: Wiley.

Schmitt, A. P., Mazzeo, J., & Bleistein, C. (1991, April). *Are gender differences between Advanced Placement multiple-choice and constructed-response sections a function of multiple-choice DIF?* Paper presented at the annual meeting of the American Educational Research Association, Chicago.

Shepard, L. (1991a). Interview on assessment issues with Lorrie Shepard. *Educational Research-er, 20*(2), 21–23, 27.

Shepard, L. (1991b). Psychometricians' beliefs about learning. *Educational Researcher, 20*(6), 2–16.

Simon, H. A. (1978). Information-processing theory of human problem solving. In W. K. Estes (Ed.), *Handbook of learning and cognitive processes: Human information processing* (Vol. 5, pp. 271–295). Hillsdale, NJ: Lawrence Erlbaum Associates.

Smith, M. L. (1991). Put to the test: The effects of external testing on teachers. *Educational Research-er, 20*(5), 8–11.

Smith, M. L., & Rottenberg, C. (1991). Unintended consequences of external testing in elementary schools. *Educational Measurement: Issues and Practice, 10*(4), 7–11.

Traub, R. E., & MacRury, K. (1990). Antwort-auswahl- vs freie-antwort-aufgaben bei lernerfolgs-tests [Multiple choice versus free response in the testing of scholastic achievement]. In K. Ingenkamp & R. S. Jäger (Eds.), *Tests und trends 8: Jahrbuch der pädagogischen diagnostik* (pp. 128–159). Weinheim, Germany: Beltz Verlag.

van den Bergh, H. (1990). On the construct validity of multiple-choice items for reading comprehension. *Applied Psychological Measurement, 14*, 1–12.

Wainer, H., & Thissen, D. (1992). *Combining multiple-choice and constructed-response test scores: Toward a Marxist theory of test construction* (RR-92-23). Princeton, NJ: Educational Testing Service.

Wainer, H., Wang, X. B., & Thissen, D. (1991). *How well can we equate test forms that are constructed by examinees* (RR-91-57). Princeton, NJ: Educational Testing Service.

Ward, W. C., Dupree, D., & Carlson, S. B. (1987). *A comparison of free-response and multiple-choice questions in the assessment of reading comprehension.* Princeton, NJ: Educational Testing Service.

Ward, W. C., Frederiksen, N., & Carlson, S. B. (1980). Construct validity of free-response and multiple-choice versions of a test. *Journal of Educational Measurement, 17*, 11–29.

Wiggins, G. (1989a). A true test: Toward more authentic and equitable assessment. *Phi Delta Kappan, 70*, 703–713.

Wiggins, G. (1989b). Teaching to the (authentic) test. *Educational Leadership, 46*(7), 41–47.

Willingham, W. W. (1985). *Success in college: The role of personal qualities and academic ability.* New York: College Entrance Examination Board.

Working Groups for the Commission on Standards for School Mathematics of the National Council of Teachers of Mathematics. (1989). *Curriculum and evaluation standards for school mathematics.* Reston, VA: National Council of Teachers of Mathematics.

2

ON THE EQUIVALENCE OF THE TRAITS ASSESSED BY MULTIPLE-CHOICE AND CONSTRUCTED-RESPONSE TESTS

Ross E. Traub
The Ontario Institute for Studies in Education

The issue of psychometric equivalence of multiple-choice and constructed-response tests has been raised in one form or another from almost the day that multiple-choice items were first used to test human subjects (Hogan, 1981; Traub & MacRury, 1990). Although a host of empirical studies on this issue has been reported during the last 70 years (Hogan, 1981), many were seriously flawed in design and analysis (Traub & MacRury, 1990). The present chapter is a review of nine relatively recent studies of trait equivalence. These investigations, better designed and conducted than many others, were examined for the purpose of (a) identifying the consistent findings, if any, produced by the investigations, and (b) deriving from a consideration of this body of work possible directions for future research.

Context is given the ensuing discussion by the answers to two questions: Which items qualify as constructed response and as multiple choice? And why the focus on trait equivalence to the exclusion of other kinds of equivalence (e.g., of difficulty or reliability)?

First is the matter of item-types. Following the typology of Bennett, Ward, Rock, and LaHart (1990; see also Bennett, this volume), a multiple-choice (M-C) item is narrowly defined as any item in which the examinee is required to choose an answer from a relatively small set of response options (e.g., four or five). The concept of constructed-response (C-R) item is defined relatively broadly in the present chapter to include any item that requires the examinee to compose an answer (as opposed to choosing among alternative answers given with the item). Possible types of C-R items range from those that can be answered with a short, discrete response—a word or a phrase, a number or a formula—to items that demand substantially more—a paragraph, an extended essay, a multistep solution to a mathematical or scientific problem. In the terminology of Bennett, Ward, et al. (1990), the concept of constructed response that is adopted here includes items in the *completion* and *construction* categories. The designations C-R (Discrete) and C-R (Extended Response) or, when appropriate, simply Essay, are used to differentiate the aforementioned types of constructed-response items.

The rationale for concentrating on the question of trait equivalence can be stated succinctly. If multiple-choice tests do not measure precisely the same characteristics as constructed-response items, then comparisons of difficulty and reliability are meaningless. Given tests that differ in format, choice of test should depend on what is measured, which is to say choice should depend on validity, not on difficulty and reliability.[1]

CULLING THE LITERATURE

The literature was searched for studies of equivalence that satisfy two requirements: (a) the investigators conducted the study in such a way that it was possible to assess whether or not the effects on performance, if any, were consistent with the hypothesis that different abilities are tapped by M-C as opposed to C-R items; (b) the research provided information as to the nature of the observed ability differences, if any.

Few studies satisfy the first of these requirements and fewer still satisfy both. In many of the studies deemed not useful to the present review, examinees were administered only two tests that differed in format, and a coefficient of correlation was computed between scores on the tests. The evidence obtained in investigations carried no further cannot be brought to bear on the trait-equivalence issue because coefficients of correlation less than one can arise as a consequence of measurement error and differences in scaling, even when both tests measure identically the same characteristics (aside from measurement error and differences in scaling). In a very few studies, the more difficult question was addressed of whether or not the coefficient of correlation, after allowance had been made for the attenuating effect of errors of measurement, was different from one. If a corrected coefficient is not different from unity, then we cannot reject the hypothesis that the tests measure equivalent characteristics. Ignoring the matter of whether or not the data

---

[1]No attempt was made to compare the relative difficulty of multiple-choice and constructed-response tests for the following reason: The true-score scales of the multiple-choice and constructed-response instruments must be equivalent for the comparison of difficulty to be meaningful. It is difficult, if not impossible, to demonstrate that this condition has been satisfied.

collected in a study allow for testing the statistical significance of the difference between the corrected correlation coefficient and unity, if it were concluded that the corrected coefficient differed from one, then it would follow that the traits measured by the two instruments are not equivalent. This result, although informative to a limited extent, gives no direct information about the nature of the different traits called into play by the formats. Other evidence is needed to elucidate the correlational result.

Stated another way, the central question is whether or not the latent abilities that can be inferred from the observed covariances among tests are the same regardless of item format, M-C versus C-R. At its simplest, this is the question of whether or not tests in different formats yield scores that are congeneric (Jöreskog, 1971). The hypothesis of congenericity can be evaluated in a study of the one-group, repeated-measures design only if it includes, at a minimum, two tests in different formats. Studies of this design suffer the limitation that repeated testing of examinees can adversely affect their motivation to perform (Traub & Fisher, 1977). When the administration of tests extends over a period of time, it is also possible that the traits measured at the beginning of the study are different from those measured at the end (van den Bergh, 1990). Repeated testing with the same item stems can only exacerbate both the foregoing limitations of the one-group design. Multiple-group designs have been used in the attempt to circumvent these criticisms (van den Bergh, 1990).

THE EVIDENCE

Nine studies were identified for close consideration. Although none of these studies satisfies in all respects the two criteria used in culling the literature, they all involved multiple measures of a particular trait or knowledge domain in each of at least two item formats, one multiple choice and one constructed response. In addition, several of the studies included tests of marker abilities, which were used in the attempt to understand possible trait differences, if any, in the characteristics measured by the different formats.

The nine studies can be classified in various ways. The main categorizing characteristic considered here is the ability or knowledge domain being tested. Two broad and familiar categories have been used: a category of language tasks and associated abilities, and a category of quantitative tasks and associated abilities. The language tasks were subclassified into writing, word knowledge, and reading comprehension.

Another characteristic of the studies, which in the extant research is not independent of the first, in the language domain at least, is the nature of the relationship between the tasks set in the multiple-choice and the constructed-response tests. This relationship has varied from one of close correspondence, where the objective has been to make the tasks in two tests as similar as format differences allow[2], to one of seemingly little similarity beyond common use of pencil-and-paper methodology. The latter circumstance is exemplified in the testing of writing ability by discrete language items on the one hand and extended essay questions on the other.

Language Domain

Writing. Studies of writing that included more than two tests in different formats have been reported by Werts, Breland, Grandy, and Rock (1980) (see also Breland, 1977; Breland & Gaynor, 1979), Quellmalz, Capell, and Chou (1982) (see also Capell & Quellmalz, 1980; Quellmalz & Capell, 1979), and Ackerman and Smith (1988). The designs of all three studies were variations of multitrait/multimethod, but differed substantially in other respects.

The most straightforward study was that by Werts et al. (1980). The data, obtained from over 200 first-year college students, were scores on six tests, three being different administrations of the Test of Standard Written English (TSWE) and three being short (20-minute) essay tests. The tests were written essentially in pairs (one TSWE, one essay), on different occasions over the course of a year. The covariance structure that fit the intercorrelations among the six variables acceptably well consisted of three occasion factors, each defined by coefficients for the two tests written on that occasion. In this structure, the three occasion factors were constrained to have intercorrelations of unity. Also, the coefficients of the TSWE variables were constrained to be identical on all three occasion factors, as were the coefficients for the essay variables. The indication that the essays measured something in common, but different from whatever the essays and TSWE shared, was the nonzero covariation permitted in the model among the essay residual variables. Had an essay method factor, orthogonal to the occasion factors, been included in the model, each essay would presumably have had coefficients on the factor of about 0.3, accounting for about 10% of the variance of each (standardized) essay variable.

---

[2]Traub and MacRury (1990) defined the notions of stem-equivalence and scoring-equivalence for multiple-choice and constructed-response tests. A multiple-choice and a constructed-response test are stem-equivalent when, item for item, the tasks posed in each test are identical except for the response required. The idea of stem-equivalence is clearly exemplified by a test of vocabulary, each item of which requires the examinee to respond with an antonym. The stems for this test can be identical for both the multiple-choice and the constructed-response versions, the only difference in versions being response mode. Scoring-equivalence occurs when responses to stem-equivalent constructed-response and multiple-choice items are scored in equivalent fashion. For example, if the responses to a multiple-choice item are scored right or wrong, 1 or 0, the answers to the constructed-response items are too. This means that no partial-credit scoring is allowed for the constructed-response item, regardless of how compelling the desire to employ such scoring might be.

Evidence of the sort provided in this, and other multitrait, multimethod studies, is necessary to the conclusion that different item formats assess somewhat different characteristics, but it is insufficient to indicate what the differences in characteristics might be. Werts et al. (1980) interpreted the covariation among the essay residual variables in terms of correlated errors, these being attributed to such irrelevancies as quality of handwriting. Another interpretation might have been made, one rooted in aspects of writing (e.g., organization, production) not directly amenable to M-C testing. Given the lack of independent measures of possible irrelevancies and possible features of writing not tested, no empirical basis exists for establishing a preference for one of these interpretations. Still, this study provides the strongest empirical evidence of the three studies of writing reviewed here that essay tests measure something in common, but different from what M-C tests measure.

Both the other investigations of writing, by Quellmalz et al. (1982) and Ackerman and Smith (1988), involved high school students. The study by Quellmalz et al. was complex, making interpretation of results hazardous. There were four tests, two of which required the writing of an essay, one the writing of a paragraph, and one the answering of a set of multiple-choice items. The M-C test included 10 paragraphs, each about 100 words long and each followed by three M-C questions. One of the three questions dealt with the main idea of the paragraph, another with ideas that would support the main idea, and the third with the organization of the paragraph—organization in the sense of being able to identify the one sentence of four that would best fit in the paragraph at a designated spot. The 10 paragraphs of the M-C test were divided into two sets of five, the sets differing by the genre of the paragraphs, expository versus narrative.

Other complicating features of the study by Quellmalz et al. (1982) were as follows: Each student in the study was assigned to one of four groups differentiated by discourse mode of the writing tasks. The members of two groups wrote all three pieces in the same genre, either two expository essays and an expository paragraph or two narrative essays and a narrative paragraph. The students in the other two groups wrote pieces in different genres, one expository essay, one narrative essay, and either a narrative paragraph or an expository paragraph. The tests were administered on three occasions over a 2-week period, with one of two orders being followed: Order I: M-C plus paragraph, Essay 1, Essay 2; Order II: Essay 1, Essay 2, M-C plus paragraph. The marking of the four tests yielded a set of 18 scores, consisting of five ratings of each of the three written pieces and three number-correct scores derived from the M-C responses. The five scores for each written piece pertained respectively to General Impression, Focus, Organization, Support, and Mechanics. (The scores on these scales were the averages of the ratings of two readers, the scale for each rating being from 1 to 4.) The M-C scales were Focus, Organization, and Support.

In preparing the data for analysis of response-mode effects, an attempt was made to remove variance due to topic and genre. The observed scores on all essay variables were standardized within genre by topic, and then standardized once again by genre (Quellmalz et al., 1982, p. 247). The paragraph variables and the M-C variables were similarly standardized within genre. The resulting score distributions were combined to obtain scores for first essay written (regardless of genre and topic), second essay written (again regardless of genre and topic), paragraph (regardless of genre), and M-C (again regardless of genre).

The scores on only 15 variables—focus, organization, and support on both essays, the paragraph and the M-C test, and mechanics on both essays and the paragraph—were intercorrelated and modeled by a 7-factor structure. This structure included three intercorrelated trait factors [(a) coherence, combining focus and organization, (b) support, and (c) mechanics], plus four orthogonal method factors, one for the variables based on the first essay the students wrote, a second for the variables based on the second essay, a third for variables based on the paragraph, which constituted the third writing task, and one factor more for variables based on the multiple-choice test. The 15 nonzero coefficients on the three trait factors were substantial (minimum of 0.4), as were the three coefficients of intercorrelation among these factors (approximately 0.8, 0.7, and 0.6). It is clear that individual differences in the qualities of essay writing called *coherence* and *support* are associated with individual differences in scores with these same names for paragraph writing and, perhaps surprisingly, paragraph reading comprehension. Also clear is the fact that individual differences in the mechanics of essay writing are (not surprisingly) related to individual differences in the mechanics of paragraph writing. More important, however, is the fact that a substantial proportion of the variance in this analysis was associated with the method factors, which is to say this variance was task specific. The proportions of total variance accounted for by the method factors were 0.24 for the four Essay 1 variables, 0.21 for the Essay 2 variables, 0.25 for the paragraph variables, and 0.20 for the three M-C variables.

The Ackerman and Smith (1988) study included one essay test (rated on six different qualities), six M-C tests of writing skills, and six stem-equivalent C-R (Discrete) versions of the M-C tests. The essay qualities that were rated—spelling, capitalization/punctuation, correct expression, usage, paragraph development, and paragraph structure—were defined to be similar to the qualities tested by the M-C and C-R (Discrete) tests. One of the models found to fit the data of this study acceptably well[3] included six correlated trait factors,

---

[3]Another good-fitting model for this study included one method factor unique to the essay variables, another unique to the essay and F-R (Discrete) variables, and a third defined by the variables of all tests, including the M-C test. This model is discussed in more detail later in the chapter, in a review of theory for format effects.

each defined by three variables with the same name, one each from the sets of six M-C, C-R (Discrete), and Essay variables, plus three uncorrelated method factors, one for the six Essay variables, another for the six M-C variables, and a third for the six C-R (Discrete) variables. But the M-C and C-R (Discrete) method factors in this structure were not very well defined and were of minor importance, accounting for only 5% and 11% respectively of the total variance of the six variables on which they were defined. Moreover, the bulk of this variance was associated with only one variable per set: capitalization/punctuation for the M-C set of variables and paragraph development for the C-R (Discrete) set. (The proportions of the total variance of the remaining five variables per set that are attributable to the M-C and C-R [Discrete] factors are 0.03 and 0.02, respectively.) As for the method factor defined by the essay scales, only the paragraph development and paragraph structure variables had substantial coefficients (0.60 and 0.79, respectively).

On the face of it, the results reported by Quellmalz et al. (1982) and Ackerman and Smith (1988) suggest that essay variables can contain reliable variance that is unrelated to the variance in M-C scores, even when, as in these studies, the latter have been intended to capture some or all of the same qualities as those reflected in the ratings of essays. A serious problem with this evidence, however, is that each method factor for writing was defined by variables derived from a single piece of writing. Clearly, these variables were not independent in the same way that the essay variables analyzed by Werts et al. (1980) were, the latter being based on three pieces of writing obtained on three different occasions. Although Quellmalz et al. did collect three samples of writing from each examinee, the method factor for one piece of writing was orthogonal to that for another piece, whereas one would hope for an essay factor defined by variables from more than one writing exercise, as in the study by Werts et al.

Word Knowledge. Two studies in this category were identified, by Traub and Fisher (1977) and Ward (1982). Traub and Fisher tested eighth-grade students with two forms of a synonyms test, the item stems being repeated, first in a C-R version of each test form and then in an M-C version. (A third item format was included, but is not pertinent to this discussion.) In addition, the students responded to tests of mathematical ability, recall memory, recognition memory, the ability to follow directions, and predisposition to guess answers to M-C items. The data from the synonym tests led to rejection of the hypothesis that the correlation between scores on the M-C and C-R versions was one, after allowance had been made for the attenuating effects of error of measurement. The obvious conclusion, that the abilities measured by an M-C synonyms test differ somehow from those measured by a C-R synonyms test, was weakened, however, by the fact that whatever the different abilities were, they were not clearly associated with any of the marker abilities—

recall memory, recognition memory, following directions ability, and/or propensity to guess.

Ward (1982) tested over 300 college students with 12 instruments. Four instruments were composed of antonym items, four of sentence completion items, and four of analogy items. The four instruments of each item type differed in format, with two of the four being the M-C and C-R (Discrete) formats. No item stems were repeated over the 12 tests. The results of an exploratory factor analysis of the intercorrelations among the tests led Ward to conclude that the C-R (Discrete) tests did not define an ability factor unique to those tests.

The conclusions drawn by Traub and Fisher and by Ward were contradictory in that Traub and Fisher claimed to have found evidence of a significant format effect, whereas Ward did not. Reconciling these results is made impossible by the very different methodologies used in each study. Traub and Fisher employed parallel test forms and repeated item stems across formats. This enabled them to use the hypothesis testing method invented by Lord (1973) for just this kind of situation. By employing stem-equivalent M-C and C-R tests, Traub and Fisher attempted to avoid confounding the effects of content and format in examinee responses. Ward, on the other hand, did not repeat item stems. This is undoubtedly a better way to maintain examinee motivation than repeating item stems, but at the cost of confounding content and format effects. Ward found no sign of format effects, although his test of equivalence was less rigorous statistically than that used by Traub and Fisher.

Reading Comprehension. Two studies addressed to the trait equivalence of reading comprehension tests have been reported by Ward, Dupree, and Carlson (1987) and van den Bergh (1990). In the former investigation, college students responded to two tests of reading comprehension. The reading passages in these instruments were followed by items testing either explicit idea, inference, or application and evaluation. Equal numbers of items in each test were in the M-C and C-R (Discrete) formats, so that when the items in each form were clustered by evaluative intent (explicit idea, inference, application and evaluation) and by format, with the clusters then scored as separate tests, 12 observed-score variables were created. Weak evidence of a format factor was obtained from an exploratory factor analysis of the intercorrelations among these variables. In addition to a factor for the variables derived from all the items of each test, the factor-analytic model accepted by Ward et al. included a bipolar factor in which the M-C variables were distinguished from the C-R (Discrete) variables by the algebraic signs of the factor coefficients of the variables. The absolute values of the coefficients were small, however, suggesting that the bipolar factor was of minor importance.

Van den Bergh's (1990) study was of a very different design from that of any other investigation considered in this review. Two more or less equivalent forms of a test were developed. By casting the items in both forms into both the C-R and M-C formats, van den Bergh obtained four tests, each of which was then administered to a different group of about 150 students. (According to van den Bergh, personal communication, February 4, 1991, the students were in the third grade of high school in The Netherlands, age about 15 years.) In addition to responding to a test of reading comprehension, all 600 students responded to 32 tests chosen to measure 16 of the semantic factors in Guilford's structure of the intellect (SI) model (Guilford, 1971; Guilford & Hoepfner, 1971). LISREL (Jöreskog & Sörbom, 1981) was used to assess whether the coefficients for the regression of the latent trait for reading comprehension on the latent traits measured by the SI tests varied with test form and test format. From the evidence obtained, van den Bergh concluded that test format did not affect the regression coefficients.[4]

The conclusion indicated by the foregoing studies of reading comprehension is that M-C and C-R items assess the same characteristics. There was no sign in either study of a strong format effect.

Quantitative Domain

Only three reports involving tests in this domain were identified for this review, these by Traub and Fisher (1977), Bennett, Rock et al. (1990), and Bennett, Rock, and Wang (1991). In the study by Traub and Fisher, two tests of mathematical knowledge and reasoning were cast in the C-R (Discrete) and M-C formats, and administered as part of a study that, as has been noted, also included verbal tests and tests marking several relatively unitary abilities. The application of Lord's (1973) test did not lead to rejection of the hypothesis of trait equivalence. Moreover, the use of factor analysis to define format factors gave only very weak results, with small coefficients for the tests on the format factors. These format factors were not substantially

---

[4]The analysis was conducted to test three regression models in sequence: In the first model, all model parameters, that is, the coefficients of regression and the residual variance, were constrained to be the same for both test forms in both formats. In the second model, parameters were free to vary by test form, but within form the parameters for both formats were constrained to be identical. In the third model, parameters were free to vary with both form and format of test. Model 2 was preferred by van den Bergh. This conclusion would have been better supported had van den Bergh also reported results for a fourth model in which parameters were free to vary by format, but within format were constrained to be the same for both test forms. Had the latter model fit the data more like Model 1 than models 2 and 3, then the conclusion favoring Model 2 would have had added support.

related to the marker abilities, which had been posited a priori to be related differentially to performance of M-C and C-R tests.

The two studies by Bennett and others were of knowledge and skill in computer programming. The responses analyzed in these studies were elicited in administrations of the Advanced Placement Computer Science (APCS) Examination to high school students. This examination includes both M-C and C-R items. The M-C items in both studies were parceled into groups of 10 items or more, with each parcel defining a separate variable. Each C-R item was treated as a separate variable, with the responses to these items rated for quality on a 10-point scale. A covariance structure model with just one factor was judged to provide an acceptable fit to the matrices of correlation coefficients for M-C and C-R variables in these studies. This model implies that the M-C and C-R variables measured the same constellation of characteristics. It is noteworthy, however, that when a model including separate factors for the variables of each format was fit to the data obtained in the study conducted by Bennett et al. (1991), the disattenuated coefficients of correlation between the two factors were significantly, albeit not substantially, less than unity.

Conclusion

To return to the question asked at the outset of this chapter: Do M-C and C-R tests of the same content measure different characteristics? There is too little sound evidence in hand for any answer to this question to be trusted. Still, if answers are attempted, then they must vary by domain. For the writing domain, the answer would appear to be that tests in different formats do measure different characteristics, although two of the three studies that were reviewed were beset by methodological problems that make it necessary to qualify the answer. For the word knowledge domain, the answer may also be "yes," but the results for the two studies in this domain are contradictory. For reading comprehension and the quantitative domain, the answer is probably that tests that differ by format do *not* measure different characteristics. Regardless of content domain, however, if differences do exist for any domain, they are very likely to be small, at least as measured by the amount of score variance accounted for.

An unsurprising corollary conclusion is that there is no good answer to the question of what it is that is different, if anything, about the characteristics measured by M-C and C-R items. Whether or not the foregoing conclusions are accepted depends perhaps as much on the theoretical perspective one brings to a review of the literature as on the evidence itself. For this reason, it is useful to consider the theories advanced in the work that has been reviewed.

THEORY ABOUT FORMAT EFFECTS

Attempts to conceptualize the possible nature of format effects are found in the papers by Ackerman and Smith (1988) for writing, by Ward et al. (1987) and van den Bergh (1990) for reading comprehension, and by Bennett et al. (1991) for computer programming. Consider each in turn.

Guided by a model of writing proposed by Hayes and Flower (1980), Ackerman and Smith (1988) hypothesized that direct methods of assessing writing ability (e.g., through use of essay tests) differ from indirect methods (e.g., through use of M-C items) in the demands the former make on ". . . the procedural components of organizing, goal setting, and translating [that] are unique to the 'direct' writing task" (p. 120). This study was conducted to see (a) whether relative examinee standing on the "generation" components of procedural knowledge would differentiate performance of the essay and the discrete C-R items from that of the M-C items, and (b) whether relative examinee standing on the "organization" components of procedural knowledge would differentiate performance of the essay and C-R (Discrete) items, and would therefore define a factor associated exclusively with the measures derived from the essay. The covariance structure consonant with this theory fit the matrix of correlations among the six M-C, six C-R (Discrete), and six Essay variables very well, apparently lending support to the theory.[5]

But support for this theory was weak, an assessment that rests principally on the fact that the essay variables had very little in common, either with the M-C and C-R (Discrete) variables or with one another. The variances of the unique factors in this analysis for the spelling, capitalization/punctuation, correct expression, and usage scales of the essay test, as proportions of the total variances of these standardized observed-score variables, were 0.74, 0.79, 0.77, and 0.66 respectively. The corresponding proportion for the unique component of the essay scale for paragraph structure was reported as 0.92. (This latter number or some of the other numbers reported for the PS variable in Table 3 of Ackerman & Smith must be in error, for the total of the contributions to the standardized variance of this variable by the orthogonal factors of the structure is greater than 1.) Only the essay scale for paragraph development was associated with a relatively small unique variance (0.07), mainly for the reason that the "organization" factor was defined primarily by this variable (with a coefficient for the factor of 0.71). Moreover, the "generation" factor was relatively weak in terms of the amount (5%) of the variance

---

[5]This covariance structure, which was fit to test the theory of Hayes and Flower (1980), is *not* the structure considered earlier in this review. Ackerman and Smith fit two different structures to their data. The structure considered previously included method factors associated with the measures differentiated exclusively by response format. It was presented to facilitate a comparison of the Ackerman and Smith results with those of Quellmalz et al. (1982) and Werts et al. (1980).

of the 12 variables it accounted for. Although the "organization" factor was stronger (16% of the variance of the six essay variables), it was defined, as would be expected a priori, by the essay variables for paragraph development and paragraph structure, and so was based on only one correlation coefficient.

The conceptualization advanced by Ward et al. (1987) for the domain of reading comprehension was that the abilities required to perform reading comprehension tests in the M-C format versus those required to perform reading comprehension tests in the C-R format will differ only if the two formats place different demands on the examinee's cognitive system for organizing, storing, and processing information. So, if the information required to respond correctly to a question (e.g., a discrete sentence completion item) is accessible in memory in the form needed to answer the question, then, according to the hypothesis, performance of recognition (M-C) and production (C-R) items will differ little, if at all. On the other hand, if the response is not accessible in memory but must be generated somehow, through manipulating data given in the question and perhaps also data drawn from memory, then ". . . the ability to recognize an appropriate solution when one is offered may not be the same as the ability to generate a solution" (Ward et al., 1987, p. 2).

To test this hypothesis, Ward et al. (1987) employed reading comprehension items presumed to differ in information-processing demands. It was expected that items based on information given explicitly in a reading passage would demand the same abilities regardless of format, whereas items requiring the examinee to make an inference or apply ideas from the passage or evaluate some aspect of the passage would require different abilities depending on item format. Contrary to hypothesis, however, the correlation between the M-C and C-R measures of explicit ideas was lower than the correlation between the M-C and C-R measures of inference and of application and evaluation of ideas.

Despite the apparently negative results, the theory proposed by Ward et al. (1987) deserves a second look. What seems incorrect are the empirical propositions deduced from the initial premises. Items that require inference or application or evaluation of ideas will require manipulation of data to obtain an answer, and these manipulations must be made regardless of the format of the item. The answers to items such as these will not be "recognized" by most examinees when the items are cast in the M-C format, and so M-C and C-R versions of the items will be answered in similar ways. On the other hand, items that test ideas stated explicitly in a reading passage may be approached differently, depending on format. In C-R format, the examinee must process the question to ascertain what is being asked (perhaps using divergent skills in the process), then he or she may scan or reread the passage, seeking the explicit information required for the response, and finally the examinee will formulate a response. In M-C format the question also has to be processed for understanding, but then the response has only to be recognized, something that may be possible from memory traces laid down in the initial reading of the passage. Moreover, a comparative analysis of the response options to M-C items that test explicit knowledge seems likely to facilitate recognition of the desired answer, even if the examinee feels the need to reread the passage. Attention during rereading will be focused by the hypothesis originating in the M-C item response options. It will be noted that the correlations Ward et al. obtained among the variables formed from the M-C and C-R items in their study were consistent with this modified version of their theory. Still, their results as a whole did not support the modified theory particularly well. The most damaging evidence was the failure to find that the tests of the marker abilities, reasoning and divergent production, were more closely related to the reading comprehension variables based on the inference/evaluation items than to the variables based on the explicit idea items.

Van den Bergh (1990) adopted a hypothesis similar in some respects to that advanced by Ward et al. (1987). Working from the belief that recognition and recall are differentially involved in performing M-C and C-R items, van den Bergh hypothesized recall to require divergent production (information retrieval) and convergent production (judging the adequacy of retrieved information); in addition, he observed that

> . . . the presentation of alternatives [in M-C items] may give rise to differences [between M-C and C-R items] in the [relative importance of the] cognition and evaluation abilities [of the Structure of Intellect (SI) model]. Cognition abilities refer to immediate awareness, immediate discovery, or rediscovery of information, whereas evaluation abilities concern comparison according to a set criterion and making a decision about criterion satisfaction. Both seem important: The respondent may "know" the answer to a multiple-choice item as soon as the alternatives are seen, or may actually compare the different alternatives presented. (p. 3)

As already noted, the data collected by van den Bergh failed to support his theory that M-C and C-R tests would be differently related to the SI abilities tested. What is not provided in van den Bergh's report is information on the task demands of the items in the reading comprehension tests. Following the modified theory of Ward et al., the results obtained (no effect associated with format differences) would be expected if van den Bergh's items tested primarily inference, application, and evaluation skills, but not explicit ideas in the passage read.

Turning from the domain of language to that of computer programming, Bennett et al. (1991) proposed the following theory for the performance of the programming items in the Advanced Placement Computer Science Examination:

. . . a free-response problem of the type presented on the APCS exam would appear to require the student to decompose the specification into goals, formulate plans to achieve each goal, translate each plan to Pascal code, and then debug that code by mentally simulating its effects. Depending on the results of this mental simulation, the examinee may return to an earlier step in this process: the simulation may suggest errors in the decomposition, the plans, or the translation of plans into code.

Accepting for the moment that this is a reasonable approximation of the processes involved in responding to the APCS free-response questions, one hypothesis . . . is that the multiple-choice items measure some of these same processes. Given the format's nature, it is difficult to imagine any single multiple-choice item assessing much more than one of these processes. However, it is plausible that, in combination, 50 such items might cover in some depth many of the processes tapped by the free-response questions. (p. 86)

Bennett, Rock, and Wang then analyzed the 50 M-C items in the version of the APCS exam that was studied, and concluded that 45 of the items tapped the processes of formulating a plan for a computer program, translating the plan into code, knowing the related rules and structures of programming, and correcting (debugging) program segments. Only five items were of a type that assessed general knowledge of a kind that might, if a sufficient number of such items were given, show reliable differences in examinee performance in M-C versus C-R formats.

THE NEXT GENERATION OF STUDIES

An expectation rooted in the foregoing review of theory for format effects is that examinees will process some kinds of items the same way, regardless of format, but will process other items in different ways, with these differences being associated with format. An implication of this theoretical perspective for future research is that care must be taken in this work to include two kinds of measures, those expected a priori to be sensitive to format effects and those expected a priori *not* to reflect format effects. An additional suggestion for research that follows from the discussion of theory is to have examinees report their thought processes as they work each item. This "think aloud" procedure has been used effectively by Norris (1990, in press) in validating tests of critical thinking. Such an approach might also provide more or less direct evidence on the differences, if any, in the cognitive processes examinees use in answering M-C and C-R items that a priori are expected to require different processes.

Another requisite of future work is to avoid, if at all possible, the inclusion of experimentally linked variables. Thus, if writing is the domain of interest, the various writing variables should be independent in the sense that each is based on examinee responses to a separate and distinct writing task, with these responses scored independently of the responses to other writing tasks.

Finally, researchers should be on the alert for variables that might differentiate M-C from C-R performance. For example, test-taking skills apparently have not been considered heretofore in format-effects research, yet these skills are thought to influence performance on M-C tests (Millman, Bishop, & Ebel, 1965). Other variables that bear consideration are described elsewhere in this volume (see, e.g., the chapter by Snow). The inclusion of measures hypothesized a priori to be associated with format factors can be expected to enhance the interpretability of the results of trait-equivalence studies.

ACKNOWLEDGMENTS

I acknowledge with gratitude the comments that T. A. Ackerman, H. van den Bergh, and especially R. E. Bennett and W. C. Ward provided on earlier drafts of this chapter, but none of these individuals is responsible for any of the errors that may remain.

REFERENCES

Ackerman, T. A., & Smith, P. L. (1988). A comparison of the information provided by essay, multiple-choice, and free-response writing tests. *Applied Psychological Measurement, 12*(2), 117–128.

Bennett, R. E., Rock, D. A., Braun, H. I., Frye, D., Spohrer, J. C., & Soloway, E. (1990). The relationship of constrained free-response to multiple-choice and open-ended items. *Applied Psychological Measurement, 14*(2), 151–162.

Bennett, R. E., Rock, D. A., & Wang, M. (1991). Equivalence of free-response and multiple-choice items. *Journal of Educational Measurement, 28*(1), 77–92.

Bennett, R. E., Ward, W. C., Rock, D. A., & LaHart, C. (1990). *Toward a framework for constructed-response items* (RR-90-7). Princeton, NJ: Educational Testing Service.

Breland, H. M. (1977). *A study of college English placement and the Test of Standard Written English* (College Entrance Examination Board Research and Development Report RDR-76-77, No. 4). Princeton, NJ: Educational Testing Service.

Breland, H. M., & Gaynor, J. L. (1979). A comparison of direct and indirect assessments of writing skill. *Journal of Educational Measurement, 16*(2), 119–128.

Capell, F. J., & Quellmalz, E. S. (1980). *Empirical validation studies of alternate response modes for writing assessment* (CSE Report No. 145). Los Angeles, CA: Center for the Study of Evaluation, University of California at Los Angeles.

Guilford, J. P. (1971). *The nature of human intelligence.* New York: McGraw-Hill.

Guilford, J. P., & Hoepfner, R. (1971). *The analysis of intelligence.* New York: McGraw-Hill.

Hayes, J. R., & Flower, L. S. (1980). Identifying the organization of writing processes. In E. W. Gregg & E. R. Steinberg (Eds.), *Cognitive processes in writing* (pp. 3–30). Hillsdale, NJ: Lawrence Erlbaum Associates.

Hogan, T. P. (1981). *Relationship between free-response and choice-type tests of achievement: A review of the literature.* Green Bay, WI: University of Wisconsin. (ERIC Document Reproduction Service No. ED 224 811)

Jöreskog, K. (1971). Statistical analysis of sets of congeneric tests. *Psychometrika, 36*(2), 109–132.

Jöreskog, K., & Sörbom, D. (1981). *LISREL: Analysis of linear structural relationships by the method of maximum likelihood. User's guide.* Chicago, IL: International Educational Services.

Lord, F. M. (1973). Testing if two measuring procedures measure the same psychological dimension. *Psychological Bulletin, 79*(1), 71–72.

Millman, J., Bishop, C. H., Ebel, R. L. (1965). An analysis of test wiseness. *Educational and Psychological Measurement, 25*(3), 707–726.

Norris, S. P. (1990). Effects of eliciting verbal reports of thinking on critical thinking test performance. *Journal of Educational Measurement, 27*(1), 41–58.

Norris, S. P. (in press). Informal reasoning assessment: Using verbal reports of thinking to improve multiple-choice test validity. In D. N. Perkins, J. Segal, & J. F. Voss (Eds.), *Informal reasoning and education.* Hillsdale, NJ: Lawrence Erlbaum Associates.

Quellmalz, E., & Capell, F. (1979). *Defining writing domains: Effects of discourse and response mode.* Los Angeles: University of California at Los Angeles, Center for the Study of Evaluation. (ERIC Document Reproduction Service No. ED 212 661)

Quellmalz, E. S., Capell, F. J., & Chou, C-P. (1982). Effects of discourse and response mode on the measurement of writing competence. *Journal of Educational Measurement, 19*(4), 241–258.

Traub, R. E., & Fisher, C. W. (1977). On the equivalence of constructed-response and multiple-choice tests. *Applied Psychological Measurement, 1*(3), 355–369.

Traub, R. E., & MacRury, K. (1990). Antwort-auswahl- vs freie-antwort-aufgaben bei lernerfolgstests [Multiple-choice vs. free-response in the testing of scholastic achievement]. In K. Ingenkamp & R. S. Jäger (Eds.), *Tests und trends 8: Jahrbuch der pädagogischen diagnostik* (pp. 128–159). Weinheim, Germany: Beltz Verlag.

van den Bergh, H. (1990). On the construct validity of multiple-choice items for reading comprehension. *Applied Psychological Measurement, 14*(1), 1–12.

Ward, W. C. (1982). A comparison of free-response and multiple-choice forms of verbal aptitude tests. *Applied Psychological Measurement, 6*(1), 1–11.

Ward, W. C., Dupree, D., & Carlson, S. B. (1987). *A comparison of free-response and multiple-choice questions in the assessment of reading comprehension* (RR 87-20). Princeton, NJ: Educational Testing Service.

Werts, C. E., Breland, H. M., Grandy, J., & Rock, D. A. (1980). Using longitudinal data to estimate reliability in the presence of correlated errors of measurement. *Educational and Psychological Measurement, 40*(1), 19–29.

3

CONSTRUCT VALIDITY AND CONSTRUCTED-RESPONSE TESTS

Richard E. Snow
Stanford University

My choice of title is meant to convey that I think the central issue for this book, and for research and development on constructed response versus multiple choice in educational tests in general, is construct validity. Messick (1989) defined validity as "an integrated evaluative judgment of the degree to which empirical evidence and theoretical rationales support the *adequacy* and *appropriateness* of *inferences* and *actions* based on test scores or other modes of assessment (p. 13)" and noted that "construct validity is based on an integration of any evidence that bears on the interpretation or meaning of the test scores. . . . [Specifically this] subsumes content relevance and representativeness as well as criterion-relatedness" (p. 17). So, for the purposes of this chapter, I am concerned mainly with the meaning or interpretation of scores derived from particular educational test designs.

The original title assigned to me was "Trait Equivalence: A Cognitive Perspective." But I think the terms *trait* and *equivalence* should be avoided, and I take a psychological, not just a cognitive, perspective.

First, I avoid *trait* because it was borrowed by early psychologists from Mendelian genetics and is to this day often misinterpreted by the public as implying a fixed, inherited characteristic. I think the term should either be abolished in psychometrics or carefully redefined to minimize the potential for public misunderstanding.

Second, I avoid *equivalence* because I doubt there is a clear meaning for such a concept in the psychology of educational tests; that is, in the consideration of construct validity for such tests. One can allow a concept of psychometric equivalence for some specified practical purpose, applying a particular statistical model to a particular level of data aggregation; but what evidence equates the constructs underlying these scores? In today's philosophy of psychological science, constructs are not even considered equated to their own indicator scores; strict operationism was rejected long ago. In other words, for example, a constructed-response test and a multiple-choice test may correlate in some student population about as high as their respective reliabilities will allow; this fact may permit the two tests to be considered psychometrically equivalent for use in rank ordering students in that population, perhaps for some specified selection purpose. But the two are not *psychologically* equated; we only act as if they were, in this specific instance. This issue is revisited later in this chapter because it is especially important in planning research on constructed-response tests.

Finally, I emphasize a psychological perspective that includes but goes beyond a purely cognitive view. Although cognitive analysis of the contrast between constructed-response and multiple-choice test formats is essential, so is analysis of the conative (i.e., motivational–volitional) and affective aspects of performance that connect to this contrast. In other words, it is not only that multiple choice and constructed response may sample different cognitive structures or demand different cognitive processing. If the two test designs evoke different motivational structures, effort investments, expectations for success, feelings of self-efficacy, or doubts or worries, that is as major an implication for test score interpretation as any cognitive difference. This issue is also exemplified later.

TOWARD A PSYCHOLOGY OF TEST DESIGN

The field of educational and psychological testing suffers today because it never developed a psychology of test design. It must do so now, not only to address questions about constructed-response formats, but to face many other new design issues and choices. Think, for example, of the myriad questions raised in planning test computerization; these questions require psychological analysis, not merely engineering decisions (see Green, Bock, Humphreys, Linn, & Reckase, 1984; Wainer, 1990).

There were scattered early steps to expand construct validation methods beyond routine psychometric analyses (e.g., French, 1965; Thurstone, 1924). Early work on response sets also contributed (see Messick, 1991). From the 1970s, with the advent of cognitive information processing research on abilities (Carroll, 1976; Embretson, 1985; Hunt & Lansman, 1975; Snow, 1978; Sternberg, 1977), evidence regarding the kinds of cognitive processing skills and strategies involved in ability performance has gradually accumulated. Some of this work also shows the influence of some test design facets on cognitive processing in test performance. More recently, cognitive research has moved to address also the knowledge-rich domains of school subject matter, and the achievement tests associated with these domains. Thus, good examples now exist of knowledge structure analysis as well as process analysis of test performance (see Snow & Lohman, 1989, for a summary).

What is still needed, however, is programmatic research from this base, to build a psychology of test design. This would involve the development of a taxonomy—a full elaboration of the facets of real and potential test designs, perhaps in the style of Guttman's use of facet theory—and programs of experimental cognitive and conative task analysis of test facets in different ability and achievement domains to build up construct descriptions associated with different test designs. Especially for achievement tests, task analytic research would need to focus on the content × process specification tables used initially to guide item development, as well as the facets of test response format. And these achievement tests must be seen from the start as psychological performance tasks; educational tests cannot be evaluated for validity simply by examining their content sampling specifications. This is not a new idea, though it has evolved considerably in the last two decades (see, e.g., Cronbach, 1971, 1988; Hofstee, 1971; Messick, 1989).

Taxonomy

People mean different things by terms such as *constructed response*, so there is a need for taxonomic work to produce a complete facet structure for test design. The contrast of constructed response versus multiple choice is but one facet in this complex facet structure, and it might take on different psychological meanings when crossed with other facets, such as group versus individual administration, oral versus written response, or degree of speededness. Furthermore, this one facet is itself complex. One can think of a whole graduated continuum of constructed-response test formats. A provisional example of such a continuum is shown in Table 3.1. It is provisional because, even in this one facet, there are several alternative possible frameworks (see, e.g., Bennett, Ward, Rock, & LaHart, 1990; also, Bennett, this volume). The point is that further research will be advanced by having a well-worked-out taxonomy of test design facets, no matter how provisional it remains with respect to research in hand at any point in time. It provides a rack on which to hang research findings as they accumulate.

Table 3.1 shows seven levels, each with some subdivisions, that might be hypothesized to have significantly different psychological features. Apparently, conventional multiple choice in which the student chooses one alternative involves the lowest degree of response construction. Multiple-choice format in which the student distributes probabilities among alternatives (see

TABLE 3.1
A Provisional Continuum of Constructed-Response Test Formats

1. *Multiple Choice*
   a) choose one
   b) distribute probabilities

2. *Multiple Choice with Intervening Construction*
   a) retrieve/reconstruct knowledge
   b) reason with knowledge

3. *Simple Completion/Cloze Procedure*
   a) insert word
   b) insert phrase

4. *Short Answer Essay/Complex Completion*
   a) produce sentence
   b) produce paragraph

5. *Problem Exercise*
   a) produce solution
   b) explain solution

6. *Teach-Back Procedure*
   a) explain concept/procedures
   b) explain structure/system

7. *Long Essay/Demonstration/Project*
   a) produce with topic constraint
   b) produce without topic constraint

8. *Collections of above over time, portfolios, and so on*

di Finetti, 1967; Shuford, Massengill, & Albert, 1966) would presumably add some degree of construction. Next comes Level 2, with a multiple-choice format in which the student is asked to construct a response before choosing among the given alternatives; such items may require retrieval, or reconstruction, or actual reasoning with knowledge. Next, Level 3 requires completing a passage by inserting a word or phrase. Then, there are various short answer formats that involve more complex completions (Level 4), problem exercises that can require construction of an explanation as well as a solution (Level 5), teach-back procedures (Level 6) in which larger domain explanations are constructed, and essays or project demonstrations constructed with or without topic constraints (Level 7). Beyond this, I note a Level 8, involving sequential collection of such constructions over time, in portfolios of school work, for example. Obviously, a much more elaborate multivariate structure for the variety of possible constructed-response formats could be fashioned.

Methodology

What methodologies can be brought to bear in analyzing and comparing the test designs at different levels in Table 3.1? Beyond psychometric analysis of contrasting test designs aimed at assessing the same construct, there are at least two other methods (or categories of methods) that should be especially useful. One method uses verbal and observational protocol analysis of task performances, interviews, and think-aloud correlates of responses to the tasks, in the style of much cognitive task analysis research of late (see Ericcson & Simon, 1984). Eye-movement recordings during test performance also fit this category. Using such records, variations in behavior prompted by different test designs can be given detailed description. The other method uses aptitude-treatment interaction (ATI) experiments perhaps suggested by the earlier protocol analyses. Individual difference constructs are chosen (as the aptitudes) that should either converge with the target construct under both test design treatments or diverge from that target construct under one of these treatments. In other words, the T variable is the test design contrast, such as constructed-response versus multiple-choice, the dependent variable is the score on each version of the test, and one or more independent A variables are chosen to represent either additional measures of the same construct, or other constructs that are alternatives or threats to the interpretation of the primary construct.

Obviously, these methods can be used in consort. The expert–novice comparison design now common in much cognitive psychological research is a special case of this combination of methods. Persons are chosen to represent experts or novices (or advanced or beginning students) in some achievement domain. This is the A variable. Then, tasks are chosen and administered to contrast performances in which novices and experts are and are not expected to differ. This is the T variable. Think-aloud protocols and related observations then provide the criterion descriptions. An important next step in research on constructed-response tests would contrast advanced and beginning students at each of the various levels of Table 3.1 in just this way.

Plausible Rival Hypotheses

Whatever the method, the main aim of this approach to construct validational research is to identify plausible rival hypotheses to the score interpretation proposed and to develop evidence that removes these rivals if possible. This is the strong form of "construct-validation-as-explanation" advocated by Cronbach (1988; see also Campbell, 1957). As Cronbach put it:

> The advice [to pursue rival hypotheses] is not merely to be on the lookout for cases your hypothesis does not fit. The advice is to find, either in the relevant

community of concerned persons or in your own devilish imagination, an alternative explanation of the accumulated findings; then to devise a study where the alternatives lead to disparate predictions. Concentrating on plausible rivals is especially important in validation because persons unfriendly to a test interpretation are likely to use a rival hypotheses as ammunition. Proponents' prior checks on the rival hypotheses provide a potent defensive weapon—or warn them to pick a line of retreat. (p. 14)

RIVAL HYPOTHESES ABOUT CONSTRUCTED-RESPONSE AND MULTIPLE-CHOICE TESTS

The emphasis on comparative studies of plausible alternatives in construct validation is particularly important in relation to research on constructed-response versus multiple-choice tests because several strong rival hypotheses have been advanced about both of these test design formats. These hypotheses have come forth in the heat of heightened public interest and political debate about education. Unfortunately, they usually do not identify precisely which of the many types of test response formats they embrace or reject.

Critics of conventional standardized testing often argue that multiple-choice format requires only a superficial, list-of-isolated-facts kind of knowledge structure, and promotes learning and instruction of this same sort, inasmuch as teachers inevitably teach to the test. Such tests are also open to invalidation due to various forms of test-wiseness, social bias, and the ease of cheating. Constructed-response format, on the other hand, involves deeper understanding and higher order, critical thinking, and thus promotes learning and instruction aimed at these higher goals. It is also fairer, because instruction and assessment are in this way more closely connected, and even potentially integrated.

Defenders of conventional standardized testing argue that multiple-choice format can be used to assess many, if not all, deeper or higher order goals of learning and instruction; the two types of tests are usually highly correlated anyway, so multiple-choice tests are entirely adequate as well as much more economical for many educational purposes. Such tests are also fairer: Major forms of bias can be detected objectively and eliminated. Constructed-response format, on the other hand, does not necessarily assess deeper or higher order understanding—it may even promote rote memorization. Furthermore, it is unreliable as well as uneconomical, and open to major sources of scoring bias, as well as unwanted correlations with non-instruction-related student characteristics such as intelligence, anxiety, and socioeconomic status.

Table 3.2 is an attempt to unpack and list these hypotheses in a form more useful for reviewing or planning research on them. Because there seems to be such a bandwagon in educational circles these days for constructed

TABLE 3.2
Some Plausible Rival Hypotheses About Constructed-Response
and Multiple-Choice Test Formats

1. *Student Attitudes*
   Students harbor attitudes about different test formats that are difficult to change and that
   influence motivation to perform well; in general, students prefer multiple-choice tests because
   they are perceived to be easier and thus less anxiety producing.

2. *Student Anxiety*
   Constructed-response format increases the correlation of achievement scores with measures
   of test anxiety; thus, constructed-response scores are contaminated with variance from this
   source.

3. *Student Motivation*
   Constructed response format increases the correlation of achievement scores with measures
   of achievement motivation; on high-stakes tests this correlation is curvilinear, indicating that
   both high and low motivation is dysfunctional on such tests. Expectations about test format
   influence learning strategies, and deviations from expected format can disrupt both learning
   and test performance.

4. *Student Ability*
   Constructed-response format increases the correlation of achievement scores with measures
   of prior ability; such test performance is particularly susceptible to interactions with ability
   (and motivation) when instruction is significantly incomplete, unstructured, unclear, or confused. Thus, constructed-response test scores are contaminated with variance from these
   sources.

5. *Influence on Instruction and Learning*
   Constructed-response format is particularly susceptible to instructional quality effects, both
   positive and negative. Although use of this format may promote emphasis on deep understanding and critical thinking in teaching and learning over the long haul, short term effects
   may include vagueness about instructional objectives and a tendency to promote rote memorization as a learning strategy.

6. *Cognitive Knowledge Structures Assessed*
   Multiple-choice and constructed-response formats do not differ in the degree to which they
   can be used to assess deep understanding and higher order thinking versus superficial isolated facts and rules.

7. *Cognitive Processing During the Test*
   Multiple-choice and constructed-response formats do not differ in the complexity of cognitive processing they evoke, despite face validity differences.

8. *Psychometric Adequacy*
   Constructed-response tests are less reliable, less economical, less representative in content
   coverage, and more subject to bias, than multiple-choice tests with the same time limit.

response and against multiple choice, and because I am playing devil's advocate here, I have worded these rival hypotheses to favor multiple-choice format. I hope this provokes more intensive research effort than would the opposite, popular wording. Also, the table gives the hypotheses within categories representing the major kinds of important research variables to be considered. But the table is not exhaustive, and it does not take the important step of connecting hypotheses to particular levels or kinds of constructed-response formats (such as those in Table 3.1). This step is necessary because hypotheses about the kinds of cognitive knowledge structuring assessed or promoted by different test formats, for example, obviously depend on the kinds of formats being compared.

In short, there are several socially, educationally, and scientifically important questions attached to the constructed-response versus multiple-choice contrast. These represent plausible, rival hypotheses about the interpretation of each kind of test score, so the time is ripe for construct validational research of the strong sort to obtain and marshall the evidence, pro and con, on each. I take no position here with respect to the hypotheses listed in Table 3.2. In the remainder of this chapter, I simply identify some example studies, methods, and questions that I think need to be considered in the continuing research. Some readers may not like some of the implications, because they raise distinct challenges to the validity of some kinds of constructed-response formats, at least for some purposes. But that is the point of viewing construct validation as research and argument about plausible rival hypotheses. We need devil's advocates as well as reformers if we want the process to produce improvement.

SOME EXAMPLE RESEARCH RESULTS

Some empirical results bear in one way or another on each of the hypotheses listed in Table 3.2. However, I have not conducted a comprehensive literature search on any of these points; even with such a review, there would be much more research to be done anyway because most of these questions are new. The following examples are organized according to the categories of Table 3.2.

Student Attitudes

Although I do not know of work on U. S. test attitudes, Zeidner (1987) surveyed two samples of Israeli junior high school students using several alternative measurement techniques to assess attitudes toward multiple-choice versus essay format for classroom tests. Attitudes favored multiple-choice over essay format on many criteria; students saw essay tests as more difficult, complex, and anxiety-producing, and felt more at ease and expectant of success with multiple-choice tests. However, a majority also thought essay tests better reflected one's knowledge of the subject matter, compared to multiple-choice tests.

Of course, student attitudes can be expected to change as experience with different test formats accumulates, and student attitude may be an arguable criterion anyway. But, clearly, research is needed on U. S. student attitudes about tests and their connection to performance. In this example, test format seems to produce both positive and negative motivational influences; test anxiety may be a particular concern.

Student Test Anxiety

Research on test anxiety is voluminous. Much work has related test anxiety to ability test performance at different educational levels, including performance on SATs and GREs (see Powers, 1988, for a summary). Beyond some concern for the role of speededness in increasing the relations between cognitive performance and test anxiety, however, most test design issues have not been addressed in this work.

There is, however, an excellent demonstration of the ATI method noted previously, with test anxiety as the *A* variable. Schmitt and Crocker (1981; see also Crocker & Schmitt, 1987) provided a striking ATI result, comparing conventional multiple-choice format with one in which construction of a response was required in an interval between presentation of the stem and choice of one of the multiple-response alternatives (that is, a comparison between Level 1a and 2a in Table 3.1). The result is shown in Fig. 3.1. In the control (regular multiple-choice) condition, there is the usually obtained,

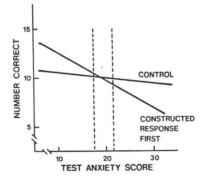

FIG. 3.1. Regression slopes of achievement test score on test anxiety score under control (conventional multiple-choice) versus constructed-response first (before multiple-choice) conditions (based on data from Schmitt & Crocker, 1981).

slightly negative relation between test anxiety and cognitive test performance; the test here assesses achievement on the statistics unit in a measurement course for college students. In the constructed-response condition, the negative relation of anxiety and performance is much more pronounced. The vertical dashed lines show the Johnson–Neyman–Pothoff region of nonsignificance. In other words, low test-anxious students (51% in the lower region) did much better with constructed-response format, whereas high test-anxious students (24% in the upper region) did much better with conventional multiple-choice format—they were penalized by constructed-response format.

The psychological interpretation is that multiple choice helps the highly anxious student maintain attention to the task; having to construct a response allows worries and self-doubts to disrupt thinking. On the other hand, constructing a reasonable response before being confronted by distractors is a good strategy for nonanxious students. The implication is that requiring constructed response allows scores to reflect test anxiety to a significantly higher degree than does multiple-choice format. Stated in another, more general way, constructed-response achievement score distributions may turn out to be significantly more highly contaminated with student anxiety variance. It is noteworthy also that in a within-person version of the Schmitt–Crocker experiment, one could find relatively high correlation between constructed-response and multiple-choice formats for the achievement test and still find noticeable differential relation of anxiety to the two; high correlation between formats certainly does not guarantee "trait equivalence."

Student Motivation

Two further hypotheses pick up on the positive side of student motivation implied in the discussion of attitudes. One concerns achievement motivation; the other, student expectations concerning test format.

In theory, test anxiety is just the negative side of achievement motivation, that is, fear of failure. The positive side is need for achievement. The two dimensions combine to predict cognitive performance as a linear or curvilinear function, depending on various characteristics of the situation. Accumulated learning from instruction would be predicted to result in linear relations between need for achievement or fear of failure and achievement. But achievement test situations, particularly when they are ego-involving, stressful, and risky, are predicted to show curvilinear relations: Both high and low need for achievement, and both high and low fear of failure, result in suboptimal performance, whereas optimal performance comes from moderate positive and/or negative motivation. At least one empirical report has shown clear curvilinear relations of this sort for both need for achievement and test anxiety measures; achievement was assessed by final, oral, constructed-response examinations in first-year college courses (Lens, 1983). The plausible hypothesis, then, is that high need for achievement, as well as high test anxiety, is more likely to be dysfunctional on constructed-response tests than on multiple-choice tests. However, even linear relations would suggest that constructed-response tests might be more contaminated with positive (as well as negative) achievement motivation variance than multiple-choice tests.

The second hypothesis arises from experiments that manipulated learner expectations to show that attention, encoding, and working memory processes in learning differ as a function of expected test format (d'Ydewalle, 1984; d'Ydewalle, Swerts, & DeCorte, 1983). Some findings on text learning suggest that learners expecting constructed-response tests pay more attention to text structure, and their performance is particularly disrupted when the text is badly structured (e.g., by scrambling sentences). Learners expecting multiple-choice tests pay less attention to structure and are less influenced by scrambling. Unexpected constructed-response tests cause the learner to try to reproduce the text structure, but this is possible only with well-structured texts. Interactions with ability appear, because learners differ in their ability to detect and reconstruct the structure of the text under different test format and expectation conditions. The hypothesis for us is that expecting constructed-response tests may motivate attentional and learning strategies during instruction different from those evoked when expecting multiple-choice tests, but that the learning effectiveness of these strategies depends crucially on the quality of instruction. Further, deviations from expectations concerning instructional structure or test format can be predicted to produce increased dependence of learning and achievement test performance on student prior ability.

Student Ability

A large volume of ATI research has shown that student prior ability predicts learning outcome more strongly when instruction is relatively unstructured and incomplete than when it is more tightly structured and complete (Cronbach & Snow, 1977; Snow, 1989). Unfortunately, previous reviews of this literature have not considered whether such results vary as a function of multiple-choice versus constructed-response tests used as measures of learning outcome. This question could be checked. Following the implication from ATI research as well as the expectation experiments cited previously, the hypothesis would be that the strongest relation of prior ability differences to learning outcome occurs when outcome is assessed by constructed-response tests following relatively unstructured, incomplete instruction. This might be a happy result for higher ability learners, but it would exacerbate the problems of lower ability learners unless the use of constructed-response formats also led to improvements in instruction designed particularly for such learners.

Influence on Instruction and Learning

This is perhaps the most difficult effect of test format to study, because adopting more constructed-response assessments presumably influences teaching and instruction over a relatively long time span, compared to other effects already discussed. But past research may hold some implications for new research. For example, the use of constructed-response versus multiple-choice format for both tests and instruction was a topic of interest in work on programmed instruction during the 1960s. To cite some results from just one relevant study, Williams (1965) found that constructed response was more effective than multiple choice as a format for programmed instruction, particularly on difficult technical material (in elementary school science in this case). Also, the more difficult constructed-response test was sensitive to these and other instructional effects, whereas the less demanding multiple-choice test was not. Hence, we might hypothesize that more use of constructed-response tests will promote more use of constructed-response format in instruction, with beneficial effects on learning. Also, using more sensitive, constructed-response criteria in instructional experiments might yield more and better suggestions for instructional improvements; if multiple-choice tests are insensitive to true improvements in learning, they may have been responsible for the rejection of many instructional innovations that showed "no gain."

On the other hand, as predicted from the previous section, Williams' (1965) constructed-response test was also more sensitive to aptitude differences; it correlated more highly with general verbal ability differences than did the multiple-choice test, even when constructed-response pretest scores were controlled (using gain scores). Strong correlation with prior ability would usually be expected to render a test less sensitive, not more sensitive, to instructional effects.

Cognitive Knowledge Structures Assessed

There is as yet little or no evidence that constructed-response tests necessarily require response construction, as opposed to rote response regurgitation. It may be that past research on constructed response, including the work on programmed instruction, did not require much more of the learner than simple reproduction verbatim of previously presented material.

Even when the constructed-response format clearly does require complex response construction, there is some evidence of high correlation with multiple-choice format. Some examples come from pilot research in my own project using teach-back procedures (as in Table 3.1, Level 6) and also short-answer essay style responses in a one-on-one interview situation (as in Table 3.1, Level 4). Of course, the high correlation comes when both types of test are scored simply for number of correct responses. In our work, however, it is also clear that the constructed-response conditions yielded many different scores and indices that allow rich description of the cognitive structuring, reorganizing, paraphrasing, elaborating, and reasoning processes in which a student is engaged, and also the kinds of conceptions, misconceptions, and associations a student may harbor. Hopefully, such indices have diagnostic value for instructional purposes even if superficial quantification of them correlates highly with a multiple-choice version of the same test domain. Unfortunately, it is also observed that the less able student tends to produce verbatim responses with little restructuring or elaborating.

In short, the research in hand is nowhere near to proving that constructed response necessarily provides deeper, richer, more diagnostic assessment for instructional purposes than does multiple choice. However, there is no good demonstration that multiple choice can be used to assess deeper higher order thinking either. Both hypotheses need much further attention.

Cognitive Processing During the Test

There has also been rather little task analytic research on achievement tests as information-processing tasks. But there has been a lot of this type of research on ability tests. The studies have included eye-movement recording during item performance as well as think aloud and interview recording, and various experimental manipulation. The general conclusion seems to be that complex cognitive processing is involved in performance even on simple tasks. In addition to multiple processes, it is clear that performers differ in strategies, and further that flexible adaptation of strategies and strategy shifting is an important source of within-person between-item variance, as well as between-person within-item variance. Of particular interest here is the finding that even minor variations in the items can drastically alter processing strategies. Important differences have been found between true–false, two-choice, and four-choice response formats (Bethell-Fox, Lohman, & Snow, 1984), and between each of these and constructed response, at least in spatial ability items (Kyllonen, Lohman, & Snow, 1984). Also, ability differences in strategic processing are marked. An able student might turn a multiple-choice item into a constructed-response item by first processing the stem to construct a possible answer, and only then scanning the response alternatives to find a match. A less able student might conduct a feature comparison search between stem and alternatives from the start in order to eliminate response alternatives, with no attempt at mental construction. Note here that ability is relative to item difficulty; the able student may also shift to a response elimination strategy on difficult items, and the less able student may use mental construction on an item that is easy enough to allow it (Snow, 1980, 1989). Thus, it can be hypothesized, for achievement tests also, that the student can make a constructed-response task out of a multiple-choice task at will, and does so as a function of ability–difficulty match.

One implication of this last hypothesis is that multiple choice is only multiple choice in the eye of the critic; in the eye of the test taker it is often constructed response. Another implication, however, is that unwanted ability variance is also involved in multiple-choice, not just in constructed-response performance, and may be involved in subtle ways. But the most important implication is that all these issues are complicated and badly in need of research.

Psychometric Adequacy

Although this chapter has centered on psychological issues deserving attention, there are, of course, plausible rival hypotheses that center on purely psychometric issues. As Table 3.2 indicates, these concern questions about the scaling, reliability, representativeness, economy, and potential biases of constructed-response tests, relative to multiple-choice tests of the same length. The complexity and subjectivity of scoring elaborate constructed responses may make such designs particularly susceptible to subtle forms of unreliability and bias. Although multiple-choice format may be susceptible to other sources of invalidity, such as cheating and test-wiseness, it at least allows more direct, objective assessment of reliability and bias. These and other psychometric issues are treated in more detail elsewhere in this volume.

A closing rival hypothesis is suggested by the concerns about bias, however. Constructed-response format may serve to increase the correlation of scores with student background variables reflecting socioeconomic and educational privileges, as it was hypothesized earlier to do when student ability and achievement motivation are the background variables. Regardless of actual biases in measurement, this result would promote the perception of social bias in the tests. It would also accentuate the educational problem to be faced, of course.

SUMMARY AND CONCLUSIONS

A brief list of conclusions can serve as summary:

1. The immediate task before us is to generate and test plausible rival hypotheses about the multiple-choice versus constructed-response contrast (but also the contrasts among other levels in Table 3.1) with respect to construct interpretation.

2. To do this, we badly need to build up a functional psychology of test design.

3. The task involves issues of cognitive process and structure but also conative and affective process and structure; we cannot ignore student personality, attitude, and belief in construct validation.

4. We must not abide arguments based on face validity or political bandwagons; constructed-response testing in one or another form may turn out to be an extremely important development in educational assessment (especially as it is wedded to advances in technology) but there are many test design questions that require careful research. Taking wrong turns at any of several points could make a monster, that is, constructed-response test designs that are worse than multiple-choice tests in their effects on today's educational problems.

5. Among the problems that need research in relation to constructed-response test design are: correlations with student attitude, anxiety, motivation, ability, and socioeconomic status; influences on instruction and learning; the kinds of knowledge structures assessed; the kinds of mental processes prompted during test performance; and a host of psychometric issues centering on scales of measurement, reliability, representativeness, and bias.

REFERENCES

Bennett, R. E., Ward, W. C., Rock, D. A., & LaHart, C. (1990). *Toward a framework for constructed-response items* (ETS RR 90-7). Princeton, NJ: Educational Testing Service.

Bethell-Fox, C. E., Lohman, D. F., & Snow, R. E. (1984). Adaptive reasoning: Componential and eye movement analysis of geometric analogy performance. *Intelligence, 8,* 205–238.

Campbell, D. T. (1957). Factors relevant to the validity of experiments in social settings. *Psychological Bulletin, 54,* 297–312.

Carroll, J. B. (1976). Psychometric tests as cognitive tasks: A new "structure of intellect." In L. B. Resnick (Ed.), *The nature of intelligence* (pp. 27–56). Hillsdale, NJ: Lawrence Erlbaum Associates.

Crocker, L., & Schmitt, A. (1987). Improving multiple-choice test performance for examinees with different levels of test anxiety. *Journal of Experimental Education, 55,* 201–205.

Cronbach, L. J. (1971). Test validation. In R. L. Thorndike (Ed.), *Educational measurement* (2nd ed., pp. 443–507). Washington, DC: American Council on Education.

Cronbach, L. J. (1988). Five perspectives on validity argument. In H. Wainer & H. I. Braun (Eds.), *Test validity* (pp. 3–17). Hillsdale, NJ: Lawrence Erlbaum Associates.

Cronbach, L. J., & Snow, R. E. (1977). *Aptitudes and instructional methods: A handbook for research on interactions.* New York: Irvington.

d'Ydewalle, G. (1984). Motivational and information processing. *Psychological Reports.* Belgium: University of Leuven.

d'Ydewalle, G., Swerts, A., & DeCorte, E. (1983). Study time and test performance as a function of test expectations. *Contemporary Educational Psychology, 8,* 55–67.

di Finetti, B. (1967). Methods for discriminating partial knowledge concerning a test item. *British Journal of Statistical Psychology, 18,* 87–123.

Embretson, S. E. (Ed.). (1985). *Test design: Developments in psychology and psychometrics.* Orlando, FL: Academic Press.

Ericsson, K. A., & Simon, H. A. (1984). *Protocol analysis: Verbal reports as data.* Cambridge, MA: MIT Press.

French, J. W. (1965). The relationship of problem-solving styles to the factor composition of tests. *Educational and Psychological Measurement, 25,* 9–28.

Green, B. F., Bock, R. D., Humphreys, L. G., Linn, R. B., & Reckase, M. D. (1984). Technical guidelines for assessing computerized adaptive tests. *Journal of Educational Measurement, 21,* 347–360.

Hofstee, W. K. B. (1971). Begripsvalidatie van studietoetsen: Een Aanbeveling [Construct validation of achievement tests: A recommendation]. *Nederlands Tijdschrift Voor De Psychologie, 26,* 491–500.

Hunt, E., & Lansman, M. (1975). Cognitive theory applied to individual differences. In W. K. Estes (Ed.), *Handbook of learning and cognitive processes: Introduction to concepts and issues* (Vol. 1, pp. 81–110). Hillsdale, NJ: Lawrence Erlbaum Associates.

Kyllonen, P. C., Lohman, D. F., & Snow, R. E. (1984). Effects of aptitudes, strategy training, and task facets on spatial task performance. *Journal of Educational Psychology, 76,* 130–145.

Lens, W. (1983). Achievement motivation, test anxiety, and academic achievement. *Psychological Reports.* Belgium: University of Leuven.

Messick, S. (1989). Validity. In R. L. Linn (Ed.), *Educational measurement* (3rd ed., pp. 13–103). New York: Macmillan.

Messick, S. (1991). Psychology and methodology of response styles. In R. E. Snow & D. E. Wiley (Eds.), *Improving inquiry in social science* (pp. 161–200). Hillsdale, NJ: Lawrence Erlbaum Associates.

Powers, D. E. (1988). Incidence, correlates, and possible causes of test anxiety in graduate admissions testings. In C. D. Spielberger & J. N. Butcher (Eds.), *Advances in personality assessment* (Vol. 7, pp. 49–75). Hillsdale, NJ: Lawrence Erlbaum Associates.

Schmitt, A. P., & Crocker, L. (1981, April). *Improving examinee performance on multiple-choice tests.* Paper presented at the American Educational Research Association, Los Angeles.

Shuford, E. H., Jr., Massengill, H. E., & Albert, A. (1966). Admissible probability measurement procedures. *Psychometrika, 31,* 125–145.

Snow, R. E. (1978). Theory and method for research on aptitude processes. *Intelligence, 2,* 225–278.

Snow, R. E. (1980). Aptitude processes. In R. E. Snow, P.-A. Federico, & W. E. Montague (Eds.), *Aptitude, learning and instruction: Vol. 1. Cognitive process analyses of aptitude* (pp. 27–63). Hillsdale, NJ: Lawrence Erlbaum Associates.

Snow, R. E. (1989). Aptitude–treatment interaction as a framework of research on individual differences in learning. In P. L. Ackerman, R. J. Sternberg, & R. Glaser (Eds.), *Learning and individual differences: Advances in theory and research* (pp. 13–59). New York: Freeman.

Snow, R. E., & Lohman, D. F. (1989). Implications of cognitive psychology for educational measurement. In R. L. Linn (Ed.), *Educational measurement* (3rd ed., pp. 262–331). New York: Macmillan.

Sternberg, R. J. (1977). *Intelligence, information processing, and analogical reasoning: The componential analysis of human abilities.* Hillsdale, NJ: Lawrence Erlbaum Associates.

Thurstone, L. L. (1924). *The nature of intelligence.* Westport, CT: Greenwood Press.

Wainer, H. (1990). *Computerized adaptive testing: A primer.* Hillsdale, NJ: Lawrence Erlbaum Associates.

Williams, J. P. (1965). Effectiveness of constructed-response and multiple-choice programming modes as a function of test mode. *Journal of Educational Psychology, 56,* 111–117.

Zeidner, M. (1987). Essay versus multiple-choice type classroom exams: The student's perspective. *Journal of Educational Research, 80,* 352–358.

4

TRAIT EQUIVALENCE AS CONSTRUCT VALIDITY OF SCORE INTERPRETATION ACROSS MULTIPLE METHODS OF MEASUREMENT

Samuel Messick
Educational Testing Service

At its core, the question of trait equivalence asks whether different methods of measurement share sufficient convergent and discriminant properties and correlates to warrant interpreting their respective scores as indicators of the same trait or construct. In the present context of contrasting construction versus choice in cognitive measurement, the method differences at issue involve different item-*response* formats, especially multiple choice versus completion and construction. This is in contradistinction to different item-*stimulus* formats, usually called "item-types," that set the task to be performed, such as antonyms, analogies, and quantitative comparisons as well as stipulated essay genres and topics.

This manner of posing the question makes it clear that trait equivalence is essentially an issue of construct validity of test interpretation and use. It is akin to that aspect of construct validity that Campbell (1960) has called "trait validity," which suggests that various approaches to the analysis of multitrait–multimethod matrices would be appropriate to its resolution (Campbell & Fisk, 1959; Messick, 1989). This construct validity view of trait equivalence is both broader and less restrictive than the traditional psychometric formulation articulated by Traub (this volume), which typically tests statistically whether or not different measures may be considered to be congeneric; that is, whether they have perfectly correlated true-scores even though their errors of measurement and scaling parameters may be different (Jöreskog, 1971; Lord, 1973).

The construct validity view is less restrictive because, when congenericness is rejected (which is ordinarily the case except under special circumstances), a kind of pragmatic trait equivalence is tolerated to facilitate effective test designs for some important testing purposes. For example, in the absence of congenericness, the presence of a dominant construct-relevant factor common to the different response formats, even though accompanied by small construct-irrelevant format-specific factors, could justify combining item responses across formats into composite scores.

The intent is for construct-relevant variance to cumulate capitalizing on the positive features of each response format (such as the greater breadth of domain coverage facilitated by multiple-choice items and the greater depth of process information promised by constructed responses), while biases attendant upon the smaller construct-irrelevant variance would not cumulate as much. This approach follows Humphreys' (1962) principle of achieving score homogeneity by the control of heterogeneity and is widely used to generate composite scores across different item-stimulus formats, or item-types, tapping a common construct. The need to capitalize on the strengths and compensate for the weaknesses of different response formats in convergent construct measurement is one of the main reasons that trait equivalence is singled out as a major issue in the construction versus choice controversy. Because of the trade-offs involved, the question is not simply which format is better for a particular purpose, but also what combination of formats serves that purpose better with fewest measurement disadvantages? Another dimension—namely, the conjunction of construction and choice, not just the contrast of construction and choice—is thereby added to the debate.

This formulation is essentially consonant with Snow's (this volume) position, but it provides a way of speaking meaningfully about trait equivalence in terms of the convergence of construct indicators as well as a way of dealing with the underlying issue in test design (i.e., which format to use and when to combine them). Trait equivalence is thus addressed through qualification rather than through Snow's (this volume) strategy of avoiding the term, although Snow is right on target in underscoring the fundamental vulnerability of the concept—namely, that trait measures cannot be considered to be equated with each other *psychologically* because, from the perspective of construct validity, the test score is not even equated with the construct it attempts to tap. Nor is the score considered to define the construct, as in strict operationism. Rather, the measure is viewed as just one of an extensible set of indicators of the construct. In these terms, the issue is whether scores for items cast in different response formats belong to the same extensible set of construct indicators or to sets associated with different constructs.

Convergent empirical relationships reflecting communality among ostensible indicators are taken to imply the operation of the construct to the degree that discriminant evidence discounts the intrusion of alternative constructs as plausible rival hypotheses. Because any suggestion of an equating of constructs with measures is immediately qualified in the construct validity framework, the full power of deductive argument, which depends upon the logical property of identity, is eroded (Cherryholmes, 1988). Hence, construct validation leads to interpretations and explanatory theories that are not only as logical and analytical as possible, but also fundamentally discursive and rhetorical, in the sense of providing persuasive data- and theory-driven argument (Cronbach, 1988).

The construct validity view of trait equivalence is also broader than the traditional psychometric view of congenericness because it leads naturally to consideration of the two major threats to construct validity, namely, construct-irrelevant variance and construct underrepresentation (Messick, 1989). That is, not only should we be concerned to demonstrate that construct-relevant variance cumulates substantially in the convergence of indicators while construct-irrelevant variance cumulates only marginally, but we should be prepared to argue that the test scores are defensibly interpretable in terms of the focal construct. Central to this argument is evidence of the extent to which salient features of the construct are well represented in the set of items or tasks while no critical aspect has been left out. This is an important point because much of the public debate about so-called authentic assessment devolves not on the relative quality of multiple-choice versus constructed-response measurement for those attributes that both formats can tap in common, but on the claim that important constructs or construct features are simply not addressed by one or the other approach.

Given these two threats to construct validity, it is fortunate that the Traub and Snow chapters in this volume offer two perspectives on the issue of trait equivalence, namely the psychometric and the cognitive-experimental. This is the case because psychometric and cognitive-experimental approaches address these two threats with somewhat different emphases, such that together they should yield a roughly balanced treatment. The psychometric perspective affords relatively direct and powerful methods for isolating and identifying construct-irrelevant variance, including factor analysis and structural-equation modeling of item or testlet interrelationships, as well as techniques for uncovering differential item functioning. In contrast, the psychometric approach to construct underrepresentation appears relatively indirect, requiring complex inferences from patterns of convergent and discriminant relationships of the focal construct with other theoretically relevant constructs and background variables.

The cognitive-experimental perspective, on the other hand, affords relatively direct methods for identifying theoretical mechanisms underlying task performance, leading to a construct representation of task requirements (Embretson, 1983). With its emphasis on construct representation through causal modeling of task performance, this approach might be expected to be more alert to problems of construct underrepresentation than of construct-irrelevant performance processes. However, both perspectives tend to rely too heavily on the construct analysis of existing tests, whether by factor analysis or task analysis, rather than focusing on theories of the construct domain as a guide to *designing* construct-relevant tests. In this connection, there is an important, if subtle, difference between the process representation of task performance and the process representation of the focal construct.

In this regard, Snow (this volume) is quite right in insisting that the cognitive perspective be broadened to encompass conative, affective, and stylistic aspects of task performance. This is apropos not only because student attitudes, interests, and anxieties clearly influence performance, but also because the appearance of different strategies or styles of responding immediately invokes the possibility of deeper personality determinants. For example, guessing on multiple-choice items or trial-and-error strategies on constructed-response tasks are not simply a function of the difference between student ability and item or task difficulty, with less proficient students expected to guess more, but also a function of risk-taking propensities at all levels of ability (Kogan & Wallach, 1964). As another instance, cognitive style preferences for broad versus narrow categorizing can influence the way in which knowledge is structured and restructured, possibly as a function of differential anxiety over the consequences of errors of inclusion as opposed to errors of exclusion (Messick, 1984). By ignoring personality influences on performance—especially conative, affective, and stylistic influences—the cognitive perspective is in danger not only of hypercognitizing its construct representations but also of hypercognitizing their implications for educational achievement and instruction (Messick, 1987).

Another advantage of the construct validity framework should be noted before commenting on some specifics of the psychometric and cognitive–experimental (or, as Snow prefers, psychological) perspectives. Namely, attention is forcefully drawn to the need for explicit scoring models, so that the way in which item or task responses are combined to produce scores rests on "knowledge of how the processes tapped by the items combine dynamically to produce effects" (Peak, 1953, p. 273). This match between the scoring model (test performance) and structural characteristics of the construct's nontest behavioral manifestations (domain performance) was called "structural fidelity" by Loevinger (1957) and constitutes a major part of the structural component of construct validity.

The predominant scoring model in education and psychology is a cumulative quantitative model in which the number of correct or keyed responses, or some weighted combination thereof, indexes the attained level of the focal construct or trait. This may be appropriate for ability or achievement constructs, but not necessarily for modeling the level of other traits or constructs such as social attitudes or creativity. Indeed, depending on the construct, perhaps it is not trait level that should be modeled but, rather, developmental level—and perhaps not level at all but, rather, membership in a latent class or diagnostic category (Loevinger, 1957; Messick, 1989). These distinctions have not been explicit in the discussions thus far but will become more so in the model-based measurement approaches to be addressed by Mislevy (this volume). The distinctions are noteworthy because preferences for multiple-choice versus constructed-response formats are likely to be contingent on the nature of the construct or construct feature that is modeled and interpreted.

SOME PSYCHOMETRIC CONSIDERATIONS

A number of psychometric considerations are raised by both Traub (this volume) and Snow (this volume) that stimulate further comment. To begin with, Traub discusses the virtues of employing stem-equivalent multiple-choice and free-response tests to control for content differences across the two formats—but at the cost of eroding examinee motivation. This is in contradistinction to using independent item stems meeting the same broad content specifications in the two formats, which better maintains examinee motivation—but at the cost of confounding format and specific-content effects. Stem-equivalence facilitates the statistical test for congenericness, but in item-level factor-analytic approaches to trait equivalence it runs the risk of elevating item-specific variance to doublet variance distorting the factor space.

Structure and Theory of Format Effects

If the hypothesis of perfectly correlated true scores across formats is not rejected, then presumably either format, or a judicious combination of both, could be employed as construct indicators. However, if the hypothesis is indeed rejected, as is likely to be the case because of differential method variance, then a number of possibilities need to be distinguished. For example, a dominant construct-relevant factor—or a dominant second-order factor generated by highly correlated first-order factors—may cut across the two formats but accompanied by small construct-irrelevant format-specific factors. This is an example of the problem of instrument factors analyzed by Cattell (1968, 1977) in his generalized treatment of perturbations in measurement. As we have seen, this situation is amenable to an appropriately weighted composite score, based on items from both formats, in which construct-relevant variance cumulates while construct-irrelevant variance does not, or at least not as much. The relative size of the format-specific factors would determine how much qualification is needed in the construct interpretation to take account of the contaminating method variance. Moreover, method contamination could be attenuated by increasing the number of response formats used from along the choice-to-construction continuum, granted that each of those selected also taps the same dominant construct factor.

Other major possibilities include the emergence of qualitatively distinct, though possibly correlated, construct-relevant factors unique to each format, such as knowledge of biological facts and principles via multiple choice in contradistinction to explanation of biological theories via constructed response. This suggests the use of separate scores separately interpreted in terms of distinct constructs. Another is the appearance of a dominant construct-relevant factor (such as quantitative reasoning) cutting across formats but accompanied by construct-*relevant* secondary factors (such as solving algebra word problems or generating geometric proofs) that are either cross-format or within-format or both. This suggests a profile of separate scores or subscores jointly interpreted in terms of a complex construct or construct network. A critical issue, of course, is whether the secondary factors qualify as construct-relevant or construct-irrelevant, and this depends on the nature of the construct theory. For example, factors for paragraph organization or for the mechanics of grammar and usage might be viewed as construct-relevant for an essay test of writing skill but not for an essay test of biology knowledge.

These matters might be substantially clarified if research on format differences were to proceed rationally from theories of task performance that take into account the cognitive processing involved in making a response, as Traub (this volume) recommends. In contrast to process representations of the focal construct, this is essentially a call for theoretical analyses of the components of method variance in test performance. In general, method variance includes all systematic effects associated with a particular measurement procedure that are extraneous to the focal construct being measured (Campbell & Fiske, 1959). Included are all of the context effects or situational factors (such as an evaluative atmosphere) that influence test performance differently from domain performance (Loevinger, 1957). Thus every measure basically consists of a construct-method unit. As a consequence, we need to distinguish, at least conceptually, those aspects of performance that are reflective of the construct from those that are responsive to the method—or, in the present context, from those that are differently responsive to different methods.

For example, Traub (this volume) proposes—modifying Ward, Dupree, and Carlson (1987)—that items requiring inference, application, or evaluation will depend on manipulations of data and of ideas from memory that must be undertaken regardless of response format. Hence, such items should appear relatively impervious to format effects. In contrast, items for which relevant material is directly accessible in memory in a form needed to satisfy the task requirements might be answered by means of recognition or some process of comparison and elimination in a multiple-choice format but require recall and reproduction in a free-response format. Hence, these items would be expected to exhibit format effects to the extent that recall is not a primary determinant of response in both formats.

This latter point serves to remind us that a format effect, like method variance in general, derives from *respondent* consistencies in item performance. These performance consistencies are influenced, but by no means determined by format characteristics. That is, for items tapping material directly accessible in memory, the multiple-choice format may allow and even facilitate recognition of the correct answer for some individuals, whereas other respondents may instead immediately recall or construct the answer and simply mark the correct alternative via matching. In any event, a major implication of this task-theoretic view of format differences is that studies of format effects should attempt to distinguish between items that, by virtue of format-related differences in their information-processing demands, would be expected to be format-sensitive as opposed to format-insensitive.

Test Design and Standardization

Another psychometric consideration that should be underscored is Snow's (this volume) call for a full elaboration of the facets of real and potential test designs. A good but provisional beginning is afforded by the continuum of response formats, ranging from multiple choice to construction and performance, proposed by Bennett and his colleagues (Bennett, Ward, Rock, & La-Hart, 1990; also, Bennett, this volume) and by the differently elaborated continuum, ranging from multiple choice to demonstration and portfolios, articulated by Snow (this volume). The main variant in these two conceptually related continua is the amount of constraint or degree of openness entailed in the response.

Further work is needed to clarify additional distinctions along these continua, as in such blends of construction and choice as multiple-choice items that require the respondent to give reasons why the chosen option is correct and possibly why each of the unchosen options is incorrect. Another possible addition is the multiple-rating format recently championed by Scriven (1990), in which each of several options is evaluated against complex standards. For example, the examinee might be asked to read a passage for main idea and then rate each of four sentences—say, by marking boxes labeled A to F—for the quality and completeness with which each captures the main idea. An added requirement might be that if none of the statements receives a grade of B or better, the respondent should write an A-quality main idea sentence of his or her own.

Other facets need to be added to a taxonomy of test design to accommodate variations in item-stimulus formats or item-types, as well as variations in content, in symbol systems, and in sense modality—although these facets may need to be nested *within* construct or type of construct. For instance, the item-stimulus format of analogies with verbal, numerical, or figural content in the stem might be used to tap verbal, quantitative, or figural reasoning, respectively, and conjointly to tap higher-order analogic reasoning; with difficult words in the stem to tap range and depth of vocabulary; possibly, with subject-matter content in the stem to tap domain-specific knowledge and reasoning; perhaps, with social stimuli in the stem to indirectly tap social attitudes; and so forth. But some cells in the taxonomy connected with the analogy format would likely be empty.

As another instance, we are familiar with the important role of content facets in designing achievement tests in subject-matter areas, but topical content is also a variant in the measurement of cognitive skills and abilities. It is not that content cells are empty for ability tests but, rather, that they are difficult to circumscribe in the absence of associated knowledge domains, curricula, and text books. Over what content should reading passages and vocabulary items range, or algebra word problems? We get some guidance here on what to leave out, not what to put in, from studies of differential item functioning. But this is really guidance about what to leave out of particular tests for particular purposes, not necessarily what to leave out of the content facet of a taxonomy of test design.

When these additional facets are crossed with the facet for response formats, one might also expect a large number of empty cells because of the construct-contingent nature of the enterprise. But a surprisingly large number will be filled, primarily because of the ubiquitousness of the multiple-choice format and the fact that anything that can be tapped by multiple choice can also be tapped by constructed response, although not necessarily equivalently. Multiple choice is used in the measurement of a wide array of cognitive skills and abilities as well as in the measurement of a wide range of subject-matter achievement. Furthermore, this measurement is not just in terms of fact retrieval, but also in terms of knowledge application, evaluation against complex standards, and problem-solving proficiency. Contingent sets of multiple-choice items might also prove useful in revealing problem-solving processes and strategies (Ebel, 1984) as well as stylistic learning preferences (Heath, 1964). Multiple choice has also been used in the measurement of social attitudes, personal needs and motives, vocational interests, aesthetic preferences, and human values (Messick, 1979). Although all of the constructs addressed by multiple choice can also be tapped by constructed responses, the reverse is not equally true. Empty cells will appear under the multiple-choice format, for instance, for organizing, synthesizing, and production skills, which inherently require some form of constructed response for their direct examination (although not necessarily for their estimation or prediction).

The daunting complexity of a fully faceted taxonomy of test design—which might be better conceived as an integrated or dovetailed set of design taxonomies for different construct domains—should not deter us from taking provisional steps in this direction. Such a move might help to clarify some widespread misconceptions, especially with respect to the design facets of standardization and objectivity of scoring. In much of the public rhetoric surrounding authentic or performance measurement, standardized testing is equated with the multiple-choice format, as is objective scoring; whereas constructed responses are viewed as nonstandardized (i.e., tailored to local needs and conditions) and subjectively scored (i.e., responsive to professional judgment). In actuality, however, the facets for standardization and objectivity are only modestly correlated with, if not orthogonal to, the facet for response formats. For example, multiple-choice items are objectively scored in that the same key is uniformly applied to all responses to an item. But the key itself is usually determined subjectively by professional judgment.

In contrast, constructed responses are also objectively scorable in many instances. An example is a science performance test requiring the qualitative analysis of an unknown chemical solution. Performance might be scored in terms of whether the correct ingredients were identified, whether the correct reagents were applied in a correct sequence, and so forth. Nor is it the case that subjective scoring of constructed responses is completely devoid of objectivity. Subjective scoring is typically constrained to be responsive to judgmental standards and score scales that are determined by professional consensus and implemented by standardized training of scorers in their use. In a sense, then, objectivity versus subjectivity of scoring refers to differences in the nature and degree of standardization of scoring procedures and the uniformity of their application. Hence it could be viewed as a subfacet of standardization. It should be noted that standardization in general, and standardization of scoring procedures in particular, is not only in the service of norm-referenced comparability of scores across examinees, which may or may not be of interest. Standardization is also in the service of criterion-referenced comparability of scores to performance standards and of the construct validity of score interpretation. Hence, standardization should not lightly be dismissed.

Other subfacets of standardization in addition to scoring include the degree to which timing, administration conditions, and items or tasks are fixed or variable across respondents. It would appear that these subfacets are roughly orthogonal to the facet for response formats because either multiple choice or constructed response could be either timed or untimed, be administered under fixed or variable conditions, and involve either a common set of tasks for each examinee or a different set. On this last point, it is usually assumed that there is more task variability with constructed responses than with multiple choice. For example, essays may be written by different examinees on different topics or in different genres, or both. Although at some level of abstraction, the test is circumscribed (for example, as a qualified writing sample), problems of equating difficulty level and discriminating power or reliability are rarely confronted. In contrast, although multiple-choice tests usually involve administration of the same items to each respondent, scores are also often determined using parallel forms for different examinees, task standardization deriving from equated forms rather than fixed items. Furthermore, computer-adaptive multiple-choice tests routinely involve different item sets for different individuals, task standardization deriving from item calibration rather than fixed equivalent forms.

In general, standardization attempts to control for known confoundings or interactions among the conditions of measurement or with examinee characteristics. It hence limits generalizability and interpretability but in *known* ways, so that interpretations can and should be qualified by the conditions that have been held constant (or that have been measured and taken into account by statistical analysis). In the absence of standardization or statistical control, interpretations still need to be qualified but the basis is fuzzy or unknown, translating into a source not just of imprecision but of invalidity. Of course, unknown interactions remain a continuing threat to generalizability and validity, until they are uncovered through construct validation and taken into account through qualified score interpretations.

SOME PSYCHOLOGICAL CONSIDERATIONS

From among the several cognitive–experimental or psychological considerations stimulated by the Traub and Snow chapters (this volume), two points are singled out for further comment. One is that unintended value implications of construct underrepresentation in educational measurement energize the public debate about measurement methods. The other is that such measurement controversies can be clarified by treating claims and counterclaims as plausible rival hypotheses to be subjected to scientific inquiry, that is, to construct validation.

Construct underrepresentation is a slippery problem in trait equivalence because two tests may be truly congeneric and yet neither may represent the focal construct adequately. The problem becomes exacerbated when the underrepresented aspects of the construct are by default tacitly viewed as being undervalued. Matters become worse still when these unintended value implications are not addressed. As an example, consider the construct of academic learning as formulated in the Beginning Teacher Evaluation Study (Denham & Lieberman, 1980), in which student engaged time was related to success on academic-learning outcomes measured by achievement test scores. A crucial distinction in the study was between academic-learning time (i.e., engaged time on activities directly pertinent to the measured outcomes) and nonacademic-learning time (i.e., everything else), with the former being valued over the latter.

Granted, the tests covered important areas of student achievement. But, as Cherryholmes (1988) elaborated:

> If academic learning time in this study bears any resemblance to academic knowledge and activities more generally, at least some of the following are involved: the abilities to provide descriptions, generate explanations, make arguments, criticize arguments, tell stories (narrations) that combine different elements (observations, facts, events), reflect on the motives or values of oneself or others, analyze decisions, communicate clearly, state novel ideas (conjectures, hypotheses), or test conjectures against evidence. It is difficult to imagine academic learning without them. The Beginning Teacher Evaluation Study, by exclusion, classifies each of these as nonacademic learning. Their construct of Academic Learning contradicts itself because their achievement tests *exclude* much that constitutes academic learning and skills. (p. 445)

The construct rhetoric and its action implications are in the name of academic learning, but the construct representation in measurement (as well as the supporting evidence) excludes much that is generally considered part of academic learning. Thus, the construct of academic learning is seriously underrepresented and, in this sense, deconstructs (Derrida, 1972, 1982). The process of reconstruction can take a number of routes. One could restrict the construct interpretation to *specific* areas of academic learning tapped by the achievement tests as opposed to academic learning more generally, making it clear that pursuit of the measured outcomes does not devalue other learning goals (which are simply not treated as part of the specific learning areas addressed). However, sooner or later one still needs to confront in the construct theory the intended and unintended implications of value conflicts implicit in trade-offs of student engaged time—trade-offs both among the measured learning areas and between measured and unmeasured learning goals.

As another instance, one could follow the original path but explicitly view the measurement representation of the construct as provisional and incomplete, deferring the fuller meaning of academic learning to a later time. In this case the insidious unintended value implications of the underrepresentation should be openly confronted, especially because there may be little disagreement about value positions once they are debated and clarified. Furthermore, any *intended* value implications should also be explicated, especially as they bear on action implications of the construct rhetoric. Indeed, one aspect of construct validation is to inquire whether the value implications and the trait implications of the construct interpretation are commensurate (Messick, 1989). As a final instance, one could strive for a fuller representation of the construct, explicitly addressing the value implications—now not so much of the construct *under*representation but, rather, of the construct representation itself. These will derive substantially from the fact that student engaged time is not unlimited.

My closing point is essentially an enthusiastic commendation of Snow's (this volume) initiative in converting the claims and counterclaims advanced in the public and political debate about educational measurement into plausible rival hypotheses to be subjected to scientific inquiry. These claims are part of the rhetoric of debate on both sides, which more often than not is a "pejorative use of rhetoric that attempts to be persuasive by using evidence selectively and appealing explicitly to biases and stereotypes" (Cherryholmes, 1988, p. 425). Snow's proposal recasts the stereotypes about test formats into testable hypotheses responsive to scientific evidence. If implemented even partially, the required research might help to elevate the debate to the level of rhetoric exemplified in strong construct validation, that is, to the level of persuasive data- and theory-based argument.

REFERENCES

Bennett, R. E., Ward, W. C., Rock, D. A., & LaHart, C. (1990). *Toward a framework for constructed-response items* (ETS-RR 90-7). Princeton, NJ: Educational Testing Service.

Campbell, D. T. (1960). Recommendations for APA test standards regarding construct, trait, or discriminant validity. *American Psychologist, 15*, 546–553.

Campbell, D. T., & Fiske, D. W. (1959). Convergent and discriminant validation by the multitrait–multimethod matrix. *Psychological Bulletin, 56*, 81–105.

Cattell, R. B. (1968). Trait-view theory of perturbations in ratings and self ratings (L(BR)- and Q-data): Its application to obtaining pure trait score estimates in questionnaires. *Psychological Review, 75*, 96–113.

Cattell, R. B. (1977). A more sophisticated look at structure: Perturbation, sampling, role, and observer trait-view theories. In R. B. Cattell & R. M. Dreger (Eds.), *Handbook of modern personality theory* (pp. 166–220). New York: Wiley.

Cherryholmes, C. H. (1988). Construct validity and discourses of research. *American Journal of Education, 96*, 421–457.

Cronbach, L. J. (1988). Construct validation after thirty years. In R. L. Linn (Ed.), *Intelligence: Measurement theory and public policy—Proceedings of a symposium in honor of Lloyd G. Humphreys* (pp. 147–171). Urbana, IL: University of Illinois Press.

Denham, C., & Lieberman, A. (Eds.). (1980). *Time to learn.* Washington, DC: National Institute of Education.

Derrida, J. (1972). Discussion: Structure, sign, and play in the discourse of the human sciences. In R. Macksey & E. Donato (Eds.), *The structuralist controversy.* Baltimore, MD: Johns Hopkins University Press.

Derrida, J. (1982). *Of grammatology.* Baltimore, MD: Johns Hopkins University Press.

Ebel, R. L. (1984). Achievement test items: Current issues. In B. S. Plake (Ed.), *Social and technical issues in testing: Implications for test construction and usage* (pp. 141–154). Hillsdale, NJ: Lawrence Erlbaum Associates.

Embretson, S. (1983). Construct validity: Construct representation versus nomothetic span. *Psychological Bulletin, 93*, 179–197.

Heath, R. W. (1964). Curriculum, cognition, and educational development. *Educational and Psychological Measurement, 24*, 239–253.

Humphreys, L. G. (1962). The organization of human abilities. *American Psychologist, 17*, 475–483.

Jöreskog, K. (1971). Statistical analysis of sets of congeneric tests. *Psychometrika, 36*, 109–132.

Kogan, N., & Wallach, M. A. (1964). *Risk taking: A study in cognition and personality.* New York: Holt, Rinehart & Winston.

Loevinger, J. (1957). Objective tests as instruments of psychological theory. *Psychological Reports, 3*, 635–694 (Monograph Supplement 9).

Lord, F. M. (1973). Testing if two measuring procedures measure the same dimension. *Psychological Bulletin, 79*, 71–72.

Messick, S. (1979). Potential uses of noncognitive measurement in education. *Journal of Educational Psychology, 71*, 281–292.

Messick, S. (1984). The nature of cognitive styles: Problems and promise in educational practice. *Educational Psychologist, 19*, 59–74.

Messick, S. (1987). Structural relationships across cognition, personality, and style. In R. E. Snow & M. J. Farr (Eds.), *Aptitude, learning, and instruction: Vol. 3. Conative and affective process analysis* (pp. 35–75). Hillsdale, NJ: Lawrence Erlbaum Associates.

Messick, S. (1989). Validity. In R. L. Linn (Ed.), *Educational measurement* (3rd ed., pp. 13–103). New York: Macmillan.

Peak, H. (1953). Problems of observation. In L. Festinger & D. Katz (Eds.), *Research methods in the behavioral sciences* (pp. 243–299). New York: Dryden Press.

Scriven, M. (1990). *Multiple-rating items.* Unpublished manuscript.

Ward, W. C., Dupree, D., & Carlson, S. (1987). *A comparison of free-response and multiple-choice questions in the assessment of reading comprehension* (ETS RR-87-20). Princeton, NJ: Educational Testing Service.

5

A FRAMEWORK FOR STUDYING DIFFERENCES BETWEEN MULTIPLE-CHOICE AND FREE-RESPONSE TEST ITEMS

Robert J. Mislevy
Educational Testing Service

Ever since Robert M. Yerkes tested a million World War I recruits with his Army Alpha Intelligence Test, multiple-choice items have dominated educational selection, placement, and assessment applications. Occasional criticism has marked their reign, from observers including no less than Banesh Hoffman, Ralph Nader, and (Educational Testing Service's own!) Norman Frederiksen. But the character of today's debates strikes at the very heart of the enterprise: The view of human ability that spawned multiple-choice tests no longer holds universal currency among psychologists and educators. The ascendant view originates from a perspective more attuned to instruction than to selection or prediction. Learners increase their competence not simply by accumulating new facts and skills at rates determined by relatively immutable "aptitudes," but by reconfiguring knowledge structures, by automating procedures and chunking information to reduce memory loads, and by developing strategies and models that tell them when and how facts and skills are relevant.

Tests can be described as mere tools to gather information in order to guide educational decisions. But an educational decision-making framework cannot be conceived except around a view of human ability, which suggests educational options, determines what information is relevant, and specifies how an implementation is to be evaluated. The pertinent questions about multiple-choice tests now are whether, when, and how these tools, developed and validated within the old paradigm, can serve useful roles within the new paradigm.

This chapter discusses an analytical framework to evaluate the contribution of different types of test items. It encompasses views of ability from the new and the old paradigms. When applied with the old, it expresses the same questions that traditional test theoretic investigations have asked. When applied with the new, it provides machinery to investigate analogous questions—about efficiency and reliability, for example. We suggest how "inference networks" can be used to model the information from various types of observations, from traditional multiple-choice items to extended performances or portfolios, in terms of skills, strategies, and states of understanding. An application in the setting of medical diagnosis introduces the ideas, and an example based on Robert Siegler's (1981) balance beam tasks illustrates their application in a simple educational setting.

This analytic framework does not deal directly with an important issue in the debate over construction versus choice, namely, the feedback effects on instruction from the content and modality of testing (see N. Frederiksen, 1984); we focus primarily on what is learned about an individual from observations. The central role of feedback in the "why's" and "when's" of construction versus choice, however, is addressed in the background section.

BACKGROUND

The Origins of Multiple-Choice Tests

The initial enthusiasm that greeted multiple-choice testing can be attributed to its neat conformance to both the psychology and the economics of the post-World War I period. The psychology was that of the IQ. To the degree that a test was reliable, ranking students in accordance with overall proficiency was thought to reflect the cardinal characteristic of human intelligence. The economic character of the decisions that shaped the evolution of testing was nearly universal in education at the beginning of this century, and it dominates practice yet today: Educators were confronted with selection or placement decisions for large numbers of students, and resources limited the information they could gather about each student, constrained the number of options they could offer, and precluded much tailoring of programs to individual students once a decision was made (Glaser, 1981).

Exposing a diverse group of students to a uniform educational treatment typically produces a distribution of outcomes, as measured by a test score at the end of the program (Bloom, 1976). Decision makers sought to identify which students would be likely to succeed in a limited number of programs. An individual's degree of success depends on how his or her unique skills, knowledge, and interests match up with the equally multifaceted requirements of a program. The Army Alpha demonstrated that at costs substantially lower than personal interviews or performance samples, responses to multiple-choice test items could provide information about certain aspects of this matchup. What is necessary in this approach is that each item tap some of the skills required for success. Even though a single item might require only a few of the relevant skills and offer little information in its own right, a tendency to provide correct answers over a large number of items supports some degree of prediction of success along this dimension (Green, 1978). A typical multiple-choice test would be used to guide infrequent, broadly cast decisions, such as college admittance, course placement, or military occupational assignment.

Stasis Assumptions

The multiple-choice educational testing enterprise evolved under two tacit assumptions of stasis:

1. *A characteristic of examinees that is stable over time is being measured.* In the Army Alpha and many educational tests, that characteristic is posited to be "intelligence," calibrated in units of IQ. "Intelligence" gave way to "aptitude." This assumption is consonant with infrequent decision making; the measure should not be easily affected by short-term instruction (e.g., the SAT should not be "coachable").

2. *The characteristics of the system affecting the examinee before the measurement is made are unaffected by the measurement process.* Focusing on the educational setting, it is assumed that the instruction prospective examinees receive and what they learn does not depend on the way their performance will be measured. It is easy to believe this assumption is satisfied when the examiners believe, as did Yerkes, that tests are measuring examinees' "innate intelligence."

The historic cost/benefit justifications for multiple-choice testing are valid to the extent that these assumptions are met in a given testing context. Current interest in alternative modes of assessment, including constructed-response formats, is spurred by the realization that these assumptions are *not* well satisfied in all educational testing problems. New types of decisions, new types of costs, and new types of benefits enter into the equation. The results in a particular context may favor multiple choice, construction, or some mix. It is clear, however, that even when multiple choice is favored, it must be justified in terms of the new paradigm rather than the old, a point to which we return later.

Dimensions of Change

Figure 5.1 offers a framework for discussing current interest in alternative modes of testing. The upper left cell represents traditional choice-type observations, used to infer overall proficiency in a specified domain. That is,

Object of Inference

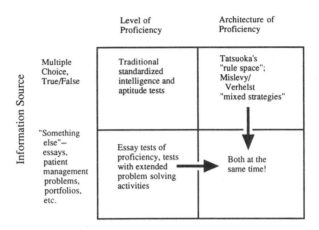

FIG. 5.1.   Modes and objects of educational testing.

it is deemed appropriate in the decision context to treat as identical all examinees with the same overall proficiency estimate, be it total score, formula score, or item response theory (IRT) ability estimate.

A first dimension of change arises from the realization that educational testing can affect educational practice. Norman Frederiksen (1984) cogently illustrated this point. During World War II, he and his co-workers encountered a gunnery course that consisted almost exclusively of bookwork and ended with a paper-and-pencil final exam. Frederiksen and his colleagues introduced a performance final requiring actual setup and operation of the equipment. Within a few sessions, the instructors had of their own volition introduced equipment into the course itself. Training now consisted of a balance of bookwork and performance, and trainees' final examination performance translated into better performance in the job. Contemporary examples include the New York Regents' physics examination, where what the Regents test the students study, and high stakes assessments in schools, where rewards for high scores on specific tests encourage, at best, emphasis of those skills, and at worst, coaching of the specific items on the test.

Once it is accepted that tests do influence instruction, attention must turn to the character of that influence. A test has "systemic validity," in J. Frederiksen and Collins' (1989) terminology, if the behaviors it encourages on the part of administrators, teachers, and students enforce the learning of desired skills. Administering a final essay test can be preferable to a final multiple-choice test with a higher reliability coefficient if, in preparing, students write more essays—*even if the final scores on the essay and multiple-choice tests are highly correlated* within a population of students at any given point in time. This realization spurs activity in the cell in the lower left. Students are still modeled in terms of overall proficiency, but the tasks are designed so as to better mirror the behaviors and the skills of the intended instruction. Steering instruction in positive directions constitutes a "consequential basis" for validating the use of a test (Messick, 1989).

A second dimension of change challenges the stasis of the examinee—or, more accurately, focuses attention on situations in which relatively short-term change is the intended outcome of the exercise, rather than a nuisance effect. Rather than seeking long-term, stable characteristics that are immune to change, a test in this context is meant to provide information about characteristics of an examinee that are ripe for change. The problem of interest is one of diagnosis or optimal assignment to instruction; the decision is viewed as shorter term; the options are cast not in terms of level of persistent proficiency but of architecture of current proficiency. Examples would include the examinee's level of understanding of phenomena in a domain of gears and pulleys problems (Hegarty, Just, & Morrison, 1988), the mental model a student is employing for series and parallel electrical circuit problems (Gentner & Gentner, 1983), and approaches to solving addition problems with mixed numbers (Tatsuoka, 1989).

The column on the right in Fig. 5.1 thus concerns applications where the inference depends on the architecture of the examinee's proficiency. Information can be obtained either from choice items or from constructed responses, as is illustrated later in a following section. These possibilities are represented by the upper and lower cells respectively. The present chapter focuses on comparisons of information about examinees from upper and lower cells, *within columns*. That is, the information from choice and construction items are compared given that one has already specified how to model examinees—according to overall proficiency or architecture of proficiency. It is clear from the preceding discussion that this logically precedent choice depends on the nature of the decision to be made about the student.

AN ANALYTIC FRAMEWORK

In this chapter, a *student model* is a caricature of a student in terms of parameters that capture distinctions that might exist among real students. A simple student model from the psychometric tradition posits a single variable—overall proficiency—that expresses all differences among students that are presumed to be relevant to the task at hand. A student model inspired by cognitive psychology might characterize a student in terms of the number of concepts and the nature of links among them. Marshall (1989, in press), for example, describes students in terms of aspects of their acquisition of schemata for arithmetic word problems. Model-based test theory consists of techniques for drawing inferences through student models, when the model for any given student cannot be specified with certainty but must be inferred imperfectly from observations.

A catalogue of such techniques has been developed over the past century for student models based on overall proficiency, from choice-type observations—the upper-left cell in Fig. 5.1. Our interest lies in analogous techniques for the remaining cells. What is required in a given application is a specification of the universe of potential student models and a way of connecting them to observations. Similar problems in such diverse areas as forecasting, troubleshooting, medical diagnosis, and animal husbandry have spurred research into *inference networks* (Lauritzen & Spiegelhalter, 1988; Pearl, 1988), or formal statistical frameworks for reasoning about interdependent variables in the presence of uncertainty. The next section introduces some of the key concepts in inference networks through a medical example. Following that, the ideas are related to student modeling in educational testing problems.

An Example from Medical Diagnosis

MUNIN is an inference network that organizes knowledge in the domain of electromyography—the relationships among nerves and muscles. Its function is to diagnose nerve/muscle disease states. The interested reader is referred to Andreassen, Woldbye, Falck, and Andersen (1987) for a more comprehensive description. The prototype discussed in that presentation and used for our illustration concerns a single arm muscle, with concepts represented by 25 nodes and their interactions represented by causal links. The ESPRIT team has generalized the application to address clusters of interrelated muscles in a network containing over a thousand nodes. A graphic representation of selected aspects of the simpler network appears in Fig. 5.2.

The rightmost column of nodes in Fig. 5.2 concerns outcomes of potentially observable variables, such as symptoms or test results. The middle layers are "pathophysiological states," or syndromes. These drive the probabilities of observations. The leftmost layer is the underlying disease state, including three possible diseases in various stages, no disease, or "Other"—a condition not built into the system. These states drive the probabilities of syndromes. It is assumed that a patient's true state can be adequately characterized by values of these disease and syndrome states. Paths indicate conditional probability relationships, which are to be determined logically, subjectively, purely empirically, or through model-based statistical estimation. Note that the probability distribution of a given observable will depend on some syndromes, but not others. The lack of a path signifies conditional independence. Note also that a given test result can be caused by different disease combinations.

As a patient enters the clinic, the diagnostician's state of knowledge about him or her is expressed by population base rates. This is depicted in Fig. 5.2

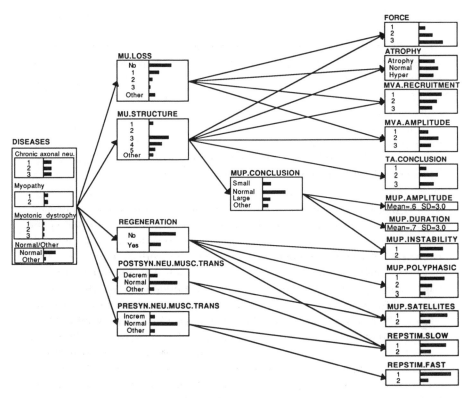

FIG. 5.2.   The MUNIN network: Initial status.

by bars that represent the base probabilities of disease and syndrome states. Base rates of observable test results are similarly shown. Tests are carried out, one at a time or in clusters, and with each result the probabilities of disease states are updated. The expectations of tests not yet given are calculated, and it can be determined which test will be most informative in identifying the disease state. Knowledge is thus accumulated in stages, with each successive test selected optimally in light of knowledge at that point in time. Figure 5.3 illustrates the state of knowledge after a number of electromyographic test results have been observed. Observable nodes with results now known are depicted with shaded bars representing observed values. For them, knowledge is perfect. The implications of these results have been propagated leftward to syndromes and disease states, as shown by distributions that differ from the base rates in Fig. 5.2. These values guide the decision to test further or initiate a treatment. Finally, updated beliefs about disease states have been propagated back toward the right to update expectations about the likely outcomes of tests not yet administered. These expectations, and the potential they hold for further updating knowledge about the disease states, guide the selection of further tests.

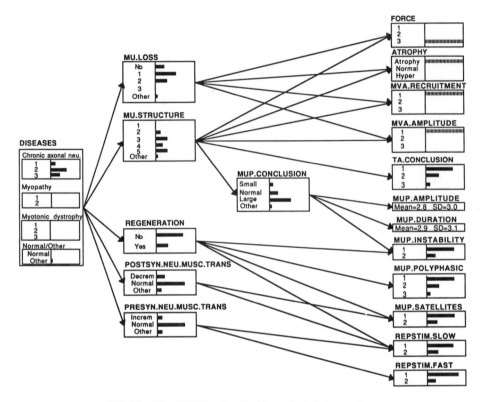

FIG. 5.3. The MUNIN network: After selected observations.

The MUNIN example described here just concerns diagnosis; the only observable nodes are tests and symptoms. The ideas can be extended to additional types of nodes. One type would be *prognostic nodes*. Probabilities would depend on underlying disease states. A network with diagnostic tests and prognostic assessments would draw inferences from current health indicators to likely outcomes, such as probability of survival after 5 years. Prognosis nodes could be potentially observable, such as whether a particular symptom will be present, or unobservable but inferable stochastically from future observables, such as the disease state that drives probabilities of new symptoms. Another type that could be introduced would be *treatment nodes*. The value of a treatment node, like an observable, would be determined with certainty when the treatment is initiated. Before this time, however, "what if" questions would be examined to explore the current projections of treatment outcomes. A prognostic node would then be affected by both disease nodes and treatment nodes; conditional probabilities of future states would depend on the current assessment of the disease state, and expected results under different treatment options. At any current state of diagnostic testing, the investigator could examine the expected results of alternative treatment options. Testing would be terminated when the additional information of subsequent tests would not provide sufficient improvement of expected treatment outcomes. For example, there may yet be several competing disease states, but if the treatment is identical in all cases, additional testing would not be warranted. (See Andreassen, Jensen, & Olesen, 1990, for a hypothetical network that encompasses diagnosis, disease identification, prognosis, and treatment selection.)

Modeling Student Understanding

To see how the ideas underlying MUNIN apply to the educational setting, consider the analogy drawn in Table 5.1. In collaboration with colleagues both within ETS and elsewhere, I am beginning to pursue a particular approach to student modeling based on this perspective (Mislevy, Yamamoto, & Anacker, 1992). In one sense it is a natural extension of traditional psychometrics: Students are described in terms of unobservable parameters, whose values, if known with certainty, would serve as the foundation for decision making; observational settings (e.g., tests, performance observations, portfolios) are devised that provide information about what these parameters might be; and statistical machinery is developed to guide decision making in the face of the uncertainty engendered by ascertaining the values of only observable variables rather than parameters.

Construction of an analytic framework for a specific application begins with a definition of a universe of student models. This "supermodel" is indexed by parameters that signify distinctions among states of students' understanding. Symbolically, we refer to the (possibly vector-valued) parameter of the student model as η. Parameters can be qualitative and quantitative, and qualitative parameters can be unordered, partially ordered, or completely

TABLE 5.1
Inference Networks in Medicine and Education

Medical Application	Educational Application
Observable symptoms, medical tests	Test items, verbal protocols, teachers' ratings of student performances
Disease states, syndromes	States or levels of understanding of key concepts, strategy choices
Interconnections based on medical theory	Interconnections based on cognitive and educational theory
Medical prognosis	Predictive distribution for criterion measures
Evaluation of potential treatment options	Expectations of student status after potential educational treatment

ordered. A supermodel can contain any mixture of these types. Their nature is derived from the structure and the psychology of the learning area, the idea being to capture the essential nature of key distinctions among students. A particular set of values of the parameters of the supermodel specifies a particular student model, or one particular state among the universe of possible states.

Any application poses a modeling problem, an item construction problem, and an inference problem. The following passages discuss each in turn.

The **modeling** problem is to delineate the states or levels of understanding in a learning domain. In meaningful applications this map would be expected to include several distinct strands, as understanding develops in a number of key concepts, and it might address the connectivity among the key concepts. Symbolically, this substep defines the *nature* of η and the *structure* of $p(\mathbf{x}|\eta)$, where $\mathbf{x}$ represents observations. Obviously any model will be a gross simplification of the reality of cognition. The objective is to capture differences among students that are important to the job at hand. As Greeno (1976) pointed out, "It may not be critical to distinguish between models differing in processing details if the details lack important implications for quality of student performance in instructional situations, or the ability of students to progress to further stages of knowledge and understanding" (p. 133). For the kinds of selection decisions that spawned traditional tests, it may indeed suffice to model students solely in terms of overall proficiency. Such applications fall in the left column of Fig. 5.1.

As useful as standard tests and standard test theory have proven in large-scale evaluation, selection, and placement problems, their focus on *who* is competent and *how many* items they can answer falls short when the goal is to improve individuals' competencies. Glaser, Lesgold, and Lajoie (1987) point out that tests can predict failure without an understanding of what causes success, but intervening to prevent failure and enhance competence requires deeper understanding. The past decade has witnessed considerable progress toward the requisite understanding. Psychological research has moved away from the traditional laboratory studies of simple (even random!) tasks, to tasks that better approximate the meaningful learning and problem-solving activities that engage people in real life. Studies comparing the ways experts differ from novices in applied problem solving in domains such as physics, writing, and medical diagnosis (e.g., Chi, Feltovich & Glaser, 1981) reveal the central importance of knowledge structures—networks of concepts and interconnections among them—that impart meaning to patterns in what one observes and how one chooses to act. The process of learning is to a large degree expanding these structures and, importantly, *reconfiguring them* to incorporate new and qualitatively different connections as the level of understanding depends. Educational psychologists have begun to put these findings to work in designing both instruction and tests (e.g., Glaser et al., 1987; Greeno, 1976; Marshall, 1985, in press). Again in the words of Glaser et al.:

> Achievement testing as we have defined it is a method of indexing stages of competence through indicators of the level of development of knowledge, skill, and cognitive process. These indicators display stages of performance that have been attained and on which further learning can proceed. They also show forms of error and misconceptions in knowledge that result in inefficient and incomplete knowledge and skill, and that need instructional attention. (p. 81)

Tests built to support such inferences lie in the rightmost column of Fig. 5.1.

Research relevant to this approach has been carried out in a variety of fields, including cognitive psychology, the psychology of mathematics and science education, artificial intelligence (AI) work on student modeling, test theory, and statistical inference. Cognitive scientists have suggested general structures such as "frames" or "schemata" that can serve as a basis for modeling understanding (e.g., Minsky, 1975; Rumelhart, 1980), and have begun to devise tasks that probe their features (e.g., Marshall, 1989, in press). Researchers interested in the psychology of learning in subject areas such as proportional reasoning have focused on identifying key concepts, studying how they are typically acquired (e.g., in mechanics, Clement, 1982; in ratio and proportional reasoning, Karplus, Pulos, & Stage, 1983), and constructing observational settings that allow one to infer students' understanding (e.g., van den Heuvel, 1990; McDermott, 1984).

Models that focus on patterns other than overall proficiency, and which constitute rudiments for student models more consonant with the results of educational and cognitive psychology, have begun to appear in the test theory literature. Examples include the following:

- Mislevy and Verhelst's (1990) *mixture models* for item responses when different examinees follow different solution strategies or use alternative mental models.

- Falmagne's (1989) and Haertel's (1984) latent class models for *binary skills*. A learner is characterized as possessing or not possessing each of a number of specified skills; a task is characterized by the subset of these its solution requires. Response probabilities are driven by the matchup between the skills he or she possesses and the skills a task demands. Also see Paulson (1986) for an alternative use of latent class modeling in cognitive assessment.

- Embretson's (1985) *multicomponent models* for integrating item construction and inference within a unified cognitive model. The conditional probabilities of solution steps given a multifaceted student model are given by IRT-like statistical structures.

- Tatsuoka's (1989) *rule space* analysis. Tatsuoka uses a generalization of IRT methodology to define a metric for classifying examinees based on likely patterns of item response given patterns of knowledge and strategies.

- Masters and Mislevy's (in press) and Wilson's (1989a) use of the *partial credit* rating scale model to characterize levels of understanding, as evidenced by the nature or approach of a performance rather than its correctness.
- Wilson's (1989b) *saltus* model for characterizing stages of conceptual development. Item responses are assumed to follow an IRT model within stages, but the characteristics of items are allowed to differ across stages.
- Yamamoto's (1987) *hybrid* model for dichotomous responses. The *hybrid* model characterizes an examinee as belonging either to one of a number of classes associated with specified states of understanding, or in a catchall IRT class. Examinees in this catchall class are characterized merely as to overall proficiency; their response patterns are not strongly associated with the states that are built into the model.

The **item construction** problem is to devise situations in which students who differ in the parameter space are likely to behave in observably different ways. The conditional probabilities of behavior of different types given the unobservable state of the student are the *values* of $p(\mathbf{x}|\eta)$, which may in turn be modeled in terms of another set of parameters, say β. The $p(\mathbf{x}|\eta)$ values provide the basis for inferring back about the student state. For measuring overall proficiency, $p(\mathbf{x}|\eta)$ might take the form of an IRT model, with item parameters β; examinees with high proficiency should be more likely than those with low proficiency to provide correct answers. As an example of the architecture of proficiency, Gentner and Gentner (1983) discussed how different parallel and series combinations of resistors and batteries prove differentially difficult for students using "water flow" as opposed to "teeming crowds" analogies to solve electrical circuit problems; items would be devised to distinguish between students using one analogy or the other, or neither or both.

Whatever the character of the student model, an element in $\mathbf{x}$ could contain a right or wrong answer to a multiple-choice test item, but it could instead be the problem-solving approach regardless of whether the answer is right or wrong, the quickness of responding, a characteristic of a think-aloud protocol, or an expert's evaluation of a particular aspect of the performance. These distinctions determine whether one is operating in the top row or the bottom row of Fig. 5.1.

Specifying a universe of student models selects a column of Fig. 5.1. This step depends on the nature of the inference or decision to be made. The question of choice versus construction is well defined when, for a given student model, observations of both types can be gathered. The decision of the mix to be observed can depend, wholly or partly, on the amount of information conveyed by alternative observations about the unobservable parameters in the student model. The effectiveness of an item is reflected in differences in conditional probabilities associated with different parameter configurations, so an item may be very useful in distinguishing among some aspects of student models but useless for distinguishing among others.

The **inference** problem is to reason from observations to student models. The model-building and item-construction steps provide η and $p(\mathbf{x}|\eta)$. Let $p(\eta)$ represent expectations about η in a population of interest—possibly noninformative, possibly based on expert opinion or previous analyses. Bayes' theorem can be employed to draw inferences about η given $\mathbf{x}$ via $p(\eta|\mathbf{x}) \propto p(\mathbf{x}|\eta)p(\eta)$. Thus $p(\eta|\mathbf{x})$ characterizes belief about a particular student's model after having observed a sample of the student's behavior. Practical problems include characterizing what is known about β so as to determine $p(\mathbf{x}|\eta)$, carrying out the computations involved in determining $p(\eta|\mathbf{x})$, and, in some applications, developing strategies for efficient sequential gathering of observations. The ESPRIT team that developed MUNIN has developed the inference network shell HUGIN (Andersen, Jensen, Olesen, & Jensen, 1989) to carry out calculations of this type, using the computational advances introduced by Lauritzen and Spiegelhalter (1988).

As mentioned previously in the MUNIN example, an inference network can be extended with prognostic nodes and treatment nodes. In educational selection, a prognostic node might be a rating of success in a training course. The goal would be to gather information about an examinee until it could be predicted with sufficient accuracy whether the rating would be above or below a cutpoint. In instructional assignment, the same prognostic node could be used but predictions would depend on instructional options as well. Now the goal would be to determine to a sufficient degree of accuracy which instructional option gives the highest expectation of success. For example, the determination may depend on identifying the mental model a student is employing, in order to explicate the limitations of that model and introduce complementary models.

APPLICATION TO OVERALL PROFICIENCY

IRT models are special instances of inference networks, with the form shown as Fig. 5.4. There is one unobservable node in a basic IRT model, the overall proficiency, often denoted θ in the IRT literature but denoted η here for consistency. There is one observable node for each test item, x_j for $j = 1, \ldots, n$. A link runs from η to each x_j, symbolizing the conditional probability distribution of the potential responses. If the only potential responses are right

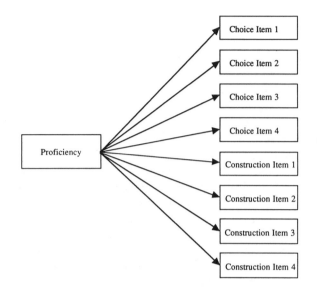

FIG. 5.4.   Network for a single proficiency, no criterion available.

or wrong, this is just a probability of a correct response at each η value; that is, $P(x_j = 1|\eta)$. The lack of links among items indicates the assumption of local, or conditional, independence of item responses given η. Most applications of IRT with multiple-choice items attend only to overall correctness, although models are also available for partial-credit scoring of choices, where the alternatives are distinguished and the conditional probabilities of each are modeled as functions of overall proficiency (e.g., Bock, 1972; Samejima, 1979; Sympson, 1983; Thissen & Steinberg, 1984).

Item response theory models can also be employed with constructed response items. What is required is that a score of some sort be assigned to a response, bringing it into the same framework as the choice items just discussed—that is, responses are mapped onto a scoring scale, and scores are mapped to η via an IRT model. The mapping of responses to item scores may be done by a human judge or mechanically in accordance with rules (Bennett, in press). An additional option is for the score to be a continuous real-valued number; Samejima (1973) provided an IRT model of this type. Figure 5.4 still represents the inference network.

Consider an application in which both choice and constructed responses can be garnered. How can the value of their information be compared? We consider four possibilities, distinguished by whether one wishes to allow for the possibility that "overall proficiency" has different meanings for choice and construction items (single proficiency vs. distinct proficiencies) and whether a prognostic node is included.

A Single Proficiency, No Criterion Available

Figure 5.4 is the appropriate inference network in this case. There is only one proficiency; probabilities of success to all items are driven by that proficiency alone, and are independent otherwise. Some of the observable nodes correspond to choice items, others correspond to construction items. A single IRT model is fit to data in which samples of examinees have been administered overlapping subsets of items of both types. Comparing information is straightforward in this case. Start with the "nothing-known-about-an-individual" state, analogous to the new patient in the MUNIN example. How much is the posterior distribution for his or her η sharpened by ascertaining a subset of choice items? How much by a subset of construction items? How much by various mixes? How much for subsets of items of the two types that take the same amount of time to administer? Do the answers vary for examinees at low, medium, or high proficiencies, as determined by entering typical responses at these various η levels? These are analyses of the accuracy with which different tests distinguish among student models within the "single-overall-proficiency" supermodel—in traditional terminology, the reliabilities of different tests that could be constructed from the full pool of items of all types.[1]

A Single Proficiency, Criterion Available

Extending the analytic framework of the preceding paragraph to predictive potential is accomplished by including one or more prognostic or criterion nodes, as illustrated in Fig. 5.5. Having assumed that the same proficiency drives probabilities for both choice and construction items means that an advantage in accuracy for η translates directly into an advantage in accuracy for the criterion. What is new is the ability to evaluate information in terms of predictive power ("predictive validity") rather than reliability.

Distinct Proficiencies, No Criterion Available

Empirical evidence suggests distinctions in at least some tests, in at least some examinee populations, between overall proficiency on choice items and overall proficiency on construction items. In the College Board's Advanced Placement (AP) history examinations, for example, girls appear to enjoy an advantage over boys on the essays compared to multiple choice, whereas

---

[1]As noted in the introduction, neither this analytic framework nor those that follow take into account feedback effects on the educational system, which can, in cost/benefit analyses, tip the balance in favor of tests with lower reliabilities and predictive potentials.

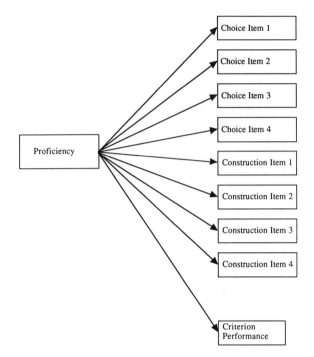

FIG. 5.5. Network for a single proficiency, criterion available.

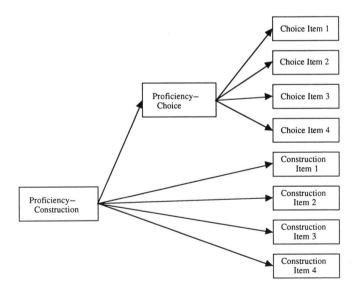

FIG. 5.6. Network for distinct proficiencies, no criterion available.

in AP in calculus, the boys do relatively better in the open-ended problems (Mazzeo, Schmitt, & Bleistein, in press). Figure 5.6 allows for the possibility of two distinct proficiencies. Choice items are driven by one, with conditional probabilities expressed perhaps through an IRT model, and construction items are driven by another. The link between the two proficiencies allows for the (possibly high) relationship between them.

The link between the two proficiencies allows belief about one proficiency to be updated by information from items of the other type. This suits an application in which one proficiency—say, the one driving construction items—is ultimately of interest, yet information about it can be obtained indirectly from the other—say, from choice items. If it is sufficiently easier or less expensive to secure, such indirect information can update belief about the node of interest more efficiently than information from nodes linked to it directly.

Distinct Proficiencies, Criterion Available

The nodes and links added in Fig. 5.7 introduce a prognostic variable. Interesting possibilities occur because information can flow to the criterion variable from both proficiencies, which can differ in their strength. The argument that in a particular application, construction items are less reliable but more

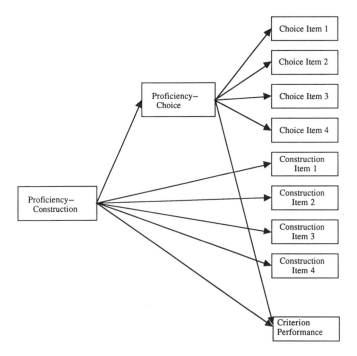

FIG. 5.7. Network for distinct proficiencies, criterion available.

valid than choice items requires the complexity of Fig. 5.7 as opposed to Fig. 5.5. This claim requires (a) weaker conditional probability links from construction item nodes to construction proficiency than those from choice item nodes to choice proficiency, (b) a commensurately stronger link from construction proficiency to the criterion than from choice proficiency to the criterion, and (c) a relatively weak link between choice and construction proficiencies.

APPLICATION TO PROFICIENCY ARCHITECTURES

This section uses similar reasoning to compare the information from choice and construction items when the latent variables are more complex than simply low-to-high proficiency. To fix ideas, we employ the balance beam example from Mislevy et al. (1992).

Siegler's Balance Beam Tasks

Piaget studied children's developing understanding of proportion with a variety of methods, including their explanations of balance beam problems (Inhelder & Piaget, 1958). Robert Siegler (1981) devised a set of balance beam tasks such that patterns of response could be predicted from the stages Piaget delineated. The tasks are exemplified in Fig. 5.8. Varying numbers of weights are placed at different locations on a balance beam; the child predicts whether the beam will tip left, tip right, or remain in balance. Piaget would posit that they will respond in accordance with their stage of understanding, the typical progression of which is outlined below. Data from the tasks are indistinguishable from standard multiple-choice test data on the surface, but there are two key distinctions:

1. What is important about examinees is not their overall probability of answering items correctly, but their (unobservable) state of understanding of the domain.

2. Children at less sophisticated levels of understanding initially get certain problems right for the wrong reasons. These items are more likely to be answered wrong at intermediate stages, as understanding deepens! They are bad items by the standards of classical test theory and IRT, because probabilities of correct response do not increase monotonically with increasing total test score. From the perspective of the developmental theory, however, not only is this reversal expected, but it is instrumental in distinguishing among children with different ways of thinking about the problems.

The usual stages through which children progress can be described in terms of successive acquisition of the following rules:

Item Type	Sample Item	Description
E	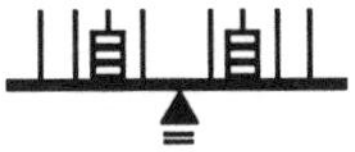	Equal problems (E), with matching weights and lengths on both sides.
D	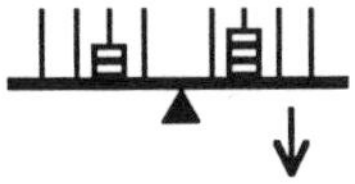	Dominant problems (D), with unequal weights but equal lengths.
S		Subordinate problems (S), with unequal lengths but equal weights.
CD	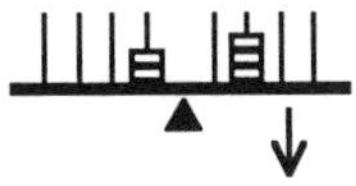	Conflict-dominant problems (CD), in which one side has greater weight, the other has greater length, and the side with the heavier weight will go down.
CS	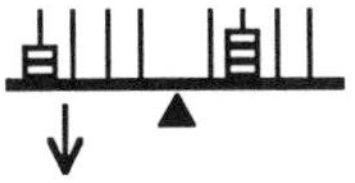	Conflict-subordinate problems (CS), in which one side has greater weight, the other has greater length, and the side with the greater length will go down.
CE		Conflict-equal problems (CE), in which one side has greater weight, the other has greater length, and the beam will balance.

FIG. 5.8. Sample balance beam items.

Rule I: If the weights on both sides are equal, it will balance. If they are not equal, the side with the heavier weight will go down. (Weight is the "dominant dimension," because children are generally aware that weight is important in the problem earlier than they realize that distance from the fulcrum, the "subordinate dimension," also matters.)

Rule II: If the weights and distances on both sides are equal, then the beam will balance. If the weights are equal but the distances are not, the side with the longer distance will go down. Otherwise, the side with the heavier weight will go down. (A child using this rule uses the subordinate dimension only when information from the dominant dimension is equivocal.)

Rule III: Same as Rule II, except that if the values of both weight and length are unequal on both sides, the child will "muddle through" (Siegler, 1981, p. 6). (A child using this rule now knows that

both dimensions matter, but doesn't know just how they combine. Responses will be based on a strategy such as guessing.)

Rule IV: Combine weights and lengths correctly (i.e., compare torques,
or products of weights and distances).

It was thus hypothesized that each child could be classified into one of
five stages—the four characterized by the rules, or an earlier "preoperation-
al" stage in which it is not recognized that either weight or length bear any
systematic relationship to the action of the beam. The classification of students is a simple example of the "architecture of proficiency," placing it in
the right-hand column of Fig. 5.1. Whereas Piaget's interviews fall in the lower
cell, Siegler's tasks fall in the upper. Table 5.2 shows the probabilities of correct response that would be expected from groups of children in different
stages, if their responses were in complete accordance with the hypothesized
rules.[2] Scanning across the rows reveals how the probability of a correct
response to a given type of item does not always increase as level of understanding increases. For example, Stage II children tend to answer Conflict-
Dominant items right for the wrong reason, whereas Stage III children, aware
of a conflict, flounder.

A Latent Class Model for Balance Beam Tasks

If the theory were perfect, the columns in Table 5.2 would give probabilities
of correct response to the various types of items from children at different
stages of understanding. Observing a correct response to a Subordinate item,
for example, would eliminate the possibility that the child was in Stage I.
But because the model is not perfect, and because children make slips and
lucky guesses, any response could be observed from a child in any stage.
A latent class model (Lazarsfeld, 1950) can be used to express the structure
posited in Table 5.2 while allowing for some "noise" in real data (see Mislevy
et al., 1992, for details). Instead of expecting incorrect responses with probability one to Subordinate items from Stage I children, we might posit some
small fraction of correct answers—p(Subordinate correct|Stage = I). Similar
probabilities of "false positives" can be estimated for other cells in Table 5.2
containing 0's. In the same spirit, probabilities less than one, due to "false
negatives," can be estimated for the cells with 1's. Inferences cannot be as

---

[2]The values in Table 5.2 assume that whenever a child's state of understanding does not
predict a particular answer, the probabilities of responding with "tip left," "tip right," and "equal"
are the same. Propensities to respond one way or another will certainly exist within particular
children in these stages, and they may vary systematically with stage of understanding. These
probabilities could be estimated from richer data, as might be gathered from the hypothetical
extension of the test described later.

TABLE 5.2
Theoretical Conditional Probabilities—Expected Proportions of Correct Response

Problem Type	Stage 0	Stage I	Stage II	Stage III	Stage IV
Equal	.333	1.000	1.000	1.000	1.000
Dominant	.333	1.000	1.000	1.000	1.000
Subordinate	.333	.000	1.000	1.000	1.000
Conflict-Dominant	.333	1.000	1.000	.333	1.000
Conflict-Subordinate	.333	.000	.000	.333	1.000
Conflict-Equal	.333	.000	.000	.333	1.000

strong when these uncertainties are present; a correct response to a Subordinate item still suggests that a child is probably not in Stage I, but no longer is it proof positive.

Expressing this model in the notation previously introduced, η represents stage membership, $\mathbf{x}$ represents item responses, and $p(\mathbf{x}|\eta)$ are conditional probabilities of correct responses to items of the various types from children in different stages—a noisy version of Table 5.2. The proportions of children in a population of interest at the different stages are $p(\eta)$, and the probabilities that convey our knowledge about a child's stage after we have observed his or her responses are $p(\eta|\mathbf{x})$.

Siegler created a 24-task test comprised of four tasks of each type. These tasks can be considered multiple-choice, because the respondent was asked to predict for each whether the beam would tip left, tip right, or balance—only one of which would actually happen. Siegler collected data from 60 children, from age 3 up through college age, at two points in time, for a total of 120 response vectors. Mislevy et al. (1992) fit a latent class model to these data using the HYBRIL computer program (Yamamoto, 1987), obtaining the conditional probabilities—$p(\mathbf{x}|\eta)$—shown in Table 5.3, and the following vector summarizing the (estimated) population distribution of stage membership:

$$p(\eta) = [\text{Prob(Stage} = 0), \text{Prob(Stage} = \text{I}), \ldots, \text{Prob(Stage} = \text{IV})]$$

$$= (.257, .227, .163, .275, .078).$$

Note that different types of items are differentially useful to distinguish among children at different levels. Equal items, for example, are best for distinguishing Stage 0 children from everyone else. Conflict-Dominant items, which would be dropped from standard tests because their probabilities of correct response do not have a strictly increasing relationship with total scores, help differentiate among children at Stages II, III, and IV.

Figure 5.9 depicts the state of knowledge about a child before observing any responses. Just one item of each type is shown rather than all four for simplicity. The corresponding status of an observable node (i.e., an item type)

TABLE 5.3
Estimated Conditional Probabilities—Expected Proportions of Correct Response

Problem Type	Stage 0	Stage I	Stage II	Stage III	Stage IV
Equal	.333*	.973	.883	.981	.943
Dominant	.333*	.973	.883	.981	.943
Subordinate	.333*	.026	.883	.981	.943
Conflict-Dominant	.333*	.973	.883	.333*	.943
Conflict-Subordinate	.333*	.026	.116	.333*	.943
Conflict-Equal	.333*	.026	.116	.333*	.943

*denotes fixed value

is the expectation of a correct response from a child selected at random from the population. The path from the stage–membership node to a particular observable node represents a row of Table 5.3.

Figure 5.9 represents the state of our knowledge about a child's reasoning stage and expected responses before any actual responses are observed. How does knowledge change when a response is observed? One of the children in the sample, Douglas, gave an incorrect response to his first Subordinate item. This could happen regardless of Douglas' true stage; the probabilities are obtained by subtracting the entries in the S row of Table 5.3 from 1.000, yielding, for Stages 0 through IV, .667, .973, .116, .019, and .057, respectively. This is the likelihood function for η induced by the observation of the response. The bulk of the evidence is for Stages 0 and I. Combining these

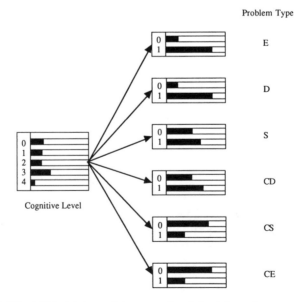

FIG. 5.9. Initial state in an inference network for balance beam exemplar.

values with the initial stage probabilities $p(\eta)$ via Bayes' theorem yields updated stage probabilities, $p(\eta|$incorrect response to a Subordinate item): for Stages 0 through IV, respectively, .41, .52, .04, .01, and .01. Expectations for items not yet administered also change. They are averages of the probabilities of correct response expected from the various stages, now weighted by the new stage membership probabilities. The state of knowledge after observing Douglas' first response is depicted in Fig. 5.10 (see Mislevy et al., 1992, for computational details; also see Macready & Dayton, 1989.)

Extending the Paradigm

The balance beam exemplar illustrates the challenge of inferring states of understanding, but it addresses development of only a single key concept. A broader view characterizes interconnections among distinct elements of understanding or lines of development. Calculating and comparing torques to solve the "conflict" problems characterizes Stage IV. But if a child at Stage IV cannot carry out the calculations reliably, his pattern of correct and incorrect responses would be hard to distinguish from that of a child in Stage III. Although the two children might answer about the same number of items correctly, the instruction appropriate for them would differ dramatically. And children at any stage of understanding of the balance beam might be able to carry out the computational operations in isolation. This section discusses a hypothetical extension to the exemplar; namely, the ability to carry out

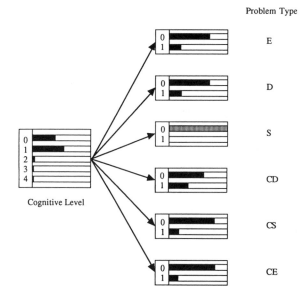

FIG. 5.10. State of knowledge after an incorrect response to an S task.

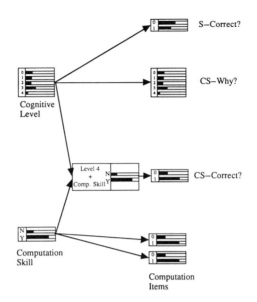

FIG. 5.11.   An inference network for an extension of the balance beam exemplar.

the arithmetic operations needed to calculate torques. For illustrative purposes, we simply posit a skill to carry these calculations out reliably, either possessed by a child or not.[3] The goal of the extended system is to infer both balance beam understanding and computational skill. To make the distinctions among states of understanding in this extended domain, we introduce two new types of observations:

1. Items isolating computation, such as "Which is greater, 3×4 or 5×2?"
2. Probes for introspection about solutions to conflict items: "How did you get your answer?" These items are construction items, in contrast to the choice items asking simply for a prediction, of "tip left," "tip right," or "remain in balance."

Figure 5.11 offers one possible structure for this network. The "S-Correct" and "CS-Correct" nodes represent the multiple-choice responses: Is the stated prediction correct? The "CS-Why" node represents the examinee's verbal explanation for a prediction for a particular Conflict-Subordinate task. To keep

---

[3]Obviously, states of understanding for calculating and comparing torques could be developed in greater detail, and would indeed have to be if one intended to remediate skill deficits in this domain. Verifying the presence of the broadly construed skill suffices to eliminate it as a source of failure on Conflict beam items. Discovering its absence could trigger further investigation with an inference network probing the details of the composite skill's architecture.

the diagram simple, only one balance beam task each for a Subordinate and a Conflict-Subordinate task are illustrated. Equal and Dominant tasks would have the same paths as the Subordinate task, and Conflict-Dominant and Conflict-Equal tasks would have the same paths as the Conflict-Subordinate tasks, although the conditional probability values would generally differ.

There are three unobservable variables in the system; that is, η has three components. The first again expresses level of understanding in the balance beam domain. The second is the ability to carry out the calculations involved in computing torques. The third concerns the integration of balance beam understanding and calculating proficiency. Specifically, it indicates whether a child both is in Stage IV *and* possesses the requisite computational skills.

Before discussing the construction versus choice tradeoffs in this network, we mention in passing some conditional independence assumptions implicit in the figure. First, note that the probabilities of the pure computation items depend on the unobservable computation variable only; they are conditionally independent of level of balance beam understanding. Secondly, for children in Stages 0 through III, both the right/wrong answers and their explanations depend only on level of understanding. Because they do not realize the connection between the problems and the torque calculations, their responses to the balance beam tasks are conditionally independent of their computational skill, even on items for which that skill is an integral component of an expert solution.

The correctness aspect of an answer has only two possibilities, right or wrong, but an explanation can fall into five categories corresponding to stages of understanding. The overt explanation is the raw observation of the constructed answer; an expert's judgment categorizes that response into one of the stage categories. Note that a Stage III child might give an explanation consistent with Stages 0, I, II, or III, but would not, by definition, give a Stage IV explanation. Theory thus posits that the conditional probability of a Stage K response from a Stage J child is zero if K > J. Conditional probabilities for K ≤ J might be estimated from data or based on experts' experience. The most likely explanation for an Equal task from people at Stage IV would probably be a Stage II explanation: "It balances because both the weights and distances are equal." A hypothetical example of the conditional probabilities of explanations of different levels for a Equal item are given in Table 5.4.

The first type of comparison of information from construction and choice items occurs when a given inference can be drawn from items of either type: To what degree do responses update the nodes of interest? In this example, probabilities of stage membership can be updated by observing either choice or construction data. Their comparative values depend on the conditional probabilities $p(\eta|\mathbf{x})$ associated with the potential responses. Specifically, the more the probabilities from a given latent state are concentrated on a few

TABLE 5.4
Conditional Probabilities of Explanations to an E Item

	Explanation				
Respondent's Stage	Stage 0	Stage I	Stage II	Stage III	Stage IV
Stage 0	1	0	0	0	0
Stage I	.20	.80	0	0	0
Stage II	.10	.10	.80	0	0
Stage III	.05	.05	.80	.20	0
Stage IV	.03	.10	.70	.02	.15

observable states, the more "reliable" the items are. The construction items in this hypothetical example would be more reliable in this sense than the choice items because a correct prediction can emanate from a student at any level, whereas a Level K verbal explanation can only come from a student at Level K or higher.

The second basis of comparison is whether certain inferences can be drawn from one type of response but not the other. For children in Stage IV, right/wrong answers to conflict items depend on the understanding/computation integration variable, but explanations depend only on understanding. As noted previously, information from choice items alone cannot determine whether poor performance on conflict items is due to Stage III reasoning or Stage IV reasoning coupled with an inability to carry out calculations reliably. This is represented in Fig. 5.12: After a correct answer to a choice-type Subor-

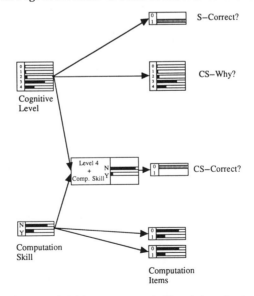

FIG. 5.12.   An extended inference network: Knowledge after two "choice" responses.

dinate item and an incorrect answer to a choice-type Conflict-Subordinate item, the state of knowledge expresses a mixture of four possibilities:

1. The student is in a low stage (0–II) and gave a correct answer to the Subordinate item without a correct rationale.
2. The student has the requisite computational skill but is in Stage III, and thus answered the Conflict-Subordinate item incorrectly because she did not have sufficient understanding.
3. The student is in Stage IV but lacks the requisite computational skill, and thus answered the Conflict-Subordinate item incorrectly because of an error when carrying the appropriate torque comparison.
4. The student is in Stage III *and* lacks the requisite computational skill.

All four of these possibilities lead to the prediction of an incorrect response to future Conflict-Subordinate items or a structurally similar proportional reasoning task such as "shadows" (Siegler, 1981). Figure 5.13 illustrates this by adding a prognostic node: a Conflict-Subordinate choice item at Time 2. For an accurate prediction, or a selection decision based on this composite skill, the distinction among the four possibilities would probably *not* be important; the child would probably perform with a similar pattern, for the same *unknown* reasons. But if the distinction were important to make—as it would be if the objective is to improve the student's chances at handling such problems—it could be accomplished by accumulating information of addi-

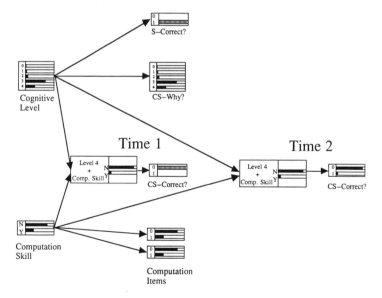

FIG. 5.13. An extended inference network: Prediction of CS at Time 2.

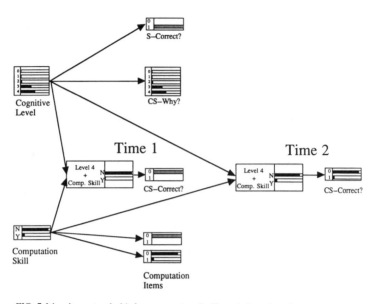

FIG. 5.14.   An extended inference network: Knowledge after three responses,
including a computation item.

tional kinds. One way would be to obtain responses to open-ended or choice-
type computation problems as in Fig. 5.14, to investigate the hypothesis of
calculation failure. Alternatively, one could obtain an open-ended answer to
the Conflict-Subordinate item: Why did you make the response you did? Figure
5.15 illustrates this possibility. The results of these types of items would inform whether the instruction should be computational or conceptual. Figure
5.16 adds instructional nodes, and illustrates the case in which information
from a choice item has indicated that the problem was computational, and
computational instruction increases the probability of a correct response at
Time 2.

A FINAL COMMENT

This chapter is based on the following premises:

1. Educational testing is gathering information to make educational decisions.
2. The type of decisions to be made determines the student model that
   is appropriate. It is assumed that the decision maker would know how
   to act if a particular student's model were known with certainty.
3. Student models cannot be known with certainty. At any point in time,

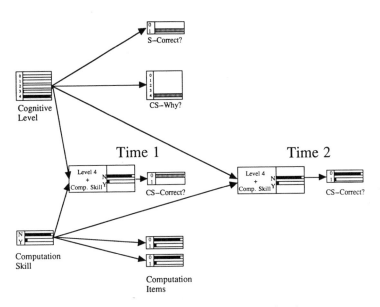

FIG. 5.15. An extended inference network: Knowledge after three responses, including an explanation.

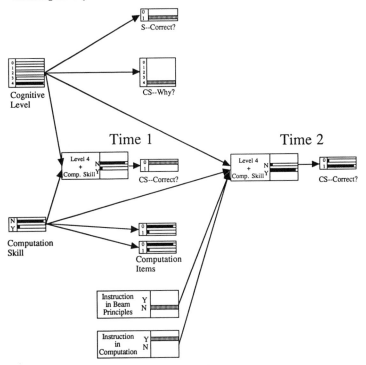

FIG. 5.16. An extended inference network: Instruction in computation.

the model for a given student is known only up to the probabilities of various alternatives.

4. Test theory consists of rules and techniques for designing observational settings to obtain information to reduce uncertainty about student models, and for carrying out inferences and making decisions in the presence of remaining uncertainty.

5. Choice and construction items are two options for obtaining information to update a student model.

6. Decisions about the type of observations to gather should be made in light of (a) the information they provide for the decision at hand, and (b) the real and potential consequences of the method of testing for the system in which the testing takes place.

The chapter's objectives are achieved to the extent that it places the debate on choice and construction in a framework wherein advocates of different approaches can ask questions that have common meanings to all participants, and that can, at least in principle, be answered.

ACKNOWLEDGMENTS

The work was supported by the Program Research Planning Council of Educational Testing Service.

REFERENCES

Andersen, S. K., Jensen, F. V., Olesen, K. G., & Jensen, F. (1989). *HUGIN: A shell for building Bayesian belief universes for expert systems* [Computer program]. Aalborg, Denmark: HUGIN Expert.

Andreassen, S., Jensen, F. V., & Olesen, K. G. (1990). *Medical expert systems based on causal probabilistic networks.* Aalborg, Denmark: Institute of Electronic Systems, Aalborg University.

Andreassen, S., Woldbye, M., Falck, B., & Andersen, S. K. (1987). MUNIN: A causal probabilistic network for interpretation of electromyographic findings. *Proceedings of the 10th International Joint Conference on Artificial Intelligence* (pp. 366–372). Milan: Kaufmann.

Bennett, R. E. (in press). Toward intelligent assessment: An integration of constructed response testing, artificial intelligence, and model-based measurement. In N. Frederiksen, R. J. Mislevy, & I. I. Bejar (Eds.), *Test theory for a new generation of tests.* Hillsdale, NJ: Lawrence Erlbaum Associates.

Bloom, B. S. (1976). *Human characteristics and school learning.* New York: McGraw-Hill.

Bock, R. D. (1972). Estimating item parameters and latent ability when responses are scored in two or more nominal categories. *Psychometrika, 37,* 29–52.

Chi, M. T. H., Feltovich, P., & Glaser, R. (1981). Categorization and representation of physics problems by experts and novices. *Cognitive Science, 5,* 121–152.

Clement, J. (1982). Students' preconceptions of introductory mechanics. *American Journal of Physics, 50,* 66–71.

Embretson, S. E. (1985). Multicomponent latent trait models for test design. In S. E. Embretson (Ed.), *Test design: Developments in psychology and psychometrics* (pp. 195–218). Orlando, FL: Academic Press.

Falmagne, J-C. (1989). A latent trait model via a stochastic learning theory for a knowledge space. *Psychometrika, 54,* 283–303.

Frederiksen, J. R., & Collins, A. (1989). A systems approach to educational testing. *Educational Researcher, 18,* 27–32.

Frederiksen, N. (1984). The real test bias: Influences of testing on teaching and learning. *American Psychologist, 39,* 193–202.

Gentner, D., & Gentner, D. R. (1983). Flowing waters or teeming crowds: Mental models of electricity. In D. Gentner & A. L. Stevens (Eds.), *Mental models* (pp. 99–129). Hillsdale, NJ: Lawrence Erlbaum Associates.

Glaser, R. (1981). The future of testing: A research agenda for cognitive psychology and psychometrics. *American Psychologist, 36,* 923–936.

Glaser, R., Lesgold, A., & Lajoie, S. (1987). Toward a cognitive theory for the measurement of achievement. In R. Ronning, J. Glover, J. C. Conoley, & J. Witt (Eds), *The influence of cognitive psychology on testing and measurement: The Buros–Nebraska Symposium on Measurement and Testing, Vol. 3* (pp. 41–85). Hillsdale, NJ: Lawrence Erlbaum Associates.

Green, B. F. (1978). In defense of measurement. *American Psychologist, 33,* 664–670.

Greeno, J. G. (1976). Cognitive objectives of instruction: Theory of knowledge for solving problems and answering questions. In D. Klahr (Ed.), *Cognition and instruction* (pp. 123–159). Hillsdale, NJ: Lawrence Erlbaum Associates.

Haertel, E. H. (1984). An application of latent class models to assessment data. *Applied Psychological Measurement, 8,* 333–346.

Hegarty, M., Just, M. A., & Morrison, I. R. (1988). Mental models of mechanical systems: Individual differences in qualitative and quantitative reasoning. *Cognitive Psychology, 20,* 191–236.

Inhelder, B., & Piaget, J. (1958). *The growth of logical thinking from childhood to adolescence.* New York: Basic.

Karplus, R., Pulos, S., & Stage, E. (1983). Proportional reasoning of early adolescents. In R. A. Lesh & M. Landau (Eds.), *Acquisition of mathematics concepts and processes* (pp. 45–90). Orlando, FL: Academic Press.

Lauritzen, S. L., & Spiegelhalter, D. J. (1988). Local computations with probabilities on graphical structures and their application to expert systems. *Journal of the Royal Statistical Society, Series B, 50,* 157–224.

Lazarsfeld, P. F. (1950). The logical and mathematical foundation of latent structure analysis. In S. A. Stouffer, L. Guttman, E. A. Suchman, P. F. Lazarsfeld, S. A. Star, & J. A. Clausen (Eds), *Studies in social psychology in World War II, Vol. 4: Measurement and prediction* (pp. 362–412). Princeton, NJ: Princeton University Press.

Macready, G. B., & Dayton, C. M. (1989, March). *Adaptive testing with latent class models.* Paper presented at the annual meeting of the American Educational Research Association, San Francisco, CA.

Marshall, S. P. (1985, December) *Using schema knowledge to solve story problems.* Paper presented at the Office of Naval Research Contractors' Conference, San Diego, CA.

Marshall, S. P. (1989). Generating good items for diagnostic tests. In N. Frederiksen, R. Glaser, A. Lesgold, & M. G. Shafto (Eds.), *Diagnostic monitoring of skill and knowledge acquisition* (pp. 433–452). Hillsdale, NJ: Lawrence Erlbaum Associates.

Marshall, S. P. (in press). Assessing schema knowledge. In N. Frederiksen, R. J. Mislevy, & I. I. Bejar (Eds.), *Test theory for a new generation of tests.* Hillsdale, NJ: Lawrence Erlbaum Associates.

Masters, G., & Mislevy, R. J. (in press). New views of student learning: Implications for educational measurement. In N. Frederiksen, R. J. Mislevy, & I. I. Bejar (Eds.), *Test theory for a new generation of tests.* Hillsdale, NJ: Lawrence Erlbaum Associates.

Mazzeo, J., Schmitt, A., & Bleistein, C. (in press). *Exploratory analyses of some possible causes for the discrepancies in gender differences on multiple-choice and free-response sections of the Advanced Placement examinations.* Princeton, NJ: Educational Testing Service.

McDermott, L. C. (1984). Research on conceptual understanding in mechanics. *Physics Today, 37,* 24–32.

Messick, S. (1989). Validity. In R. L. Linn (Ed.), *Educational measurement* (3rd ed.) (pp. 13–103). New York: American Council on Education/Macmillan.

Minsky, M. (1975). A framework for representing knowledge. In P. H. Winston (Ed.), *The psychology of computer vision* (pp. 211–277). New York: McGraw-Hill.

Mislevy, R. J., & Verhelst, N. (1990). Modeling item responses when different subjects follow different solution strategies. *Psychometrika, 55,* 195–215.

Mislevy, R. J., Yamamoto, K., & Anacker, S. (1992). Toward a test theory for assessing student understanding. In R. A. Lesh & S. Lamon (Eds.), *Assessments of authentic performance in school mathematics* (pp. 293–318). Washington, DC: American Association for the Advancement of Science.

Paulson, J. A. (1986). *Latent class representation of systematic patterns in test responses* (Tech. Rep. ONR-1). Portland, OR: Portland State University, Psychology Department.

Pearl, J. (1988). *Probabilistic reasoning in intelligent system: Networks of plausible inference.* San Mateo, CA: Kaufmann.

Rumelhart, D. A. (1980). Schemata: The building blocks of cognition. In R. Spiro, B. Bruce, & W. Brewer (Eds.), *Theoretical issues in reading comprehension* (pp. 33–58). Hillsdale, NJ: Lawrence Erlbaum Associates.

Samejima, F. (1973). Homogeneous case of the continuous response level. *Psychometrika, 38,* 203–219.

Samejima, F. (1979). *A new family of models for the multiple-choice item* (ONR Research Report 79-4). Knoxville, TN: University of Tennessee.

Siegler, R. S. (1981). Developmental sequences within and between concepts. *Monographs of the Society for Research in Child Development, 46* (2, Serial No. 189).

Sympson, J. B. (1983). *A new item response theory model for calibrating multiple-choice items.* Paper presented at the annual meeting of the Psychometric Society, Los Angeles, CA.

Tatsuoka, K. K. (1989). Toward an integration of item response theory and cognitive error diagnosis. In N. Frederiksen, R. Glaser, A. Lesgold, & M. G. Shafto (Eds.), *Diagnostic monitoring of skill and knowledge acquisition* (pp. 453–488). Hillsdale, NJ: Lawrence Erlbaum Associates.

Thissen, D., & Steinberg, L. (1984). A response model for multiple-choice items. *Psychometrika, 47,* 201–214.

van den Heuvel, M. (1990). Realistic arithmetic/mathematics instruction and tests. In K. Gravemeijer, M. van den Heuvel, & L. Streefland (Eds.), *Context free productions tests and geometry in realistic mathematics education* (pp. 53–78). Utrecht, The Netherlands: Research Group for Mathematical Education and Educational Computer Center, State University of Utrecht.

Wilson, M. R. (1989a). A comparison of deterministic and probabilistic approaches to measuring learning structures. *Australian Journal of Education, 33,* 125–138.

Wilson, M. R. (1989b). Saltus: A psychometric model of discontinuity in cognitive development. *Psychological Bulletin, 105,* 276–289.

Yamamoto, K. (1987). *A model that combines IRT and latent class models.* Unpublished doctoral dissertation, University of Illinois.

6

ITEM CONSTRUCTION AND PSYCHOMETRIC MODELS APPROPRIATE FOR CONSTRUCTED RESPONSES

Kikumi K. Tatsuoka
Educational Testing Service

Recent developments in cognitive theory suggest that new achievement tests must reflect several important aspects of performance, including the cognitive processes underlying problem solving, dynamic changes in students' strategies, and the structure or representation of knowledge and cognitive skills (Glaser, 1985). These measurement objectives require a new test theory that is both qualitative and quantitative in nature. Achievement measures must be both descriptive and interpretable in terms of the processes that determine performance. Traditional test theories have shown a long history of contributions to American education through supporting norm-referenced and criterion-referenced testing.

Scaling of test scores has been an important goal in these types of testing, but individualized information such as diagnosis of misconceptions has never been a main concern. In these contexts the information objectives for a test will depend on its intended use. Standardized test scores are useful for admissions or selection purposes, but such scores cannot provide teachers with useful information for designing remediation. Formative uses of assessment require new techniques; this chapter tries to introduce one such example.

Constructed-response formats are desirable for measuring complex and dynamic cognitive processes (Bennett, Ward, Rock, & LaHart, 1990), whereas multiple-choice items are suitable for measuring static knowledge. Birenbaum and K. Tatsuoka (1987) examined the effect of the response format on diagnosis and concluded that multiple-choice items may not provide appropriate information for identifying students' misconceptions. The constructed-response format, on the other hand, appears to be more appropriate, supporting the assertion of Bennett et al.

As for the second objective, dynamic strategy change, several studies on "bug" stability suggest that bugs, and therefore strategies, tend to shift with "environmental challenges" (Ginzburg, 1977) or "impasses" (Brown & Van-Lehn, 1980). Sleeman and his associates (Sleeman, Kelly, Martinak, Ward, & Moore, 1989) developed an intelligent tutoring system aimed at the diagnosis of bugs and their remediation in algebra. However, bug instability made diagnosis uncertain and hence remediation could not be directed. K. Tatsuoka, Birenbaum, and Arnold (1989) conducted an experimental study to test the stability of bugs and also found that inconsistent rule application was common among students who had not mastered signed-number arithmetic operations. By contrast, mastery-level students showed a stable pattern of rule application. These studies strongly indicate that the unit of diagnosis should be neither erroneous rules nor bugs, but somewhat larger components such as sources of misconceptions or instructionally relevant cognitive components. The primary weakness of attempts to diagnose bugs is that bugs are tentative solutions for solving the problems when students don't have the right skills. However, the two identical subtests (32 items each) used in the signed-number study had almost identical true score curves for the two-parameter logistic models (K. Tatsuoka & M. Tatsuoka, 1991). This means that bugs are unstable, but total scores are very stable. Therefore, searching for the stable components that are cognitively relevant is an important goal for diagnosis and remediation.

The third objective, evaluating the structure or representation of cognitive skills, requires response formats different from traditional item types. We need items that ask examinees to draw flow charts in which complex relations among tasks, subtasks, skills, and solution path are expressed graphically, or that ask examinees to describe such relations verbally. Questions can be figural response formats in which examinees are asked to order the causal relationships among several concepts and connect them by a directed graph.

These demanding measurement objectives apparently require a new psychometric theory that can accommodate more complicated forms of scoring than just right or wrong item-level responses. The correct response to the item is determined by whether all the cognitive tasks involved in the item can be answered correctly. Therefore, the hypothesis would be that if any of the tasks would be wrong, then there would be a high probability that the final answer would also be wrong.

These item-level responses are called *macrolevel responses*, and those of the task-level are called *microlevel responses*. This chapter addresses such issues as follows. The first section discusses macrolevel analyses versus microlevel analyses and focuses on the skills and knowledge that each task requires. The second section introduces elementary graph theory as a tool to organize various microlevel tasks and their directed relations. Third, a theory for designing constructed-response items is discussed and illustrated with real examples. Further, the connection of this deterministic approach to the probabilistic Item Response Theory and Rule space models (K. Tatsuoka, 1983, 1990) is explained. These models are demonstrated as a computation device for drawing inferences about microlevel performances from the item-level responses. Finally, possible scoring rubrics suitable for graded, continuous, and nominal response models are addressed.

MACRO- AND MICROLEVEL ANALYSES

Making Inferences on Unobservable Microlevel Tasks from Observable Item-Level Scores

Statistical test theories deal mostly with test scores and item scores. In this chapter, these scores are considered to be macrolevel information, and the underlying cognitive processes are viewed as microlevel information. Here we are using a much finer level of *observable performance* than the item level or the macrolevel.

Looking into underlying cognitive processes and speculating about examinees' solution strategies, which are unobservable, may be analogous to the situation that modern physics has come through in the history of its development. Exploring the properties of and relations among microlevel objects such as atoms, electrons, neutrons, and other elementary particles has led to many successes in theorizing about physical phenomena at the macrolevel, such as the relation between the loss and gain of heat and temperature. Easley and M. Tatsuoka (1968) state in their book *Scientific Thought* that "the heat lost or gained by a sample of any non-atomic substance not undergoing a change of state is jointly proportional to the number of atoms in the sample and to the temperature change. This strongly suggests that both heat and temperature are intimately related to some property of atoms" (p. 13). Heat and temperature relate to molecular motion and the relation can be expressed by mathematical equations involving molecular velocities.

This finding suggests that, analogously, it might be useful to explore the properties and relations among microlevel and invisible tasks, and to predict their outcomes. These are observable as responses to test items. Our aim is to explore a method that can scientifically explain macrolevel phenomena—in our context, item-level or test-level achievement—derived from microlevel tasks. The method should be generalizable from specific relations in a specific domain to general relations in general domains. In order to accomplish our goal, elementary graph theory is used.

Identification of Prime Subtasks or Attributes

The development of an intelligent tutoring system or cognitive error diagnostic system involves a painstaking and detailed task analysis in which goals, subgoals, and various solution paths are identified in a procedural network (or a flow chart). This process of uncovering all possible combinations of subtasks at the microlevel is essential for making a tutoring system perform the role of the master teacher, although the current state of research in expert systems only partially achieves this goal. According to Chipman, Davis, and Shafto (1986), many studies have shown the tremendous effectiveness of individual tutoring by master teachers.

It is very important that analysis of students' performances on a test be similar to the analyses done by human tutors. Although the context of this discussion is task analysis, the methodology to be introduced can be applied in more general contexts such as skill analysis, job analysis, or content analysis.

Identifying subcomponents of tasks in a given problem-solving domain and abstracting their attributes is still an art. It is necessary that the process be made automatic and objective. However, we here assume that the tasks are already divided into components (subtasks) and that any task in the domain can be expressed by a combination of cognitively relevant prime subcomponents. We denote these by $A_1, \ldots, A_k$ and call them a set of attributes (see Fig. 6.1).

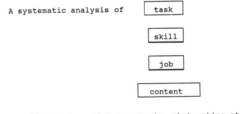

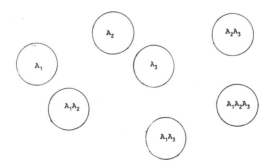

FIG. 6.1. Examples of attributes.

Determination of Direct Relations Between Attributes

Graph theory is a branch of mathematics that has been widely used in connection with tree diagrams consisting of nodes and arcs. In practical applications of graph theory, nodes represent objects of substantive interest, and arcs show the existence of some relationship between two objects. In the task-analysis setting, the objects correspond to attributes. Definition of a direct relation is determined by the researcher using graph theory on the basis of the purpose of his or her study.

For instance, $A_k \to A_l$ if A_k is an immediate prerequisite of A_l (Sato, 1990), or $A_k \to A_l$ if A_k is easier than A_l (Wise, 1981). These direct relations are rather logical but there are also studies using sampling statistics such as proximity of two objects (Hubert, 1974) or dominance relations (Takeya, 1981). (See M. Tatsuoka, 1986, for a review of various applications of graph theory in educational and behavioral research.)

The direct relations as defined can be represented by a matrix called the adjacency matrix $\mathbf{A} = (a_{kl})$ where

$$\begin{cases} a_{kl} = 1 \text{ if a direct relation exists from } A_k \text{ to } A_l \\ a_{kl} = 0 \text{ otherwise} \end{cases}$$

If a direct relation exists from A_k to A_l and also from A_l to A_k, then A_k and A_l are said to be equivalent. In this case, the elements a_{kl} and a_{lk} of the adjacency matrix are both one.

There are many ways to define a direct relationship between two attributes, but we use a "prerequisite" relation in this chapter. One of the open-ended questions shown in Bennett, Sebrechts, and Yamamoto (in press) is used to illustrate various new terminologies and concepts in this study:

Item 1: How many minutes will it take to fill a 2,000-cubic centimeter tank if water flows in at the rate of 20-cubic centimeters per minute and is pumped out at the rate of 4-cubic centimeters per minute?

This problem is a two-goal problem, and the main canonical solution is that:

1. Net filling rate = 20 cc per minute − 4 cc per minute
2. Net filling rate = 16 cc per minute
3. Time to fill tank = 2000 cc/16 cc per minute
4. Time to fill tank = 125 minutes.

We define attributes involved in this problem:

A_1: First goal is to find the net filling rate.
A_2: Compute the rate.

A_3: Second goal is to find the time to fill the tank.

A_4: Compute the time.

In this example, A_1 is a prerequisite of A_2, A_2 is a prerequisite of A_3, and A_3 is a prerequisite of A_4. This relation can be written by a chain, $A_1 \rightarrow A_2 \rightarrow A_3 \rightarrow A_4$. This chain can be expressed by an adjacency matrix whose cells are $a_{12} = a_{23} = a_{34} = 1$, and others are zeros.

$$
\text{Adjacency matrix } \mathbf{A} =
\begin{array}{c}
\begin{array}{cccc}
A_1 & A_2 & A_3 & A_4
\end{array} \\
\left[
\begin{array}{cccc}
0 & 1 & 0 & 0 \\
0 & 0 & 1 & 0 \\
0 & 0 & 0 & 1 \\
0 & 0 & 0 & 0
\end{array}
\right]
\begin{array}{c}
A_1 \\ A_2 \\ A_3 \\ A_4
\end{array}
\end{array}
$$

This adjacency matrix $\mathbf{A}$ is obtained from the relationships among the attributes that are required for solving Item 1. The prerequisite relations expressed in the adjacency matrix $\mathbf{A}$ in this example may change if we add new items. For instance, if a new item—which requires only the attributes A_3 and A_4 to reach the solution—is added to the item pool consisting of only Item 1, then A_1 may not be considered as the prerequisite of A_3 anymore. The prerequisite relation, in practice, must be determined by a task analysis of a domain and usually it is independent of items that are in an item pool.

Reachability Matrix: Representation of All the Relations, Both Direct and Indirect

Warfield (1973a, 1973b) developed a method called "interactive structural modeling" in the context of switching theory. By his method, the adjacency matrix shown in the preceding section indicates that there are direct relations from A_1 to A_2, from A_2 to A_3, and from A_3 to A_4, but no direct relations other than among these three arcs. However, a directed graph (or digraph) consisting of A_1, A_2, A_3, and A_4 shows that there is an indirect relation from A_1 to A_3, from A_2 to A_4, and from A_1 to A_4.

Warfield showed that we can get a reachability matrix by multiplying the matrix $\mathbf{A} + \mathbf{I}$ (the sum of the adjacency matrix $\mathbf{A}$ and the identity matrix $\mathbf{I}$) by itself n times in terms of Boolean algebra operations. The reachability matrix indicates that reachability is at most n steps (A_k to A_l), whereas the adjacency matrix contains reachability in exactly one step (A_k to A_l). (A node is reachable from itself in zero steps.) The reachability matrix of the example in the previous section is:

$$R = (A + I)^3 = (A + I)^4 = (A + I)^5 = \ldots$$

$$R = \begin{array}{cccc} A_1 & A_2 & A_3 & A_4 \end{array}$$
$$R = \begin{bmatrix} 1 & 1 & 1 & 1 \\ 0 & 1 & 1 & 1 \\ 0 & 0 & 1 & 1 \\ 0 & 0 & 0 & 1 \end{bmatrix} \begin{array}{c} A_1 \\ A_2 \\ A_3 \\ A_4 \end{array}$$

where the definition of Boolean operations is as follows:

$1 + 1 = 1, 1 + 0 = 0 + 1 = 1, 0 + 0 = 0$ for addition and
$1 \times 1 = 1, 0 \times 1 = 1 \times 0 = 0, 0 \times 0 = 0$ for multiplication.

The reachability matrix indicates that all attributes are related directly or indirectly. From the chain shown, it is obvious that although A_k and A_{k+1} relate directly, A_k and A_{k+2} relate indirectly.

This form of digraph representation of attributes can be applied to evaluation of instructional sequences, curriculum evaluation, and documentation analysis, and has proved to be very useful (Sato, 1990). Moreover, a reachability matrix can provide us with information about the cognitive structure of attributes. However, application to assessment analysis requires extension of the original method introduced by Warfield.

A THEORY OF ITEM DESIGN APPROPRIATE
FOR THE CONSTRUCTED-RESPONSE FORMAT

An Incidence Matrix in Assessment Analysis

The adjacency matrix (a_{kl}) is a square matrix of order $K \times K$, where K is the number of attributes and a_{kl} represents the existence or absence of a direct relation from A_k to A_l. We now consider a special case.

When the adjacency matrix $\mathbf{A}$ is a null matrix, hence $\mathbf{A} + \mathbf{I}$ is the identity matrix of the order k, there is no direct relation among the attributes. Let Ω be a set $\{A_1, A_2, \ldots, A_k\}$ and L be the set of all subsets of Ω, $L = [\{A_1\}, \{A_2\}, \ldots, \{A_1, A_2\}, \{A_1, A_3\}, \ldots, \{A_1, A_2 \ldots, A_k\}, \{\ \}]$, then L is called a lattice in which the number of elements in L is 2^k.

In this case, we should be able to construct an item pool of 2^k items in such a manner that each item involves only one element of L. There is a row for each attribute and a column for each item, and the element of 1 in (k,j)-cell indicates that Item j involves attribute A_k whereas 0 indicates that Item j does not involve A_k. Then this matrix of order $K \times 2^k$, or $K \times n$ for short, is called an incidence matrix, $\mathbf{Q} = (q_{kj})$, $k = 1, \ldots K \& j = 1, \ldots n$.

For example, in the following matrix $\mathbf{Q}$, the $(k + 1)$th column (Item $k + 1$) has the vector of $(1\ 1\ 0 \ldots 0)$, which corresponds to the $(k + 1)$th set,

$\{A_1, A_2\}$ in L.

$$
\mathbf{Q}(k \times n) \;=\;
\begin{array}{c}
\begin{array}{ccccccccc}
i1 & i2 & .\,. & ik & i(k+1) & i(k+2) & \cdots & i(2_k-1) & i(2^k)
\end{array}\\[4pt]
\left[
\begin{array}{ccccccccc}
1 & 0 & .\,. & 0 & 1 & 1 & \ldots\ldots & 1 & 0\\
0 & 1 & .\,. & 0 & 1 & 0 & \ldots\ldots & 1 & 0\\
0 & 0 & .\,. & 0 & 0 & 1 & \ldots\ldots & 1 & 0\\
. & . & \cdots & . & . & . & \ldots\ldots & . & .\\
0 & 0 & .\,. & 1 & 0 & 1 & \ldots\ldots & 1 & 0
\end{array}
\right]
\begin{array}{c}
A_1\\ A_2\\ A_3\\ .\\ A_k
\end{array}
\end{array}
$$

However, if K becomes large, say $K=20$, then the number of items in the item pool becomes astronomically large, $2^{20} = 1,048,576$. In practice, it might be very difficult to develop a pool of constructed-response items so that each item requires only one independent attribute. Constructed-response items are usually designed to measure such functions as cognitive processes, organization of knowledge and cognitive skills, and theory changes required in solving a problem. These complex mental activities require an understanding of all the relationships that exist in the elements of Ω. Some attributes are connected by a direct relation, and others are isolated.

In general, the manner in which the attributes in Ω interrelate bears a closer resemblance to the arc/node tree configuration than to the unidimensional chain shown in the previous section.

Suppose we modify the water-filling-a-tank problem (see Item 1) to make four new items that include the original attributes.

Item 2   What is the net filling rate of water if water flows in at the rate of 50 cc/min and out at the rate of 35 cc/min?

Item 3   What is the net filling rate of water if water flows in at the rate of h cc/min and out at the rate of d cc/min?

Item 4   How many minutes will it take to fill a 1,000-cubic-centimeter tank if water flows in at the rate of 50-cubic centimeters per minute?

Item 5   How many minutes will it take to fill an x-cubic-centimeter water tank if water flows in at the rate of y-cubic centimeters per minute?

The incidence matrix $\mathbf{Q}$ for the five items will be:

$$
\mathbf{Q}(4 \times 5) \;=\;
\begin{array}{c}
\begin{array}{ccccc}
i1 & i2 & i3 & i4 & i5
\end{array}\\[4pt]
\left[
\begin{array}{ccccc}
1 & 1 & 1 & 0 & 0\\
1 & 1 & 0 & 0 & 0\\
1 & 0 & 0 & 1 & 1\\
1 & 0 & 0 & 1 & 0
\end{array}
\right]
\begin{array}{c}
A_1\\ A_2\\ A_3\\ A_4
\end{array}
\end{array}
$$

The prerequisite relations among the four attributes are changed from the "totally ordered" chain, $A_1 \to A_2 \to A_3 \to A_4$ to the partially ordered relation as stated in the following. That is, A_1 is a prerequisite of A_2, A_3 is a prerequisite of A_4, but A_2 is not a prerequisite of either A_3 or A_4. The relationship among the attributes is no longer a totally ordered chain but two totally ordered chains, $A_1 \to A_2$ and $A_3 \to A_4$.

Tatsuoka (1991) introduced the inclusion order among the row vectors of an incidence matrix and showed that a set of the row vectors becomes a Boolean algebra with respect to Boolean addition and multiplication. In this Boolean algebra, the prerequisite relation of two attributes becomes equivalent to the inclusion order between two row vectors—that is, the row vectors A_1 and A_3 include the row vectors A_2 and A_4, respectively, in the $\mathbf{Q}(4 \times 5)$ matrix shown.

There is an interesting relationship between an incidence matrix $\mathbf{Q}(k \times n)$ and the reachability matrix $\mathbf{R}(k \times k)$. A pairwise comparison over all the combinations of the row vectors of $\mathbf{Q}(k \times n)$ matrix with respect to the inclusion order will yield the reachability matrix $\mathbf{R}(k \times k)$ in which all the relations logically existing among the k attributes, both direct or indirect, are expressed. This property is very useful for examining the quality and cognitive structure of an item pool.

The adjacency and reachability matrices of the items given earlier are:

$$\mathbf{A}(4 \times 4) \;=\; \begin{bmatrix} 0 & 1 & 0 & 0 \\ 0 & 0 & 0 & 0 \\ 0 & 0 & 0 & 1 \\ 0 & 0 & 0 & 0 \end{bmatrix} \qquad \mathbf{R}(4 \times 4) \;=\; \begin{bmatrix} 1 & 1 & 0 & 0 \\ 0 & 1 & 0 & 0 \\ 0 & 0 & 1 & 1 \\ 0 & 0 & 0 & 1 \end{bmatrix}$$

However, the reachability matrix of the case given in $\mathbf{Q}(k \times n)$, in which k attributes have no relations, will be the identity matrix of the order k. This result can be easily confirmed by examining the inclusion relation of all pairs of the row vectors of the matrix $\mathbf{Q}(k \times n)$.

Connection of Our Deterministic Approach to Probability Theories

K. Tatsuoka and M. Tatsuoka (1987) introduced the slippage random variable S_j, which is assumed to be independent across the items, as follows:

If $S_j = 1$, then $X_j = 1 - R_j$ and if $S_j = 0$, then $X_j = R_j$

or, equivalently, $S_j = |X_j - R_j|$.

A set $\{X_m\}$ forms a cluster around R (where X_m is an item response pattern that is generated by adding different numbers of slips to the ideal item pattern R). The Tatsuokas showed that the total number of slippages, s, in these "fuzzy" item patterns follows a compound binomial distribution with the slippage probabilities unique to each item. They called this distribution the "bug distribution."

However, it is also the conditional distribution of **s** given R, where R is a state of knowledge and capabilities. This is called a "state distribution" for short. Once a distribution is determined for each state of knowledge and capabilities, then Bayes' decision rule for minimum errors can be applied to classify any student's response pattern into one of these predetermined states of knowledge and capabilities (K. Tatsuoka & M. Tatsuoka, 1987).

The notion of classification has an important implication for education. Given a response pattern, we want to determine the state to which the student's misconception is the closest and we want to answer the question: "What misconception, leading to what incorrect rule of operation, did this subject most likely have?" or "What is the probability that the subject's observed responses have been drawn from each of the predetermined states?" This is error diagnosis.

For Bayes' decision rule for minimum errors, the classification boundary of two groups of "fuzzy" response patterns becomes the linear discriminant function when the state distributions are multivariate normal and their covariance matrices are approximately equal. Kim (1990) examined the effect of violation of the normality requirement, and found that the linear discriminant function is robust against this violation. Kim further compared the classification results using the linear discriminant functions and K-nearest neighbors method, which is a nonparametric approach, and found that the linear discriminant functions are better. However, the classification in the n-dimensional space with many predetermined groups (as many as 50 or 100 states) is not practical.

K. Tatsuoka (1983, 1985, 1990) proposed a model, called "rule space," that is capable of diagnosing cognitive errors. Rule space uses item response functions where the probability of correct response to Item j is modeled as a function of the student's "proficiency" (which is denoted by Θ) as $P_j(\Theta)$, and $Q_j(\Theta) = 1 - P_j(\Theta)$. The rule space model maps all possible item response patterns into ordered pairs of (Θ, ζ), where ζ is an index measuring atypicality of response patterns, thus all the error groups will also be mapped into this Cartesian Product space. The mapping is one-to-one almost everywhere if the item response functions are monotone increasing (Dibello & Baillie, 1991; K. Tatsuoka, 1985).

Figure 6.2 illustrates the rule space configuration.

Rule space can be regarded as a technique for reducing the dimensionality of the classification space. Furthermore, because the clusters of "fuzzy" response patterns that are mapped into the two-dimensional space follow approximately bivariate normal distributions (represented by the ellipses shown in Fig. 6.2), Bayes' decision rules can be applied to classify a point in the space

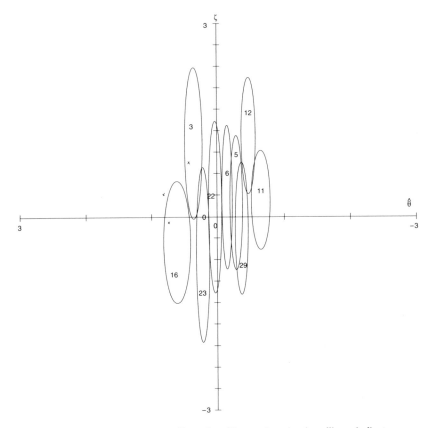

FIG. 6.2. The rule space configuration. The numbers in nine ellipses indicate error states (e.g., No. 5 state is "One cannot do the operation of borrowing in fraction subtraction problems.") and "x" marks represent students' points (θ, ζ).

into one of the ellipses shown in Fig. 6.2 (K. Tatsuoka, 1990; M. Tatsuoka & K. Tatsuoka, 1989).

Kim also compared the classification results using rule space with Bayes' classifiers—the discriminant function approach—and the nonparametric K-nearest neighbors method. He found that the rule space approach was efficient in terms of CPU time, and that the classification errors were as small as those created by the other two methods. Moreover, states located in the two extreme regions of the θ scale tended to have singular within-groups covariance matrices in the n-dimensional space; hence, classification using discriminant functions could not be carried out for such cases. The rule space classification, on the other hand, was always obtainable and reasonably reliable.

We assumed the states for classification groups were predetermined. However, determination of the universal set of knowledge states is a complicated task and it requires a mathematical tool, Boolean algebra, to cope with the problem of combinatorial explosion (K. Tatsuoka, 1991).

We utilized a deterministic logical analysis to narrow down the fuzzy region of classification as much as possible without losing the interpretability of misconceptions and errors. Then the probability notion, used to explain such uncertainties as instability of human performance on items, was used to express perturbations.

Correspondence Between the Two Spaces, Attribute Responses and Item Responses

K. Tatsuoka (1991) and Varadi and K. Tatsuoka (1989) introduced a "Boolean descriptive function" f to establish a relationship between the attribute responses and item responses. For example, in the matrix $Q(4 \times 5)$, a subject who cannot do A_1 but can do A_2, A_3, and A_4, will have the score of 1 for those items that do not involve A_1 and the score of 0 for those that do involve A_1. Thus, the attribute pattern (0 1 1 1) corresponds to the observable item pattern (0 0 0 1 1). By making the same kinds of hypothesis on the different elements of L and applying these hypotheses to the row vectors of the incidence matrix Q, we can derive the item patterns that are logically possible for a given Q matrix. These item patterns are called "ideal item patterns" (denoted by Ys).

Generally speaking, the relationship between the two spaces, the attribute space and the item space, is not as straightforward as the example of $Q(4 \times 5)$. This is because partial-order relations among the attributes almost always exist and a given item pool often does not include the universal set of items that involves all possible combinations of attributes.

A Case When There is No Relation Among the Attributes

Suppose there are four attributes in a domain and that the universal set of 2^4 items are constructed, then the incidence matrix of 2^4 items is given as follows:

$$
Q(4 \times 16) = \begin{matrix} & \begin{matrix} & & & & & & & & 1 & 1 & 1 & 1 & 1 & 1 & 1 \\ 1 & 2 & 3 & 4 & 5 & 6 & 7 & 8 & 9 & 0 & 1 & 2 & 3 & 4 & 5 & 6 \end{matrix} & \\ \begin{bmatrix} 0 & 1 & 0 & 0 & 0 & 1 & 1 & 1 & 0 & 0 & 0 & 1 & 1 & 1 & 0 & 1 \\ 0 & 0 & 1 & 0 & 0 & 1 & 0 & 0 & 1 & 1 & 0 & 1 & 1 & 0 & 1 & 1 \\ 0 & 0 & 0 & 1 & 0 & 0 & 1 & 0 & 1 & 0 & 1 & 1 & 0 & 1 & 1 & 1 \\ 0 & 0 & 0 & 0 & 1 & 0 & 0 & 1 & 0 & 1 & 1 & 0 & 1 & 1 & 1 & 1 \end{bmatrix} & \begin{matrix} A_1 \\ A_2 \\ A_3 \\ A_4 \end{matrix} \end{matrix}
$$

An hypothesis that states "this subject cannot do A_l but can do $A_1, \ldots A_{l-1}, A_{l+1}, \ldots A_k$ correctly" corresponds to the attribute pattern (1 ... 1 0 1

. . . 1). Let us denote this attribute pattern by Y_l; then Y_l produces the item pattern X_l where $x_j = 1$ if Item j does not involve A_l, and $x_j = 0$ if Item j involves A_l. This operation is defined as a Boolean descriptive function.

Sixteen possible attribute patterns and the images of $\mathbf{f}$ (16 ideal item patterns) are summarized in Table 6.1.

For instance, attribute response pattern 10 indicates that a subject cannot do A_1 and A_3 correctly but can do A_2 and A_4. Then, from the incidence matrix $\mathbf{Q}(4 \times 16)$ shown previously, we see that the scores of items 2, 4, 6, 7, 8, 9, 11, 12, 13, 14, 16 must be zero, and the scores of 1, 3, 5, 10 must be 1.

Table 6.1 indicates that responses to the 16 items can be classified into one of the 16 predetermined groups. They are the universal set of knowledge and capability states that are derived from the incidence matrix $\mathbf{Q}(4 \times 16)$ by applying the properties of Boolean algebra. In other words, the 16 ideal item patterns exhaust all the possible patterns logically compatible with the constraints imposed by the incidence matrix $\mathbf{Q}(4 \times 16)$. By examining and comparing a subject's responses with these 16 ideal item patterns, one can infer the subject's performances on the unobservable attributes. As long as these attributes represent the true task analysis, any response patterns of these 16 items that differ from the 16 ideal item patterns are regarded as fuzzy patterns or perturbations resulting from some lapses or slips on one or more items, reflecting random errors.

A Case When There Are Prerequisite Relations Among the Attributes

So far we have not assumed any relations among the four attributes in Table 6.1. It is often the case that some attributes are directly related one to another. Suppose A_1 is a prerequisite of A_2, A_2 is a prerequisite of A_3, and A_1, is also a prerequisite of A_4.

If we assume that a subject cannot do A_1 correctly, then A_2 and A_3 cannot be correct because they require knowledge of A_1 as a prerequisite. Therefore, the attribute patterns 3, 4, 5, 9, 10, 11, and 15 in Table 6.1 become (0 0 0 0), which is Pattern 1. By an argument similar to the previous paragraph, "cannot do A_2" implies "cannot do A_3." In this case the attribute patterns 2 and 7, and the patterns 8 and 14 are respectively no longer distinguishable. Table 6.2 summarizes the implication of the relations assumed among the four attribute set.

The number of attribute patterns has been reduced from 16 to 7. The item patterns associated with these seven attribute patterns are given in the right-hand column, in which each pattern still has 16 elements. It should be noted that we do not need 16 items to distinguish seven attribute patterns. Items 2, 3, 4, 5, 10, and 11 are sufficient to provide the different ideal item pat-

TABLE 6.1
A List of 16 Ideal Item Response Patterns Obtained from 16 Attribute
Response Patterns by a Boolean Description Function

	Attribute Response Patterns	Ideal Item Response Patterns
1	0000	1000000000000000
2	1000	1100000000000000
3	0100	1010000000000000
4	0010	1001000000000000
5	0001	1000100000000000
6	1100	1110010000000000
7	1010	1101001000000000
8	1001	1100100100000000
9	0110	1011000010000000
10	0101	1010100001000000
11	0011	1001100000100000
12	1110	1111011010010000
13	1101	1110110101001000
14	1011	1101101100100100
15	0111	1011100011100010
16	1111	1111111111111111

terns, (0 0 0 0 0 0), (1 0 0 0 0 0), (1 0 0 1 0 0), (1 1 0 1 1 0), (1 1 0 0 0 0),
(1 1 1 0 0 0), (1 1 1 1 1 1), which are obtained from the second through
fifth columns, and the 10th and 11th columns of the ideal item patterns in
Table 6.2.

The seven reduced attribute patterns given in Table 6.2 can be considered
as a matrix of the order 7 × 4. The four column vectors, which associate
with attributes A_1, A_2, A_3, and A_4, satisfy the partial order defined by the inclusion relation. Expressing the inclusion relationships among the four
attributes—A_1 (Column 1), A_2 (Column 2), A_3 (Column 3) and A_4 (Column 4)—
in a matrix results in the following reachability matrix **R**:

TABLE 6.2
A List of Attribute Response Patterns and Ideal Item Response Patterns
Affected by Direct Relations of Attributes

Original Patterns	Attribute Patterns	Ideal Item Patterns
1,3,4,5,9,10,11,15	0000	1000000000000000
2,7	1000	1100000000000000
8,14	1001	1100100100000000
13	1101	1110110101001000
6	1100	1110010000000000
12	1110	1111011010010000
16	1111	1111111111111111

$$
\mathbf{R} = \begin{bmatrix} 1 & 1 & 1 & 1 \\ 0 & 1 & 1 & 0 \\ 0 & 0 & 1 & 0 \\ 0 & 0 & 0 & 1 \end{bmatrix}
$$

It is easy to verify that $\mathbf{R}$ can be derived from the adjacency matrix of $\mathbf{A}$ obtained from the prerequisite relations among the four attributes; $A_1 \rightarrow A_2 \rightarrow A_3$ and $A_1 \rightarrow A_4$ (see Fig. 6.3).

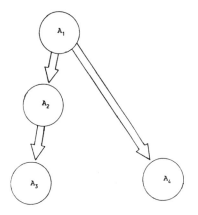

FIG. 6.3.   An example of partially ordered attributes.

An Approach to Designing Constructed-Response Items for a Diagnostic Test

Notwithstanding the foregoing, it is sometimes impossible to construct items like 2, 3, 4, and 5 that involve only one attribute per item. This is especially true when we are dealing with constructed-response items and have to measure much more complicated processes such as organization of knowledge and cognitive tasks. In these cases, it is natural to assume that each item will involve several attributes. By examining Table 6.2, one can find several sets of items for which the seven attribute patterns produce exactly the same seven ideal item patterns as those in Table 6.2.

Examples are the sets {2, 3, 4, 5, 10, 11} and {2, 3, 4, 5, 13, 11}. There are 128 different sets of items that produce the seven ideal item patterns when the seven attribute patterns in Table 6.2 are applied. This means that there are many possibilities for selecting an appropriate set of six items so as to maximize the diagnostic capability of a test. The common condition for selecting these sets of items can be generalized by the use of Boolean algebra, but detailed discussion is not given in this chapter.

This simple example implies that this systematic item construction method enables us to measure unobservable underlying cognitive processes via observable item response patterns. However, if the items are constructed without taking these requirements into account, then instructionally useful feedback or cognitive error diagnoses may not be always obtainable.

Explanation With Math Items

The five items associated with the tank filling problem were given earlier. The incidence matrix $Q(4 \times 5)$ produces nine ideal item patterns and attribute patterns using the BUGLIB program (Varadi & K. Tatsuoka, 1989). Table 6.3 summarizes them.

The prerequisite relations, $A_1 \rightarrow A_2$ and $A_3 \rightarrow A_4$ imply some constraints on attribute patterns: The attribute pattern, (0 1) for A_1, A_2, and A_3, A_4, cannot exist logically. A close examination of Table 6.1 reveals that the constraints result in nine distinguishable attribute patterns. They are: 3, 5, 10

TABLE 6.3
A List of Nine Knowledge and Capability States and Nine Ideal Item Patterns
for Five Items Associated with the Tank-Filling Problem

	Attribute Patterns	Ideal Item Patterns	Description of States
1	1111	11111	Can do everything
2	1110	01101	Can do $A_1{}^*$, A_2, A_3 Cannot do A_4
3	1100	01100	Can do A_1, A_2 Cannot do A_3, A_4
4	1011	00111	Can do A_1, A_3, A_4 Cannot do A_2
5	1010	00101	Can do A_1, A_3 Cannot do A_2, A_4
6	1000	00100	Can do A_1 Cannot do A_2, A_3, A_4
7	0011	00011	Can do A_3, A_4 Cannot do A_1, A_2
8	0010	00001	Can do A_3 Cannot do A_1, A_2, A_4
9	0000	00000	Cannot do anything

$^*A_1$: Goal is to find the net filling rate.
A_2: Compute the rate.
A_3: Goal is to find the time to fill the tank.
A_4: Compute the time.

result in Pattern 1, that is, (0000); 8 results in Pattern 2, that is, (1000); 9 results in 4, (0010); 13 in 6, (1100); 15 in 11, (0011); and the Patterns 7, (1010); 12, (1110); 14, (1011) and 16 (1111) remain unchanged.

It can be easily verified that the reachability matrix given in an earlier section is the same as the matrix that is obtained by examining the inclusion relationships among all combinations of the four column vectors of the attribute patterns in Table 6.3. This means that all possible knowledge states obtainable from the four attributes with the structure represented by **R** can be used for diagnosing a student's errors. Thus, the five tank-filling items should serve to diagnose the nine states of knowledge and capabilities listed in Table 6.3.

ILLUSTRATION WITH REAL EXAMPLES

Example I: A Case of Discrete Attributes in Fraction Addition Problems

Birenbaum and Shaw (1985) used Guttman's facet analysis technique (Guttman, Epstein, Amir, & Guttman, 1990) to identify eight task-content facets for solving fraction addition problems. There were six operation facets that described the numbers used in the problems and two facets dealing with the results. Then, a task specification chart was created based on a design that combined the content facets with the procedural steps. Figure 6.4 shows the task specification chart.

The task specification chart describes two strategies to solve the problems, Methods A and B. Those examinees who use Method A convert a mixed number $(a\,b/c)$ into a simple fraction, $(ac+b)/c$, and the users of Method B separate the whole number part from the fraction part and then add the two parts independently. In these cases, it is clear that when the numbers become larger in a fraction addition problem, Method A requires computational skills to get the correct answer. Method B, on the other hand, requires a deeper understanding of the number system.

Sets of attributes for the two methods are selected from the task specification chart in Fig. 6.4 as follows:

Problem: $a\,b/c + d\,e/f$		Method A	Method B
A_1	Convert $(a\,b/c)$ to $(ac+b)/c$	used	not used
A_2	Convert $(d\,e/f)$ to $(df+e)/f$	used	not used
A_3	Divide fraction by a common factor	used	used
A_4	Find the common denominator of c & f	used	used
A_5	Make equivalent fractions	used	used

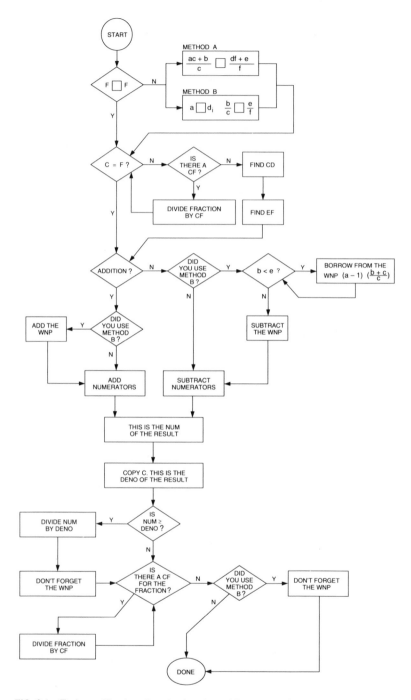

FIG. 6.4. Task specification chart for fraction addition and subtraction problems. *Note.* The symbol used to denote the general fraction form used in this figure is a(b/c) + d(e/f); F is fraction; CD is common denominator; CF is common factor; WNP is whole number part; NUM is numerator; DENO is denominator; EF is equivalent fraction.

A_6	Add numerators	used	used
A_7	Divide numerator by denominator	used	used
A_8	Don't forget the whole number part	used	used
B_1	Separate a & d and b/c & e/f	not used	used
B_2	Add the whole numbers, including 0	not used	used

The two methods share all of the attributes in common, except for B_1 and B_2, A_1 and A_2. The incidence matrices for the 10 items in Birenbaum and Shaw (1985), for Methods A and B, are given in Table 6.4.

A computer program written by Varadi and Tatsuoka (BUGLIB, 1989) produces a list of all the possible "can/cannot" combinations of attributes, otherwise known as the universal set of attribute-response patterns.

For Method A, 13 attribute patterns are obtained. The attribute patterns and their corresponding ideal item patterns are given in Table 6.5 where the attributes are denoted by the numbers 1 through 8 for A_1 through A_8, and 9 and 10 for B_1 and B_2, respectively. For instance, the second state, 2, has the attribute pattern 11111110 and the ideal item pattern is represented by 1111000100.

TABLE 6.4
Ten Items with Their Attribute Characteristics by Method A and Method B

	Method A	
1	2 8/6 + 3 10/6	A_1, A_2, A_3, A_6, A_7
2	3/5 + 1/5	A_6
3	3 10/4 + 4 6/4	A_1, A_2, A_3, A_6, A_7
4	7/4 + 5/4	A_6, A_7
5	3/4 + 1/2	A_4, A_5, A_6, A_7, A_8
6	2/5 + 12/8	$A_3, A_4, A_5, A_6, A_7, A_8$
7	1/2 + 1 10/7	$A_2, A_4, A_5, A_6, A_7, A_8$
8	1/3 + 1/2	A_4, A_5, A_6
9	3 1/6 + 2 3/4	$A_1, A_2, A_4, A_5, A_6, A_7, A_8$
10	5/6 + 1/3	A_4, A_5, A_6, A_7, A_8

	Method B	
1	2 8/6 + 3 10/6	$B_1, A_3, A_4, A_5, A_6, A_7, B_2$
2	3/5 + 1/5	same as by Method A
3	3 10/4 + 4 6/4	$B_1, A_3, A_6, A_7, A_8, B_2$
4	7/4 + 5/4	same as by Method A
5	3/4 + 1/2	same as by Method A
6	2/5 + 12/8	same as by Method A
7	1/2 + 1 10/7	$B_1, A_4, A_5, A_6, A_7, A_8, B_2$
8	1/3 + 1/2	same as by Method A
9	3 1/6 + 2 3/4	B_1, A_4, A_5, A_6, B_2
10	5/6 + 1/3	same as by Method A

TABLE 6.5
A List of All the Possible Sets of Attribute Patterns Derived from the Incidence
Matrices Given in Table 6.4

	Method A		Ideal Item
States	Cannot	Can	Response Pattern
1	none	1,2,3,4,5,6,7,8	1111111111
2	8	1,2,3,4,5,6,7	1111000100
3	4,5,8	1,2,3,6,7	1111000000
4	1	2,3,4,5,6,7,8	0101111101
5	2,1	3,4,5,6,7,8	0101110101
6	3	1,2,4,5,6,7,8	0101101111
7	3,1	2,4,5,6,7,8	0101101101
8	3,2,1	4,5,6,7,8	0101100101
9	1,2,3,8	4,5,6,7	0101000100
10	1,2,3,4,5,8	6,7	0101000000
11	7,1,2,3,8	4,5,6	0100000100
12	1,2,3,8,7,4,5	6	0100000000
13	1,2,3,4,5,6,7,8	none	0000000000

	Method B		Ideal Item
States	Cannot	Can	Response Pattern
1	none	3,4,5,6,7,8,9,10	1111111111
2	8	3,4,5,6,7,9,10	1101000110
3	4,5	3,6,7,8,9,10	0111000000
4	9,10	3,4,5,6,7,8	0101110101
5	3	4,5,6,7,8,9,10	0101101111
6	3,9,10	4,5,6,7,8	0101100101
7	3,8	4,5,6,7,9,10	0101000110
8	3,8,9,10	4,5,6,7	0101000100
9	3,4,5,8,9,10	6,7	0101000000
10	7,3,8	4,5,6,9,10	0100000110
11	3,7,8,9,10	4,5,6	0100000100
12	3,4,5,7,8,9,10	6	0100000000
13	3,4,5,6,7,8,9,10	none	0000000000

It is interesting to note that there is no state including "cannot do an item that involves both of the attributes, A_1 and A_2, but can do items that involve either A_1 or A_2 alone" in the list given in Table 6.5. If one would like to diagnose such a compound state, then a new attribute should be added to the list.

Another interesting result is that A_5 cannot be separated from A_4 as long as we use only these 10 items. In other words, the rows for A_4 and A_5 in the incidence matrix for Method A are identical. Needless to say, Birenbaum and Shaw (1985) found many different errors that originated in attribute A_5—making equivalent fractions—and they must be diagnosed for remediation

(Bunderson & Olsen, 1983). In order to separate A_5 from A_4, we must add a new item that involves A_4 but not A_5, thereby making Row A_5 different from Row A_4.

Beyond asking the original "equivalent fraction" question, we now add an item to the existing item pool, which asks, "What is the common denominator of $2/5$ and $1/7$?" This is a way to test the skill for getting common denominators correctly and also distinguishes the separate skill required for making equivalent fractions. However, because the solutions to each of these questions are so closely related and interdependent, it may not be possible to separately measure the examinees' skills in terms of each function. If an examinee answers this item correctly but gets a wrong answer for items involving addition, such as $2/5 + 1/7$, then it is more likely that the examinee has the skill for getting correct common denominators but not the skill for making equivalent fractions correctly.

Thirteen knowledge and capability states are identified from the incidence matrix for Method B, and they are also summarized in Table 6.5. Some ideal item response patterns can be found in the lists for both Methods A and B. This means that for some cases we cannot diagnose a student's underlying strategy for solving these 10 items. Our attribute list cannot distinguish whether a student converts a mixed number $(a\,{}^b/_c)$ to an improper fraction, or separates the whole number part from the fraction part. If we can see the student's scratch paper and can examine the numerators prior to addition, then we can find which method the student used. There are two solutions to this problem. One might use a computer for testing so that crucial steps during problem-solving activities can be coded. The second possibility is to add new items so that these three attributes, A_1, A_2, and B_1, can be separated in the incidence matrix for Method B.

Example 2: The Case of Continuous and Hierarchically Related Attributes in the Adult Literacy Domain

Kirsch and Mosenthal (1990) have developed a cognitive model that underlies the performance of young adults on so-called document literacy tasks. They identified three categories of variables that predict the difficulties of items with a multiple R of .94.

The three categories are defined as follows:

- "Document" variables are based on the structure and complexity of the document.
- "Task" variables are based on the structural relation between the document and the accompanying question or directive.
- "Process" variables are based on strategies used to relate information in the question or directive to information in the documents. (p. 5)

The "Document" variables comprise six specific variables including the number of organizing categories in the document, the number of embedded organizing categories in the document, and the number of specifics. These three variables are considered in our incidence matrix as the attributes for "Document" variables.

The "Task" variables are determined on the basis of the structural relations between a question and the document to which it refers. The larger the number of units of information required to complete a task, the more difficult the task. Four attributes are picked up from this variable group.

The "Process" variables in Kirsch and Mosenthal's (1990) regression analysis influenced the item difficulties to a large extent. One of the variables in this category is the degree of correspondence, which is defined as the degree to which the information given in the question or directive matches the corresponding information in the document. The next variable represents the type of information that has to be developed to locate, identify, generate, or provide the requested information based on one or more nodes from a document hierarchy. Five hierarchically related attributes are determined from this variable group. The last variables are Plausibility of Distractors, which measure the ability to identify the extent to which information in the document matches features in a question's given and requested information.

A total of 22 attributes are selected to characterize the 61 items. The attributes in each variable group are totally ordered, that is, $A_1 \rightarrow A_2 \rightarrow A_3 \rightarrow A_4 \rightarrow A_5$, therefore the number of possible combinations of "can/cannot" attributes is drastically reduced (Tatsuoka, 1991). One hundred fifty-seven possible attribute response patterns were derived by the BUGLIB program and hence 157 ideal item response patterns are produced. As was explained in an earlier section, these 157 ideal item response patterns correspond to 157 state distributions that are multivariate normal. These states are used for classifying an individual examinee's response pattern. A sample of 10 states with their corresponding attribute response patterns are shown in Table 6.6.

As can be seen in Table 6.6, several subsets of attributes are totally ordered and the elements of the subset form a chain. Fifteen hundred subjects were classified into one of the 157 misconception states by a computer program entitled RULESPACE (Tatsuoka, Baillie, & Sheehan, 1991). The number of subjects who were classified into each state was: 157 subjects in State No. 1, 46 in No. 4, 120 in No. 11, 81 in No. 12, 37 in No. 14, 68 in No. 50, 12 in No. 32, 27 in No. 102, 11 in No. 138, and 4 in No. 156. The interpretation of misconceptions for these results is described in detail elsewhere (Sheehan, Tatsuoka, & Lewis, 1991), but State No. 11 (into which the largest number of subjects were classified) is described here.

"Cannot" attributes A_{18} and A_{19} relate directly from A_{18} to A_{19}. Therefore, as represented in Table 6.6, the statement can be made that "a subject classified in this state cannot do A_{18}, and hence cannot, by default, do A_{19}." Thus,

TABLE 6.6
The Ten States Selected from 157 Possible States Yielded
by Boolean Operation (via BUGLIB Program)

		Attribute Pattern	Directed Direct Relation
		1111111111222	Among Attributes
States		1234567890123456789012	Not Mastered
1	No. 1	1111111111111111111111	None
2	No. 4	1111111111111111110111	None
3	No. 11	1111111111111111100111	$A_{18} \rightarrow A_{19}$
4	No. 12	1111011111111111100111	$A_{18} \rightarrow A_{19}$
5	No. 14	1111011110111111100111	$A_{18} \rightarrow A_{19}$
6	No. 30	1111011100111111100111	$A_9 \rightarrow A_{10}, A_{18} \rightarrow A_{19}$
7	No. 32	1100011100111111100110	$A_3 \rightarrow A_4 \rightarrow A_5, A_9 \rightarrow A_{10}$
8	No. 102	1000011111111111111111	$A_2 \rightarrow A_3 \rightarrow A_4 \rightarrow A_5$
9	No. 138	1000011111111011110111	$A_2 \rightarrow A_3 \rightarrow A_4 \rightarrow A_5$
10	No. 156	1000010000001110000100	$A_2 \rightarrow A_3 \rightarrow A_4 \rightarrow A_5$
			$A_7 \rightarrow A_8 \rightarrow A_9 \rightarrow A_{10}$
			$A_{11} \rightarrow A_{12} \rightarrow A_{13}$
			$A_{16} \rightarrow A_{17} \rightarrow A_{18} \rightarrow A_{19}$
			$A_{21} \rightarrow A_{22}$

the prescription for these subjects' errors is likely to be that they make mistakes when items have the following specific feature: "Distractors appear both within an organizing category and across organizing categories, because different organizing categories list the same specifics but with different attributes" (Kirsch & Mosenthal, 1990, p. 30).

PSYCHOMETRIC THEORIES APPROPRIATE FOR A CONSTRUCTED RESPONSE FORMAT

An incidence matrix suggests various scoring formulas for the items. First, the binary scores of right or wrong answers can be obtained from the condition that if a subject can perform all the attributes involved in an item correctly, then the subject will get a score of one on that item; otherwise the subject will get a score of zero. With this scoring formula, the simple logistic models (Lord & Novick, 1968) for binary responses can be used for estimating the scaling variable θ.

Second, partial credit scores or graded response scores can be obtained from the incidence matrix if performance dependent on the attributes is observable and can be measured directly. This condition permits applicability of Masters' partial credit models (Masters, 1982) or Samejima's general graded-response models (Samejima, 1988) to data.

As far as error diagnoses are concerned, simple binary response models always work even when performances on the attributes *cannot* be measured directly and are *not* observable. However, computer scoring (Bennett, Rock, et al., 1990) or scoring by human raters can be used to assign *graded* scores to the items. For example, the number of correctly processed attributes for each item could be represented as a graded score.

Muraki (1991) wrote a computer program for his modified version of Samejima's (1969) original graded response model. Muraki's program can also be used to apply Samejima's model.

Third, a teacher may assign different weights to the attributes and give a student a score corresponding to the percentage of correct answers achieved, depending on how well the student performed on the attributes. Thus, the final score for the item becomes a continuous variable. Then Samejima's (1974, 1988) general continuous IRT model can be used to estimate the ability parameter θ. If the response time for each item is available, then her multidimensional continuous model can be applied.

Fourth, if a teacher is interested in particular combinations of attributes and assigns scores to nominal categories, say 1 = {can do A_1 and A_3}, 2 = {can do A_1 and A_2}, and 3 = {can do A_2, A_3, and A_4}, and so on, then Bock's (1972) polychotomous model can be utilized for estimating θ.

CONCLUSION

A wide variety of Item Response Theory models accommodating binary scores and graded, polychotomous, and continuous responses have been developed in the past two decades. These models are built upon a hypothetical ability variable θ. We are not against the use of global item scores and total scores—for example, the total score is a sufficient statistic for θ in the Rasch model—but it is necessary to investigate microlevel variables such as cognitive skills and knowledge and their structural relationships in order to develop a pool of cognitively sound constructed-response items. The systematic item construction method enables us to measure unobservable underlying cognitive processes via observable item response patterns.

This chapter has introduced an approach for organizing several dozen such microlevel variables and for investigating their systematic interrelationships. The approach utilizes deterministic theories, graph theory, and Boolean algebra. When most microlevel variables are not easy to measure directly, an inference must be made from the observable macrolevel measures. An incidence matrix for characterizing the underlying relationships among microlevel variables is the first step toward achieving our goal. Then a Boolean algebra that is formulated on a set of sets of attributes, or a set of all possible item response patterns obtainable from the incidence matrix, enables us to establish relationships between two worlds: attribute space and item space (K. Tatsuoka, 1991).

A theory of item construction was introduced in conjunction with K. Tatsuoka's (1991) work in Boolean algebra. If a subset of attributes has a connected, directed relation and forms a chain, then the number of combinations of "can/cannot" attributes will be reduced dramatically. Thus, it will become easier for us to construct a pool of items by which a particular group of misconceptions of concern can be diagnosed with a minimum of classification errors.

One of the advantages of the rule space model (K. Tatsuoka, 1983, 1990) is that the model relates a scaled ability parameter θ to misconception states. For a given misconception state, one can always identify the particular types of errors that relate to ability level θ. If the centroid of the state is located in the upper part of the rule space, then one can conclude that this type of error is rare. If the centroid lies on the θ axis, then this error type is observed very frequently.

Although rule space was developed in the context of binary IRT models, the concept and mathematics are general enough to be extended for use in more complicated IRT models. Further work to extend the rule space concept to accommodate complicated response models will be left for future research.

ACKNOWLEDGMENTS

The author gratefully acknowledges and thanks several people for their help: Randy Bennett, Robert Mislevy, Kathy Sheehan, Maurice Tatsuoka, and Bill Ward for valuable comments and suggestions, John Cordery for editorial help, and Donna Lembeck for various help.

REFERENCES

Bennett, R. E., Rock, D. A., Braun, H. I., Frye, D., Spohrer, J. C., & Soloway, E. (1990). The relationship of constrained free-response to multiple-choice and open-ended items. *Applied Psychological Measurement, 14*, 151–162.

Bennett, R. E., Sebrechts, M. M., & Yamamoto, K. (in press). *Fitting new measurement models to GRE General Test constructed-response item data*. Princeton, NJ: Educational Testing Service.

Bennett, R. E., Ward, W. C., Rock, D. A., & LaHart, C. (1990). *Toward a framework for constructed-response items* (RR-90-7). Princeton, NJ: Educational Testing Service.

Birenbaum, M., & Shaw, D. J. (1985). Task Specification Chart: A key to better understanding of test results. *Journal of Educational Measurement, 22*, 219–230.

Birenbaum, M., & Tatsuoka, K. K. (1987). Open-ended versus multiple-choice response formats—It does make a difference for diagnostic purposes. *Applied Psychological Measurement, 11*, 329–341.

Bock, R. D. (1972). Estimating item parameters and latent ability when the responses are scored in two or more nominal categories. *Psychometrika, 37*, 29–51.

Brown, J. S., & VanLehn, K. (1980). Diagnostic models for procedural bugs in basic mathematical skills. *Cognitive Science, 4,* 370–426.

Bunderson, V. C., & Olsen, J. B. (1983). *Mental errors in arithmetic: Their diagnosis in precollege students* (Final Project Report, NSF SED 80-12500). Provo, UT: WICAT.

Chipman, S. F., Davis, C., & Shafto, M. G. (1986). Personnel and training research program: Cognitive science at ONR. *Naval Research Review, 38,* 3–21.

Dibello, L. V., & Baillie, R. J. (1991). *Separating points in rule space.* (CERL Research Report). Urbana, IL: University of Illinois.

Easley, J. A., & Tatsuoka, M. M. (1968). *Scientific thought, cases from classical physics.* Boston, MA: Allyn & Bacon.

Ginzburg, H. (1977). *Children's arithmetic: The learning process.* New York: Van Nostrand.

Glaser, R. (1985). *The integration of instruction and testing.* Paper presented at the ETS Invitational Conference on the Redesign of Testing for the 21st Century, New York.

Guttman, R., Epstein, E. E., Amir, M., & Guttman, L. (1990). A structural theory of spatial abilities. *Applied Psychological Measurement, 14,* 217–236.

Hubert, L. J. (1974). Some applications of graph theory to clustering. *Psychometrika, 39,* 283–309.

Kim, S. H. (1990). *Classification of item-response patterns into misconception groups.* Unpublished doctoral dissertation, University of Illinois, Champaign.

Kirsch, I. S., & Mosenthal, P. B. (1990). Document literacy. *Reading research quarterly, 25,* 5–29.

Lord, F. M., & Novick, M. R. (1968). *Statistical theories of mental test scores.* Reading, MA: Addison-Wesley.

Masters, G. N. (1982). A Rasch model for partial credit scoring in objective tests. *Psychometrika, 47,* 149–174.

Muraki, E. (1991). *Comparison of the graded and partial credit item response models.* Unpublished manuscript. Princeton, NJ: Educational Testing Service.

Samejima, F. (1969). Estimation of ability using a response pattern of graded scores. *Psychometrika Monograph,* 17.

Samejima, F. (1974). Normal ogive model on the continuous response level in the multidimensional latent space. *Psychometrika, 39,* 111–121.

Samejima, F. (1988). *Advancement of latent trait theory* (ONR Final Report). Knoxville, TN: University of Tennessee.

Sato, T. (1990). *An introduction to educational information technology* (D. L. Harnisch & M. L. Connell, Trans.). Kawasaki, Japan: NEC Technical College. (Original work published 1987)

Sheehan, K., Tatsuoka, K. K., & Lewis, C. (1991). *Using the rule space model to diagnose document processing errors.* Paper presented at the ONR Conference Workshop on Model-Based Measurement, Princeton, NJ: Educational Testing Service.

Sleeman, D., Kelly, A. E., Martinak, R., Ward, R., & Moore, J. (1989). Studies of diagnosis and remediation with high school algebra students. *Cognitive Science, 13,* 551–568.

Takeya, M. (1981). *A study on item relational structure analysis of criterion referenced tests.* Unpublished doctoral dissertation, Waseda University, Tokyo.

Tatsuoka, K. K. (1983). Rule space: An approach for dealing with misconceptions based on item response theory. *Journal of Educational Measurement, 20,* 345–354.

Tatsuoka, K. K. (1985). A probabilistic model for diagnosing misconceptions in the pattern classification approach. *Journal of Educational Statistics, 12,* 55–73.

Tatsuoka, K. K. (1990). Toward an integration of item-response theory and cognitive error diagnoses. In N. Frederiksen, R. L. Glaser, A. M. Lesgold, & M. G. Shafto (Eds.), *Diagnostic monitoring of skill and knowledge acquisition* (pp. 453–488). Hillsdale, NJ: Lawrence Erlbaum Associates.

Tatsuoka, K. K. (1991). *Boolean algebra applied to determination of the universal set of knowledge states* (Tech. Rep. ONR-1, RR-91-4). Princeton, NJ: Educational Testing Service.

Tatsuoka, K. K., Baillie, R., & Sheehan, K. (1991). *RULESPACE: Classifying a subject into one of the predetermined groups.* Unpublished computer program.

Tatsuoka, K. K., Birenbaum, M., & Arnold, J. (1989). On the stability of students' rules of operation for solving arithmetic problems. *Journal of Educational Measurement, 26,* 351–361.

Tatsuoka, K. K., & Tatsuoka, M. M. (1987). Bug distribution and pattern classification. *Psychometrika, 52,* 193–206.

Tatsuoka, K. K., & Tatsuoka, M. M. (1991). *On measures of misconception stability* (ONR-Tech. Rep. No. ONR-91-1). Princeton, NJ: Educational Testing Service.

Tatsuoka, M. M. (1986). Graph theory and its applications in educational research: A review and integration. *Review of Educational Research, 56,* 291–329.

Tatsuoka, M. M., & Tatsuoka, K. K. (1989). Rule space. In S. Kotz & N. L. Johnson (Eds.), *Encyclopedia of statistical sciences* (pp. 217–220). New York: Wiley.

Varadi, F., & Tatsuoka, K. K. (1989). *BUGLIB.* Unpublished computer program.

Warfield, J. N. (1973a). On arranging elements of a binary in graphic form. *IEEE Transaction on Systems, Man, and cybernetics, SMC-3,* 121–132.

Warfield, J. N. (1973b). Binary matrices in system modeling. *IEEE Transactions on Systems, Man, and Cybernetics, SMC-3,* 441–449.

Wise, S. L. (1981). *A modified order-analysis procedure for determining unidimensional items sets.* Unpublished doctoral dissertation, University of Illinois, Champaign.

7

CONSTRUCTED RESPONSE AND DIFFERENTIAL ITEM FUNCTIONING: A PRAGMATIC APPROACH

Neil J. Dorans
Alicia P. Schmitt
Educational Testing Service

From the test practitioner's point of view, constructed-response items transfer the bulk of arduous labor that goes into producing a test item and its score from the test developer to the test scorer. Quality multiple-choice items are difficult to produce but easy to score and analyze. Constructed-response items are relatively easy to produce, but difficult to score and complicated to analyze. For multiple-choice items, the psychometrics are well developed and procedures for performing microscopic dissections of items are well established. These procedures include techniques for assessing differential item functioning (DIF). Two DIF procedures routinely used at Educational Testing Service are the Mantel–Haenszel procedure (Holland & Thayer, 1988) and the standardization approach (Dorans & Kulick, 1986), both of which are described in detail in Dorans and Holland (1992). Other procedures, based on item response theory (IRT), are described by Thissen, Steinberg, and Wainer (1992).

Mislevy, Yamamoto, and Anacker (1992) contrasted the well developed body of psychometrics for multiple-choice items with the nascent state of psychometrics for constructed-response items. To the extent that a constructed-response item is unconstrained and examinees are free to produce any response they wish, the test scorer has a difficult and challenging task of extracting information from examinee responses. To date the psychometrics for dealing with this unconstrained response type have lagged behind the development and administration of these items. Until psychometrics finds ways of extracting replicable and valid information from these responses,

135

constructed-response applications will remain the exception in high-volume, "high-stakes" testing applications.

Differential item functioning analysis, which is defined later, provides secondary psychometrics, usually performed in areas where the primary psychometrics associated with descriptions of item performance, test performance, and examinee performance are well established, as is the case with multiple-choice items. Given the current state of psychometrics and cognitive theory for constructed-response testing, we have no alternative but to rely on a class of DIF procedures that is descriptive and can be applied in the absence of cognitive and related psychometric models, making the procedures, in this sense, "model-free."

Constructed-response items move beyond traditional multiple-choice items, for which DIF methodology is well-defined, toward item types involving selection or identification, reordering or rearrangement, substitution or correction, completion, construction, and presentation (Bennett, this volume). Model-free DIF assessment requires both a rule for scoring items and a matching variable on which different subpopulations can be viewed as comparable for purposes of assessing their item performance. This chapter focuses primarily on DIF assessment and secondarily on constructed-response. The DIF portions draw heavily on earlier work, most notably, Dorans and Holland (1992). The standardization and Mantel–Haenszel approaches are described in some detail to give the reader an appreciation of state of the art, model-free DIF assessment, and because these procedures can be extended to assess DIF among some constructed-response formats.

The structure of the chapter is as follows: DIF is defined and then is contrasted with impact via Simpson's paradox, which demonstrates the importance of matching in DIF studies. The standardization approach is defined as a flexible procedure for describing DIF, while the Mantel–Haenszel (MH) procedure is described as a statistically powerful method for detecting DIF. A common framework from which to view these two related procedures is then presented, from which the essence of model-free DIF is extracted. A general procedure for DIF assessment is outlined, followed by a taxonomy of item responses, and then each option within the taxonomy is evaluated in terms of its amenability to DIF analysis using the general procedure. Next, empirical findings from other studies are discussed in terms of their relevance to constructed-response DIF assessment. Finally, future directions in constructed-response DIF analysis are considered.

DIFFERENTIAL ITEM FUNCTIONING

Differential item functioning (DIF) refers to a psychometric difference in how an item functions for two groups. DIF indicates a difference in item performance between two comparable groups of examinees, that is, groups that are matched with respect to the construct being measured by the test. The comparison of matched or comparable groups is critical because it is important to distinguish between differences in item functioning and differences in group ability.

In the first chapter of the book, *Handbook of Methods for Detecting Test Bias*, Shepard (1982) defined DIF, or what was then called "item bias," as psychometric features of the item that can misrepresent the competence of a group. She provided some conceptual definitions of the term offered by other authors, including: "An item is unbiased if, for all individuals having the same score on a homogeneous subtest containing the item, the proportion of individuals getting the item correct is the same for each population group being considered" (Scheuneman, 1975, p. 2). This definition underlies the model-free DIF approaches described in Dorans and Holland (in press) and in this chapter.

Lord (1980) provided the item response theory definition of DIF:

> If each test item in a test had exactly the same item response function in every group, then people of the same ability or skill would have exactly the same chance of getting the item right, regardless of their group membership. Such a test would be completely unbiased. If on the other hand, an item has a different item response function for one group than for another, it is clear that the item is biased. (p. 212)

This model-based definition underlies the DIF procedures described by Thissen, Steinberg, and Wainer (1992).

Thissen (1987) added to these definitions by referring to DIF as:

> . . . an expression which describes a serious threat to the validity of tests used to measure the aptitude of members of different populations or groups. Some test items may simply perform differently for examinees drawn from one group or another or they may measure "different things" for members of one group as opposed to members of another. Tests containing such items may have reduced validity for between-group comparison, because their scores may be indicative of a variety of attributes other than those the test is intended to measure. (p. 1)

Statistical methods used to identify DIF were defined by Shepard (1982) as: "internal methods designed to ensure that the meaning, which individual items attribute to the total test, is the same for all subgroups" (p. 23). A variety of methods have been used since the 1950s. Two methods for DIF assessment presently employed at Educational Testing Service are the standardization approach (Dorans & Kulick, 1986) and the Mantel–Haenszel approach (Holland & Thayer, 1988). Both procedures compare matched groups and are used primarily with multiple-choice items.

DIF VERSUS IMPACT

It is important to make a distinction between DIF and impact. Impact refers to a difference in performance between two intact groups. Impact is pervasive in test and item data because individuals differ with respect to the developed abilities measured by items and tests, and intact groups, such as those defined by ethnicity and gender, differ with respect to the distributions of developed ability among their members. For example, on a typical SAT mathematics item it is usually the case that Asian-Americans score higher than Whites, males score higher than females, and high school juniors and seniors score higher than junior high school students.

In contrast to impact, which can often be explained by stable consistent differences in examinee ability distributions across groups, DIF refers to differences in item functioning *after* groups have been matched with respect to the ability or attribute that the item purportedly measures. Unlike impact, where differences in item performance reflect differences in overall ability distributions, DIF is an *unexpected* difference among groups of examinees who are supposed to be comparable with respect to the attribute measured by the item and the test on which it appears.

Simpson's Paradox

Simpson's paradox (Simpson, 1951) illustrates why one should compare the comparable, as is done in DIF analyses. Table 7.1 summarizes the performance of two hypothetical groups, A and B, on an imaginary item. This table contains four rows and six columns of numbers. The first three columns pertain to Group A, and the last three pertain to Group B. The first three rows show three different ability levels ranging from the lowest to the highest, and the fourth row sums across ability levels. (In the case of the third and

TABLE 7.1
Summary of the Performance of Two Hypothetical Groups on an Imaginary Item

Ability Level	Group A			Group B		
	N_m	N_{cm}	N_{cm}/N_m	N_m	N_{cm}	N_{cm}/N_m
1	400	40	.10	10000	2000	.20
2	1000	500	.50	10000	6000	.60
3	1000	900	.90	4000	4000	1.00
Weighted Sum	2400	1440	.60	24000	12000	.50

Note. The symbols N_m, N_{cm}, and N_{cm}/N_m refer to the number of people at the ability level m, the number of people at ability level m who answered the item correctly, and the proportion at ability level m who answered the item correctly, respectively.

sixth columns, the sum in the fourth row is a weighted sum.) The symbols N_m, N_{cm}, and N_{cm}/N_m refer to the number of people at the ability level m, the number of people at ability level m who answered the item correctly, and the proportion at ability level m who answered the item correctly, respectively.

Of the 2,400 examinees in Group A, 1,440 or 60% answered the item correctly. In contrast, only 50%, 12,000 of 24,000, of Group B answered the item correctly. The impact on this item is $.6 - .5 = .1$ in favor of Group A.

Upon closer examination, however, the ratio N_{cm}/N_m at each of the three ability levels for Group A is actually .1 *lower* than the corresponding ratio for Group B. These conditional proportions are .1, .5, and .9 for Group A, and .2, .6, and 1.0 for Group B. Hence, when we compare comparable groups at each ability level m, we find that this item actually favors Group B over Group A, not vice versa as suggested by impact. This contradiction between impact and DIF is due to unequal distributions of ability in Groups A and B, as seen in the N_m columns. The imaginary item actually disadvantages Group A, but because Group A is more able than Group B, the overall impact suggests that the item favors Group A.

Simpson's paradox illustrates the importance of comparing the comparable. Both the standardization approach (Dorans & Kulick, 1983, 1986), which has been used on the Scholastic Aptitude Test (SAT) since 1982, and the Mantel–Haenszel method (Holland & Thayer, 1988), which has been used with most ETS testing programs since 1987, emphasize this principle as well. In practice, both approaches use total test score as a measure of comparability. They share a common definition of "Null DIF," namely that there is no differential item functioning between groups *after* they have been matched on total score. Neither method requires a psychometric or a cognitive model of item or test performance.

These two DIF assessment procedures are highly related and complement each other well. The Mantel–Haenszel is a statistically powerful technique for detecting DIF. Standardization is a very flexible, easily understood descriptive procedure that is particularly suited for assessing plausible and implausible explanations for DIF. Standardization is described first because of its flexibility and the ease with which it can be generalized to constructed-response DIF assessment.

STANDARDIZATION: A FLEXIBLE METHOD FOR DESCRIBING DIF

Before the mid-1980s, the Mantel–Haenszel (1959) procedure had not been applied to DIF assessment. Dorans (1982) reviewed item bias studies that had been conducted on SAT data in the late 1970s and concluded that these studies were flawed, because either DIF was confounded with lack of model fit (delta plot approach) or it was contaminated by impact (as a result of "fat matching," the practice of grouping scores into broad categories of roughly comparable ability). A new method was needed, and Dorans and Kulick (1983, 1986) developed the standardization approach.

Standardization's Definition of DIF

An item exhibits DIF when the expected performance on the item differs for matched examinees from different groups. Expected performance can be operationalized by nonparametric item-test regressions. Differences in empirical item-test regressions are indicative of DIF.

One of the main principles underlying the standardization approach is to use *all* available appropriate data to estimate the conditional item performance of each group at each level of the matching variable. The matching done by standardization (and Mantel–Haenszel) does *not* require the use of stratified sampling procedures that yield equal numbers of examinees at a given score level across groups. In fact, throwing away data in this fashion just leads to poorer estimates of effect sizes that have larger standard errors associated with them than effect sizes based on all the data.

The first step in the standardization analysis is to use all available data to estimate nonparametric item-test regressions in the reference group and in the focal group. The *focal* group is the focus of analysis, and the *reference* group serves as a basis for comparison. At ETS, the current practice is to do analyses in which Whites are the reference group, and Blacks, Hispanics, Asian-Americans, and in some cases, Native Americans, serve as the focal groups, and analyses in which females are the focal group and males are the reference group.

Let $E_f(I|M)$ define the empirical item-test regression for the focal Group F, and let $E_r(I|M)$ define the empirical item-test regression for the reference Group R, where I is the item score variable and M is the matching variable. The definition of DIF employed by the standardization approach implies that $E_f(I|M) = E_r(I|M)$.

The most detailed definition of DIF is at the individual score level, m,

$$D_m = E_{fm} - E_{rm},$$

where E_{fm} and E_{rm} are realizations of the item-test regressions at score level m. The D_m are the fundamental measures of DIF according to the standardization method because these quantities are differences in item performance between focal group and reference group members who are matched with respect to the attribute measured by the test. Any differences that exist after matching cannot be explained or accounted for by ability differences, as measured by total score. Plots of these differences, as well as plots of $E_f(I|M)$ and $E_r(I|M)$, provide visual descriptions of DIF in fine detail. For illustrations of nonparametric item test regressions and differences for a rare actual SAT item that exhibits considerable DIF, see Dorans and Kulick (1986).

Standardization's Primary Item Discrepancy Index

The sheer volume of the SAT item pool precludes sole reliance on plots for DIF assessment. There is a clear need for some numerical index that targets suspect items for close scrutiny, while allowing acceptable items to pass swiftly through the screening process. Standardization has such an index: the standardized p-difference (STD P-DIF). This index uses a weighting function supplied by the standardization group to average differences across levels of the matching variable. The function of the standardization group, which may be a real group or a hypothetical group, is to supply specific weights for each score level. These are used in weighting each individual D_m before accumulating the weighted differences across score levels to arrive at a summary item-discrepancy index.

The Standardized P-Difference. The standardized p-difference is defined as:

$$STD\ P\text{-}DIF = \Sigma_m w_m (E_{fm} - E_{rm})/\Sigma_m w_m = \Sigma_m w_m D_m/\Sigma_m w_m,$$

where $(w_m/\Sigma_m w_m)$ is the weighting factor at score level m supplied by the standardization group to weight differences in item performance between the focal group (E_{fm}) and the reference group (E_{rm}). The standardized p-difference is so named because the original applications of the standardization methodology defined expected item score in terms of proportion correct at each score level,

$$STD\ P\text{-}DIF = \Sigma_m w_m (P_{fm} - P_{rm})/\Sigma_m w_m = \Sigma_m w_m D_m/\Sigma_m w_m,$$

where P_{fm} and P_{rm} are the proportions correct (i.e., the number of examinees who answer correctly over the total number of examinees), in the focal and reference groups at score level m,

$$P_{fm} = R_{fm}/N_{fm}; \qquad P_{rm} = R_{rm}/N_{rm}.$$

In contrast to impact, in which each group has its relative frequency serve as a weight at each score level,

$$IMPACT = P_f - P_r$$
$$= \Sigma_m N_{fm} P_{fm}/\Sigma_m N_{fm} - \Sigma_m N_{rm} P_{rm}/\Sigma_m N_{rm},$$

STD P-DIF uses a standard or common weight on both P_{fm} and P_{rm}, namely, $(w_m/\Sigma_m w_m)$. The use of the same weight on both P_{fm} and P_{rm}, or more generally, E_{fm} and E_{rm}, is the essence of the standardization approach. In the foregoing equation, P_r is the proportion correct observed in the reference group, and P_f is the proportion correct observed in the focal group. The particular set of weights employed for standardization depends on the purposes of the investigation. In practice, $w_m = N_{fm}$ has been used because it gives the greatest weight to differences in P_{fm} and P_{rm} at those score levels most frequently attained by the focal group under study. Use of N_{fm} means that *STD P-DIF* equals the difference between the observed performance of the focal group on the item and the predicted performance of selected reference group members who are matched in ability to the focal group members. This can be derived very simply (Dorans & Holland, 1992).

STD P-DIF can range from -1 to $+1$ (or -100% to 100%). Positive values of *STD P-DIF* indicate that the item favors the focal group, and negative *STD P-DIF* values indicate that the item disadvantages the focal group. *STD P-DIF* values between $-.05$ and $+.05$ are considered negligible. *STD P-DIF* values between $-.10$ and $-.05$ and between $.05$ and $.10$ are inspected to insure that no possible effect is overlooked. Items with *STD P-DIF* values outside the $\{-.10, +.10\}$ range are more unusual and should be examined very carefully.

Differential Distractor Functioning, Speededness, and Omission

DIF assessment does not stop with the flagging of an item for statistical DIF. In fact, the flagging step can be viewed as just the beginning. The next step is to try to understand the reason or reasons for the DIF. Green, Crone, and Folk (1989) have developed a log-linear approach for assessing what they call *differential distractor functioning* (DDF). The standardization approach to distractor analysis is also quite helpful.

The generalization of the standardization methodology to all response options including omission and "not-reached" is straightforward and is known as standardized distractor analysis (Dorans, Schmitt, & Bleistein, 1988, 1992). It is as simple as replacing the keyed response with the option of interest in all calculations. For example, a standardized response rate analysis on Option A would entail computing the proportions choosing A (as opposed to the proportions correct) in both the focal and reference groups,

$$P_{fm}(A) = A_{fm}/N_{fm}; \quad P_{rm}(A) = A_{rm}/N_{rm},$$

where A_{fm} and A_{rm} are the number of people in the focal and reference groups, respectively, at score level m who choose Option A. The next step is to compute differences between these proportions,

$$D_m(A) = P_{fm}(A) - P_{rm}(A).$$

Then these individual score level differences are summarized across score levels by applying some standardized weighting function to these differences to obtain $STD\ P\text{-}DIF(A)$,

$$STD\ P\text{-}DIF(A) = \Sigma_m w_m D_m(A)/\Sigma_m w_m,$$

the standardized difference in response rates to Option A. In a similar fashion one can compute standardized differences in response rates for Options B, C, D, and E, and for nonresponses as well, which means standardization can be used to assess *differential distractor functioning* (Schmitt & Dorans, 1990), *differential speededness* (Dorans, Schmitt, & Bleistein, 1988; Schmitt, Dorans, Crone, & Maneckshana, 1990), and *differential omission* (Rivera & Schmitt, 1988; Schmitt & Dorans, 1990; Schmitt et al., 1990).

As an example from Schmitt and Dorans (1990), consider the standardized distractor analysis for an SAT antonym item from a disclosed 1984 test form for which the key, distractors, and DIF information are provided in Table 7.2.

As can be seen in the table, standardization identifies DIF on the key opposite of *practical* is *(D) having little usefulness* for Black examinees (*BLK STD P-DIF* = −16%) and for Puerto Rican examinees (*PR STD P-DIF* = −11%). In addition, standardization indicates to us where the "anti-DIF" may lie, and the plots for the Black group corroborate these indications. Clearly, the Black and Puerto Rican focal groups are drawn towards *(A) difficult to learn*, which suggests that they have confused the word *practical* with the word "practice." See Schmitt, Holland, and Dorans (1992) for examples in which the standardized distractor analysis corroborates DIF hypotheses for Hispanics.

MANTEL–HAENSZEL: TESTING
THE CONSTANT ODDS RATIO HYPOTHESIS

In their seminal paper, Mantel and Haenszel (1959) introduced a new procedure for the study of matched groups. Holland (1985), and later Holland and Thayer (1988), adapted the procedure for use in assessing DIF. This adapta-

TABLE 7.2
The Standardized Distractor Analysis for an SAT Antonym Item
from a Disclosed 1984 Test Form

STD P-DIF (Option)			
MA	PR	BLK	PRACTICAL:
.04	.09	.12	(A) difficult to learn
.00	.00	.00	(B) inferior in quality
.01	.01	.01	(C) providing great support
−.05	−.11	−.16	*(D) having little usefulness*
.00	.00	.00	(E) feeling great regret

tion is used at Educational Testing Service as the primary DIF detection device. The basic data used by the MH method are in the form of M 2-by-2 contingency tables or one large three-dimensional 2-by-2-by-M table.

The 2-by-2-by-M Contingency Table

Under rights scoring for the items in which responses are coded as either correct or incorrect (including omissions), counts of rights and wrongs on each item can be arranged into a 2-by-2-by-M contingency table for each item being studied. There are two levels for group: the *focal* group that is the focus of analysis, and the *reference* group that serves as a basis for comparison. There are also two levels for item response: right or wrong; and there are M score levels on the matching variable (e.g., total score). Finally, the item being analyzed is referred to as the *studied item*. The 2(groups)-by-2(item scores)-by-M(score levels) contingency table for each item can be viewed in *2-by-2 slices* (there are M slices per item) as shown in Table 7.3.

The null DIF hypothesis for the Mantel–Haenszel method can be expressed as

$$H_0: [R_{rm}/W_{rm}] = [R_{fm}/W_{fm}] \quad m = 1, \ldots, M.$$

In other words, the odds of getting the item correct at a given level of the matching variable is the same in both the focal group and the reference group across all M levels of the matching variable.

The Constant Odds Ratio Hypothesis

In their original work, Mantel and Haenszel (1959) developed a chi-square test of the null DIF hypothesis against a particular alternative hypothesis known as the *constant odds ratio hypothesis*,

$$H_a: [R_{rm}/W_{rm}] = \alpha [R_{fm}/W_{fm}] \quad m = 1, \ldots, M \text{ and } \alpha \neq 1.$$

Note that when $\alpha = 1$, the alternative hypothesis reduces to the null DIF hypothesis. The parameter α is called the *common odds ratio* in the M 2-by-2

TABLE 7.3
2-by-2-by-M Contingency Table for an Item, Viewed in 2-by-2 Slices

	Item Score		
Group	Right	Wrong	Total
Focal group (f)	R_{fm}	W_{fm}	N_{fm}
Reference group (r)	R_{rm}	W_{rm}	N_{rm}
Total group (t)	R_{tm}	W_{tm}	N_{tm}

tables because under H_a, the value of α is the odds ratio that is the same for all m,

$$\alpha_m = [R_{rm}/W_{rm}]/[R_{fm}/W_{fm}] = [R_{rm}W_{fm}]/[R_{fm}W_{rm}].$$

Holland and Thayer (1988) reported that the MH approach is the test possessing the most statistical power for detecting departures from the null DIF hypothesis that are consistent with the constant odds ratio hypothesis.

Estimate of Constant Odds Ratio

Mantel and Haenszel also provided an estimate of the constant odds-ratio,

$$\alpha_{MH} = [\Sigma_m R_{rm}W_{fm}/N_{tm}]/[\Sigma_m R_{fm}W_{rm}/N_{tm}].$$

This estimate is an estimate of DIF effect size on a metric that ranges from 0 to ∞ with a value of 1 indicating null DIF. This odds-ratio metric is not particularly meaningful to test developers who are used to working with numbers on an item difficulty scale. In general, odds are converted to log odds because the latter is symmetric around zero and easier to interpret.

MH DIF in Item Difficulty Metrics

At ETS, item difficulty estimates in the "delta metric," which has a mean of 13 and a standard deviation of 4, are used by test developers. Large values of Δ correspond to difficult items, and easy items have small values of delta. Holland and Thayer (1985) converted α_{MH} into a difference in deltas via:

$$MH\ D\text{-}DIF = -2.35\ ln[\alpha_{MH}].$$

Note that positive values of *MH D-DIF* favor the focal group, whereas negative values favor the reference group.

Another metric that is used more universally to describe item difficulty is the p-metric, percent correct or proportion correct metric. The α_{MH} can also be expressed in the metric used by standardization,

$$MH\ P\text{-}DIF = P_f - P_f\dagger,$$

where

$$P_f\dagger = [\alpha_{MH}P_f]/[(1 - P_f) + \alpha_{MH}P_f].$$

As with the standardization approach, the Mantel–Haenszel procedure does not require a psychometric or a cognitive model of item performance. In this sense, both Mantel–Haenszel and standardization are model-free DIF assessment procedures.

A COMMON FRAMEWORK AND THE ESSENCE
OF MODEL-FREE DIF

A Common Framework

Up to now, the Mantel–Haenszel method and the standardization method
have been described in terms of the frameworks from which they evolved:
Mantel–Haenszel as a powerful statistical test of the constant odds ratio model,
and standardization as a nonparametric, model-free alternative to item
response theory for describing item-ability regressions. The two procedures,
however, share a common framework. Dorans (1989) utilized this framework
to spell out the similarities and dissimilarities of these two procedures for
DIF assessment. Dorans and Holland (1992) demonstrated analytically that
for rights-scored tests, Mantel–Haenszel and standardization share a common
definition of null DIF that is stated in different metrics. The two procedures
differ with respect to how they measure departures from null DIF.

Under rights scoring for items in which responses are coded as either correct or incorrect (including omissions), both the standardization procedure
and the Mantel–Haenszel procedure use the same basic data, which takes
the form of counts of rights and wrongs on each item arranged into a 2(groups)-
by-2(item scores)-by-M(score levels) contingency table for each item being
studied. The Mantel–Haenszel and standardization procedures operate on the
contingency table in different ways.

The first difference is in the metric for defining DIF. Standardization uses
differences in conditional proportions correct D_m, whereas Mantel–Haenszel
uses conditional odds ratios α_m. The second difference is in the choice of
weights used to average the D_m or the α_m across levels of the matching variable. The Mantel–Haenszel approach uses weights that are nearly optimal
statistically for testing a constant odds-ratio model. In contrast, the weights
employed in the standardization approach are not defined statistically. Instead they may be chosen to suit the needs of a particular investigator. The
intuitively appealing focal group frequency distribution, which was employed
by Dorans and Kulick (1983) in their original work on the SAT, has continued
to be used to describe departures from null DIF. The third difference between
the two methods is the metric in which the final statistic is portrayed. Although
a delta metric version of the standardization DIF statistic has been developed,
the primary metric used by standardization has been the p-metric, even with
formula-scored tests where an item formula-scored metric would seem superior on logical grounds. In contrast, delta has been the metric of choice
for the Mantel–Haenszel method. One consequence of this difference in metrics is that standardization tends to attenuate DIF in easy and hard items because the p-metric is bounded at both the top and bottom. In contrast, the

delta metric is unbounded and, consequently, differences for easy and hard items are magnified.

Despite these differences in choice of metric and weighting, standardization and Mantel–Haenszel agree very closely with respect to measurement of departures from null DIF for the vast majority of items. In fact, correlations across items between these two methods in the same metric (e.g., delta) are typically close to unity and slightly higher than within-method correlations between metrics, which are in the high .90s. Cross-metric, cross-method correlations are usually in the middle .90s. These correlations indicate that the two methods are measuring essentially the same DIF in slightly different ways: Standardization uses intuitively appealing weighting of conditional differences in proportions correct whereas the Mantel–Haenszel method uses statistically driven weighting of conditional odds ratios. The correlations also indicate that the choice of metric for describing the DIF effect may be more critical from a practical point of view than the choice of method.

The Essence of Model-Free DIF

Although we have just pointed out differences between the statistically powerful Mantel–Haenszel procedure and the flexible standardization approach, their similarities form the essence of what we are calling empirical, as opposed to model-based, DIF assessment. First, **both procedures require a well-defined and appropriate matching variable** in order to detect DIF. Inadequate matching variables allow impact to creep back into the results. The importance of the matching variable has been discussed often in the DIF assessment literature. The matching variable should measure the same construct as the items being studied for DIF.

Second, both procedures require that **some rule exists for scoring items**. The typical rule is to assign a 1 to a correct answer and a 0 to an incorrect answer though, as Dorans and Holland (1992) demonstrate, the standardization approach is also easy to use with formula-scored multiple-choice items.

Third, both procedures typically use an internal criterion or total score as the matching variable, which implies **the existence of a rule for combining information across items**. An internal criterion is typically employed because the collection of items with which an item is administered often measures a common construct and leads to a single score. For most tests, this combination rule is simply the sum of item scores.

The applicability of existing DIF assessment procedures to constructed-response data hinges on all three of these points, but particularly on the existence of an appropriate matching variable, often obtained by combining information across items, and the existence of a well-defined item scoring rule. If the matching variable exists and the items can be scored right/wrong, both Mantel–Haenszel and standardization can be used for DIF assessment. For nonbinary item scoring, some form of the standardization model can be used for DIF assessment, as can a "successive chops" version of the Mantel–Haenszel method.

MODEL-FREE DIF ASSESSMENT
FOR CONSTRUCTED-RESPONSE ITEMS

The importance of the matching variable cannot be overstated in a DIF analysis, especially for constructed-response items, which tend to be more time consuming to administer than multiple-choice items. More time per item translates to administering fewer items in a given unit of time, which may imply less reliable internal matching variables. Using an external matching variable may have its own problems, as is discussed later. For the purposes of this section, however, a well-defined and appropriate matching variable is assumed.

Nominal Data

Also assumed is that responses to a constructed-response item can be clustered on logical grounds into a limited set of score categories. When the item scoring rule yields only nominal data that cannot be ordered, and when no one category is viewed as "correct" (as in describing alternative response strategies), the standardization procedure can be applied via its standardized differential distractor mode. All response categories are treated in turn "as if" they were the correct response, and proportions choosing each category are computed across focal and reference groups at each score level of the matching variable M. Then, a set of standardization weights can be applied to differences in proportions between focal and reference group members to average differences across levels of the matching variable. This type of analysis, which may have important diagnostic value, can be used with ordered categories as well.

Successive Binary Chops on Ordered Data

If the scoring rule for a constructed-response item results in an ordered score that ranges from less correct to more correct, and numbers can be attached to each level of this score, then two options are available. Either the binary version of the standardization procedure and the Mantel–Haenszel procedure can be applied to successive binary chops of the data, or a continuous version of the general standardization framework can be applied to these scores.

The successive binary-chop application of existing DIF procedures treats item scores at or above a certain level as correct, and those below that level are incorrect. The binary version of standardization or Mantel–Haenszel is applied to the data at each of several successive chops. Each chop reveals whether DIF is evident at that level. A partial application of this notion occurs with formula scored tests, where the standardization procedure is applied routinely in binary-chop mode (omits and "not-reached" are treated as incorrect) along with the Mantel–Haenszel method; and for some tests, like the SAT, in formula-scored mode where rights are scored as 1, wrongs are scored as $-1/(k-1)$, and omits and "not-reached" are scored as zero. In fact, the formula-score DIF version of the general standardization model, described in Dorans and Holland (1992), represents an application of the standardization model that illustrates how the method can be used with constructed-response data.

Extended Standardization on Ordered Data

The second approach to ordered data, which provides us with an average value for describing DIF on a constructed-response item, uses the general form of the standardization method. At each matching score level, there exist distributions of constructed-response item scores, I, for both the focal group (e.g., females), and the reference group (e.g., males). The expected item scores for each group at each matching score level can be computed by using the frequencies to obtain a weighted average of the score levels. These expected item scores define the empirical item-test regressions that are the basic building blocks for the standardization approach.

Earlier, we let $E_f(I|M)$ define the empirical item-test regression for the focal Group F, and let $E_r(I|M)$ define the empirical item-test regression for the reference Group R. The definition of DIF employed by the standardization approach implies that $E_f(I|M) = E_r(I|M)$. The most detailed definition of DIF is at the individual score level m, $D_m = E_{fm} - E_{rm}$, where E_{fm} and E_{rm} are realizations of the item-test regressions at score level m. The D_m are the fundamental measures of DIF according to the standardization method because these quantities are differences in item performance between focal group and reference group members who are matched with respect to the attribute measured by the test.

The standardized p-difference was so named because the original applications of the standardization methodology defined expected item score in terms of proportion correct at each score level. For the purposes of constructed-response DIF assessment, we let *STD P-DIF* refer more generally to a standardized difference in performance on the item.

For illustrative purposes, suppose responses to a constructed-response item can be clustered into four categories, A, B, C, and D, and that these four categories receive scores of 9, 8, 7, and 6, respectively. As stated earlier, the standardized p-difference is defined as:

$$STD\ P\text{-}DIF = \Sigma_m w_m(E_{fm} - E_{rm})/\Sigma_m w_m = \Sigma_m w_m D_m/\Sigma_m w_m,$$

where $(w_m/\Sigma_m w_m)$ is the weighting factor at score level m supplied by the standardization group to weight differences in item performance between the focal group (E_{fm}) and the reference group (E_{rm}). Instead of scoring the item 1 if correct and 0 if incorrect or omit as for binary scoring of multiple-choice items, the item is scored 9 if the response is in Category A, 8 if the response is from Category B, 7 if the response is from Category C, and 6 for Category D. Under this type of scoring, the expected item performance in the focal group at score level m is:

$$E_{fm} = \{A_{fm}*(9) + B_{fm}*(8) + C_{fm}*(7) + D_{fm}*(6)\}/N_{fm},$$

where A_{fm}, B_{fm}, C_{fm}, and D_{fm} are counts of the number of focal group members at score level m who produced responses in categories A, B, C, and D, and N_{fm} is the total number of focal groups members at score level m. Likewise, for the reference group, we have

$$E_{rm} = \{A_{rm}*(9) + B_{rm}*(8) + C_{rm}*(7) + D_{rm}*(6)\}/N_{rm}.$$

Unlike the $STD\ P\text{-}DIF$ for multiple-choice items, this $STD\ P\text{-}DIF$ does not range from -1 to $+1$. Instead, its theoretical range is -3 to $+3$, as would have been the case had the item been scored 0, 1, 2, and 3.

How Big Is Big?   A very practical issue that must be addressed with this general approach is the set of flagging rules used to identify too much DIF. Under right/wrong scoring, any difference that exceeds null DIF by 10% in either the positive or negative direction is flagged as large enough to merit careful investigation. With more complicated scoring (e.g., ordered category scoring as was illustrated), one possibility is to convert all differences to a percent-of-maximum-difference scale, and continue to use the 10% rule (5% for distractor analyses). Another option would be to define the effect size in terms of its ultimate impact on the score that is assigned to examinees. This more practical approach would take into account the number of distinct pieces of information (items) contributing to the reported score, and the importance of the studied item to the combination rule that produces this reported score. More needs to be learned about optimal flagging rules in this context.

The Need for Smoothing.   The standardization procedure works well with moderate-to-large data sets, but it runs into trouble with small data sets—especially when the reference group is small. A standard data analytic strategy for dealing with sparse data is to use some kind of statistical model to smooth away sampling irregularities in the observed data. Ramsay (1991) recently developed a kernel-based procedure for smoothing nonparametric item characteristic curves, such as those used in the standardization method, for binary-scored items. This procedure should readily be adapted to the polytomous case. Ramsay and Holland (1989) have developed a kernel-based procedure for smoothing the log-odds ratio for the Mantel–Haenszel method, which could also readily be adapted to estimate conditional differences in constructed-response item score/matching variable regressions. More theoretical work is needed on these extensions.

THE ITEM TYPE CONTINUUM, SCORING RULES, AND DIF

In this section, we focus on a framework for constructed-response items developed by Bennett, Ward, Rock, and LaHart (1990; see also Bennett, this volume), and evaluate the amenability of these different item types to analysis by our general model-free DIF procedure. Bennett et al. presented a scheme for categorizing item types into seven categories that ranges from the highly constrained, artificial, and easy-to-score *multiple-choice* item to the virtually unconstrained, naturalistic, and much harder to score *presentation* item type. For DIF purposes, we once again assume that a well-defined and adequate matching variable exists, even though we would question the tenability of this assumption in practice.

The *multiple-choice* item type is highly constrained in that examinees are required to choose a single best answer from a limited number of options, usually four or five. For multiple-choice items, the standardization method and the Mantel–Haenszel method can be and have been used repeatedly. In addition, model-based IRT methods (Thissen, Steinberg, & Wainer, 1992) have also been used successfully in smaller scale applications. DIF for multiple-choice items is essentially under control. See Dorans and Holland (1992) for a discussion of some sticky, but small, unsolved problems.

Items in the *selection/identification* class are answered by choosing one or more responses from a stimulus array where the number of choices is large enough to preclude guessing the correct answer. Note that in contrast to the multiple-choice item type, this class of items is less constrained with respect to selection or identification of the correct response. DIF on selection/identification items can be assessed via the model-free approaches of standardization or Mantel–Haenszel or the model-based IRT approaches because these items can easily be scored correct or incorrect. In fact, standard DIF detection techniques probably would work better with this item class than with multiple-choice items because of the near elimination of guessing.

As with selection/identification items, *reordering/rearrangement* responses are chosen from a stimulus array. The task is to place items in the correct sequence or alternative correct sequence. The elementary probability theory of permutations and combinations tells us that the number of response options grows rapidly when we move from selection/identification to reordering/rearrangement. Hence we have increased the amount of potential diversity or chaos permitted in the response space. Reordering/rearrangement items are less likely to be amenable to standard DIF analyses unless possible orders or arrangements can clearly be split into correct and incorrect sets. If the sets can be ordered and different degrees of partial credit awarded, the general model-free standardization method could readily be applied. Even if these categories could not be ordered, the "distractor analysis" could be used to study differential performance.

Substitution/correction items require that the examinee replace what is presented with a correct alternative. At first glance it appears that this item type has a smaller response space than the reordering/rearrangement item type. In fact, it is the first item type in the continuum that has an infinite response space, albeit in practical terms, the number of plausible responses is limited. Substitution/correction items may or may not be amenable to standard multiple-choice DIF analyses. If the items can easily be scored correct/incorrect, as is most likely the case with correcting grammatical and spelling errors, then the arsenal of DIF techniques widely used with multiple-choice items are readily applicable. If partial credit orderings are obtainable or if the categories are only nominal, then the general model-free standardization model can be used.

The *completion* type allows for a slightly greater complexity of responses than the preceding one. Here, the task is to respond correctly to an incomplete, as opposed to incorrect, stimulus. Completion items are probably amenable to standard DIF analyses, especially when there is a clearly defined class of correct answers, as is the case with the mathematical grid-in item type (Braswell & Kupin, this volume). If the completion item is carefully crafted, a single class of equivalent responses should be identifiable. In practice, however, clever examinees may demonstrate that what the test developer thought was a complete set was missing one or two unusual members. A limited set of ordered categories may also be extracted from completion items, in which case the general model-free DIF procedure could be used. Even in the unusual case where only nominal categories could be found, the distractor analysis mode of the general standardization procedure could still be applied.

Instead of merely completing a stimulus or correcting one, the examinee presented with a *construction* type item has to produce a complete response to a stimulus. The range of possible responses here is very large and the degree of chaos that can swamp any signal in the response space can be imposing.

Construction items will be difficult to assess for DIF because they tend to be very time consuming (e.g., a 30-minute essay) and because the literature (Mazzeo, Schmitt, & Bleistein, 1991; Traub & MacRury, 1990) suggests that essays, the most widely used construction item, do not necessarily measure the same construct as multiple-choice items, the most widely used basis for creating a matching variable. In other words, the matching variable problem that affects all DIF analyses, even those for multiple-choice items, is particularly severe for the construction item types. The best solution to the problem would be to extract as much relatively independent information from these items as possible via a partial-scoring scheme, cumulate the resulting scores across the limited number of items that can be administered, and use this aggregate as the matching variable for a DIF analysis involving the general procedure. Even here, the limited number of stimuli may preclude using this approach.

Presentation items permit the largest amount of freedom on the part of the examinee and, as importantly, allow for the most noise to enter into the response space. Here, the examinee is required to make a physical presentation or performance delivered under real or simulated conditions in which the object of the assessment is, in some substantial part, the manner of performance and not simply its result. The testing conditions as well as the response options are relatively unconstrained in order to observe a realistic performance. To the extent that the conditions are realistic, they will not be controlled, and comparability across presentations will be hard to achieve. DIF analysis for this item type is probably not possible. In practice, very few of these items will be administered, the testing conditions may be too uncontrolled to permit even consistent scoring across examinees, and the number of examinees tested would probably be too small to permit any reasonable DIF assessment.

In summary, current DIF procedures can be used with multiple-choice items and selection/identification items. These procedures also may work for reordering/rearrangement, substitution/correction, and completion. The more general model-free standardization approach would probably be as applicable, if not more applicable, for these three partially constrained item types. DIF analysis for the construction and presentation items is either very problematic (construction) or virtually impossible (presentation). In the next section we review results from other studies that support some of the positions we have just expressed.

EMPIRICAL FINDINGS PERTINENT TO DIF ASSESSMENT FOR CONSTRUCTED-RESPONSE ITEMS

Since the late 1960s there has been much interest in comparisons of multiple-choice and constructed response item formats. Little has been done, however, with respect to comparisons of differential performance by subgroups. In Traub and MacRury's (1990) review, only four studies were referenced. In addition, we located three other studies. All seven studies address the differential performance of males and females only at the total score level. Moreover, the results of these studies are confounded by factors affecting item format comparisons. Traub and MacRury specified that in order to compare performance, it is essential that item formats be equivalent with respect to trait, scale, instrument, and scoring method. In addition, the selection of an appropriate matching criterion should also be a requirement to avoid confounding DIF with impact.

The purpose of this section is to summarize empirical findings pertinent to constructed-response DIF assessment. First, several studies comparing the performance of men and women on total scores obtained under the two item formats are briefly described. Second, an illustration of DIF assessment on a constructed-response completion item is presented. Third, a major constraint that may affect constructed-response DIF assessment is addressed.

Studies Comparing Subgroup Performance on Total Score

Comparison of male and female performance on multiple-choice and constructed-response formats has been reported by Bell and Hay (1987), Bolger (1984), Breland and Griswold (1981), Mazzeo, Schmitt, and Bleistein (1991), Murphy (1980, 1982), Petersen and Livingston (1982), and Schmitt and Crone (1991). All but the last study have focused on total-score test differences.

The studies by Bolger (1984) and Murphy (1980, 1982) were based on comparisons of converted raw scores to percentages of marks attained. They found that males performed better than females on multiple-choice items than would be expected on the basis of their performance on constructed-response items. Although these researchers attempted to equate the multiple-choice and constructed-response scales by using percentages, this is a questionable scale equivalency method. No instrument equivalency or differences in test performance by ability level were reported.

Bell and Hay (1987) considered item-format ability differences by comparing males and females with either arts or science subject background across an external ability composite. They did not find crossover of the male and female regression lines for the multiple-choice items nor did they find crossover for a particular type of constructed-response item type, comprehension essays. For both of these item types, females outperformed males all along the ability continuum, but the differences were smaller for the multiple-choice items after the raw score differences were converted to percentages in order to permit some degree of comparison. Results for the other constructed-response item type (composition essay) were not easily interpreted because of the interaction between ability and group membership. No special method to attain scale equivalency, other than percentages, was used.

Breland and Griswold (1981) compared male and female performance on several basic skills measures. One of these measures consisted of an English Placement Test with one essay and three multiple-choice sections. Linear regression analyses were computed to compare the prediction equations of males and females using each of the three multiple-choice sections as predictors of the essay portion. They found parallel slopes but different intercepts; for each of the multiple-choice predictors, the expected essay performance of females was higher than the expected essay performance of males across all score levels. Using the reported means and standard deviations on the four sections of the English Placement Test provided by Breland and Griswold (1981), Mazzeo, Schmitt, and Bleistein (1991) calculated standardized differences between males and females and found considerably large differences only for the essay portion of the examination, where females did better than males.

Studies reported by Mazzeo et al. (1991) on four different examinations of the Advanced Placement Program, and by Petersen and Livingston (1982) on the Admissions Testing Program English Composition Test are all consistent with the previously summarized findings. Relative to males, female examinees perform better on the constructed-response sections than they do on the multiple-choice sections. These findings do not bode well for using scores on multiple-choice sections as a matching variable for DIF analyses on constructed-response items.

An Illustration of DIF on a Completion Type Item

Differential item performance analyses were computed by Schmitt and Crone (1991) on two mathematics examinations consisting of items in both multiple-choice and constructed-response formats. The constructed-response items consisted of a completion type where students gridded the correct numeric response. The total mathematics score, composed of both constructed-response items (grid-ins) as well as multiple-choice items (four-option algebra placement, four-option quantitative comparison, and five-option regular math items), was used as an internal matching criterion. DIF analyses indicated that female and Black examinees had differentially lower performance on grid-in items than did comparable groups of males and White examinees. Table 7.4 presents *STD P-DIF* summary information for the grid-in items in one of these mathematics forms. Comparable results were obtained with the other form and with the Mantel–Haenszel delta-difference DIF statistic, as well. Sample sizes for these DIF analyses ranged from 9,943 for White examinees to 641 for Hispanic examinees. There were 7,129 females, 6,088 males, 1,742 Blacks, and 728 Asian-American examinees.

In Table 7.4 the 20 grid-in items were categorized into six groups according to their *STD P-DIF* values. Three of these groups represent positive DIF values (i.e., the focal group did differentially better than its reference group) and three groups represent negative DIF values (i.e., the focal group did

TABLE 7.4
Differential Item Functioning (DIF) Summary
for GRID-IN Items Using an *Internal Criterion—Math Form A*

			Category of DIF Value For All Comparisons			
	Cross-Group	Cross-Group	Male/Female	White/Black	White/Hispanic	White/Asian
STD P-DIF Category	Number	% of Items	Percent of Items by DIF Category			
DIF ≥ .10	0	0.0	0.0	0.0	0.0	0.0
05≤ DIF < .10	0	0.0	0.0	0.0	0.0	0.0
.00≤ DIF < .05	7	35.0	25.0	15.0	40.0	40.0
−.05< DIF < .00	4	20.0	45.0	60.0	5.0	20.0
−.10< DIF ≤ −.05	4	20.0	15.0	15.0	5.0	40.0
DIF ≤ −.10	5	25.0	15.0	10.0	0.0	0.0
Total	20	100.00	100.00	100.00	100.00	100.00
Mean	—	—	−0.03	−0.03	−0.01	−0.02
S.D.	—	—	0.05	0.04	0.02	0.04
Maximum	—	—	0.03	0.02	0.05	0.05
Minimum	—	—	−0.12	−0.12	−0.06	−0.09

differentially worse than its reference group). $|STD\ P\text{-}DIF|$ values greater than or equal to .10 define the two extreme categories. The middle categories, one for positive DIF and one for negative DIF, correspond to $|STD\ P\text{-}DIF|$ values between .05 and .10. $|STD\ P\text{-}DIF|$ values between .00 and .05 are categorized in the two least extreme groupings. Analyses were done to compare the performance on grid-in items between matched White examinees and each of the following focal groups: Black, Hispanic, and Asian-American test takers; and between matched male and female (focal group) examinees. Although all focal groups demonstrated negative DIF, female and Black examinees had more extreme negative DIF items and larger negative $STD\ P\text{-}DIF$ means across both forms. The percentage of negative items across both forms ranged from 75% to 80% for these two focal groups.

Examination of the multiple-choice items indicated negligible differential performance for female and for Black test takers on all but one item type, algebra placement. Female and Black examinees demonstrated differentially higher performance on the algebra placement items.

In order to evaluate whether the internal matching criterion was related to the high negative DIF findings for the grid-in item type, DIF analyses for the grid-in items were redone using an external matching criterion that did not include either grid-ins or algebra placement items. The criterion was composed of 60 multiple-choice math items (40 regular math and 20 quantitative comparison). The same six $STD\ P\text{-}DIF$ groupings were used to summarize results of this re-analysis. Table 7.5 presents the classification of grid-in DIF

TABLE 7.5
Differential Item Functioning (DIF) Summary for GRID-IN Items Using an
External Criterion—Math Form A

			Category of DIF Value For All Comparisons				
	Cross-Group	Cross-Group	Male/Female	White/Black	White/Hispanic[a]	White/Asian
STD P-DIF Category	Number	% of Items	Percent of Items by DIF Category				
DIF ≥ .10	0	0.0	0.0	0.0	N/A	0.0
.05 ≤ DIF < .10	5	25.0	5.0	0.0	N/A	20.0
.00 ≤ DIF < .05	4	20.0	25.0	5.0	N/A	35.0
−.05 ≤ DIF < .00	3	15.0	35.0	60.0	N/A	15.0
−.10 < DIF ≤ −.05	4	20.0	20.0	25.0	N/A	30.0
DIF ≤ −.10	4	20.0	15.0	10.0	N/A	0.0
Total	20	100.00	100.00	100.00	N/A	100.00
Mean	—	—	−0.03	−0.04	N/A	0.00
S.D.	—	—	0.05	0.04	N/A	0.06
Maximum	—	—	0.06	0.00	N/A	0.10
Minimum	—	—	−0.12	−0.11	N/A	−0.09

[a]N/A: Insufficient sample size (N < 200) for DIF analysis.

values into the six *STD P-DIF* groupings for the first form. Results for the second form were comparable.

Because the re-analysis using an external matching criterion had to be restricted to those examinees who took the external test, sample sizes for all the groups were considerably reduced. A minimum sample size of 200 was specified for focal or reference groups. Sample size was insufficient for the Hispanic focal group. For the external criterion analysis, there were 2,717 White, 1,992 female, 1,655 male, 527 Black, and 202 Asian-American examinees.

Results of the DIF analyses using the external all multiple-choice matching criterion did not reduce the magnitude or direction of the DIF found using the internal criterion. The external criterion seemed to increase the negative DIF found for the Black focal group for the grid-in items on both forms. The *STD P-DIF* means increased in magnitude from −.03, based on DIF computations with the internal matching criterion, to −.04, based on DIF computations with the external criterion. The percentage of negative items across both forms for the Black group also increased, from 85% to 95%. Results for the female/male comparison using the external criterion were also mostly negative across both forms.

Dimensionality analyses for both the internal matching test and especially the external matching test indicated that these tests were basically unidimensional in the general population (Lehman & Mazzeo, 1991), which was consistent with earlier, more extensive analyses conducted on other versions of the external matching test (Dorans & Lawrence, 1987). The DIF results, however, question the appropriateness of either the total math internal or external matching criterion for some subgroups and indicate the possibility that these tests are multidimensional for the subgroups, despite their overall unidimensionality for the total group. Thus, these total scores might not be an appropriate matching criterion for all item types.

An extreme example of a matching variable that was clearly inappropriate occurred in preliminary analyses done by Mazzeo, Schmitt, and Bleistein (personal communication) where a constructed-response essay section was used as the matching variable to compute DIF on a multiple-choice section. They found extreme and pervasive negative DIF for the multiple-choice items that had not been evident when the analyses were computed using an internal multiple-choice matching criterion. Obviously, essays and multiple-choice tests did not measure the same construct in the same way or with the same degree of accuracy in this instance.

Matching Criterion

Evaluations of the trait equivalence of multiple-choice and constructed-response items seem to indicate that these two item formats are not equivalent even when the item content and the scoring are maintained across the two item formats. Traub and MacRury (1990) concluded that multiple-choice and constructed-response tests measure different configurations of knowledge and ability. Thus, the total score matching criteria used for constructed-response DIF analyses may, based on these conclusions, have to consist of constructed-response items. If a non-constructed-response matching criterion is used, the comparability of the groups for constructed-response DIF may not be achieved. Because some constructed-response tests consist of a limited number of items, which in turn sample only a very restricted domain pertinent to the primary construct, finding an appropriate constructed-response matching criterion may be almost impossible. In such cases, DIF analyses also may be impossible to do.

BEYOND DESCRIPTION AND DETECTION

Levels of Proficiency and Constructed Response

Mislevy (this volume) makes a distinction between *levels of proficiency* and the *architecture of proficiency* when describing psychometric models for educational and psychological test data. In a recent book entitled *A Century* of *Ability Testing*, Thorndike and Lohman (1990) sketched a history of testing and, as their title implies, most of this testing is of the "levels-of-proficiency" type. Examinees are administered tests, usually multiple-choice but sometimes constructed-response, their responses are recorded and scored, and they are ultimately ordered on a continuum. The model-free DIF procedures that have been described in this chapter and elsewhere (Dorans, 1989; Dorans & Holland, 1992; Dorans & Kulick, 1986; Holland & Thayer, 1988), as well as those based on IRT models (Thissen, Steinberg, & Wainer, 1992) can be used successfully on levels-of-proficiency items and tests when the items are binary-scored multiple-choice questions. When the level-of-proficiency items are what Mislevy (this volume) calls "something else," (e.g., one of the several constructed-response item types described in this chapter), then the general standardization approach can be used, provided that an adequate matching variable, such as level of proficiency, exists along with a well-defined item scoring rule.

Other model-based DIF procedures can undoubtedly be developed from the various IRT models that exist for the nonbinary item data case. Thissen and Steinberg's (1986) taxonomy of IRT models is a lodestone for psychometricians interested in developing IRT-based DIF assessment procedures. Thissen and Steinberg make distinctions among: *binary models*, such as the normal ogive models developed by Lawley (1943), Tucker (1946), and Lord (1952), and the one- and two-parameter logistic models introduced by Rasch (1960) and Birnbaum (1968); *difference models*, epitomized by Samejima's (1969) "graded-response" model, a pertinent model for constructed-response data; *divide-by-total models*, such as Master's (1982) "partial credit" model, Andrich's (1978) "rating scale" model, and Bock's (1972) "nominal" model, all of which would seem particularly applicable to level-of-proficiency constructed-response data; *left-side added models*, epitomized by the three-parameter logistic model (Birnbaum, 1968); and *left-side added multiple category models*, which modify divide-by-total models to account for guessing, such as is done with Thissen and Steinberg's (1984) "multiple-choice" model.

The binary and left-side added models can be used with binary-scored multiple-choice items. DIF procedures based on these models also exist (Thissen et al., 1992). The difference, divide-by-total, and left-side added models exist for multiple-category responses that are likely to be by-products of well-scored constructed-response items. Our cursory review of the literature uncovered very few DIF applications employing these models. Ferrara and Walker-Bartnick (1990) used the "partial credit" model to assess DIF in an essay test, an application involving real data. Thissen et al. (1992) presented an illustrative application of the "multiple-choice" model to assess differential alternative functioning, their expression for differential distractor functioning. More importantly, these authors provide a general IRT likelihood ratio definition of DIF, analogous to the general model-free standardization definition, that holds for all the IRT models described in the Thissen and Steinberg (1986) taxonomy. Thus, in theory, model-based IRT DIF assessment alternatives to the general standardization procedure could be devised for multiple category constructed responses.

The reasons for not using the more elegant model-based DIF assessment procedures for multiple-category responses include some old complaints: complexity, cost, and relative lack of user-friendly software, not to mention understanding and experience. The latter reasons are remediated by proper training and besides, ignorance rarely stands in the way of application, viz., factor analysis in the 1960s and 1970s, binary IRT in the 1980s, and more recently the widespread misuse of the Mantel–Haenszel chi-square test as a measure of DIF effect size. The real stumbling blocks will be availability of user-friendly software and cost. As Thissen et al. (1992) point out, the cost of IRT likelihood ratio DIF assessment, as well as other types of IRT-based DIF assessment, is steep compared to the model-free methods of standardization and Mantel–Haenszel.

A more recent issue concerns the desire to avoid confounding model misfit with DIF. The standardization procedure was originally developed as an alternative to IRT-based procedures, which were in vogue in the early 1980s, not because it was less expensive—standardization DIF analyses involving hundreds of thousands of examinees (all the data) are cheaper than IRT calibrations involving $1/_{100}$ of the data (a spaced random sample of a few thousand)—but because it was model-free, and Dorans and Kulick (1983, 1986) did not want to confound model misfit with DIF. The clearest example of model misfit confounding DIF assessment is the Rasch model, which, like Angoff and Ford's (1973) transformed item difficulty approach, confounds DIF with differences in item acuity or quality. Although appropriate IRT models (e.g., the three parameter logistic model) have been shown to be powerful tools in analyzing multiple-choice item data, their applicability to constructed-response data is yet to be demonstrated. Until such time, the prudent course is to use the more descriptive model-free approaches.

Architecture of Proficiency

Mislevy et al. (1992) left behind the century-old world of level-of-proficiency testing and delved into the relatively unchartered waters of architecture of proficiency (Mislevy, this volume). Here the psychometrics are less well developed. Instead of the simple model of cognitive ability that underlies much of classical test theory and item response theory, namely "the more proficient you are, the better you will do on items and tests of proficiency," these new models attempt to incorporate more complex, maybe more realistic, conceptions of cognition. The authors cited some instances of this new type of psychometric modeling, most of which are theoretical papers or papers involving limited examples. Mislevy and Verhelst (1990) have developed "mixture models" for item responses when different examinees follow different solution strategies or use alternative mental models. This approach involves the identification of classes of examinees who follow distinct solution strategies. Falmagne (1989) and Haertel (1984) employed "binary skills" models that describe competence in terms of the presence or absence of many elements of skill or knowledge. Masters and Mislevy (in press) and Wilson (1989a) used the "partial credit rating scale" model to characterize levels of understanding with respect to their nature as opposed to their correctness. Wilson (1989b) described a "Saltus" model to categorize stages of conceptual development by parameterizing the differential patterns of strength and weakness expected as learners progress through successive conceptualizations of a domain. Yamamoto's (1987) "Hybrid" model characterized an examinee as either belonging to one of a number of classes associated with states of understanding or being placed in a catchall IRT class. Tatsuoka's "rule space" approach (1983, 1985, 1990) used a joint distribution of IRT proficiency estimates *and* indices of lack of fit for individuals to identify systematic patterns of response to particular solution strategies, both correct and incorrect.

The waters of the architecture of proficiency are, as water invariably is, quite fluid. Hence, the cognitive and psychometric models are in their early stages of development. Until an island of psychometric understanding emerges from this sea of exploration and innovation, the prudent thing to do is leave the DIF apparatus ashore. As stated earlier, DIF is "secondary" psychometrics that needs a firm psychometric foundation from which to study group similarities and differences. Mislevy (personal communication, October, 1990) viewed DIF as an unwelcome group interaction term connecting observations and inferences, and recommended that we need to have a scoring model or at least a scoring procedure to know whether the interaction term is needed. With levels-of-proficiency testing, the foundation of scoring models and scoring rules exists. As the waters of the architecture of proficiency undergo an elemental change and solidify, the time will be ripe for developing DIF procedures based on emerging models. These procedures are likely to be either directly based on the new models or on extensions of old procedures; for example, using a multivariate matching variable with the Mantel–Haenszel and standardization frameworks (Dorans & Holland, 1992). The adaptations of Mantel–Haenszel and standardization are likely to be easier to use and less subject to the side effects of model misfit.

Water has three states: liquid, solid, and gaseous. The waters of the architecture of proficiency may appear perilous to many land-locked level-of-proficiency types. A temptation that must be avoided is to "stay ashore," using binary scoring on constructed responses only because it is easier to defend a simple scoring rule than a complicated one. The cost of constructed response necessitates that we extract as much relatively independent and useful information as we can out of each response. At the very least, we need to use graded responses or ordered multiple category scoring. We may, however, very well need to immerse ourselves in the seas of architecture-of-proficiency models. Otherwise, constructed-response testing, which is a rather fluid endeavor itself, may vaporize for cost reasons before it ever establishes a firm foothold in the history of testing.

ACKNOWLEDGMENTS

The opinions expressed in this chapter are those of one or both of the authors and should not be misconstrued to represent official policy of either the College Board or Educational Testing Service. The authors thank Randy Bennett and William Ward for their reviews and comments on earlier versions of the chapter and Elise Sharrett for her assistance in revising the chapter.

REFERENCES

Andrich, D. (1978). A rating formulation for ordered response categories. *Psychometrika, 43,* 561–573.
Angoff, W. H., & Ford, S. F. (1973). Item-race interactions on a test of scholastic aptitude. *Journal of Educational Measurement, 10,* 95–105.
Bell, R. C., & Hay, J. A. (1987). Differences and biases in English language examination formats. *British Journal of Educational Psychology, 57,* 212–220.
Bennett, R. E., Ward, W. C., Rock, D. A., & LaHart, C. (1990). *Toward a framework for constructed-response items* (RR-90-7). Princeton, NJ: Educational Testing Service.
Birnbaum, A. (1968). Some latent trait models and their uses in inferring an examinee's ability. In F. M. Lord & M. R. Novick, *Statistical theories of mental test scores* (pp. 397–479). Reading, MA: Addison-Wesley.
Bock, R. D. (1972). Estimating item parameters and latent ability when the responses are scored in two or more nominal categories. *Psychometrika, 37,* 29–51.
Bolger, N. (1984). *Gender differences in academic achievement according to method of measurement.* Paper presented at the annual meeting of the American Psychological Association, Toronto. (ERIC Document Reproduction Service No. ED 255 555)
Breland, H. M., & Griswold, P. A. (1981). *Group comparisons for basic skills measures* (College Board Report No. 81-6). New York: College Entrance Examination Board.
Dorans, N. J. (1982). *Technical review of item fairness studies: 1975–1979* (SR-82-90). Princeton, NJ: Educational Testing Service.
Dorans, N. J. (1989). Two new approaches to assessing differential item functioning: Standardization and the Mantel–Haenszel method. *Applied Measurement in Education, 2,* 217–233.
Dorans, N. J., & Holland, P. W. (1992). DIF detection and description: Mantel–Haenszel and standardization. In P. W. Holland & H. Wainer (Eds.), *Differential item functioning: Theory and practice* (pp. 35–66). Hillsdale, NJ: Lawrence Erlbaum Associates.
Dorans, N. J., & Kulick, E. (1983). *Assessing unexpected differential item performance of female candidates on SAT and TSWE forms administered in December 1977: An application of the standardization approach* (RR-83-9). Princeton, NJ: Educational Testing Service.

Dorans, N. J., & Kulick, E. (1986). Demonstrating the utility of the standardization approach to assessing unexpected differential item performance on the Scholastic Aptitude Test. *Journal of Educational Measurement, 23,* 355–368.

Dorans, N. J., & Lawrence, I. M. (1987). *The internal construct validity of the SAT* (RR-87–35). Princeton, NJ: Educational Testing Service.

Dorans, N. J., Schmitt, A. P., & Bleistein, C. A. (1988). *The standardization approach to assessing differential speededness* (RR-88-31). Princeton, NJ: Educational Testing Service.

Dorans, N. J., Schmitt, A. P., & Bleistein, C. A. (1992). The standardization approach to assessing comprehensive differential item functioning. *Journal of Educational Measurement, 29,* 1–11.

Falmagne, J-C. (1989). A latent trait model via a stochastic learning theory for a knowledge space. *Psychometrika, 54,* 283–303.

Ferrara, S., & Walker-Bartnick, L. (1990, April). *Detecting and analyzing differential item functioning in an essay test using the partial credit model.* Paper presented at the annual meeting of the National Council on Measurement in Education, Boston, MA.

Green, B. F., Crone, C. R., & Folk, V. G. (1989). A method for studying differential distractor functioning. *Journal of Educational Measurement, 26,* 147–160.

Haertel, E. H. (1984). An application of latent class models to assessment data. *Applied Psychological Measurement, 8,* 333–346.

Holland, P. W. (1985). *On the study of differential item performance without IRT.* Paper presented at the annual meeting of the Military Testing Association, San Diego, CA.

Holland, P. W., & Thayer, D. T. (1985). *An alternative definition of the ETS delta scale of item difficulty* (RR-85-43). Princeton, NJ: Educational Testing Service.

Holland, P. W., & Thayer, D. (1988). Differential item performance and the Mantel–Haenszel procedure. In H. Wainer & H. I. Braun (Eds.), *Test validity* (pp. 129–145). Hillsdale, NJ: Lawrence Erlbaum Associates.

Lawley, D. N. (1943) On problems connected with item selection and test construction. *Proceedings of the Royal Society of Edinburgh, 62-A* (Part I), 74–82.

Lehman, J. D., & Mazzeo, J. (1991, April). *Confirmatory factor analyses of mathematical prototypes.* Paper presented at the annual meeting of the National Council on Measurement in Education, Chicago, IL.

Lord, F. M. (1952). A theory of test scores. *Psychometrika Monograph No. 7, 17* (4 part 2).

Lord, F. M. (1980). *Applications of item response theory to practical testing problems.* Hillsdale, NJ: Lawrence Erlbaum Associates.

Mantel, N., & Haenszel, W. M. (1959). Statistical aspects of the analysis of data from retrospective studies of disease. *Journal of the National Cancer Institute, 22,* 719–748.

Masters, G. N. (1982). A Rasch model for partial credit scoring. *Psychometrika, 47,* 149–174.

Masters, G. N., & Mislevy, R. J. (in press). New views of student learning: Implications for educational measurement. In N. Frederiksen, R. J. Mislevy, & I. I. Bejar (Eds.), *Test theory for a new generation of tests.* Hillsdale, NJ: Lawrence Erlbaum Associates.

Mazzeo, J., Schmitt, A. P., & Bleistein, C. A. (1991, April). *Do women perform better, relative to men, on constructed-response tests or multiple-choice tests? Evidence from the advanced placement examinations.* Paper presented at the annual meeting of the National Council of Measurement in Education, Chicago, IL.

Mislevy, R. J., & Verhelst, N. (1990). Modeling item responses when different subjects employ different solution strategies. *Psychometrika, 55,* 195–215.

Mislevy, R. J., Yamamoto, K., & Anacker, S. (1992). Toward a test theory for assessing student understanding. In R. Lesh & S. L. Lamon (Eds.), *Assessment of authentic performance in school mathematics* (pp. 293–318). Washington, DC: Association for the Advancement of Science.

Murphy, R. J. L. (1980). Sex differences in GCE examination entry statistics and success rates. *Education Statistics, 6,* 169–178.

Murphy, R. J. L. (1982). Sex differences in objective test performance. *Journal of Educational Psychology, 52,* 213–219.

Petersen, N. S., & Livingston, S. A. (1982). *English Composition Test with Essay: A descriptive study of the relationship between essay and objective scores by ethnic group and sex* (SR-82-96). Princeton, NJ: Educational Testing Service.

Rasch, G. (1960). *Probabilistic models for some intelligence and attainment tests.* Copenhagen: Denmarks Paedagogiske Institute.

Ramsay, J. O. (1991). Kernel smoothing approaches to nonparametric item characteristic curve estimation. *Psychometrika, 56,* 611–630.

Ramsay, J. O., & Holland, P. W. (1989). *Smoothing the Mantel–Haenszel estimator to estimate nonconstant odds ratios.* Unpublished manuscript.

Rivera, C., & Schmitt, A. P. (1988). *A comparison of Hispanic and White students' omit patterns on the Scholastic Aptitude Test* (RR-88-44). Princeton, NJ: Educational Testing Service.

Samejima, F. (1969). Estimation of latent ability using a response pattern of graded scores. *Psychometrika Monograph No. 17, 34* (4 Part 2).

Scheuneman, J. D. (1975, April). *A new method of assessing bias in test items.* Paper presented at the annual meeting of the American Educational Research Association, Washington, DC. (ERIC Document Reproduction Service No. ED 106 359)

Schmitt, A. P., & Crone, C. R. (1991, April). *Alternative mathematical aptitude item types: DIF issues.* Paper presented at the annual meeting of the National Council of Measurement in Education, Chicago, IL.

Schmitt, A. P., & Dorans, N. J. (1990). Differential item functioning for minority examinees on the SAT. *Journal of Educational Measurement, 27,* 67–81.

Schmitt, A. P., Dorans, N. J., Crone, C. R., & Maneckshana, B. T. (1990, April). *Differential item omit and speededness patterns on the SAT.* Paper presented at the annual meeting of the National Council on Measurement in Education, Boston, MA.

Schmitt, A. P., Holland, P. W., & Dorans, N. J. (1992). Evaluating hypotheses about differential item functioning. In P. W. Holland & H. Wainer (Eds.), *Differential item functioning: Theory and practice* (pp. 281–315). Hillsdale, NJ: Lawrence Erlbaum Associates.

Shepard, L. A. (1982). Definitions of bias. In R. A. Berk (Ed.), *Handbook of methods for detecting test bias* (pp. 9–30). Baltimore: Johns Hopkins University Press.

Simpson, E. H. (1951). The interpretation of interaction contingency tables. *Journal of Royal Statistical Society* (Series B), *13,* 238–241.

Tatsuoka, K. K. (1983). Rule space: An approach for dealing with misconceptions based on item response theory. *Journal of Educational Measurement, 20,* 345–354.

Tatsuoka, K. K. (1985). A probabilistic model for diagnosing misconceptions by the pattern classification approach. *Journal of Educational Statistics, 10,* 55–73.

Tatsuoka, K. K. (1990). Toward an integration of item-response theory and cognitive error diagnosis. In N. Frederiksen, R. Glaser, A. Lesgold, & M. Shafto (Eds.), *Diagnostic monitoring of skill and knowledge acquisition* (pp. 453–488). Hillsdale, NJ: Lawrence Erlbaum Associates.

Thissen, D. (1987). Discussant comments on the NCME symposium, Unexpected Differential Item Performance and its Assessment Among Black, Asian-American, and Hispanic Students. In A. P. Schmitt & N. J. Dorans (Eds.), *Differential item functioning on the Scholastic Aptitude Test* (RM-87-1). Princeton, NJ: Educational Testing Service.

Thissen, D., & Steinberg, L. (1984). A taxonomy of item response models. *Psychometrika, 51,* 567–577.

Thissen, D., & Steinberg, L. (1986). A response model for multiple choice items. *Psychometrika, 49,* 501–519.

Thissen, D., Steinberg, L., & Wainer, H. (1992). Detection of differential item functioning using the parameters of item response models. In P. W. Holland & H. Wainer (Eds.), *Differential item functioning: Theory and practice* (pp. 67–113). Hillsdale, NJ: Lawrence Erlbaum Associates.

Thorndike, R. M., & Lohman, D. F. (1990). *A century of ability testing.* New York: Riverside.

Traub, R. E., & MacRury, K. (1990). Antwort-auswahl- vs freie-antwort-aufgaben bei lernerfolgs-
tests [Multiple-choice vs. free-response in the testing of scholastic achievement]. In K. Ingenkamp & R. S. Jäger (Eds.), *Tests und trends 8: Jahrbuch der Pädagogischen Diagnostik*
[Tests and trends: Eighth yearbook of educational measurement] (pp. 128–159). Weinheim
und Basel, Germany: Beltz Verlag.

Tucker, L. R. (1946). Maximum validity of a test with equivalent items. *Psychometrika, 11*, 1–13.

Wilson, M. R. (1989a). A comparison of deterministic and probabilistic approaches to measuring
learning structures. *Australian Journal of Education, 33*, 125–138.

Wilson, M. R. (1989b). Saltus: A psychometric model of discontinuity in cognitive development.
Psychological Bulletin, 105, 276–289.

Yamamoto, K. (1987). *A model that combines IRT and latent class models.* Unpublished doctoral
dissertation, University of Illinois.

8

ITEM FORMATS FOR
ASSESSMENT IN MATHEMATICS

James Braswell
Jane Kupin
Educational Testing Service

Assessment provides indicators of educational success for a variety of purposes and audiences. The purposes include individual student evaluation, curriculum evaluation, and national assessment. The audiences include the individuals who are assessed, curriculum developers, educators charged with planning and decision making, and the public. In general, for reasons of efficiency and cost, most standardized examinations consist entirely of multiple-choice questions. Because scores on these examinations affect perceptions of individual and school success, attention is given toward preparing students to do well on them. Increasingly, standardized tests are being criticized for failing to provide an appropriate instructional target (Shavelson, 1990).

In particular, multiple-choice examinations are frequently criticized because the task posed requires students to recognize a correct answer rather than to generate one. This criticism is in part true but it is more valid of certain questions and types of questions than of others. This chapter takes the position that multiple-choice questions are reliable indicators of student ability and achievement in mathematics, but that complementary formats can provide a more appropriate target for instruction. The use of multiple-choice items in mathematics testing is discussed first. Then, essay and short-answer questions ("construction" and "completion" in the Bennett, Ward, Rock, & LaHart, 1990, and Bennett, this volume, terminology), are considered. Finally, machine-scorable alternatives to standard multiple-choice items are introduced and findings from their use are presented.

MULTIPLE-CHOICE FORMATS

Mathematics examinations are different from examinations in other domains (e.g., verbal). In mathematics, there is frequently a standard algorithm or procedure that can be applied to solve a problem. Although the student must decide which procedures to apply, the procedures, when selected and applied correctly, generally yield a unique solution.

In certain questions, the choices serve to focus the test taker, and the correct answer cannot be determined without them. Consider, for example, the following question.

A jar contains 10 pencils, some sharpened and some unsharpened. Each of the following could be the ratio of sharpened to unsharpened pencils EXCEPT

(A) 1:1
(B) 3:2
(C) 4:1
(D) 5:1
(E) 9:1

Although a student could list various possible ratios of sharpened to unsharpened pencils, there is no way a student can answer this question without considering the various choices. Because 10 is a small number, perhaps the most reasonable approach to solving the problem is to consider each choice. This seems like a reasonable question to pose in a multiple-choice format, even though the student is only required to recognize instances and one noninstance of the situation.

The following example is somewhat different in that a unique solution exists and it can be determined without considering the choices.

Which of the following is the greater of two numbers whose product is 220 and whose sum is 10 more than the difference between the two?

(A) 5   (B) 10   (C) 22   (D) 44   (E) 55

Although it is not difficult to set up an appropriate equation to find the solution directly, for example, $(x + y) - (x - y) = 10$, the test-wise individual can use the choices to find the solution indirectly. If each choice is considered as a candidate for the greater number, then the lesser number possibilities can be placed beside them:

(A) 5, 44

(B) 10, 22

(C) 22, 10

(D) 44, 5

(E) 55, 4

Clearly, Choices A and B are out as candidates for the solution since the first number is not the greater of the two. For Choices C, D, and E, the sums and differences are:

(C) 32 and 12

(D) 49 and 39

(E) 51 and 59

Only in Choice D is the sum 10 more than the difference. One might argue that the test-wise approach weakens the validity of the question. Notice, however, that the test-wise analysis is not at all trivial, even though the ability required might not be at the same level as that required to solve the problem directly.

The first of these examples is given to illustrate the fact that some good multiple-choice questions cannot straightforwardly be turned into constructed response items because the choices are an essential part of the question. Although the second example affords the opportunity to manipulate the choices to reach a solution, the analysis required by this approach is not simple. Thus, the breadth of measurement can be enhanced by retaining multiple-choice questions and introducing other, less constrained formats.

ESSAY AND SHORT-ANSWER ITEM TYPES USED IN LARGE-SCALE ASSESSMENT PROGRAMS

Without doubt, the essay question has greater face validity and acceptability than other item formats. The reasons for this are obvious. The student is required to interpret, analyze, solve, and produce. Scoring such questions is not simply an issue of right or wrong, but affords the possibility of awarding partial credit, evaluating approaches/techniques, and tracking interesting correct and incorrect approaches that could provide suggestions for improving instruction.

In the College Board's Advanced Placement (AP) Program, all subject examinations have some essay questions. This program consists of syllabi and examinations that represent a wide range of college-level courses (e.g., calculus, physics, American history, French) offered in high schools. A primary reason that the program is widely recognized by colleges is that essay questions make up about half of most examinations. For each subject, a faculty committee is appointed by the College Board to prepare and maintain course syllabi, develop and review test questions, and assist in setting scoring rubrics for essay questions. The essay questions are graded by high school and college readers who receive thorough training on scoring procedures so that uniform standards are applied. For example, on the AP Calculus AB examination there are five essay questions, each worth nine points. There is also a 45-question multiple-choice section that is given the same weight as the essay section in determining scores. The multiple-choice questions are machine scored and each essay is read by one or more readers, each of whom reads only one question on a particular student's paper.

Students who sit for AP examinations may take the essay questions with them at the end of the examination. Later, the scoring rubrics are compiled and a report of the results is prepared. This information is shared with teachers as an aid in improving their courses and in helping students prepare for future examinations.

A question from the 1990 AP Calculus AB examination is shown in Fig. 8.1. The scoring rubric is provided in Fig. 8.2.

Those who read AP examinations come from all areas of the country representing numerous institutions and disciplines. Their housing, meals, and travel are paid for and each reader receives an honorarium for approximately 5 days of reading. These operational details illustrate the fact that scoring essay questions is much more expensive and time-consuming than scoring multiple-choice questions. Just how much more expensive is suggested by the fee charged in 1990–1991 for taking a 3-hour AP examination versus the fee for the 3-hour multiple-choice Scholastic Aptitude Test. The AP fee was $65 per examination, whereas the SAT fee was $16. Scoring-related costs account for a major part of this fee difference.

Another program of national scope that uses open-ended and short-answer exercises is the National Assessment of Educational Progress (NAEP). This program is funded by the U.S. Department of Education to collect and report data over time on the performance of students in the nation's schools. The trend in NAEP has been to increase the proportion of questions that require students to produce solutions. As is the case for the AP program, the essay and short-answer questions must be scored by trained readers.

---

5. Let f be the function defined by $f(x) = \sin^2 x - \sin x$ for $0 \le x \le \frac{3\pi}{2}$.

    (a) Find the x-intercepts of the graph of f.

    (b) Find the intervals on which f is increasing.

    (c) Find the absolute maximum value and the absolute minimum value of f. Justify your answer.

FIG. 8.1.   Question 5 from 1990 Advanced Placement Calculus AB Examination.

Solution	Distribution of Points

(a) $\sin^2 x - \sin x = 0$

Therefore $x = 0, \dfrac{\pi}{2}, \pi$

(a) 1: $\sin^2 x - \sin x = 0$
     1: all correct answers,
2:   0/1: any extra answers
     0/1: for answer points if answers in
          degrees in part (a) and/or (b)

(b) $f'(x) = 2\sin x \cos x - \cos x$
      $= \cos x (2\sin x - 1)$

$f'(x) = 0$ when $x = \dfrac{\pi}{6}, \dfrac{\pi}{2}, \dfrac{5\pi}{6}, \dfrac{3\pi}{2}$

$$
\begin{array}{ccccc}
 & - & + & - & + \\
f' & \vdash\!\!\!+\!\!\!\!\!\!+\!\!\!\!\!\!+\!\!\!\!\!\!\dashv & & & \\
 & 0 \quad \frac{\pi}{6} \quad \frac{\pi}{2} \quad \frac{5\pi}{6} & & \frac{3\pi}{2} & \\
\end{array}
$$

Therefore $\dfrac{\pi}{6} \le x \le \dfrac{\pi}{2}$ and $\dfrac{5\pi}{6} \le x \le \dfrac{3\pi}{2}$

(b) 1: $f'(x)$
     1: any two correct interior
         critical points for candidate's f'
     1: all other correct interior critical
         points and no incorrect ones
         0/1: if there is not a third correct
              interior critical point
4:   1: answer
         0/1: if interior critical points are
              incorrect for candidate's f'
         0/1: if candidate's f' has less than 2
              interior critical points
         Note: If part (b) is blank,
                the point for $f'(x)$ may
                be earned in part (c)

(c)   The function is continuous on
$\left[0, \dfrac{3\pi}{2}\right]$, so the function should be
evaluated at critical points and
endpoints

x	$f(x)$
0	0
$\dfrac{\pi}{6}$	$-\dfrac{1}{4}$
$\dfrac{\pi}{2}$	0
$\dfrac{5\pi}{6}$	$-\dfrac{1}{4}$
$\dfrac{3\pi}{2}$	2

Therefore

maximum value = 2
and
minimum value = $-\dfrac{1}{4}$

(c) 1: maximum value = 2
     1: minimum value based on candidate's
         interior critical points
         0/1: if finds less than 2 interior
              critical points
     1: justification
         0/1: if finds less than 2 interior
3:            critical points

     1/1: maximum at $\dfrac{3\pi}{2}$, if value at
          $x = \dfrac{3\pi}{2}$ is displayed

     0/1: maximum = $\dfrac{3\pi}{2}$ (comparable ruling
          for minimum)

FIG. 8.2. Scoring rubric for Question 5 from the 1990 Advanced Placement
Calculus AB Examination.

NAEP exercises are written to fit assessment objectives developed through
a national consensus process. In addition to providing reports of student performance at Grades 4, 8, and 12 for the nation, NAEP also provides state-
level comparative data at selected grade levels. For the 1990 assessment,
the 40 participating states and territories were to receive Grade 8 results comparable to other participating states and to the nation. For 1992, NAEP's state
assessment program calls for expansion to Grades 4 and 8. The following

Content Area					
Mathematical Ability	Numbers & Operations	Measurement	Geometry	Data Analysis, Statistics, & Probability	Algebra & Functions
Conceptual Understanding					
Procedural Knowledge					
Problem Solving					

FIG. 8.3. NAEP content/ability grid.

policy statement included in the *Mathematics Objectives, 1990 Assessment* (NAEP, 1988) booklet gives the purpose of the state comparisons.

> The purpose of a state-level student achievement comparison is to provide data on student performance to assist policymakers and educators to work toward the improvement of education. Such data can be useful by encouraging and contributing to a discussion of the quality of education and the conditions that determine it. (p. 7)

In mathematics, items are written to fit specifications so that the total pool of questions will enable those who interpret and use NAEP results to make educationally sound inferences and decisions about results. The ability/content matrix shown in Fig. 8.3 was used to control coverage.[1] Each content area is broken down into topics and subtopics and each ability category is also subdivided. For example, Problem Solving consists of the following abilities:

1. Recognize and formulate problems.
2. Understand data sufficiency and consistency.
3. Use strategies, data, models, and relevant mathematics.
4. Generate, extend, and modify procedures.
5. Reason (spatially, inductively, deductively, statistically, and proportionally).
6. Judge the reasonableness and correctness of solutions.

One purpose of the matrix approach is to help ensure that items included in the assessment cover a wide range of skills and topics—some very basic and some that require higher order thinking. Some exercises written to fit the matrix require the use of calculators, protractors, rulers, and various other materials.

---

[1]The National Assessment Governing Board has revised the matrix for the 1994 mathematics assessment.

In the rectangle ABCD below, explain why triangles AED, AFD, and
AGD have equal areas.

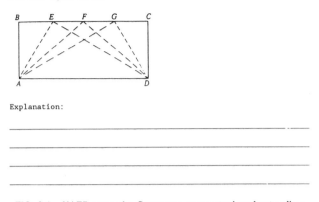

Explanation:

_____ ____

_____

_____

_____ ____

FIG. 8.4. NAEP example: Geometry, conceptual understanding.

An example from the Grade 12 1990 assessment is shown in Fig. 8.4. This
item was classified as Geometry, Conceptual Understanding. The scoring
rubric is shown in Fig. 8.5. More information about NAEP content and procedures can be found in *The NAEP Guide* (Mullis, 1990).

Interesting assessments can also be found at the state level. In Massachusetts, public school students in Grades 4, 8, and 12 are tested every 2
years in order to compare schools and suggest improvements to curriculum.
The tests, administered by the Massachusetts Educational Assessment Program (MEAP), are in the subject areas of reading, mathematics, science, and
social science.

Although school comparisons are based on the results of multiple-choice
questions, students are also tested with open-ended questions designed to
measure reasoning and problem-solving approaches. An example of a MEAP
open-ended mathematics question for Grades 8 and 12 is given in Fig. 8.6.

Asking students for an explanation is common in these questions. The goal
is to find out how students think, including their misconceptions. For this question, the explanation also serves as a guide to the reasonableness of the graph.
For example, if a student draws the graph about running as a line sloping
downwards, and then explains that running improves from childhood to age
20, the answer is counted as correct because the graph is consistent with
the explanation. A U-shaped graph that reflected childhood, youth, and old
age would demonstrate a more complete understanding of the relationship
over time.

Trained readers classify and evaluate student's answers. The results are
reported with some interpretation, such as a discussion of common errors.
(Badger, 1989).

The results on the open-ended questions are not used to compare schools.
They are intended to assist schools and teachers in curriculum planning. The

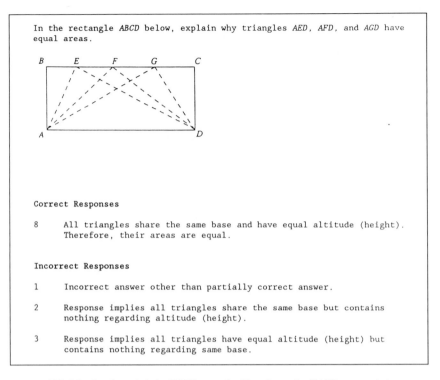

In the rectangle *ABCD* below, explain why triangles *AED, AFD,* and *AGD* have equal areas.

Correct Responses

8   All triangles share the same base and have equal altitude (height). Therefore, their areas are equal.

Incorrect Responses

1   Incorrect answer other than partially correct answer.

2   Response implies all triangles share the same base but contains nothing regarding altitude (height).

3   Response implies all triangles have equal altitude (height) but contains nothing regarding same base.

FIG. 8.5. Scoring rubric for NAEP example. (*Note*: In scoring NAEP open-ended items, a code of 8 generally denotes a correct answer and codes of 1, 2, 3, etc., generally denote incorrect answers. The different incorrect response codes are used to track interesting incorrect or partially correct alternatives.)

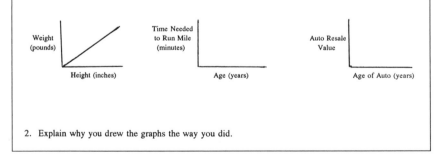

1. Two of the three graphs below have not been completed. Draw lines in the last two so that the graphs look the way they would if you had real numbers to use. (Hint: Look at the labels along the axes first. Then pretend there are numbers along them. Think about how the two quantities are related. Use the first graph as an example.)

2. Explain why you drew the graphs the way you did.

FIG. 8.6. MEAP example: Open-ended mathematics question for Grades 8 and 12.

use of the open-ended questions also sends a message to schools about the importance of activities that focus on the reasoning behind the answer, rather than just the answer.

In addition to the comparative assessment, MEAP administers in alternate years mathematics and science performance assessments at Grades 4, 8, and 12. The performance tasks are done by pairs of students working as teams. Each task is planned so that it provides an interesting context for problem solving and so that it evaluates understanding and skills. An example of a performance task administered in Grades 4 and 8 is given in Fig. 8.7.

The performance tasks tend to have less in the way of written explanations than the open-ended questions. Rather, students communicate about the task by talking with their teammates while trained administrators observe the students' work and report on their conversations and approaches.

The results of the performance assessment, like those of the open-ended questions, are not used to compare schools, but are reported so that teachers can understand students' strengths and weaknesses. They are also intended as model assessments for schools and teachers (Badger, Thomas, & McCormick, 1990).

MACHINE-SCORABLE ALTERNATIVES
FOR LARGE-SCALE ASSESSMENT

The preceding discussion described questions that require students to produce written responses. Evaluating and scoring these responses is generally expensive and the human resources and logistical organization required are difficult to manage. In this section, machine-scorable alternatives to essay and short-answer items are discussed.

Popcorn Estimation

Description of the Task: Students were told to use whatever they wanted from a set of materials to estimate the number of kernels in a container. The administrator observed and recorded their strategy. When they had reached a solution, they were asked to describe an alternate method and, if appropriate, to carry it out.

Concepts/Skills Evaluated:

- identification of problem
- appropriate procedures
- correct use of apparatus (balance)
- proportional reasoning
- computation
- understanding of large numbers
- accuracy/precision judgments

FIG. 8.7.   MEAP example: Performance task for Grades 4 and 8.

Much of the criticism leveled against multiple-choice questions is directed toward the choices and not the questions. To be sure, multiple-choice questions are also criticized as being trivial, but this need not be the case. There are many examples of multiple-choice mathematics questions that test important concepts, procedures, and higher order thinking. Nevertheless, the fact that the correct answer is included in a list of alternatives reduces face validity. Critics charge with some justification that recognition, plug-in approaches, and various other test-wise strategies can be used to home in on the correct answer. Test questions that illustrate the various criticisms unfortunately abound. Given this situation, machine-scorable alternatives to multiple-choice questions that permit students to solve a problem and record their own answers would be a step in the right direction. Two possibilities appear reasonable given the current scanning technology. The first is the use of a grid in which the student's answer can be recorded and later scanned and scored. The second is a handwritten answer that can be optically interpreted. Both of these variations have been tried. The first of these has met with greater success.

In the first case, 12 mathematics questions of the type used on the College Board's Scholastic Aptitude Test (SAT) were administered in different formats to two student groups. One group received the 12 questions in the standard multiple-choice format; the other received the same questions without choices, and recorded their answers on grids that allowed for integer solutions from 0 to 999. In providing their answers, students were asked to write the solution at the top of the grid and then grid in the corresponding result. An example of a gridded response is found in Fig. 8.8. Students were asked to write their answers at the top of the grid for two reasons: (a) it has been found that the gridded results are more accurate if the written form is present, and (b) the written form provides a basis for evaluating gridding accuracy.

Another phase of the investigation involved the use of a more elaborate gridding format. For this phase, the grid allowed for fractions and decimals in addition to integer answers. Such a grid extends the range of problems

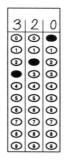

FIG. 8.8. Example of 3-digit grid format.

The last 10 questions on the Mathematics test will have no answer choices. Instead, you must solve each problem and enter your answer in a special grid as shown in the following examples.

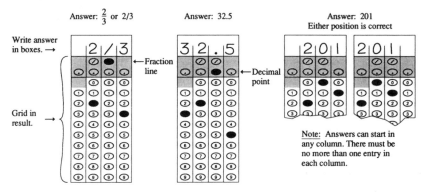

FIG. 8.9.   Directions used on prototype examinations.

Write your answer in the boxes at the top of each column. Then fill in the corresponding oval beneath each box. *Because the answer sheet will be machine scored, you will receive credit only if the ovals are filled in correctly.* No question has a negative answer. No more than four columns are needed to answer any question.

Some problems may have more than one correct answer. In such cases, enter only one answer. For example, see sample question 6 below.

If you obtain an answer such as 0.6666 . . . , you may record the result as .666 or .667. Do not enter less accurate values such as .66 or .67.

In each of the following sample questions, solve the problem and record your answer. Be sure to fill in the correct oval beneath each box.

that can be posed, but introduces additional complexity and requires slightly more time for responding. Figure 8.9 shows the more elaborate format along with its directions.

Answers such as 1/4 could be gridded as .25 or 1/4. A total of 20 questions were presented with grids of this type. Two questions were presented that allowed for the possibility of more than one correct answer. One of these questions is shown in Fig. 8.10.

The following questions were of interest for both types of grids.

- What are the statistical characteristics of items?
- Does the gridded-response format require more time than the standard multiple-choice format?
- What do students think of questions that require gridded solutions?
- How frequently do students make gridding errors and how do the error rates compare on the two types of grids?
- What questions seem best suited to the grid-in format?

Properties of the Whole Number n
I. n is even.
II. n is a multiple of 3.
III. n is between 20 and 70.
IV. $n - 1$ and $n + 1$ are prime numbers.

4. Grid in a value that satisfies all of the properties of n listed in the table above.

4.

Note: Correct answers are 30, 42, or 60

FIG. 8.10. Question with more than one correct answer.

Findings: 3-Digit and 4-Digit Formats

The 3-digit grid format was tried out in the fall of 1988 in high schools throughout the nation. The 4-digit grid format was piloted in the spring of 1989. Sample questions, one of each type, are shown in Fig. 8.11.

Item Functioning and Timing. In general, the item statistics for questions present in these formats were as good as or better than those for the same or similar items presented in the regular multiple-choice format. The percentages of students responding correctly to the grid versions were generally less than for comparable multiple-choice versions, as guessing and backdoor approaches are virtually eliminated. The reliability of the questions presented in the 3-digit grid format was about the same as that of corresponding questions presented in multiple-choice form. The reliability of the 20 questions presented in the 4-digit grid format was considerably higher than for the same number of multiple-choice questions of similar content.

The gridded-response format generally required more time to answer than did similar multiple-choice questions. Two factors seemed to account for this: (a) students must write and then grid their solutions, and (b) students may

Question Accompanied by 3-Digit Grid	Question Accompanied by 4-Digit Grid
A tower sends a signal every 8 seconds. At this rate, how many signals would the tower send in $\frac{2}{3}$ of an hour?	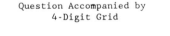 In the figure above, segment PT has length 36, Q is the midpoint of PR, R is the midpoint of QS, and S is the midpoint of QT. What is the length of segment QS?
Answer: 300	Answer: 14.4 or 72/5

FIG. 8.11. Examples of 3- and 4-digit grid format questions.

work more carefully and check their work because there are no choices to confirm their solutions. Comments made by some students following the trials indicated that the multiple-choice options did indeed function in this way. For questions like those used on the SAT, the average multiple-choice question requires about 1.2 minutes to answer. The average gridded-response type (4-digit grid) requires about 1.6 minutes.

Students' Opinions.   In general, students expressed a strong preference for multiple-choice type questions over the grid type. However, for the 3-digit grid, over half of the students responded that the grid type was a better measure of their mathematics ability. This opinion did not hold for the 4-digit grid, where over half of the sample felt that the multiple-choice questions were a better measure of their ability. One possible explanation for this finding is that students in the 4-digit field trial had no advanced preparation with the examination format and answer sheet design. This lack of preparation could have caused confusion in working with the format that was not present in the 3-digit field trial where students received advanced information.

Accuracy of Gridded Solutions.   A thorough analysis was made of the accuracy of students' gridded responses. Such a study was possible because students were instructed to write their answers and then grid them. Over 2,000 answer sheets were analyzed for gridding errors. There were 101 students who made a total of 109 gridding errors. Thus, approximately 5% of the students made a gridding error and virtually all of these students made only one error. Surprisingly, the frequency of errors for the 4-digit grid was lower than for the simpler 3-digit grid. However, there was a greater tendency for an error to be made on the 4-digit grid when the answer involved a fraction or decimal. This result might be expected because students had no advance preparation for the format.

Suitable Questions for This Format.   The gridded-response format is not suitable for certain types of questions because of the nature of the answers. For the 4-digit grid used on the SAT, ungriddable answers include irrational numbers, algebraic expressions, negative numbers, numbers with too many digits, and verbal answers. In addition, questions whose chief distracters are ungriddable, even if the correct answer is griddable, should be avoided. For example, if the correct answer to a question is 2, and the most likely wrong answers are $2x$ and x^2, the question would probably be better presented in a multiple-choice format if it has to be machine-scorable.

Some questions written for the multiple-choice format are not suitable for the gridded response format, but can be made suitable by minor revision. Figure 8.12 gives an example. For the multiple-choice version, the correct answer is (E). For the gridded response version, any multiple of 12 greater than 30 is acceptable, so long as it fits into the grid. The scoring program for the

Multiple-Choice Version

> If x is an even integer and y is an integer divisible by 6,
> which of the following could be the value of xy?
>
> (A) 18   (B) 27   (C) 30   (D) 32   (E) 36

Gridded Response Version

> If x is an even integer and y is an integer divisible by 6,
> what is a possible value of xy that is greater than 30?

FIG. 8.12. Example of multiple-choice question revised for gridded response.

gridded response version would have to be written to recognize all such multiples of 12 as correct answers.

Scoring. Even when there is only one correct answer, there can be many ways to grid it. Scoring programs will need to accommodate the different answer forms. For example, an answer of 3 can be entered on the 4-digit SAT grid as a single digit in any one of the spaces on the grid, and it can also be entered as 03, 3.0, 6/2, and so on.

Some rules about acceptable variations need to be established and communicated to students. For example, 2/3 can be entered in fraction form. Is it acceptable to enter 2/3 as a decimal? If so, what degree of accuracy is required (.66 vs. .666)? Should such decimals be rounded to .667 or truncated to .666? For the SAT gridded response questions, the tentative decision is to accept either .666 (the most accurate truncated value accommodated by the grid) or .667 (the most accurate rounded form accommodated by the grid) as acceptable decimal forms of 2/3, but not .6, .66, 0.67, and so on. This decision will be reevaluated as additional data become available.

Before SAT gridded responses are scored, they will go through an editing process in which multiple forms of the same answer will be represented in one way. For example, 1/2, 4/8, 0.5, and .50 would all appear as 0000.500. In this process, blank spaces are disregarded, fractions are translated into decimals, and other interpretations of the answer are made, such as interpreting ..5 as .5. Once each answer has been machine edited and translated into its canonical representation, the responses are scored by a program that compares the translated answer with the correct answer (or the set of correct answers, if there are several correct answers of different values).

Machine Recognition of Handwritten Digits

Another possibility explored was the use of handwritten calculator-like digits. Rather than gridding ovals corresponding to the digits 0–9, students recorded their answers on a template like the one shown in Fig. 8.13. Up to 3-digit

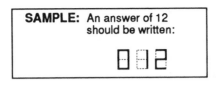

FIG. 8.13.   Example of handwritten digit template.

integer solutions could be formed, each on a lightly colored figure-eight background. If a computer program could be developed to accurately scan these characters, the handwritten option would seem viable. When pilot testing was conducted in the fall of 1988, the scanning algorithm was under development. However, the answer sheets were not scored because (a) a sufficiently reliable scanning algorithm was not developed, and (b) students disliked having to mechanically form the digits more than they disliked having to grid in answers.

Additional work on machine recognition of handwritten digits has since been done (Reid-Green, 1990). Although this work did not focus on mathematics testing, it has implications for that activity. A program to interpret data on financial aid forms was developed by the Advanced Technology Systems group at Educational Testing Service. The forms were scanned and the accuracy of the interpreted characters was evaluated. Six categories of readily detectable scanning errors were identified:

1. Badly formed characters.
2. Erasures or stray marks.
3. Digits overwritten so that lines were too thick.
4. Non-numeric characters in the fields (e.g., a comma).
5. Unrecognizable cursive characters.
6. Extra characters in the field.

In addition to these error types, less easily detected scanning errors proved a problem. Such errors result when the scanning program substitutes another character for the intended one. Poorly formed characters accounted for the majority of substitution errors (e.g., 6 read as 8). The frequency of scanning error suggests that this technology, although promising, is not ready for use in large-scale assessment programs like the SAT.

SUMMARY

The ideal alternatives to multiple-choice questions are short-answer and essay questions scored by readers. Because the scoring process is involved and expensive, these item formats are frequently avoided in large-scale testing programs.

The alternative presented in this chapter is to have candidates produce their answers and enter them in a machine-scorable form. One of the formats discussed was a scannable grid and the other was a scannable template for handwritten numbers. Of these two formats, only the grid was accurate enough to be used at the time of this writing.

Although the overall statistical characteristics of questions presented in the 4-digit grid format were very good, additional investigation is needed to make decisions about how to deal with decimal equivalents of certain fractions, whether questions with more than one correct answer can be handled by the system, and the impact of this format on various population subgroups. In the tryout phase, the grid format was unexpectedly more difficult for females and Blacks (see Dorans & Schmitt, this volume). Two hypotheses have been advanced to explain this finding: (a) anxiety, and (b) lack of familiarity with the gridding procedure. Each of these conditions could affect population subgroups differently. Students received no advanced notice concerning the 4-digit grid format, but subsequent investigations will provide students with directions and samples. It seems clear that any novel item format should be thoroughly explained in advance of the test administration so that examinees are appropriately prepared.

Both the scannable grid and the scannable template should be considered forerunners to a computer-delivered test in which students would enter answers by typing on a keyboard. The widespread use of such a test awaits, among other things, a network of computerized centers in which to administer it. Some of the same questions raised about item suitability and rules for interpreting responses would also apply to responses gathered through this medium.

REFERENCES

Badger, E. (1989). *On their own: Student response to open-ended tests in mathematics.* Quincy, MA: Massachusetts Educational Assessment Program, Massachusetts Department of Education.

Badger, E., Thomas, B., & McCormick, E. (1990). *Beyond paper & pencil.* Quincy, MA: Massachusetts Educational Assessment Program, Massachusetts Department of Education.

Bennett, R. E., Ward, W. C., Rock, D. A., & LaHart, C. (1990). *Toward a framework for constructed-response items* (RR-90-7). Princeton, NJ: Educational Testing Service.

Mullis, I. V. S. (1990). *The NAEP guide.* Princeton, NJ: National Assessment of Educational Progress, Educational Testing Service.

National Assessment of Educational Progress. (1988). *Mathematics objectives, 1990 assessment.* Princeton, NJ: Educational Testing Service.

Reid-Green, K. S. (1990). *Analysis of a pilot study of machine recognition of handwritten digits* (RM-90-3). Princeton, NJ: Educational Testing Service.

Shavelson, R. J. (1990, April). *Can indicator systems improve the effectiveness of mathematics and science education? The case of the U. S.* Paper presented at the annual meeting of the American Educational Research Association, Boston, MA.

10

ASSESSMENT AS AN
EPISODE OF LEARNING

Dennie Palmer Wolf
Harvard Graduate School of Education

Jules Henry, a sociologist and anthropologist, was absorbed with the human inability to focus on one thing at a time. He was struck in particular by our capacity to take in not only the stated message, but what he called the "noise" around that message, which is nothing less than its other aspects or layers of meaning. In his book of essays, *Culture Against Man* (1963), Henry had much to say about how many implicit lessons are taught in classrooms:

> A child writing the word "August" on the board . . . is not only learning the word "August" but also how to hold the chalk without making it squeak, how to write clearly, how to keep going even though the class is tittering at his slowness, how to appraise the glances of the children in order to know whether he is doing it right or wrong, et cetera. If the spelling, arithmetic, or music lesson were only what it appeared to be, the education of the American child would be much simpler; but it is all the things the child learns *along with* his subject matter . . . that really constitute the education process. (p. 289; italics added)

By custom, assessment falls outside the definition of lessons. But it is as laminated and as full of implications as is writing "August." At first glance, assessments are simply a moment of being measured: Did I study hard enough to slip by with a respectable C, or at least to pass? Was it the proportional reasoning problems or the geometry that tripped me up? Will I have to repeat, or can I progress to the next level?

But any assessment is also a head-on encounter with a culture's models of prowess. It is an encounter with a deep-running kind of "ought." Assessments publish what we regard as skill and what we will accept or reject as a demonstration of accomplishment, whether those assessments take the form of an SAT exam, shooting your first deer, or surviving boot camp. Assessments—particularly high-stakes ones—take stock of much more than knowledge. Failing to finish a timed, multi-item achievement test in biology is a lesson in the American romance with speed, efficiency, and technology, as much as in the structure of a scientific domain. Failing to come up with radical and plentiful revisions to a first draft is to fall short of contemporary writing process expectations that everyone is an author and that authorship entails revision. In short, any assessment anoints certain characteristics, ways of being, and kinds of information, while underplaying, ignoring, or outrightly suppressing others. It is because of this power that the issues of cultural bias in testing and major changes to gate-keeping tests like the SAT and the National Teachers Examinations have been, and should be, the occasions for intense debate.

Finally, and least acknowledged, any assessment is—or could be—an occasion when a participant learns something about the nature of assessment itself. It is a moment when he or she suddenly, painfully, or with delight, sees his or her work as someone else might, either because the participant can no longer dodge their commentary, or because the participant, himself or herself, steps outside and becomes an onlooker. It is a moment when we make use of what William James realized:

> Our considering our . . . self at all is a reflective process, it is the result of our abandoning our outward-looking point of view, and of our having become able to think of subjectivity as such, *to think of ourselves as thinkers* . . . (1890/1950, pp. 296–297; italics added)

> In the thoughts that do resemble the things they are "of" (percepts, sensations), we can feel, alongside of the thing known, the thought of it going on as an all together separate act and operation in the mind . . . personality implies the incessant presence of two elements, an objective person, known by a passing subjective Thought and recognized as continuing in time. *Hereafter let us use the words ME and I for the empirical person and the judging Thought.* (James, (1890/1950, p. 371; italics added)

Currently, all of these faces of assessment are undergoing scrutiny and change. First, there is much discussion of what knowledge to measure. The very notion of a fixed canon is no longer tenable in the strictest sense: *The Autobiography of Frederick Douglass* and Martin Luther King's *Letter from a Birmingham Jail*, once virtually invisible, are now widely taught, read, and tested. It is equally true that we are changing our minds about whether we want to know only about student knowledge. Some would teach and test explicitly for familiarity with a body of cultural knowledge, whatever its shifting margins are, leaving implicit questions of the learner's mastery of skills like questioning, writing, and investigation (Cheney, 1991; Hirsch, 1987). Others want the focusing power of assessment turned on strategies and essential understandings: how to do science (Baron, 1990; Tinker, in press) or how to unpack the narrative of history made available in primary sources (Holt, 1990; Neumann, 1991; Resnick & Resnick, in press; Wiggins, 1991; Zessoules & Gardner, 1991). Both of these discussions are important—in fact, necessary, given the changing demographics of American schools and colleges. At the same time, they are ancient and familiar. They probably raged among scholars setting exams in Mandarin China, they have peppered the evolution of the British examining systems, and they have fueled American debates about public testing since there were enough children in school to make it worth someone's time to sort them into types and tracks.

The frontier in assessment has a different address. It has to do with seizing that third, and unrecognized, aspect of assessment, which is neither measurement, nor simple acculturation, but an occasion for learning. An example will illustrate. It is taken from the autobiography of the dancer and choreographer, Paul Taylor. In this episode, Taylor (1987) remembers reading the original critical response to one of his most acclaimed dances, "Auerole," and then he recalls a later time, when he watched the dance in performance:

> After the premiere, critics . . . write that "Auerole" typifies just about everything that modern dance has been trying to do away with. Allen Hughes of the *New York Times* says it's "different, daring, and delightful."
>
> "Delightful." I was to argue with the *Times*? Yet there's something . . . If I could only duplicate myself and send one of me out front to see what it looks like.
>
> Later on, when out with an injury, I was able to see it, and my nagging doubts were confirmed. The dance had been good to me. I appreciated it, valued and trusted it, but was out of sympathy. Though I understood its audience appeal, for me it had little. I, too, enjoyed seeing dances that required little effort to understand, ones that gave uplift and caused a smile. Yet I was not smiling. I couldn't forget how relatively easy the dance had been to make and how previous dances, both larger and smaller scaled, had stretched my goals much further. "Auerole" had been child's play compared with others that I had to dig for, grapple with, and slave over, ones that had a more developed craft to them but weren't as popular. It was impossible to know if it would continue to be appreciated: yet for all its success, perhaps because of it, "Auerole" filled me with resentment. I was wary of it. It caused me to see a time coming when a choice would have to be made—to remain on the comfortably safe side of the doorway to success, or to pass through it and into a tougher and lot less familiar place. (pp. 140–147)

Lauren Resnick (1987) described higher order thinking as involving the application of multiple criteria, as demanding self-regulation of the thinking process, and as effortful. Taylor's work at the back of the auditorium surely has these hallmarks. What this points out is that assessment is not a post hoc event that occurs once the thinking has quit. Without the discontents, dance— or writing, or science—becomes smug and still.

Taylor was a lucky man: He had a troupe of dancers, his own critical eye, and a very public chorus of reviewers urging him to learn the craft of responding to and revising his own work. But some version of this capacity for self-monitoring and some version of this chorus of opinions is essential to the gradual achievement of good work in any field. As Lampert (1990) suggested, "mathematics develops as a process of 'conscious guessing' about relationships among quantities and shapes, with proof following a zig-zag path starting with conjectures and moving to the examination of premises through the use of counterexamples and refutations" (p. 30). Thus, even in fields like mathematics, if we want students to be able to pursue this "zig-zag path," we have to consider just which assessment practices will protect, nudge, and inform that long course of work.

THE CHARACTER OF FAMILIAR ASSESSMENTS

By now the list of sins ascribed to standardized IQ and achievement testing rivals Don Giovanni's own catalogue of evil deeds. We know, for instance, about how these forms of assessment have characteristically tested for the simplest forms of achievement and made students fluent in artifactual displays of knowledge (e.g., selecting multiple-choice answers) that bear little or no resemblance to the extended performances that underlie the solving of genuine problems or the generation of worthwhile understanding. Most tests consist of simple forms of knowledge display that must be generated quickly—the estimated time per item on most multiple-choice tests is no more than 1 minute. Responses remain at the level of first drafts, there is neither time nor encouragement to revise or reconsider. Given the determination to have individual performance data, no test performance gathers to it any of the distance, leveraging, or robustness that is the result of critique and the consideration that follows it. Achievement is measured through a series of curriculum-independent questions, and scores are handled chiefly as rank-orderings, thus conventional tests promote notions of intelligence that are virtually independent of either effort or growth (Resnick, 1987; Wolf, Bixby, Glenn, & Gardner, 1991). Such tests have also ratified separate standards for different groups of students by providing an all-too-easy way to sort students into Chapter 1 classes, tracks, or gifted and talented programs where materials, teaching styles, and the curriculum simply reinforce the initial classification (Oakes, 1985; Rand Corporation, 1990). Finally, the call for objectivity and secrecy in the design of many tests has insulated most assessments from discussion by teachers, families, and community members (Schwartz & Viator, 1990).

Less often noticed is that tests routinely fail to inform learning. The efficient collection of data about a sample of student performance for an outside audience (school boards or legislatures) has come to dominate over the first audiences and obligations for assessment: to make students and teachers acute critics of the quality of work and able discussants of what should count as excellence. Students rarely receive samples of different levels of performance and the criteria that define them prior to any assessment. It is infrequent that students see their whole graded test booklets again; more typically they receive summary reports of their scores. Few are the occasions when testers (whether teachers, state departments, or independent testing companies) present, never mind discuss, the range of approaches provoked by different questions. Finally, students infrequently have the opportunity to make use of what they learn from earlier performances to inform a second try. In essence, rarely are school assessments the occasion for making public the standards and strategies for doing good work. Yet all that we know regarding the generation of worthwhile work tells us that it requires incubation, revision, collaboration, and the public display of and debate about failure, risk, and excellence (John-Steiner, 1987; Perkins, 1982).

This silence over the achievement of excellence is not uniquely the fault of standardized, multiple-choice tests. The New Jersey state writing test requires students to generate an essay. They are explicitly given time for writing notes. But only the resulting first draft essay is scored. Moreover, once it has been assessed, students get back only their scores. If the score is poor, students can only re-take the test without a critique to use in a second-round attempt. Thus, even in the heart of what has come to be lionized as performance testing, we throw away the opportunity to teach students how to become adept critics of their own work, how to provoke responses from others, and how to make wise use of what they learn from those responses.

THE ECOLOGY OF WISE ASSESSMENT: EXAMPLES FROM THE ARTS AND HUMANITIES

Anthony Burgess, reflecting on the work of making art, once wrote: "Art begins with craft, and there is no art until craft has been mastered. You can't create unless you are willing to subordinate the creative impulse to the constriction of form. But the learning of craft takes time and we all think we are entitled to short-cuts . . . Art is rare and sacred and hard work, and there ought to be a wall of fire around it" (quoted by L. Wolf, personal communication, 1990).

As a part of this "sacred and hard work," artists, musicians, and writers keep sketchbooks, practice scales, and pin-up work for critique. Dance companies hold open rehearsals, ensemble players raise questions about one another's playing, and poets give readings. Books and movies are greeted with a brawling chorus of opinions. Consequently, artists, musicians, writers, and scholars have invented a kind of culture thick with multiple forms of ongoing assessment. When they are interviewed about the place of assessment in their work, these individuals underscore several ways in which it affects and informs them (Wolf, 1989, 1990). First, it is of cardinal importance that the assessment is conducted as a part of ongoing work that the individual sees as meaningful. Assessment matters and is sought when it is integral to polishing an enterprise that is evolving and in which the individual has a keen sense of being an agent. Second, individuals reiterate the place of learning about excellence in the process of coming to know what "counts." In making this point, many stress the place of models, live experts, or peers who they know plot a zigzag course between humility and excellence. Third, these adults mention how critical it is to learn that excellence is composite; that it involves diverse aspects of work including *know-how* (knowledge and craft); *pursuit* (the long-term performance that includes initiation, work, and revision); *force* (style, insight, and innovation), and *accomplishment* (punctuality, effort, being able to work effectively with others, and being curious enough to learn from the work of others). These individuals claim that it is this understanding that permits them to see excellence as achievable, not as a matter of raw talent or lightning flashes of insight. Finally, many artists, writers, and performers insist on the importance of *sustained assessment*, by which they mean the ongoing appraisal of their work over time in a way that allows for both self-assessment, or reflection, and social assessment, or response and critique. In the case of self-assessment, virtually each individual spoke about what one respondent called "being in charge, taking responsibility for standing outside your own work and for deciding when to keep still and when to ask out loud for help." Each could detail moments when that kind of internal reflection had pulled together what might have otherwise escaped as fleeting insights about the work at hand through the use of sketchbooks, journals, or simply notes penciled on scraps of itinerant paper. Equally as often, these individuals recall the provocation of someone who had played the role of a tough outside critic. Thus, emerging from these interviews is the strong confirmation that productive assessment teaches. It combines a kind of unsparing reflection from within and the skill of provoking wise, even ruthless, criticism from without. When these two lines of assessment work effectively in tandem, one spurring and correcting the other, an individual has powerful resources for pushing work beyond where it has coasted, foundered, or lain.

For example, Catherine Hammond, a poet preparing a manuscript for publication, kept religiously numbered sets of sequential drafts in a notebook, with each emergent set of changes highlighted in fluorescent pink. At points of major difficulty or change she made the effort to describe what was happening in her writing in notes that she interleaved with the drafts or scribbled in the margin. Her work allows a look at the interlocking uses of reflection and critique. For instance, early in the genesis of a poem, "The Drone Note of Bee Trees," Hamond (1990) returned to older work that remained unfinished, noting that themes recur, and pushing herself to wonder:

Is the Mrs. Gatz poem
The Jenny Innes poem
The Booth poem

Are they all one poem?
About mutilations

Are they all love poems
About loss?

A second note, commenting on the first, explains: "These handwritten notes mean a couple of things. Probably my computer's not booted up. Or I'm trying to sort out what this is all about. Sometimes I walk around a lot. I'm like a cat here, with a feeding dish. In for a bite or so." It is a similar moment of reflection that reminded Hammond that any poem is a part of a much larger conversation among generations of poems (see Burke, 1974; Scholes, 1990): "At some point I realized that Tito Rios' poem, 'The Good Lunch of Oceans' had influenced 'The Drone Note of Bee Trees' in ways perhaps similar to Robert Lowell's response in 'Skunk Hour' to Elizabeth Bishop's 'The Armadillo.' I added the dedication [to Rios]" (Hammond, 1990). To add the dedication is not mere courtesy, it fills out the poem, reminding readers about the inseparability of reading and writing, the lineage of any poem, and the life history of the particular one they hold in their hands. It also helps her to pin down that lineage, for use in the poem on which she is at work.

All the while that she writes, Hammond monitors, crossing out words, tinkering with punctuation so as to get pause, rush, and flow just right. But even as she spends her craft, she is hanging fire, constantly asking, "Is this good enough, is this going to be an exercise or a poem?" Finally, it comes: "We have ignition. I can tell this is going to be a poem. I call it cracking the poem, breaking the poem. But I usually feel more exhilarated, joyful, when I do that."

Her own second thoughts, the catch in the exhilaration, send her into the arms of a second kind of assessment. She puts her poem in the hands of fellow writers, seeking not so much critique, but response. She wants to know what will they remember of it in 2 weeks, and what passages are dangerously forgettable:

> I take it to a writing friend who tells me the end is boring. That the poem has all this electricity and then duds out. I know he's right. I do this over and over. I keep trying to bury the passion in me and in the work, wash it away—exactly what this poem is about. I'm real uncomfortable being this way. It's why I tried being any kind of writer but a poet. This place I am going to have to go to finish this poem is real scary to me—and embarrassing . . . I have to be careful about trying to hit the ball out of the park. Too big an ending will betray the poem. However, I can't wimp out. What I do is not write for a day. I have put in the request.

It takes time, and experiment, to find out which changes should be swallowed and kept and which are foreign and ill-fitting. The first impulse is often to make the work over in the image legislated by critics: "Norman was worried about the apostrophe to van Gogh [an image at the close of the poem where she speaks of van Gogh 'hacking his head/to a boiled potato.'] I didn't want to lose the boiled potato line so I moved it up."

She lives with the re-ordered poem for several days and then reconsiders: "I'm going to bite the bullet. Despite criticism from Norman about the end section with the sun and hay and stuff, I really have a problem with changing the order. The progression gets totally messed. Oh well."

This conversation between self-assessment and socially generated criticism recurs throughout the notebooks. It is there, not as a distraction, but as a force that pushes work along. When the intuitions in both overlap (as in Catherine and Norman's agreement about the importance of the ending), there is an underscored reason to struggle towards changes, even when those changes involve difficult negotiations between external critique and tightly held intuitions.

The implication for the redesign of current testing is that a major portion of school-based assessment should be conceived as an episode in which students learn how to write (or experiment, or do research) using the power of assessment to push them along the "zigzag path" that Lampert described. In more specific terms, assessment ought to be live: that is, conducted in the face and threat and promise of real work. It ought also to offer clear and very human models of how good work is gradually achieved in a process that may involve revision, brutal cutting, harsh critique, and blind alleys. Also, assessment must take the form of a series of iterative episodes of work followed by time for personal reflection and the gathering of responses from peers, mentors, and outside judges. In this way, it should allow an individual ways and time for making use of that chorus of opinion so as to make it possible to decide what in the criticism is apt, and what misses the mark. Finally, and far from incidentally, productive forms of assessment permit an individual to plow the fruits of that critique and reflection back into his or her final response.

This kind of assessment would complicate the reform of testing vastly—it would demand that we do much more than turn our attention to performance assessments. We would have to redesign the entire envelope of assessment, replacing singular tests with extended, iterative processes, agreeing that we are interested in what students produce when they are given access to models, criticism, and the option to revise. But only if we go that distance will the skills of self-appraisal and critical conversation belong to more than a few skilled and determined adults.

DO STUDENTS HAVE WHAT IT TAKES? EVIDENCE FROM METACOGNITIVE RESEARCH

William James' insistence on the "I" and the "me" is actually only one sample of a new characterization of human mind that emerged at the turn of the century. Across disciplines as diverse as philosophy, poetry, and neurology, the new argument was that the mind is naturally fractured. Charcot, Freud, and Janet wrote of the unconscious and the conscious mind. The poet Rimbaud investigated the experience of dreams in which sleepers observed themselves in acts that were both imagined and experienced, writing the curiously 20th-century phrase, "*on me pense*" (loosely translated "One is aware of me"). None of these writers had assessment in mind, yet they effectively picked out just that quality of doing and observing, of being in two places at once, that makes it possible either to reflect on ongoing work or to understand what it is that someone else has to say about one's own work.

In the ensuing 100 years, these writers' hunches about the fundamental nature of the ability to be "in two places at once" have been borne out. Research on 2-year-olds shows that they can act and then judge and be ashamed or pleased about their own actions (Kagan, 1982). As they play with small toys, 3-year-olds can slip in and out of different voices, at one moment offering a story, and then stepping out of the imagined scene to comment, "No, no, pretend that didn't happen." Four-year-olds are keenly aware that people have minds that perform many distinct acts: remembering, thinking, dreaming, pretending, and believing. Even then, children understand the possibility of false beliefs—the recognition that one can believe fervently, but be deceived. This is an essential element in being able to generate self-criticism that is based on the realization that something you once thought of as grand is, on second thought, closer to ordinary. Thus, the capacity for reflection and for changing one's appraisal of something as apparently immaterial as thoughts is an early-emerging, and in that sense basic, human capacity.

Consequently, self-assessment is open to students at all levels. It does not wait for twelfth grade, nor does it depend on being gifted. It does, however, demand time and invitation. By way of example, consider what happens when a student in a mixed class of ninth and tenth graders is asked to keep a journal while he reads Primo Levi's *Moments of Reprieve*, an account of life in a German prisoner-of-war camp. What follows here is the evolution of that student's thought about a particular vignette, "The Last Christmas of the War," a sketch in which Levi describes what happened when he received a package of holiday food in the midst of the starvation of a camp (Wolf, 1988).

The student begins by reading independently and taking notes in his journal, recording what surprises, puzzles, or amuses him. The point of the journal is to make him alert to the pulse and pattern of his responses as a reader. In this first pass, the student writes a kind of patchwork of comments that includes everything from his reactions to characters to his reactions to reading nonfiction. No one thing stands out as central, consuming, or pointed:

The Last Christmas
Levi is smart, smart enough not to get killed. A survivor even when he was still in the camp.

True friends, him and Alberto, don't betray each other/wiling to sacrifice for each other.

Breaking stereotypes—the German girl who gave them food for fixing her bike wasn't an awful German. Within a couple million people there's bound to be some good.

History vs. story: I took a course on the Holocaust and it was about the whole thing, this is about one moment. You get detail from the story. You get someone's feelings.

Later, having read more, and having talked about the sketches, the student goes back to his original comments on "The Last Christmas of the War." Reading over them, he finds a thread that interests him, a kind of path through the essay. He writes a note in the margin: "something about the details under everything . . ." This barely held idea crystallizes as he writes some additional comments about his original observations:

The Last Christmas
I am used to hearing about the Holocaust as a gory event, through adult eyes which are concerned more with the allies [*sic*] success than with everyday events. Here you see the war through tiny details. He writes about all the thinking and planning that goes into rationing out a week's supply of candy. The war is larger due to these tiny things. He makes you see this awful mix. Like when he takes off his hat to salute, trying not to lose the cookie crumbs in it.

At this point the student has an idea about the particular sense he can or wants to make out of "The Last Christmas." Of all the various observations that showed up in his original entries, it is this idea of human specifics that he wants to track down.

But he isn't working alone. His journal shuttles back and forth between him and his teacher, who takes an important role in questioning and probing what is emerging as an idea. The student writes the first draft of a paper that is, in many ways, a catalog of sharply observed moments framed by the student's understanding of the power of the particular to be human:

> Levi expresses his feelings through seemingly trivial details. He twists these trivial details into much bigger ideas and conclutions [sic]. He selects unhappy memories and uses them to teach others.

In the margins of this draft, the teacher raises a pointed question to prompt further thought:

> Why do all these details matter? What happens because the points are made with details?

In the second draft of the paper, the student answers:

> Primo Levi is odd among camp survivors. Even though he lived through the mud and the hunger and the fear, he doesn't blame anyone. His stories are of his experiences rather than his abuses. His stories are not meant as revenge for the past. Insted [sic] he uses the little details of his memories to uncover the human sense in bad things.

The student is reading, not as a consumer, but as a writer—someone who understands that effects are the result of choices. He knows that the details have been set out deliberately like a trail into the narrative. The details matter because they trace a map of effort, cause, and hope onto the barren face of camp life. The student has learned some history, he may have picked up something about what re-reading can yield, but chiefly he has learned how to turn first-run curiosity into inquiry, and how to drive inquiry home to understanding. Just as for the poet Catherine Hammond, this requires that a reader have time, the right to re-enter work, and the dialectic of reflection and response.

Three questions arise from these examples of a writer and a reader. The first is whether or not we will come around to thinking about assessments as including more than the cold-start, first-draft performances we have traditionally seen as the "right" measures of student ability. The second is whether or not we can harness the heat and light that assessment generates to underscore, or even to teach, the place of reflection and critical response in the generation of a quality performance. The third is whether or not we want to or can find ways to assess students' understanding of reflection and response as a part of their competence in reading, writing, or doing science.

ASSESSMENTS AS EPISODES OF LEARNING

To pursue these ideas, researchers from Harvard Project Zero, Educational Testing Service, and the Pittsburgh public schools have collaborated on a project designed to extend the most worthwhile assessment practices in the arts and humanities to urban public school classrooms. The assessments were designed to monitor and report on what students learned working on sustained projects focused on the "big ideas" in a range of disciplines. For instance, students worked for several weeks on reading, scene writing, casting, and directing activities that led, eventually, towards their understanding of drama as performance, rather than text. Other students spent a semester learning to compose and notate original songs, discussing how performers inevitably have to re-realize a score as music (Winner, in press; Wolf & Pistone, 1992). Along with these practices, teachers instituted a range of ways of encouraging reflection: classroom discussion of works in progress, journals, and the formation of a portfolio of representative works. Equally, their classrooms came to include multiple forms of critical response: peer editing, exhibitions, and portfolio reviews by outside readers.

The work of the collaborative was designed to try to find answers to the preceding questions about assessments as occasions for learning. First, we were interested in developing modes of assessment that would, in their very structure, focus on work that was enhanced by occasions of reflection and critique. Second, we believed that these modes of assessment might provide a diverse range of students with opportunities to learn the skills of reflection and critique and, in that way, permit more students to exhibit proficiency. In this light, we were committed to investigating the idea that teachers participating in these forms of assessment would develop the kinds of critical judgment that would permit them to see, value, and nurture possibilities in the work of students from a range of backgrounds and exhibiting varying levels of school achievement. Finally, we wanted to design assessments that provided information, not just about final products, but also about students' capacity to take a work from first draft to finished piece. In this way, we were interested in a form of dynamic assessment that would yield information about students' entry level of performance and their performance when they had the scaffolding provided by models, consultation, resources, and their own option to appraise and re-enter a project. Thus, we wanted assessments that provided a view of student achievement that encompassed development (or longitudinal growth) as well as a clear reading of where a student's work stood in relation to the standards of excellence in a particular field.

The chief result has been the development of what has come to be called the *process-portfolio*. Based on forms of portfolio work common in the visual arts and extended in recent years by any number of writing projects, process-portfolios are distinguished by a constellation of four significant characteristics: (a) the conception of assessment as a part of a larger episode of learning; (b) the creation of a portfolio culture, (c) the scaffolding of reflective and critical capacities; and finally, (d) the inclusion of reflection and response as part of what assessments should examine.

The first hallmark of a process-portfolio is the way in which ongoing assessment is viewed as a part of learning. Students regularly return to earlier works to revise or make comparisons with later ones. Students use the samples of their own work to reflect on the changing nature of their own standards. Having chosen and reflected on one comparison of satisfying and unsatisfying pieces, at a later date they are invited to reassess and change or preserve that earlier choice. This process of selecting and shaping a representative collection of work yields a kind of autobiographical understanding that includes knowledge of past change and the prospect of future development. Here, one eighth-grade student writes an entry in which his own development as a writer becomes clear:

> When I look back, (my beginning poems) were very basic. In the beginning they were all rhymed haiku because that is all I knew about. . . . Then I experimented with going more with the feelings or ideas . . . don't kill yourself going over the rhymes, go with what you feel. I did that for two months. Then— that's now—I started compacting them, shortening them to make deeper meaning. I could see that it would make more of a point, so I washed out the "the's" and "and's" and "if's." Now I am working on something different, sort of the morals. Like if one day my mom's car broke down, I might write that night about how a fish got caught, or the feeling of not being able to swim. I am not trying to write like just how I feel, but metaphors, I think you call them. (Wolf, 1987, p. 21)

As a part of this sequence, students may continue to craft a particular work, expanding and revising it. Often, such continued revision leads to insight about the very nature of writing. For example, as she talks about finishing an essay on her sister's death, a high school senior comments that she would have "about 10 more drafts." When asked why so many, she explains:

> **Student**: Well, I realize I have to put more of when she is well into the story. Because otherwise all you do is see her when she is sick and then you would say to yourself, "Why is it a terrible thing that she died"? You need the contrast of what came before to really appreciate it. And what comes after when I could write about how we all changed—I think me and my sister changed, and my mother and father changed—I would put in how she loved going out with her friends and what she did and what she used to say. And exact memories like what we used to do at Christmas, in the morning. And how our house was so different after she died. That's the only way the person could really see what I lost. You need the comparison.

Interviewer: Would you tell it just like that, in order: first she was well, then she got sick, she struggled and died, and then the family changed?

Student: All I know is that I could do it lots of different ways. Like start at the beginning. Or start in the middle of when she is sick and work backwards to before and ahead to when she is really dying and couldn't go outside even any more.

Interviewer: So you don't imagine sticking to what happened in the order it happened?

Student: No, I think the point is to see which way works. I mean I would have to choose the way that I could do, and the way that made it clear what I was trying to say about her life.

Interviewer: Well, but since it really happened isn't that the one way to tell it?

Student: Well, no, not really, it's up to me. I might like working back and forth to the memories. That might work better. I would really have to try it to see. (Holt, 1990, p. 5)

This life history can be told "lots of different ways." The facts here are not self-evident; their resonance, acceptance, and comprehension depends on the author's creative manipulation and insight. Here she can see that it makes a difference if the reader knows what her sister was like before her illness ("You need the contrast . . ."). She realizes that it will be different if told chronologically or as a memoir or as a movement back and forth in time. No, the facts do not speak for themselves. Order alters meaning. It conveys to the reader what's important and what is not. To make sense, the narrative must have a point, so the correct way to represent the facts of that narrative is not through some slavish fidelity to their chronological order. With the time to re-enter the work and to reflect, the writer realizes that the correct way is the one that will make it clear "what I was trying to say about her life" (Holt, 1990, pp. 2–5).

The second distinguishing feature of process-portfolio work is that this work takes place in a *portfolio culture*, that is, a setting in which there is frequent and public discussion about what makes for good work and a clear sense that good work takes a long time to emerge. Students have access to the criteria that will be used to score their work and those criteria are explained, even debated. Students also have access to samples of work that have been scored and commented on. The point is to provide students with a clear sense for the multidimensional nature of good work: that it involves much more than neatness, length, or correct grammar. They learn something about the place of qualities like the ability to pose an interesting problem, to learn from and comment on someone else's work, or to revise an earlier draft.

The third feature of process-portfolio work is the way in which it functions to help students formulate a reflective autobiography of themselves as learners. Process-portfolios are longitudinal collections of work that contain much in addition to the range of finished works entered into traditional portfolios. They may contain an actual autobiography of the writer that stresses the language resources that the individual brings to writing. Also present are what we call "biographies of a work": documentation of the various stages of development of a text. When collected at diverse points, these biographies permit a longitudinal look at a student's changing control of the processes for shaping a final piece. In addition, students often keep journals and write reflections about their work. They include comments or comparisons between pieces that are satisfying and unsatisfying or discussions of pieces in which they have learned something about the connections between usually separate activities, such as reading and writing (Camp, 1990a, 1990b; Seidel & Zessoules, 1990; Winner, in press). The process-portfolios are live, rather than archival; they are constantly in use and under revision. Students are regularly asked to re-enter the stream of their work, reflecting on how they have changed as writers, comparing what were once their best works with more current selections, or returning to earlier works to revise them in the light of new understandings. In all of these ways, students are encouraged to make use of criticism and reflection to improve their skills and understandings (Brewer, 1990; California Assessment Program, 1990a, 1990b).

Table 10.1 contains one highly schematized outline for the generation and use of process-portfolios in writing. (It is important to understand, however, that whereas philosophies and basic procedures are common, the specific steps vary considerably from class to class.) What this schematization highlights is the ongoing nature of assessment and the ways in which students are helped to become adept at using their own reflections, as well as the response from other readers, to inform their work. Nowhere is this more evident than in the final selection of work for the process-portfolio. Part way through the semester or year, students compile a draft of the final contents. They collect a chorus of opinions around that portrait of themselves as writers, meaning that they collect critical readings of their work from their teacher, peers, and a parent or another adult (Howard, 1990). They are given time and help in considering what sense to make of the critiques they have received. They are encouraged to consider what their own reflections add to that chorus—that is, to entertain the possibility of not swallowing all suggestions whole. Near the close of a semester or year, students make a final selection of biographies, reflections, and final pieces that can function as the basis for a course grade, a document they can pass to introduce themselves to their teacher the following year, or the data for district-wide evaluation of the writing program and the writing achievement of students (Camp, 1990a, 1990b; Howard, 1990; Wolf, 1989b).

TABLE 10.1
An Outline for Generating a Process-Portfolio

1. *Autobiography of a writer:* Students write or talk about the language resources they bring to writing, what they already know about writing, what kinds of resources they have as writers (e.g., memory, reading, knowledge of another language, etc.).

*2. *Begin chronological collection of writing:* Students assume responsibility for building a developmentally organized sample of their work. In that sample, students routinely collect notes, drafts, reflections, and final versions.

*3. *Early experiences with explicit response and reflection:* Students are given class time as well as guided instruction in appraising their work. This takes the form of questions that students can apply to their writing. Sample reflections might include:

- Choose a satisfying and unsatisfying piece of work and comment on what makes them different.
- Select and comment on a piece in which you learned something as a writer.
- Choose a piece you love and explain what you would still like to change in it.

The social side of appraisal begins with response, rather than critique, from other readers (peers, teachers). In these responses, readers pick out for students what they find memorable or worth pursuit in their pieces. Readers also indicate moments where they loose the thread, are puzzled, or disinterested.

*4. *Continue chronological collection:* Students return to the work of forming a longitudinal sample of their work.

*5. *Later experiences with reflection:* In these experiences, young writers begin to look across their works, asking questions about how they are changing as writers.

(This cycle of writing experience followed by reflection and response may recur any number of times throughout the semester or year.)

6. *Research:* Students use the materials of their own writing folders to ask questions about writing. Such questions might include:

- Compare the writing you do in two different classes; how is it different?
- What is different about the writing that you do inside and outside of school?

7. *Family review of writing folders:* Students take their writing folders home, presenting them to a member of the family. Families read and respond, writing or recording comments.

*8. *Initial creation of a process-portfolio:* Students make a selection from the entire corpus of work available to them in their writing folders in an effort to present the most effective picture of themselves as writers. They use the criteria for scoring their process-portfolios to guide them, looking for evidence of their growth as a writer, their control of a range of different types of writing, and so on.

*9. *Review of the process-portfolio:* Students and teachers review the portfolio, discussing where it is successful and where it is still in need of work. Teachers may suggest the inclusion of different pieces of work, or pieces of work that could be revised.

(Continued)

TABLE 10.1
Continued

---

*10. *Revision of the process-portfolio:* Students consider the comments on their portfolios, work on the portfolios, and submit them in their final form.

*11. *Process-portfolio assessment:* Teachers, acting as scorers, read the portfolios, generating profiles (cf. the criteria in Fig. 10.1). These data are returned to students, used to evaluate the health of the writing program in the schools, and provide a basis for reports of student writing achievement in the district.

Note. These materials were developed in close collaboration with a group of teachers and administrators in Pittsburgh, as well as colleagues Roberta Camp, Steve Seidel, and Rieneke Zessoules.
*Starred items are of major importance. Unmarked items are optional. Individual teachers and students can make additions to this process.

Process-portfolios are promising forms of assessment in several ways. Like traditional portfolios, they sample the range of a student's writing, not merely a single performance. In addition, they hold open the option of indexing development or growth, in addition to achievement. But perhaps more significantly, they are a form of assessment that teaches skills that schools have typically kept implicit. These are the metacognitive skills of judging the sufficiency and quality of one's own work and developing strategies for improvement (Brown, 1984, 1988; Brown & Palincsar, 1986; Hatano, 1982). The technology of the process-portfolios makes the body of a student's work into a palpable display that affords frank and informed conversations.

As part of the process-portfolio process, the targets of assessment have also shifted. Teachers and students alike now think about writing performance as including much more than the finished product. They have expanded their notions of the dimensions of writing skill to include reflection and critique, as well as the resulting evidence of development. A draft of the summary sheet that students and teachers use in appraising process-portfolios is reprinted in Fig. 10.1.

IMPLICATIONS FOR LARGE-SCALE ASSESSMENTS

It is crucial that the sorts of access to understanding standards and strategies provided by process-portfolios find their way into the assessments that districts, states, and perhaps even the nation will use to certify students and evaluate schools. Quite simply, if these skills are not recognized as worthy of scrutiny and scoring, they will not be widely taught. If they are not widely taught, they become the sole and private property of the few who pick them up in advanced courses or in reading and redrafting under some parent's eagle eye. They become, not a part of an explicit and public curriculum, but

PORTFOLIO EXIT ASSESSMENT

Student writer_____ Grade_____

Teacher_____ School_____

The contents of this student's portfolio demonstrate:
(Please check where appropriate)

	Significant Evidence Present	Satisfactory Evidence Present	Some Evidence Present	Little Evidence Present
Accomplishment in writing	____	____	____	____

- setting and meeting worthwhile challenges
- establishing and maintaining purpose
- use of the techniques and choices of the genre
- organization, development, use of detail
- control of conventions, vocabulary, sentence structure
- awareness of the needs of the audience
- use of language, sound, images, tone, voice
- humor, metaphor, playfulness

Use of processes and resources for writing	____	____	____	____

- awareness of strategies and processes for writing
- use of processes: prewriting, drafting, revision
- awareness of features important to writing
- ability to see strengths and opportunities in own and others' writing
- ability to describe what one sees and knows about writing
- use of the classroom social context for writing
- use of available experience and resources
  (one's own, the school's, the community's)

Development as a writer	____	____	____	____

- progress from early to late pieces, growth, development
- increased understanding of features and options important to writing
- engagement with writing, investment, pursuit
- use of writing for different purpose, genres, and audiences
- sense of self as a writer, achievements and purposes as a writer
- personal criteria and standards for writing

This student's strengths in writing include:

This student's developmental needs as a writer include:

FIG. 10.1.   Draft of criteria for assessing process-portfolios.

230

an implicit set of expectations that can be used to sort the gifted from the average and the at-risk student.

With these issues in mind, researchers at Performance Assessment Collaborative for Education at the Harvard Graduate School of Education have begun to design assessments that carry the demand for reflection, response, and re-drafting. These assessments are intended to provide useful data about essential understandings in the arts and humanities. They are meant to work at a district, state, or even a regional level. Consequently, the effort has been to carry many characteristics of process-portfolio work over into the necessarily more compact format of widely applicable performance assessments.

Throughout this project we have worked on creating assessments that will underscore how quality work evolves over time, results in part from the use of reflection and critique, and often demands re-entry. Because assessments with this character inevitably take time, we have sought to design integrated assessments, ones that examine multiple understandings at once. At the same time, we have taken on the demand to formulate assessments in which wide numbers of students can participate and potentially do well—without in any sense lowering standards. That has meant providing a range of ways in which students can exhibit their knowledge, including visual and oral presentations. It has also meant finding materials that relate to the diversity of students in public schools, without dodging the issue that school is a place to learn about things you didn't already know.

The particular example sketched here is an assessment in American history. It is an assessment that focuses on the Reconstruction period and the question of whether or not the freed people were given anything like the resources they needed in order to take up their newly offered civil rights. The assessment has been developed for use as one of several performance assessments in American history, which is only one section of a much larger set of social studies assessments. It could be administered at the end of the required American history course or as part of a series of history projects adding up to a final exit credential in history. It might be used as a part of district, state, or national level assessments of programs of student achievement (Resnick & Resnick, 1990).

The assessment grows out of an essay on learning in history by Tom Holt, an American historian. In that essay, *Thinking Historically*, Holt reflected on how students might be welcomed into the process of actually doing, rather than merely memorizing history (Holt, 1990). In particular, he argued that students must learn how to raise questions about the materials they confront. He made the point that interrogation is most likely to arise when students have in their hands not the univocal, averaged, and apparently complete accounts of textbooks, but the multivocal, situated, and clearly partial visions that primary sources such as letters, diaries, or theatre posters offer. Finally, he suggested that the originality of history lies in opening up new veins in the evidence. This happens, he suggested, only when students (or historians) enter the implied lives of other places and eras fully—that is, with imagination. Consequently, the assessment has been framed to examine a cluster of related abilities: the capacity to read and enter primary source materials; the ability to formulate a point of view about the evidence contained therein; and the ability to present this point of view persuasively.

Although this assessment occurs in a compact period of time (approximately a week), it preserves many of the features of the more extended portfolio work: the agency of students; the emphasis on *the biography of effort* that underlies good work; and time for personal reflection, response from others, and the option to integrate that response. In that sense, it is also an assessment of students' ability to develop an initial idea through collaboration, reflection, critique, and re-drafting.

The project is also an effort to move towards a more authentic display of understanding than the usual series of questions on traditional tests. In it students take on the responsibilities of a historical museum curator who must find both visual and textual ways of portraying a particular vision of the Reconstruction period to a diverse audience. In this way, it is based on a model of expert knowledge as it is practiced and applied by historians.

The whole is structured into three episodes, each designed to provide a different kind of data about students' historical understanding. In the first episode (Day 1), students are introduced to the project. They read a short document that reminds them of the major dimensions and events of the Reconstruction period. Then they look at a videotape with segments taken from other history exhibitions or displays (e.g., the use of letters in the 1990 public television series on the Civil War). Students and teachers discuss the way in which an exhibition of this kind is an argument—a way of presenting data so that it affects an audience in a particular manner. They examine the video samples as instances of strong performances, examining how historical facts, the cracking of stereotypes, and powerful modes of presentation are used. Thus, the focus of Day 1 is to introduce students not only to their assignment but to the dimensions of strong work and the idea of an expert performance.

Day 2 provides a look at students' entry-level understanding, at the same time that it also introduces them to working with primary source documents. Students listen to a taped, dramatic reading of a series of short, personal documents, such as letters that freed people who went North wrote home to relatives or even former owners. Students produce a reader's journal (akin to that of the student reading Primo Levi), containing a set of initial responses to these documents. Based on these readings, students draft a short paragraph about what they would like their exhibition to show. Figure 10-2 contains a sample document, a letter written home to a former owner by a freed

To My Old Master, Colonel, P. H. Anderson
Big Spring, Tennessee

Sir: I got your letter and was glad to find you had not forgotten Jourdon, and that you
wanted me to come back and live with you again, promising to do better for me than
anyone else can. I have often felt uneasy about you... I thought the Yankees would have
hung you long before this for harboring Rebs they found at your house...Although you
shot at me twice before I left you, I did not want to hear of your being hurt, and am glad
you are still living...

[handwritten: ?]

I am doing tolerably well here; I get $25 a month, with victuals and clothing; have a
comfortable home here for Mandy (the folks her call her Mrs. Anderson), and the children,
Milly, Jane and Grundy, go to school and are learning well....

[handwritten: NEW]

As to my freedom, which you say I can have, there is nothing to be gained on that score, as
I got my free papers in 1864....Mandy says she would be afraid to go back without some
proof that you are sincerely disposed to treat us justly and kindly -- and we have concluded
to test your sincerity by asking you to send us our wages for the time we served you. This
will make us forget and forgive old scores, and rely on your justice and friendship in the
future. At $25 a month for me, and $2 a week for Mandy, our earnings would amount to
$11, 680. Add to this the interest for the time our wages have been kept back and deduct
what you paid for our clothing and three doctor's visits for me, and pulling a tooth for
Mandy, and the balance will show what we are in justice entitled to. Please send the money
by Adams Express...We trust the good Maker has opened your eyes to the wrongs which
you and your fathers have done to me and my fathers in making us toil for you for
generations without recompense...Surely there will be a day of reckoning for those who
defraud the laborer of his hire.

[handwritten: 25-2 / NO / FAIR]

[handwritten: FANCY? / HOW?]

In answering this letter please state if there would be any safety for my Milly and Jane,
who are now grown up and both good-looking girls...You will also please state if there
are any schools opened for the colored children in your neighborhood, the great desire of
my life now is to give my children an education, and have them from virtuous habits.

[handwritten: JOKE / REEL?]

P. S. Say howdy to George Carter, and thank him for taking the pistol from you when you
were shooting at me.

From your old servant,

Jourdan Anderson

FIG. 10.2. Sample document with student notes (from *A Collection of Reconstruction Era Documents* collected by K. Jennings, unpublished manuscript).

man who traveled north. On this document a student has made comments as she listened to the taped reading. Even though the margin notes are short and contain spelling and arithmetic errors, they are indicative of the kinds of critical insights that can be generated at this point in the assessment, even by students who are struggling with reading and writing. This particular student, for example, is aware that despite the Emancipation Proclamation, men and women are hardly equal (cf. her note beside the comments on salaries). She also attends to the document closely enough to wonder whether its sometimes exaggerated tone indicates that it might not be "reel." Students' entries serve to document their skills at the opening, or the base-line moment, of the assessment. These initial documents become the first entry in a brief portfolio of work to be assessed by teacher-readers at a later date.

A second episode, lasting 3 days, provides information on students' performance in group settings. On Day 3, students work in small groups of approximately four, discussing what they have noticed about the documents and working on drawing inferences about the nature of the Reconstruction period. They make notes to keep track of questions that arise for which they want the answer. Individual students write additional insights into the journals they began earlier. Based on this work, students talk about what it takes to read a primary source document well and what it is to write about it powerfully. In this phase of their work, they have access to resources including readings on the Civil War and Reconstruction periods from a variety of viewpoints and an additional set of photographs and ephemera from the Reconstruction period.

On Day 4, students are asked to construct a basic plan for their exhibition. As they work, each group is asked to generate a collection of work concerning the exhibition they would propose: a title, a sketch, or list showing the sequence and grouping of items with a short rationale for that particular design; interpretive labels for at least four of what they take to be major pieces in the exhibition; and notes indicating which of the graphic images will be used to document or underscore the point of the exhibition.

On Day 5, groups make oral presentations about their exhibitions, taking critical questions and suggestions from the floor. This segment of work yields assessments of the products that groups of students generate, with each student in a group receiving the same score as others. Individual students take notes on revisions they would want to make, based on the questions they get and the other presentations they hear.

In a third episode (homework, or Day 6 of class time), students work individually, still in the role of the curator. This time, however, they are asked to revise the group's work, based on the critique received and their own reflections. As evidence of this rethinking of the exhibition, individual students submit the text for an introductory panel to accompany the exhibition, as well a revised set of labels and sequence of presentation. In this period of work, students continue to have access to a wide range of historical resources that represents a diversity of opinion on the Reconstruction. This final segment yields assessment information about how individual students perform, given the benefit of resources, social interaction, and the time to develop thoughtful responses.

As suggested previously, teachers who have helped to outline this assessment hope that it can be used to examine multiple dimensions of historical understanding: *embedded accuracy* (e.g., the ability to use the facts of history in the service of forming a larger historical argument); *forceful reading* (e.g., the ability not only to comprehend, but to enter the era and lives portrayed in primary source materials); *the orchestration of multiple sources of evidence* (e.g., the ability to research and use primary and secondary sources, interviews, artifacts, etc.); *argument and point of view* (e.g., the ability to form an interpretation of the data and to argue for it powerfully); *the capacity to reconsider stereotypes and received views* (e.g., the capacity to get under the skin of the customary characterizations of slaves, slave-owners, the North, the South, etc.); and *power* (e.g., the ability to use the resources of language, visual images, and oral delivery to make their points compelling). These dimensions of performance are examined in the context of both individual work and group collaborations.

This kind of assessment uproots some of our oldest and deepest habits. First, there is the conception of assessment as a terminal episode, something that follows after, rather than informs, ongoing work. Here, we have deliberately blurred the borders between instruction and assessment, using episodes of ongoing assessment to feed later segments of work. This is dramatically different from the cold-start, first draft performances we have traditionally used in schools.

Second, these forms of assessment challenge our traditional preference for highly individualistic approaches that avoid the noise and support of collaboration or the use of tools and resources. In this new view, students are working together, looking over one another's shoulders, and consulting what other people have already had to say about the Reconstruction period. In so doing, we are turning away from sealed test booklets and turning toward the traditions of dynamic assessment inspired by much more social notions of mind (Hatano, 1982; Luria, 1976; Vygotsky, 1962).

Third, we are lessening the concern for test security and secrecy (Schwartz & Viator, 1990). Nothing like that really survives in this assessment. Questions and tasks, as well as the standards of strong performance, are made public. But as we move in this direction, there will be additional questions. We have to think about publishing sample work and scoring rubrics ahead of time. In this light, we will have to do away with the destructive tradition of different standards for different students that is so much a part of our practice of sorting students into distinct tracks. We will have to consider how students in general math, bilingual students, or dyslexic individuals can participate without either being handicapped or being allowed to slip through the cracks. Incipient in this proposal is the possibility that evaluators will be confronted with a wider range of work that varies in values, outlook, or rhetorical approach. This range will raise the challenge of scoring systems that can acknowledge varieties of excellence, rather than a homogenized high standard.

Such assessment also challenges the conventional psychometrics that we have come to rely on for recording, presenting, and aggregating information on student or school performances. For instance, the history task described here requires multidimensional or profile scoring to capture differences in students' control of relevant historical information, their capacity to formulate arguments, and the power of their presentations. Such tasks also carry the obligation to think about models that include individual and group performance, as well as differences in students' unsupported and supported performances.

Finally, we are running at odds with the urge to stay with machine-storable, single-sitting assessments for the sake of efficiency, cost, and apparent objectivity. The new assessment forms are costly and require a level of teacher judgment that we have systematically tried to circumvent. The wager is that once we internalize the costs and demands of such assessments, they will prove their worth: They will enhance student performance, they will act as a form of professional development for teachers, and they will promote renewed confidence in public schools as institutions where standards can be promulgated and pursued.

CONCLUSION

Despite a decade of educational reform leading to many statutes and considerable mandatory statewide testing in 47 states, little has changed in schools. There are stricter attendance rules, minimum grades required for participation in extracurricular activities, stricter conduct rules, longer school days, more competency testing, more homework, better teacher pay, and a longer school year. At the same time, there are no gains in reading proficiency, little improvement in mathematics, no improvement in civics, and no progress in writing skills (Hechinger, 1990). Thus, one resounding lesson of this early wave of efforts is that regulation is not the same as deep reform.

If genuine school reform is to take root, working lasting changes in student achievement, it must reach the most fundamental constituents of education. We will have to move from a curriculum of basic skills to one that privileges thoughtfulness and values. We must develop a corps of professionally skilled teachers sensitive to the potentials of a diverse school population.

And finally, we must undo those practices like standardized testing that have ratified a curriculum of minimum skills and provided the rationale for practices like tracking, which make it acceptable to offer the privileged access to knowledge and the poor access only to schooling.

Thus, it is essential to invent a new vision of student assessment as a productive force in American education. In essence, we need a major transition from testing to assessment. This transition is and will continue to be complex. It entails not one, but two, goals. The first is to replace the technology of standardized testing with the technologies of performance assessment (i.e., ways of directly assessing whether students have the strategies and the essential understandings of a domain like physics or a critical skill such as writing). Standardized testing was designed to be a post-hoc episode of measurement, independent of the curriculum, serving chiefly the purposes of certification and accountability. Assessment is meant to be an episode in which both students and teachers learn about the standards of good work and how to achieve them. If well designed, it should inform learning and program design, as well as provide measures of accountability. As such, it is meant to grow out of the curriculum and to involve human judgments about what constitutes failure, competence, and excellence. Consequently, assessment inevitably involves debate.

Through the civil rights reforms of the 1950s and 1960s, many students previously excluded from integrated and fully funded schooling gained access. In the ensuing 30 years we have made very gradual progress toward ensuring that *all* children have access to the basic skills of arithmetic, reading, and writing. However, there are still chronic problems of access. Now the issue is access to what Goodlad has termed *understanding*, as opposed to mere *schooling*. Put plainly, anyone is welcome to learn to add, but few are ushered into Algebra 1 (Goodlad & Keating, 1990).

Much the same might be said about standards, the second goal. Everyone has access to the standards of punctuality, neatness, and correctness. But we leave implicit other, fiercer, and more powerful standards—what it takes to write a powerful essay, to do science, or to develop new interpretations as a historian. What makes for an A, or a pass, is not debated in most classrooms. Few high school or middle school students know if there are varieties of excellence or whether the only route is to come up with a perfect match to the answer key. Equally few students are forced to become agents in appraising their own work. But if we believe Paul Taylor and Catherine Hammond, knowledge of standards, the capacity to apply them, and the ability to provoke and use criticism selectively, are absolute ingredients in the generation of strong work. To be kept or deemed ignorant of these skills is to be, silently and legally, but very effectively, crippled and walled out (Michaels & O'Connor, 1990). In this light, assessment reform is not just a technical nicety. It is about providing access to standards and the routes to their attainment.

But the same romance with technology that ushered in standardized and machine-scorable tests in the early 20th century could have a second, equally devastating, chapter. Currently, in the context of American schools, changes in assessment are being heralded as the levers for a wide spectrum of changes: substantial revisions in the curriculum, the professionalization of teaching, and a transition from a conception of schooling based on minimum competency to one informed by considerably higher standards of achievement for all students. As a result, assessment has become not an end, but a major means, in a very high-stakes effort to change American public schooling. It is frankly doubtful whether even the best of assessment programs can work such extensive changes. Assessment cannot countermand the effects of poverty, racism, and a long history of the neglect of schools. It is at best an exponent of, not a substitute for, a system of values. Assessments can insist and model, but not create, wise and fair forms of education.

ACKNOWLEDGMENTS

The research reported here was funded through a grant from the School Reform Program of the Rockefeller Foundation. Much of the student work was collected during a project that was supported by the Office of Academic Affairs at the College Board. It was informed by comments from Sylvia T. Johnson and the other participants at the original conference and grows out of prolonged collaboration with colleagues: Roberta Camp, JoAnn Doran, JoAnne Eresh, Kathy Howard, Steve Seidel, and Rieneke Zessoules.

REFERENCES

Baron, J. (1990, July). *Blurring the edges between instruction and assessment.* Paper presented at the Institute on New Modes of Assessment, Harvard University, Cambridge, MA.

Brewer, R. (1990, July). *The development of portfolios in writing and mathematics for statewide assessment in Vermont.* Paper presented at the Institute on New Modes of Assessment, Harvard University, Cambridge, MA.

Brown, A. L., & Palincsar, S. (1986). *Guided, cooperative learning and individual knowledge acquisition* (Tech. Rep. No. 372). Champaign, IL: Center for the Study of Reading.

Brown, A. S. (1984). The role of strategic memory in retardates' memory. In N. R. Ellis (Ed.), *International Review of Research in Mental Retardation* (Vol. 7, pp. 55–108). New York: Academic Press.

Brown, A. S. (1988). Motivation to learn and understand: On taking charge of one's own learning. *Cognition and Instruction, 5,* 311–321.

Burke, K. (1974). *A philosophy of literary form.* Berkeley, CA: University of California Press.

CAP (California Assessment Program) (1990a). *The California assessment program: A position paper on testing and instruction.* Sacramento, CA: Author.

CAP (California Assessment Program) (1990b). *Guidelines for the mathematics portfolios.* Sacramento, CA: Author.

Camp, R. (1990a). *Arts PROPEL: Ideas for stimulating reflection.* Unpublished manuscript, Educational Testing Service.

Camp, R. (1990b). Thinking together about portfolios. *The Quarterly of the National Writing Project and the Center for the Study of Writing, 12*(2), 8–14, 27.

Cheney, L. (1991). *Tyrannical machines.* Washington, DC: The National Endowment for the Humanities.

Goodlad, J., & Keating, P. (1990). *Access to knowledge.* New York: The College Entrance Examination Board.

Hammond, C. (1990). *Manuscript notes for poems.* Tucson, AZ. Unpublished manuscript.

Hatano, G. (1982). Cognitive consequences of practice in culture specific procedural skills. *Quarterly Newsletter of the Laboratory of Comparative Human Cognition, 4,* 15–18.

Hechinger, F. (1990, November 21). About education. *New York Times,* p. B11.

Henry, J. (1963). *Culture against man.* New York: Random House.

Hirsch, E. D. (1987). *Cultural literacy: What every literate American needs to know.* Boston: Houghton-Mifflin.

Holt, T. (1990). *Thinking historically Narrative, imagination, and understanding.* New York: The College Entrance Examination Board.

Howard, K. (1990). Making the writing portfolio real. *The Quarterly of the National Writing Project and the Center for the Study of Writing, 12*(2), 4–8, 27.

James, W. (1890/1950). *The principles of psychology.* New York: Dover.

Jennings, K. (1990). *A collection of Reconstruction era documents.* Unpublished manuscript.

John-Steiner, V. (1987). *Notebooks of the mind.* Albuquerque, NM: University of New Mexico Press.

Kagan, J. (1982). *The second year.* Cambridge, MA: Harvard University Press.

Lampert, M. (1990). When the problem is not the questions and the solution is not the answer: Mathematical knowing and teaching. *American Educational Research Journal 27,* (1), 29–64.

Luria, S. (1976). *Cognitive development.* Cambridge, MA: Harvard University Press.

Michaels, S., & O'Connor, C. (1990). *Literacy as reasoning within multiple discourses: Implications for policy and educational reform.* Paper presented to the Chief State School Officers Summer Institute, Washington, DC.

Neumann, F. (1991). *Sample assessments in social studies.* Center on Organization and Restructuring of Schools. Madison, WI: University of Wisconsin.

Oakes, J. (1985). *Keeping track: How schools structure inequality.* New Haven, CT: Yale University Press.

Perkins, D. (1982). *The mind's best work.* Cambridge, MA: Harvard University Press.

Rand Corporation. (1990). *Multiplying inequalities: The effects of race, social class, and tracking on opportunities to learn mathematics and science.* Santa Monica, CA: Rand Publications.

Resnick, L. B. (1987). *Education and learning to think.* Washington, DC: National Academy Press.

Resnick, L. B., & Resnick, D. (1990). *A proposal for a national examining system.* Pittsburgh, PA: Learning, Research, & Development Center.

Resnick, L. B., & Resnick, D. (in press). Assessing the thinking curriculum: New tools for educational reform. In B. R. Gifford & M. C. O'Connor (Eds.), *Future assessments: Changing views of aptitude, achievement, and instruction.* Boston: Kluwer Academic.

Scholes, R. (1990). *Protocols of reading.* New Haven, CT: Yale University Press.

Schwartz, J., & Viator, K. (Eds.) (1990). *The prices of secrecy: The social, intellectual, and psychological costs of current assessment practices.* Cambridge, MA: Educational Technology Center.

Seidel, S., & Zessoules, R. (1990, July). *Through the looking glass: Student reflections in portfolios.* Paper presented at the Institute on New Modes of Assessment, Harvard University, Cambridge, MA.

Taylor, P. (1987). *Private domain.* New York: Alfred Knopf.

Tinker, R. (in press). *Doing science.* Technical Educational Resources Corporation. Cambridge, MA: Unpublished manuscript.

Vygotsky, L. (1962). *Thought and language.* Cambridge, MA: MIT University Press.

Wiggins, G. (1991). *Sample history assessment.* Rochester, NY: Consultants in Learning, Assessment, & School Structure.

Winner, E. (Ed.). (in press). *A handbook for Arts PROPEL.* Cambridge, MA: Harvard University.

Wolf, D. (1987). *Interviews of student writers in Arts PROPEL.* Unpublished manuscript, Harvard University Graduate School of Education, Cambridge, MA.

Wolf, D. (1988). *Reading reconsidered. Literature and literacy in high school.* New York: The College Entrance Examination Board.

Wolf, D. (1989a). Artistic learning: Where and what is it? *Journal of Aesthetic Education, 22*(1), 143–155.

Wolf, D. (1989b). Portfolio assessment: Sampling student work. *Educational Leadership, 46*(7), 35–39.

Wolf, D. (1990, August). *Assessment as an episode of learning.* Paper presented at the annual meeting of the American Psychological Association, Boston.

Wolf, D., Bixby, J., Glenn, J., & Gardner, H. (1991). To use their minds well: Investigating new forms of student assessment. In G. Grant (Ed.), *Review of research in education* (pp. 31–74) Washington, DC: American Educational Research Association.

Wolf, D., & Pistone, N. (1992). *Taking full measure: Rethinking assessment through the arts.* New York: The College Entrance Examination Board.

Zessoules, R., & Gardner, H. (1991). Authentic assessment: Beyond the buzzword and into the classroom. In V. Perrone (Ed.), *Expanding student assessment.* Washington, DC: The Association for Supervision & Curriculum.

11

PERFORMANCE ASSESSMENT AND EDUCATIONAL MEASUREMENT

Drew H. Gitomer
Educational Testing Service

Good readers can recognize printed words more quickly than can poor readers (Perfetti, 1985). Chess experts can remember game positions more accurately than novices (Chase & Simon, 1973). Skills such as reading recognition and chess memory are emergent properties stemming from well-developed, easily accessible knowledge bases built from extensive reading or chess experience. These skills also can serve as limited proxy measures for assessing reading and chess ability, particularly if one wants to make a crude cut between good and poor performers. That is not to say, however, that such proxy measures are adequate for all assessment decisions, particularly those associated with instruction, for at least two reasons. First, these findings do not necessarily imply that training the emergent properties will benefit the criterion performance. Teaching someone skill at remembering chess positions is not likely to improve their overall chess playing ability. Second, because these proxy measures are not tied to the epistemology of a domain, the relationship of the skill to the domain is murky. Such tenuous relationships frequently lead to misleading instructional advice.

Although it is recognized that assessment must be considered in the context of its consequences, both intended and unintended (Messick, 1989), and that different educational decisions require correspondent approaches to assessment (LeMahieu & Wallace, 1986; Mislevy, this volume), a fairly rigid model of assessment has dominated in this country (Resnick & Resnick, 1985). Assessments designed to assist in selection decisions (e.g., the SAT), or to make broad evaluative claims about institutional performance (e.g., norm-referenced standardized achievement tests) are setting the instructional agenda of schools. However, standardized achievement tests are inconsistent with instructional decision making needs for several reasons, including the fact that they are not closely tied to instructional content and are one-time affairs (LeMahieu & Wallace, 1986). These instruments, because they tend to be administered on a large scale, use proxy measures to probe wide coverage of domains rather than in-depth examination of any specific area.

Though inappropriate for instructional decision making, proxy measures have been used to such ends, with pernicious effects on education (Resnick & Resnick, 1985; Wiggins, 1989). They have become instructional ends in and of themselves, rather than being indicators of emergent properties that naturally develop out of serious learning experiences. So instead of children expanding their vocabulary through extensive reading experience, students receive direct vocabulary instruction to improve test scores. Their vocabulary may consist of dictionary-like definitions, not the type of contextually related meanings that arise out of normal encounters with language (e.g., Gross, Fischer, & Miller, 1989). Students are spending a great deal of time learning things because they are measured on current test instruments, not because these things have intrinsic value as instructional goals. Because traditional formats such as multiple-choice items are limited in the range of student skills and knowledge that can be assessed (e.g., N. Frederiksen, 1984), the result is a correspondingly limited curriculum.

If, in fact, teachers and schools are "teaching to the test," then we ought to develop assessments in which teaching to the test is a valid use of instructional time. J. Frederiksen and Collins (1989) argued that systemically valid assessment instruments are those that foster the type of learning and performance that is deemed critical to the educational mission. Assessment activities that are systemically valid are worthwhile learning tasks in and of themselves. Wolf and Camp (both in this volume) describe ways in which such assessment activities can serve as critical learning opportunities.

Assessment of students, formal or informal, is a major activity in the classroom, taking up to one half of classroom time (Stiggins & Conklin, 1988). With so much time and effort given to assessment, together with the impact it has on curricular content and pedagogy, there is a groundswell of support for the development of performance assessments. The purpose of this chapter is to present a framework for performance assessments that have the goal of improving the systemic validity of educational practice.

DEFINING PERFORMANCE ASSESSMENT

Performance assessment has a long history in work settings, and has been used for a number of purposes: administrative decisions such as promotion and compensation; guidance and counseling decisions by supervisors; and validation research for selection, training, and intervention efforts (Berk, 1986; Landy & Farr, 1983). Smith (1976) has proposed a three-dimensional model of performance assessment that is adapted here for educational purposes and is presented in Fig. 11.1.

The first dimension, *time span covered*, refers to the temporal duration of the assessment task. Traditional testing situations are immediate in that the student is being assessed on performance during the very limited test administration. *Specificity* refers to the generality of the assessment information. If we were to look at student writing, an assessment of noun–verb agreement would be specific, whereas a judgment of communicative effectiveness would be more general. Finally, *closeness to educational objectives* refers to the proximity of assessment goals to the ultimate objectives of an educational institution. So, for example, if we were going to examine students' literacy, the *behaviors* category might include a measure of decoding speed. *Results* would subsume a measure of the reading levels of students within a school. *Educational effectiveness* might be assessed by examining the proportion of students who successfully completed post-high school educational or training programs.

Current educational testing generally can be characterized as falling somewhere in the left, front, lower corner of this cube. Traditional tests frequently are one-time measures of very specific pieces of knowledge and are seldom

DIMENSIONS OF PERFORMANCE ASSESSMENT

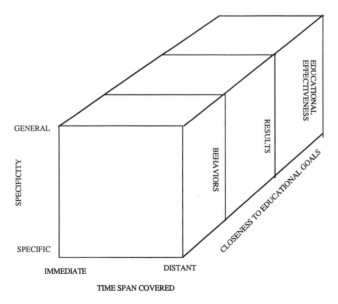

FIG. 11.1.   Dimensions of performance assessment in an educational context. Adapted from Smith (1976), p. 749, and used by permission of Marvin D. Dunette.

linked to broader criteria of educational effectiveness, such as successful program completion. At best, these test measures are used as predictors of broader educational measures (e.g., Willingham, 1985). For example, SAT scores are frequently correlated with grade point average. However, because of the limited inferences that can be drawn from correlational data, they do not provide much other information helpful to instructional decision making (see Wolf, Bixby, Glenn, & Gardner, 1991).

Performance assessment can be thought of as a methodology by which a greater area of the cube can be addressed. In practice, performance assessment has become a catchall concept encompassing virtually any non-multiple-choice assessment task. A performance is simply the execution of an action; it is little wonder that even a simple fill-in-the-blank item is put forth as a performance assessment task. Yet, performance assessment can be considered more narrowly. Its characteristics are evident in the following definition:

> A performance task is one that simultaneously requires the use of knowledge, skills, and values that are recognized as important in a domain of study and is qualitatively consistent with tasks that members of discipline-based communities might conceivably engage in. Assessment entails judgments and reports of the quality of performance by community members.

This definition has implications for the entire educational enterprise, including the epistemological basis for instruction, the methods and outcomes of assessment, and the roles of those involved in assessment.

EPISTEMOLOGY AND PERFORMANCE ASSESSMENT

Doyle (1986) argued that the way in which teachers present the curriculum, through teaching and assessment, reflects the way that content is represented. So, if in designing assessment or instruction the teacher partitions the content into discrete skills and pieces of knowledge, then it is more than likely that the student will represent the content of the domain similarly. Different ways of structuring assessment and instructional tasks lead to distinct content representations of the same surface curriculum.

Brown and Palincsar (1989) advocated *proleptic teaching*, an approach that maintains the integrity of a target task. Teachers may give less-skilled students greater support and/or more accessible materials, but the goals, strategies, desired outcomes, and essential task are preserved. The frequent discontinuity between what is asked of students in schools and the important tasks of a discipline is reduced. Schoenfeld (1985), for example, noted that the algorithmic focus of mathematics education has little to do with genuine mathematical problem solving. Correspondent performance assessment examines students on tasks that are qualitatively consistent with tasks that members of discipline-based communities might conceivably engage in. That is not to say that classroom mathematics tasks are isomorphic with those encountered by the mathematician, or that the art student's task is precisely consistent with that of the artist. It is to say, however, that there is more coherence between student tasks and tasks engaged in by members of a discipline in a proleptic teaching approach than exists in traditional curricula. Proleptic teaching and assessment implies a view of learning and understanding that is qualitatively different from teaching and assessment that emphasize basic skill and knowledge components isolated from integrated activities. One goal is for students to realize that academic work can be an apprenticeship activity (Collins, Brown, & Newman, 1989) whereby students become part of a community of learners (e.g., Bartholomae, 1985). A brief review of some of the critical distinctions between traditional assessment and performance assessment follows.

The Nature of Problems

Traditional testing assesses the ability to answer what can be called *well-structured, unconditional, knowledge-lean tasks* (Gitomer, 1991a). A well-structured problem is one in which the given state is clearly defined, the goal state is clearly recognized, and there are clear rules or methods for getting from one state to the other (Newell & Simon, 1972). Unconditional refers to the fact that the problem interpretation is not subject to dependent considerations. A knowledge-lean (VanLehn, 1989) problem is so named because limited external world knowledge is needed to solve the problem. The problem $2 + 3 = x$ is an example of a highly structured, unconditional, knowledge-lean task.

Most problem solving in real-world contexts is not nearly so circumscribed. First, most problems are ill-structured. The critical skill is to come to understand a problem and to formulate it in a way so that solutions can be devised. Individuals need to conceptualize the entire problem-space, including defining the current and goal states, and discovering the problem-solving procedures and techniques that would be appropriate to navigating the problem. It has been said that "much problem solving is directed at structuring problems, and only a fraction of it at solving problems once they are structured" (Simon, 1973). Second, virtually all real-world problems encountered by experts in a domain require extensive subject matter knowledge. Identifying relevant knowledge and applying it in the course of problem solving is a mark of expertise. Third, almost all problem interpretations are conditionally dependent on a particular set of givens.

We are only beginning to attend to the variety of problem-solving situations that exist. Traditional models of cognition emphasized understanding and problem solving as purely solitary enterprises. However, one need only examine many real-world tasks to recognize that a great deal of problem solving is collaborative. Groups can facilitate problem-solving performance by breaking down tasks into manageable components, by assigning specific tasks to those most able to do them, and by providing a forum in which ideas and arguments can be presented, evaluated, and improved (Brown & Palincsar, 1989). The ability to work within groups and to manage groups so that they are most effective are skills that have not been addressed in traditional assessment instruments.

Because people learn in specific situations, the knowledge involved in problem solving is initially tied to those situations. Thus, we have examples of individuals who are effective proportional reasoners in informal situations like supermarkets (e.g., which is the better buy: 12 oz. at $2.69 or 16 oz. at $3.39?), but who are unable to handle analogous problems if presented in formal school settings (Rogoff & Lave, 1984). The epistemological consequence is that knowledge can no longer be thought of as an abstract set of cognitively represented concepts, but only considered relative to a constrained set of situations. Thus, a single blanket statement about an individual's skill in proportional reasoning has less meaning than a claim about proportional reasoning skill in either school or shopping tasks.

Recognizing that knowledge has a situated basis has several implications for assessment and instruction. First, problems can be designed that encourage students to demonstrate the depth of their understanding of target principles, even if not evinced in traditional, structured school settings. Presumably, we would want to include a range of problems that demand collaborative problem solving. We might even ask students to take on different roles within the group in order to assess the strengths and weaknesses of an individual problem solver within a group context. Second, we need to clarify claims about a student's ability. Failure to respond correctly to problems in a structured, formal setting does not necessarily mean that the targeted skill or understanding would not be manifest in other situations. From an instructional perspective, it makes greater sense to build on the knowledge and skill a student has, even if severely context specific, and develop it towards a more abstract, principled, and generally useful form, than to deny its presence absolutely and begin instruction *de novo*. Third, we need to provide students with a variety of contexts in which to exercise newly acquired problem-solving skills if we are to promote generalizability beyond a single situation-specific context. We should attempt to understand task and student characteristics that lead to differentially successful solutions in seemingly analogous situations. This type of understanding could lead to more adaptive forms of instruction (e.g., Snow, 1989).

We contrast two items, presented in Fig. 11.2, to illustrate some of these differences. The first is taken from the Graduate Management Admissions

Multiple-choice problem

> If each photocopy of a manuscript costs 4 cents per page, what is the cost, in cents to
>
> reproduce x copies of an x-page manuscript?
>
> (A)$4x$　　　B)$16x$　　　(C) x^2　　　(D) $4x^2$　　　(E)$16x^2$

Performance assessment item

> The printing department is thinking about upgrading its duplication equipment to become more
>
> efficient. What should be done?

> FIG. 11.2.　Sample multiple-choice and performance assessment problem-solving
> items.

Test and is designed to measure general mathematical problem solving. The purpose of this item is to predict success in graduate management programs. However, the skills such an item taps are, at best, a limited subset of skills needed by management students to succeed. The solver must represent the word problem algebraically, apply multiplication operators, and evaluate the answer with respect to the given options. There is no conditional interpretation that will alter the correctness of (D).

Thus, this item can be considered a proxy measure of a larger complex of skills. Although it may be an effective problem for predicting future success, at least two concerns arise. First, because of the high-stakes nature of an admissions test like this, if student work is oriented towards mastery of the proxy measures, rather than mastery of the broader problem-solving tasks that the proxies are part of, then educational programs may become oriented in ways that are inconsistent with educational theory. Second, the instructional implications for management education that derive from performance on this item are extremely limited.

A performance task in management is likely to be very different. We can envision a problem such as the one presented in the lower half of Fig. 11.2. There is no simple formula that can be applied. Rather, the manager must first understand the current problem state, identifying variables that are going to weigh in any determination. The astute manager will not only consider the average number of pages printed monthly and the cost per page, but will also factor in variations in print demands during the month (Are there heavy demands at the end of the month? Are large jobs done overnight?), the range in the number of copies per print job, delays, rush jobs, maintenance and electrical costs, support staff needed, types and cost of printing jobs not done in-house, and so on.

The manager must also define the goal state or anticipated outcome, a task that is even more complicated. Changes in efficiency are not evaluated simply by comparing copies per minute from one system to another. What are the additional costs incurred by selecting a new system, in terms of equipment, maintenance, staff, and training? The new machine is likely to have new features (e.g., a fax) that can bring benefits not previously associated with an older generation of duplication technology. What difficulties are likely to be solved by introducing new technology and what new ones may emerge? What are future projections for all relevant variables?

Failure to gather advice and information from people likely to be affected by this decision would be foolish. Not only is the contributed information likely to be valuable, but the participation of others is necessary to improve the likelihood of their accepting a given solution. Thus, group problem-solving skills are critical.

After evaluating a multitude of factors, it is unlikely that a good manager would make an unconditional recommendation of System 123 from Company XYZ. More likely, a conditional set of scenarios would be presented. Option A might assume steady printing demand and thus, the hiring of an overnight person, rather than the purchase of a new machine. Option B might assume increasing demand, but no changes in the basic responsibilities of the printing department, leading to a recommendation of a moderate upgrade. Option C might assume a restructuring of document-related services and lead to a recommendation of state-of-the-art technology.

Not only is this problem conditional, but it requires the good solver to use a tremendous amount of subject matter knowledge. In the language of cognitive science, the solver represents knowledge about duplication technology and organizational management in *schemas* that help to shape the problem definition into a structured form. The particular value for any schema variable is determined by the specific context of the company purchasing the technology, but the recognition of the importance and relationship of variables derives from an understanding of complex systems that has been acquired through learning and experience.

The very constrained nature of problem solving portrayed not only on standardized tests, but throughout the educational system, delivers a skewed message about the nature of problems in a domain. The absence of problem-finding demands together with the overwhelming emphasis on distinctly correct solutions depicts knowledge as absolute, unconditional, discrete, individual, and subject to algorithmic manipulation. Ironically, as technology advances, the need for human execution of algorithmic methods will be increasingly deemphasized. Important skills will involve constructing problem representations with precise specification and making sense of the resultant analyses.

Asking students to construct a problem representation, rather than simply to recall answers or procedures, represents an implicit epistemological shift. It requires that students shift from a "knowledge telling" strategy (e.g., Bereiter & Scardamalia, 1987) to a more constructivist "knowledge transformation" role. They are asked to use their knowledge and skills to make meaning of new situations. Learning, then, is not viewed as simply the accretion of facts and procedures. Rather, it is seen as a restructuring activity in which new relationships are forged, perhaps into radically different conceptual structures (e.g., Carey, 1985).

Thus, performance assessment problems should derive from an epistemological view of the structure of a domain. Not only should they require skills deemed important to a domain, but those skills ought to be embedded in contexts that reflect a significant portion of the epistemological structure. The parsing of tasks into discrete skills harkens back to the "fallacy of pure insertion" (Donders, 1969) in which it was incorrectly assumed that the character of a mental process remained intact regardless of whether it was combined with other processes or tasks. Simple additive models tend to be inadequate and inaccurate representations of human cognition.

METHODS AND OUTCOMES OF ASSESSMENT

Using the types of problems just described necessarily entails judgments by assessors. Solutions must be considered in terms of their soundness rather than in absolute terms of right and wrong. Because the scope of solutions cannot be fully anticipated, it is impossible to assess this class of performances without relying on the interpretations of skilled judges. Johnston (1989) argued that the "objectivity" in psychometrics has been a search for tools that will provide facts that are untouched by human minds. He was realistic when he said, "We are stuck with interpretation, so we might as well get used to it and make the most of it" (p. 511).

In the discussion that follows I have separated performance assessment into three primary components. First, standards are needed against which performance is judged. Second, a protocol for making judgments is necessary. Third, methods are needed for reporting outcomes in ways useful for decision making by participating constituencies.

Standard Setting

Problems as described previously do not lend themselves to ideal answers against which examinees' responses can be gauged. The development of standards occurs through careful consideration of quality within a domain and derives from the epistemology of the discipline. Two widely disparate answers can both be of high quality, and two superficially similar responses can vary drastically on that same dimension. For example, an astute political thinker may reach the same conclusion as an uninformed individual on some issue, yet the argument from the former may be much more convincing, or at least more coherent.

Voss and his colleagues (Voss, Blais, Means, Greene, & Ahwesh, 1989; Voss, Tyler, & Yengo, 1983) have examined the quality of argument structure in the social sciences. One can examine structure quality independent of the position adopted. Adapting Toulmin's (1958) argument structure, Voss et al. have observed that quality in a political science argument depends on evidential support for claims made and the overall coherence of the argument structure.

Toulmin's argument structure is presented in Fig. 11.3. In an argument, an individual makes a *claim* based on one or more pieces of information, the *data*. A simple data-claim structure in social science might be "The unemployment rate is high; therefore, the economy is weak." However, because that assertion can be challenged, it needs to be supported by *warrants* or premises such as "Unemployment is a sign of a weak economy." The quality of a warrant is often determined by its *backing*, the claims that establish the authority of the warrant. The backing for this warrant might be an appeal to economic theory or historical economic relationships among variables. Often, a claim is subject to *qualification*; it is only germane under certain conditions. Finally, the *rebuttal* or counterargument specifies the conditions under which the warrant, and therefore the claim, might not hold. A hypothetical rebuttal in this case might be that the relationship between unemployment and the economy does not hold when interest rates are below a certain level.

Voss and his colleagues have compared individuals with differing levels of expertise in terms of the quality of their arguments in ill-structured social

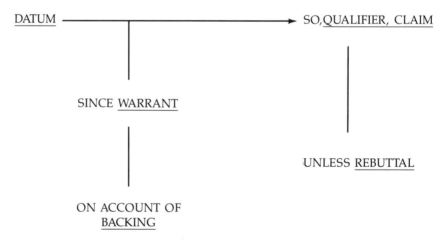

FIG. 11.3. A model of Toulmin's (1958) argument structure.

science domains. Voss et al. (1983), for example, compared experts and novices on a political science problem. They found that novices made many more direct datum-claim statements. They failed to develop the complex, supporting arguments complete with explicit warrants and backing that experts constructed. There was a very low proportion of direct datum-claim arguments for experts. The argument's structure, rather than the posited claim, is the final determinant of quality.

Note that ill-structured domains cannot be submitted to a formal logical analysis. Standards of what constitute acceptable warrants and backings are determined by a relevant community. Thus, the criteria for acceptable backing might be quite different for the economist and the physicist. Nevertheless, comparable schemes for evaluating the quality of an argument have been put forth in the natural sciences as well (Giere, 1984; Root-Bernstein, 1984). In fact, Duschl (1990) stated that one of the goals of science education ought to be to teach students to evaluate scientific claims by examining the background knowledge claims included in the argument.

Standard setting within an assessment context requires more than the identification of important features to be considered. There must be a sense of levels of performance that is shared by judges. Although scientific explanation is valued in the fourth grade science fair competition as well as in the journal review process, the expectations for performance in these two contexts are vastly different. Models of performance assessment have been developed in a number of educational contexts, including the holistic scoring of some College Board Advanced Placement exams (e.g., College Board, 1989), artistic competitions, and science fairs.

Standard setting ought to include the following:

A Shared Understanding of Criteria Used to Judge Performance. The same term can mean very different things to different judges. It is important that a standard setting discussion be directed at achieving a shared understanding of the concepts and issues being assessed. One way to ensure this understanding is to ground the standards in students' work.

Table 11.1 is an excerpt from a discussion of teachers, language arts supervisors, and participating researchers in developing standards for how to look at student work in a writing portfolio.[1] The participants are searching for an understanding of one important feature of student writing—the student's self-concept as a writer—by examining student reflections as well as

[1]The work described is being done with colleagues at Educational Testing Service, Harvard Project Zero, and Pittsburgh Public Schools as part of the Arts PROPEL project. Specifically, I would like to acknowledge the work of Roberta Camp, Joann Doran, Joanne Eresh, Kathy Howard, Paul LeMahieu, Steve Seidel, Dennie Wolf, and Rieneke Zessoules. The interpretation presented here is the author's and does not necessarily reflect the views of these individuals.

Teacher 1	I think she was trying to be different because obviously chronological order would be most logical—but she tried to organize it a different way.
Teacher 2	I didn't do creative writing. I made them do all the research, all the notes, and then they did the creative writing. They chose either a monologue, dialogue, or short story and kids came up with other ideas. When they were finished they were pleased with the results, and so was I. Someone wrote about George Washington's thoughts on his deathbed, Langston Hughes when he visits his father in Mexico including the background of their relationship. They have to incorporate facts into the creative piece.
Researcher 1	She also says here (there's a really strong thing) about getting control in the sense of not needing a whole lot of help from anyone else and being able to see where she's having problems. Also, she liked having a paper where she could get all her points down and not have to struggle all the time.
Supervisor 1	Well that's part of the "less pressure" of the term paper.
Researcher 2	I really got the sense somehow that she was taking responsibility as a critical reader and particularly in the longer piece about Evaluation of Self as a Writer. I don't even know what I could point out to show her meaning, but she has a good sense of herself as a writer.
Teacher 1	But it's true—she definitely developed that.
Researcher 1	It's partly in the Evaluation of Self as a Writer. She's very specific about before—"I'm writing about more realistic issues. I write better and more efficient. I start off with powerful paragraphs, my sentence structure has improved and I can develop my body slowly at this point . . ." She has a sense of process. She has specifics about what she looks at.
Teacher 1	And she understands *why* she's getting better—"I have written more this year, which expanded my success. I didn't have a chance to get lazy."
Researcher 1	It's almost as if you need to read the Portfolio and then look at the folder. Then come back and look at the Evaluation of Self as a Writer—You read it and there's a real person who seems to be saying things that make sense, but you don't have any evidence for it. Then you need to go through all the other pages to see what she did and come back and ask, "What did she say?"
Supervisor 2	My sense was that from the first page through the tenth page I wasn't sure that anything she said was so—and if I were the next years teacher . . . It wasn't until I read the Dear Senior letter that I thought, yes, this is so. It seemed that the Portfolio had to include something more for me as the teacher receiving this child so I had some sort of substantiation that she really did grow as a writer. It wasn't until I reached that piece (the letter) that I felt she had the control of language that she talked about—She varied the sentence structure, had interesting beginnings . . .
Teacher 1	And towards the middle, you start to see it.
Supervisor 2	But if I had just seen this documentation at the beginning, the questionnaires. . . The Evaluation of Self as a Writer helps because I start to see her control of language. But that one really locked it in. I can see what kind of writer I'm receiving when I read that Dear Senior piece. If I had this and the research paper, I wouldn't know her as a writer at all.
Supervisor 1	I want to have the option of teacher-improved solutions.
Teacher 1	I was going to say, "How can you guarantee you're going to get that?"
Supervisor 2	That's what I'm going to argue for then, as each teacher reviews what a student puts in the Portfolio there's a possibility that the teacher can add a piece to the Portfolio.

(Continued)

TABLE 11.1
Continued

Teacher 3	Is there another possibility? Every time we talk about having a selection we say the students select, but we always place some kind of parameter—even if it's general such as "most satisfying" or "I like best" it's still a parameter. Do we ever explore just allowing free pick to see if the students will see the gaps and take steps to fill them in? Hopefully that would happen. The teacher would be the fail-safe plan. I wonder if the student could not, given the opportunity, make some kind of selection.
Researcher 1	And the question of whether we need a range of writing just like we need different kinds of writing—when you say Free Pick and filling in the gaps, we need a sense of what's needed to know if they're filling in the gaps.

the student's writing samples. They are also considering how to construct a portfolio so as to provide a representative picture of the student. Several features of the discussion are salient:

1. *Specificity:* Participants are adept at supporting their claims with specific evidence. For example, the comment by Researcher 2 refers to the student taking responsibility as reader and writer in the student's Self Evaluation piece.

2. *Search for evidential sources:* Participants are willing to consider the entire portfolio in making claims about the student. Thus, Supervisor 1 considers the student's Self Evaluation with some reservation until she perceives a confirmation from the Dear Senior writing selection. Note that the conversation then turns to a discussion of how to ensure that evidence is available to assessors. The two supervisors argue that teachers should include work they feel is revealing about a student. Teacher 3, for pedagogical reasons, wants to leave the student with as much control over portfolio selection as possible, but is willing to consider teacher selection as a "fail-safe plan."

3. *Sincere negotiation:* I hope it is as evident to the reader as it was to me as an observer, that this was an honest dialogue. Each participant listened, responded, and integrated the viewpoints of the others. No one tried to dominate the conversation. Rather, there was a working-through to achieve a collective understanding.

Scale Definition. It is more than likely that especially when one steps outside of the classroom, some sort of scaling of individuals' performance will be required. Educational policy and decision making often require the characterization of individuals in reference to specified criteria. These characterizations will vary in the extent to which they are normative or criterion referenced. Scaling is used for two primary reasons. First, scales serve to discipline the assessment report in form and function. Performance that can be characterized in many different ways is structured within a common framework and reported on a common scale. The second purpose of scaling is to reduce data efficiently for communication and aggregation. Reducing complex performance to one, or even a limited set of numbers, enables aggregation procedures that permit comparisons of groups to standards, either normative or criterion referenced.

Scales can take a variety of forms. Two of the most common types are graphical scales and behaviorally anchored rating scales (BARS). Each has a multitude of variations and some examples are presented in Fig. 11.4. BARS were designed to reduce the ambiguity of scale anchors associated with most graphical schemes (Landy & Farr, 1983).

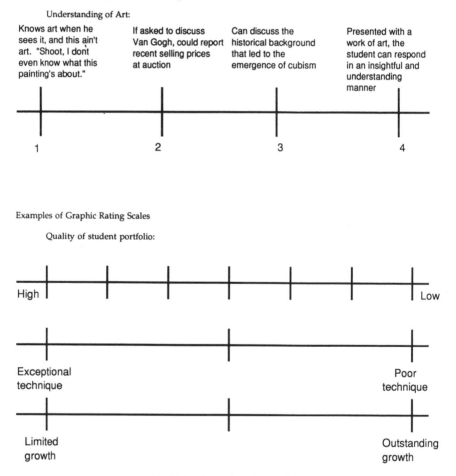

FIG. 11.4. Example rating scales.

Calibration Exemplars. Individuals will be rated differently on the criteria defined during the preceding activity. Samples of student work that represent the full range of performance for a particular population are needed to illustrate both different levels of quality and the different ways of achieving defined levels of quality. Judges should rate these exemplars on the scale as defined and then discuss those judgments as a means for clarifying judgment criteria. The calibration exercise is designed to ensure that judges' rank-orderings of individuals are reasonably consistent. It is also desirable that absolute ratings are similar, so that post-scoring adjustments for harshness or leniency are not necessary.

Judgment and Moderation

In addition to standard setting and calibration procedures, a structure or protocol is necessary in order to guide judges in the assessment of student performance. Many of the related issues are strictly pragmatic, but need to be addressed nevertheless. All have implications for the quality of assessment.

Interestingly, Robert Wherry (1983) provided many guidelines for assessment in an employee context that have direct implications for performance assessment in educational settings. His theory is based on years of theoretical and empirical work in performance assessment. Where appropriate, I have borrowed from Wherry's theory and adapted them to an educational context. Important issues include:

1. *How much time is given to the assessment?* Compromises are usually necessary between the amount of time one would like to have to examine student work and the time available to look at a relatively large number of productions. A fair assessment requires that all students be afforded similar depth of review.

2. *How much context is provided about the performance?* When we examine a student's performance, at issue is the extent to which we understand the conditions under which the student was working. How circumscribed was the assignment? Is a relatively impoverished problem solution a function of the constraints of the assignment or due to the student's inability to develop anything more impressive? It is difficult to get a sense of a student's scientific capabilities, for example, if he or she has only been asked to complete the periodic table. How much time did the student have to work on the performance being assessed? We would expect more from a student working on a year-long project than one which was completed in 2 weeks.

Wherry claimed that "tasks in which the performance is maximally controlled by the ratee rather than by the situation will be more favorable to accurate ratings" (p. 293). His argument is that performance tasks ought to facilitate the exhibition of optimum performance. In educational settings this will not always be the case. What seems critical then, is that judges understand the context within which the work was done. Performance assessments may require submission of a discussion of the context for the performance along with a product.

3. *Who are the judges and what is their relationship to the individual being assessed?* Wherry claimed that the accuracy of ratings was "in direct proportion to the number of previous relevant contacts with the ratee" (p. 294). This alters the traditional model of standardized assessment in a very significant way. First, this claim turns on end the conventional wisdom that objective assessment is best achieved when there is no relationship between the assessor and the student. It claims that performance judgments will be most accurate when there is a great deal of contact and available relevant information. Judgments about an individual based on a single contact around an assessment activity will be less reliable than judgments based on ongoing observation of relevant performance. Thus, teachers and other regular observers of student performance are likely to be more reliable raters of student performance than will be the outside judge. Note also that Wherry claimed that the sheer number of contacts is not the determining factor, but rather the number of contacts that are *relevant* to the performance being examined.

4. *What is the interaction between judges?* Educational assessment has employed models that vary widely in the level of interaction among judges. For example, dissertation committees fall at one end of a continuum that represents significant negotiation and exchange among assessors. Typically, the result of that negotiation is a single judgment of performance quality. The British APU (Assessment Performance Unit) model (Burstall, 1991) represents an intermediate point of the spectrum in which each judge renders his or her own rating of the individual. If there is significant disagreement, a moderating activity that can entail third-party negotiation is employed to bring the judgments into alignment. The other extreme is represented by judgments in many scholastic sporting events such as gymnastics. Here, judges independently rate each performance. Judge's ratings are then averaged, with extreme scores sometimes discarded. Differences in judgments are settled on strictly algorithmic terms, rather than through interaction or negotiation. There is no definitive answer as to which of these models is most appropriate or results in the highest quality judgments. Obviously, serious examination will be required as educational performance assessments become widespread.

5. *What is the assessor's perception of the use of assessment information?* Wherry argued that judgments are affected both by how the assessor perceives the information will be used and by the nature of the justification for

the assessment that will be required. He claimed that "Any setting that facilitates the increase of bias, such as knowledge that the rating will have an immediate effect upon the recipient, will decrease the accuracy of raters, whereas any setting that stresses the importance [of ratings] to the organization or to society as a whole will decrease perceived bias elements and thus increase accuracy" (p. 296). Bias here refers to a systematic effect on performance rating that is based on factors not related to the performance itself. If teachers are judging their own students and teacher performance is judged by student accomplishment, then we can add a second potential source of bias, knowledge of an immediate effect on the assessor (i.e., over and above knowledge of an immediate effect on the recipient). An assessment model must recognize this potential conflict of interest; it must take steps to ensure that performance assessments are perceived as fair and provide safeguards to minimize bias. In this context, there exists an inherent conflict, not easily resolved, between the desire to employ familiar assessors and the potentially biasing effects of familiarity on their judgments.

Wherry also posited that having to justify the judgment can affect the way performance is rated. Specifically, he argued that "knowledge that the rating may have to be justified to the ratee may cause the rater to recall a higher proportion of favorable perceptions and thus lead to leniency" and also that "knowledge that the rating may have to be justified to the rater's superior may cause the rater to recall a higher proportion of perceptions related to actions known to be of particular interest to the superior whether such actions are pertinent or not" (p. 297). To reconcile these two potential sources of bias Wherry said "To assure that neither of the distorting effects just mentioned shall take place alone, it is better to assure their mutual cancellation by requiring that both types of review shall take place" (p. 297). In a healthy educational assessment environment, there ought to be a public accounting that justifies itself to all of the relevant stakeholders (Gitomer, 1991b). Thus, it seems perfectly reasonable that assessment justifications be provided to both students and institutional users. The benefit is that justification contributes to a public and shared sense of performance criteria that can be continuously monitored and adjusted in light of possible changes in the educational goals of a system.

Reporting Assessment Information

Perhaps the biggest obstacle to educationally useful assessment models is that the reported information is not amenable to the needs of particular constituencies. There is a clear mismatch between the needs of educational users and the information provided to them. Percentile rankings provide teachers with little or no information useful for instruction at the classroom level. Knowing this information doesn't suggest what to do next, short of studying similar assessment items that one hopes will increase the student's subsequent percentile rank. Unfortunately, this form of "teaching to the test" is too often the resulting scenario.

Similarly, the public reporting of assessment information for institutional purposes cannot possibly be done at the level of detail that might benefit students in the classroom. Procedures for aggregating and reducing information are necessary in order to support the information needs of school districts, states, and national constituencies. The challenge is to develop an integrated system that at once respects the pedagogical and epistemological goals in the classroom and still satisfies institutional needs. We are attempting to develop such a model in the context of Arts PROPEL in writing assessment around student portfolios.

Writing portfolios, elaborated on by Camp (this volume; see also Camp, 1990, and Howard, 1990) have been developed in classrooms. They have become, among other things, vehicles to provide assessment information for understanding students' writing processes and their development. The assessment is ongoing, relatively informal, and reported to students in nonstandardized formats.

Several steps designed to satisfy institutional needs have been or are being implemented. They include the following:

1. Teacher–Supervisor Conferences. As described by Doran (1990), the school district has developed a system whereby supervisors like Doran regularly meet with teachers to review a sampling of student portfolios. Teachers are asked to bring portfolios that illustrate a range of student performance. By explicitly asking to review a range of students, the supervisor is able to avoid the tendency to see only the "best" students. The discussion focuses on the teacher's reactions to student work, teacher understanding of different students, teacher ability to respond to the variety of children in the classroom, and teacher perception of the instructional program. Thus, it becomes an opportunity for district administrators to check whether desired educational practice is occurring. Conferences also provide supervisors with an in-depth sense of performance for a sample of students, a useful complement to the broad, but limited, information that is usually given by standardized test scores. Finally, the conferences are an outstanding vehicle for professional development of teachers, and as Doran admitted, supervisors.

2. District Portfolio Guidelines. After working through portfolio processes in a number of classrooms, teachers, district personnel, and researchers developed a set of minimum portfolio guidelines that all teachers are required to implement. Each student's portfolio must contain, at the least, examples of the student's writing, evidence of diversity, and reflections on writing and its development. Despite the district mandate, flexibility is inherent in this system. There is no requirement that students must, for example, have a particular fixed balance of narrative and expository pieces.

3. Sampling of District Performance. Most district-level decisions do not require data from each student. In order to get a sense of performance across an institution, sampling is appropriate. We are developing a district assessment system whereby a sample of student writing portfolios will be assessed on a limited set of criteria. The criteria emanate from the in-depth discussions that have been held around student portfolios by classroom teachers. Thus, the criteria, though fairly general, maintain the basic epistemological and pedagogical structure seen as important in the classroom. Second, there are multiple criteria that reflect the multifaceted nature of writing. There is no attempt to aggregate scores on individual criteria into an arbitrary summary that eliminates meaningful references to writing. Instead, aggregation procedures will preserve unique criteria to delineate a picture of student performance. Reports will take the form of "Eight percent of students in Grade 10 exhibit satisfactory evidence of being able to communicate in writing for a variety of purposes." The standards that determine what constitutes satisfactory evidence will be determined in the manner detailed earlier.

The public reporting of data has several salubrious effects for educational accountability purposes. First, by using sampling techniques within an institution, one should be able to make defensible claims about performance, including any relevant breakdowns (e.g., female vs. male performance). Second, the characteristics of performance that are reported make clear to the public those curricular goals that are deemed important by the institution. Claiming that most students are, for example, able to critically analyze a scientific argument describes more about the goals of a science education system than simply saying that the mean percentile ranking of students in science on some standardized instrument is 75. Third, the relationship between classroom goals and institutional goals is sympathetic. Because the characteristics described in the institutional summary emanate from classroom goals, the mixed message "This isn't important, but we need to do it for the test" is not in evidence. Thus, we are hoping to create a situation in which students, teachers, and institutions are judged on performance that they value.

CONCLUSIONS

Educational performance assessment in this country is very much in its formative stages. The following lists some of the most important issues that need to be addressed:

1. The educational assessment community must understand the nature of the inferences made on the basis of performance assessment and develop

a methodology to support them. It is interesting to note that performance assessments have often been criticized because they cannot be scored objectively. Yet, the real issues include obtaining agreement on what the scoring criteria should be, ensuring that judges share an understanding of the criteria definition, and determining the level at which inferences are made. In traditional assessment, scoring requires no inference, although determining the meaning of scores clearly does. The interpretive scoring of performance assessment requires inference by judges, but only moderate inferences to the type of tasks encountered in criterion performance are required beyond this level.

That said, there still remains the critical issue of how far performance can be generalized. To what extent do we have confidence that a particular student's performance is indicative of the broader constructs and the claims we wish to make about the student? What are the chances that success on one performance task suggests success on related tasks? How do we go about defining a universe of tasks and skills that we believe are represented in the performance of the assessment task and how do we know when we have adequately sampled from that domain? These questions are not easily answered, and have implications for performance task design, supplementary evidential support about the student, as well as the assessment of performance. For many assessment decisions, performance tasks will only be useful to the extent that we have confidence that performance represents a level of competence that is not strictly responsive to a single task. We want to be able to make broader claims about the student's general understanding.

2. Equity issues are critical in performance assessment, as they are with any assessment enterprise. Villegas (1990) argued that equity goes beyond selecting tasks that are culturally representative. Especially in performance situations, there must be a fundamental understanding and respect for the ways in which members of different social groups communicate, particularly as this affects the performance. For example, the reticence of one group in certain situations may be a function of social values and must be accounted for within the assessment model. Cultural differences may affect the ways in which one formulates a problem or develops a solution. Also, cultural groups may be differentially familiar with the context surrounding a given problem.

3. Inherent in performance assessment is a dynamic mechanism that permits the assessment process to keep pace with changes in our understanding. Judgments of performance quality are clearly relative and depend on the effective use of accepted knowledge claims and world views. Thus, Newton's arguments were scientifically compelling in his day because they were consistent with then-current knowledge claims and world views. However, the same reasoning would fall short today, given the scientific knowledge now accepted. All fields, from the arts to the sciences, undergo fundamental

shifts in views of quality and acceptability. An assessment system needs to explicitly recognize that by providing mechanisms that correspondingly facilitate the evolution of assessment standards.

ACKNOWLEDGMENTS

The work reported here was generously funded by the Rockefeller Foundation and by Educational Testing Service. The author is grateful to Roberta Camp, Dick Lesh, Carol Myford, Howard Wainer, and the editors for their helpful comments on previous drafts. The views presented here are strictly those of the author.

REFERENCES

Bartholomae, D. (1985). Inventing the university. In M. Rose (Ed.), *When a writer can't write: Studies in writer's block and other composing process problems* (pp. 134–166). New York: Guilford.

Bereiter, C., & Scardamalia, M. (1987). *The psychology of written composition.* Hillsdale, NJ: Lawrence Erlbaum Associates.

Berk, R. A. (1986). *Performance assessment: Methods and applications.* Baltimore: The Johns Hopkins University Press.

Brown, A. L., & Palincsar, A. S. (1989). Guided, cooperative learning and individual knowledge acquisition. In L. B. Resnick (Ed.), *Knowing, learning, and instruction* (pp. 393–451). Hillsdale, NJ: Lawrence Erlbaum Associates.

Burstall, C. (1991). The British experience with national educational goals and assessment. In *The assessment of national educational goals: Proceedings of the 1990 ETS Invitational Conference* (pp. 71–79). Princeton, NJ: Educational Testing Service.

Camp, R. (1990). Thinking together about portfolios. *The Quarterly of the National Writing Project and the Center for the Study of Writing, 12*(2), 8–14, 27.

Carey, S. (1985). *Conceptual change in childhood.* Cambridge, MA: MIT Press.

Chase, W. G., & Simon, H. A. (1973). The mind's eye in chess. In W. G. Chase (Ed.), *Visual information processing* (pp. 215–281). New York: Academic Press.

College Board. (1989). *The Advanced Placement examination in United States history.* New York: Author.

Collins, A., Brown, J. S., & Newman, S. E. (1989). Cognitive apprenticeship: Teaching the crafts of reading, writing, and mathematics. In L. B. Resnick (Ed.), *Knowing, learning, and instruction* (pp. 453–494). Hillsdale, NJ: Lawrence Erlbaum Associates.

Donders, F. C. (1969). On the speed of mental processes (1868–1869). *Acta Psychologica, 30*, 412–431.

Doran, J. (1990). *Portfolios for professional development: An administrator's story.* Presentation at Annual Meeting of the National Council of Teachers of English, Atlanta.

Doyle, W. (1986). Content representation in teachers' definitions of academic work. *Journal of Curriculum Studies, 18*, 365–379.

Duschl, R. A. (1990). *Restructuring science education: The importance of theories and their development.* New York: Teachers College Press.

Frederiksen, J. R., & Collins, A. (1989). A systems approach to educational testing. *Educational Researcher, 18*(9), 27–32.

Frederiksen, N. (1984). The real test bias. *American Psychologist, 39,* 193–202.

Giere, R. (1984). *Understanding scientific reasoning.* New York: Holt, Rinehart, & Winston.

Gitomer, D. H. (1991a). Cognitive science perspectives on problem solving: Implications for assessment in graduate management education. *Selections,* Spring, 39–46.

Gitomer, D. H. (1991b). The angst of accountability in arts education. *Visual Arts Research, 17,* 1–10.

Gross, D., Fischer, U., & Miller, G. A. (1989). The organization of adjectival meanings. *Journal of Memory and Language, 28,* 92–106.

Howard, K. (1990). Making the writing portfolio real. *The Quarterly of the National Writing Project and the Center for the Study of Writing, 12*(2), 4–7, 27.

Johnston, P. (1989). Constructive evaluation and the improvement of teaching and learning. *Teachers College Record, 90,* 509–528.

Landy, F. J., & Farr, J. L. (1983). *The measurement of work performance: Methods, theory, and applications.* Orlando, FL: Academic Press.

LeMahieu, P. G., & Wallace, R. C. (1986). Up against the wall: Psychometrics meets praxis. *Educational Measurement: Issues and Practice,* Spring, 12–16.

Messick, S. (1989). Validity. In R. L. Linn (Ed.), *Educational measurement* (3rd ed., pp. 13–103). New York: Macmillan.

Newell, A., & Simon, H. A. (1972). *Human problem solving.* Englewood Cliffs, NJ: Prentice-Hall.

Perfetti, C. A. (1985). *Reading ability.* New York: Oxford University Press.

Resnick, D. P., & Resnick, L. B. (1985). Standards, curriculum, and performance: A historical and comparative perspective. *Educational Researcher, 14*(1), 5–21.

Rogoff, B., & Lave, J. (1984). *Everyday cognition: Its development in social context.* Cambridge, MA: Harvard University Press.

Root-Bernstein, R. (1984). On defining scientific theory: Creationism considered. In A. Monague (Ed.), *Science and creationism* (pp. 64–94). New York: Oxford University Press.

Schoenfeld, A. H. (1985). *Mathematical problem solving.* New York: Academic Press.

Simon, H. A. (1973). The structure of ill-structured problems. *Artificial Intelligence, 4,* 181–201.

Smith, P. C. (1976). Behaviors, results, and organizational effectiveness: The problem of criteria. In M. D. Dunnette (Ed.), *Handbook of industrial and organizational psychology* (pp. 745–775). Chicago: Rand McNally.

Snow, R. E. (1989). Aptitude-treatment interaction as a framework for research on individual differences in learning. In P. L. Ackerman, R. J. Sternberg, & R. Glaser (Eds.), *Learning and individual differences* (pp. 13–60). New York: W. H. Freeman.

Stiggins, R. J., & Conklin, N. F. (1988). Teacher training in assessment (Tech. Rep.). Portland, OR: Northwest Regional Educational Laboratory.

Toulmin, S. (1958). *The uses of argument.* Cambridge, England: Cambridge University Press.

VanLehn, K. (1989). Problem solving and cognitive skill acquisition. In M. I. Posner (Ed.), *Foundations of cognitive science* (pp. 527–580). Cambridge, MA: MIT Press.

Villegas, A. M. (1990). *Culturally responsive pedagogy for the 1990s and beyond.* Princeton, NJ: Educational Testing Service.

Voss, J. F., Blais, J., Means, M. L., Greene, T. R., & Ahwesh, E. (1989). Informal reasoning and subject matter knowledge in the solving of economics problems by naive and novice individuals. In L. B. Resnick (Ed.), *Knowing, learning, and instruction* (pp. 217–249). Hillsdale, NJ: Lawrence Erlbaum Associates.

Voss, J. F., Tyler, S. W., & Yengo, L. A. (1983). Individual differences in the solving of social science problems. In R. F. Dillon & R. R. Schmeck (Eds.), *Individual differences in cognition* (pp. 205–232). New York: Academic Press.

Wherry, R. J. (1983). Wherry's theory of rating. In F. J. Landy & J. L. Farr (Eds.), *The measurement of work performance: Methods, theory, and applications* (pp. 283–303). Orlando, FL: Academic Press.

Wiggins, G. (1989). A true test: Toward more authentic and equitable assessment. *Phi Delta Kappan,* *70,* 703–713.

Willingham, W. W. (1985). *Success in college: The role of personal qualities and academic ability.* New York: College Entrance Examination Board.

Wolf, D., Bixby, J., Glenn, J., & Gardner, H. (1991). To use their minds well: Investigating new forms of student assessment. In G. Grant (Ed.), *Review of Research in Education* (Vol. 17, pp. 31–74). Washington, DC: American Educational Research Association.

12

INNOVATION AND REFORM: EXAMPLES FROM TEACHER ASSESSMENT

Carol Anne Dwyer
Educational Testing Service

Rather than discussing construction versus choice in cognitive measurement for its own sake, I begin this chapter by asserting that we are instead taking part in a broad reform movement that encompasses both education and measurement. We need to understand what goals and assumptions are behind this broader reform context if we are to act in concert with others to improve education. If we fail to act in concert, measurement will once again find itself talking at cross-purposes not only with its critics, but with those we hope to serve. Once again, we will find ourselves deeply embroiled in devising technically sound and logically rigorous measures that will eventually prove off-target with respect to what we and others had hoped to accomplish. Our efforts will ultimately have been fruitless and our conversations frustrating.

The 1980s saw great activity in high-level, officially sanctioned educational reform, and the reform of teaching and teacher assessment was at the heart of much of this activity. Reports such as *A Nation at Risk* (National Commission on Excellence in Education, 1983), *Who Will Teach Our Children?* (California Commission on the Teaching Profession, 1985), *A Nation Prepared* (Task Force on Teaching as a Profession, 1986), *Tomorrow's Schools* (Holmes Group, 1990), and *The Educational Reform Decade* (Policy Information Center, 1990) showed the depth of public concern over the quality of teaching and learning in America, and the thirst for educational reform. In the sections that follow, the forces behind this drive for reform are discussed, particularly their interrelationships with teaching and teacher assessment. I take the current call for "authentic assessment" as an example of an attempt to translate broad educational

265

reform goals into measurement and instructional practice. Then, primarily in the context of teacher assessment, I contrast this attempt with the response of the measurement and educational research communities to these same reform goals.

The past decade's reform activities were highly diverse. They included attention to student achievement, teacher qualifications and supply, school management, the qualifications of school administrators, the nature and quality of research on teaching and teacher education, and curriculum reform, particularly in mathematics and science. The initial wave of reform emphasized instituting testing requirements for students as a means to educational accountability. A second wave of reform efforts was built on the recognition of the central role of the teacher in bringing about improved student learning, and the necessity of involving teachers themselves in the reform process. Improvements in individual teacher performance, the perception and reality of the quality of teaching as a profession, and the content and quality of the education of teachers are all key issues that recur throughout these educational reform initiatives.

Although proponents of these reforms differ in their basic assumptions and goals, there appear to be some common themes in teaching reform:

- Improving the quality of teaching in order to improve student performance.
- Professionalizing teaching, and elevating the status and responsibility of those who teach.
- Improving the supply of teachers, particularly teachers of mathematics and science, and minority teachers.
- "Weeding out" incompetents from the teaching force.
- Developing a better understanding of the process of teaching.

Underlying these themes are competing goals and interests. For example, the struggle for power over educational decision making is evident in debates over accountability. Calls for higher standards for teacher licensing, for teachers to be held responsible for student performance, and for recertification of practicing teachers all reflect a press for accountability through external control. On the other hand, calls for increased roles for teachers in school and district decision making, in assessment, and in research on teaching reflect the desire to establish accountability and control through the teaching profession and through individual teachers themselves. Such differences in orientation reflect the competing values and interests of regulatory groups such as state and national governments on the one hand and of teachers on the other. The differences also reflect the diversity of value orientations in the general public, between those who would cure education's ills through increased external control and those who believe that the individuals who comprise the educational system can best heal themselves.

Numerous other examples of the importance of understanding the underlying goals of educational reform and the conflicts that surround them can be found. Reform efforts related to the educational achievements of minorities are abundant and diverse, although not always openly acknowledged. The focus of these efforts is on both teachers and students: minority student achievement, the ability of nonminority teachers to deal with minority students, the need for more minority teachers, and the quality of preparation of minority teachers. Reformers differ in their perceptions of how critical these issues are and in the solutions that they propose. More importantly, they differ in their fundamental notions of the meaning of "equality" and the means for achieving it.

Underlying a number of proposals for educational and assessment reform is the question of the value of competition and interpersonal comparisons. Discussions of this question frequently invoke the concept of "educational excellence" and its importance to our national social and economic welfare. Although virtually no one disputes this as a legitimate educational goal, there are sharp differences of opinion about the precise meaning of excellence and how to achieve it. One discernible viewpoint emphasizes the importance of individual competition as a means to educational excellence, and accepts a view of teaching and learning that highly values objectivity and standardization, and that approaches knowledge acquisition as a process of transfer of knowledge from teacher to learner. A contrasting viewpoint that is a major theme of current educational reform is that education should be less concerned with competition and more encouraging of cooperation. Characteristic of this point of view are the call for teaching styles and curriculum materials that involve cooperative learning, problem solving, and the concern with the educational and personal achievement needs of individual students and teachers. More broadly, there is an increased valuing of the personal and particular relative to group interests, of concrete and contextualized forms of knowledge relative to the abstract and generalized. Knowledge acquisition is seen as a process by which the learner constructs knowledge through interactions with the teacher and the subject matter. The theoretical manifestations of this reform conflict include more attention in the research and measurement communities to integrative, synthetic, and complex views of teaching and learning (with all the lack of control that this implies), relative to more fragmented (but more controllable) forms of investigation and interpretation.

Perhaps most importantly for assessment, these educational reform efforts give clear indications that their orientation includes increasing tolerance for subjectivity, and a valuing of human judgment—and even intuition—over precise decision rules and logical operations.

THE ROLE OF ASSESSMENT IN REFORM

Although the surface text of educational reform agendas may be clear, the underlying forces that drive these initiatives are more complex than they first appear. These underlying forces are sometimes contradictory and are, in general, ill-articulated by their proponents and poorly understood by their target audiences. Assessment has played a central but paradoxical role in recent educational and social reforms. This role has been two-fold: Assessment has been viewed positively (if simplistically), as one of the principal tools for effecting reform; but it has also been viewed much more negatively, as an area that is in need of basic reform in its own right.

Calls for reform of assessment include concerns about tests' fairness, their relationship to instruction, and their emotional impact on test takers. Most importantly for teacher assessment, there is also clear indication of increasing acceptance of subjectivity or professional judgment in measurement.

Cole (1981) characterized researchers in test bias as constituting two distinct groups: "defenders" of testing and "reformers" of testing. This categorization continues to be apt for assessment reform: Defenders of assessment expect that assessment can be a positive force in effecting educational reform by providing objective information about the status quo and the effects of reform interventions; reformers of assessment view testing as a major area of the educational system needing reform, and seek to force that reform as an explicit part of their educational improvement agendas. In both camps, assessment is the vehicle for educational reforms, often in a form that is technically simplistic or practically unrealistic. When assessment itself is the subject of reform efforts, twin pitfalls exist: Responses can be improvements in traditional measurement terms, but substantively off-track; or they can be directly responsive to the reform interests but with low measurement credibility. Increasingly, however, parallels are becoming evident between the assumptions of many educational reform agendas and long-term trends in the theory and practice of educational and psychological measurement, particularly in our conceptions of validity.

As has often been the case with educational reforms, assessment continues to play a central role. Assessment can provide a concrete example of how reforms are to be made, and how their effects can be demonstrated for public consumption as well as for professional improvement. Both those who give priority to accountability goals, and those who give priority to professional and personal autonomy goals, make the reform of teacher assessment a central element.

This conversation about assessment reform echoes the educational reform conversation. In discussions of both student and teacher assessment, there is a call for authentic assessment. It is clear that authentic assessment is both more and less than innovative assessment, but the terms remain inchoate, characterized by overdrawn contrasts with the status quo, a disproportionate emphasis on assessment, exaggerated expectations for its power to cure educational ills, and a conspicuous lack of consensus on central definitional issues.

Because many definitions of authentic assessment show considerable overlap with certain views of constructed-response testing, it is instructive to compare the predominant characteristics of each, as well as to link them with the major themes of broader educational reform. In the sections that follow, these differing views and their underlying links to reform are explored. I then provide examples of innovative practice in teacher assessment. Finally, these examples are compared with the themes of educational reform efforts and are used to suggest educationally and psychometrically constructive actions and research.

"Authentic Assessment"

"Authentic assessment," associated with both student and teacher assessment, is a highly charged yet elusive concept. Many definitions exist, but close inspection reveals considerable disparity among them, and considerable differences in their authors' basic assumptions. Authentic assessment is not simply a different kind of testing, and it is not synonymous with constructed-response testing or performance assessment. It is fundamentally a criticism of the status quo of testing. In contrast with constructed-response testing, its arguments are not those of the traditional measurement value system, although they may share a common vocabulary. Authentic assessment is variously defined with reference to its content (usually thinking skills or problem solving), level of difficulty, authorship, impact on the curriculum, and purposes. In almost all cases, however, its fundamental characteristic is its departure from the perceived characteristics and consequences of current forms of assessment, particularly multiple-choice testing. In this regard, the contrast is stark: authentic assessment is not, for example, standardized, imposed, objective, norm-referenced, timed, concerned with knowledge of facts, or external to the educational process. Multiple-choice testing is viewed as being all of these things.

Mitchell (1989, 1990) has provided one of the most comprehensive views of authentic assessment. Her view includes the assessment method used, the content covered, the uses of the assessment, the consequences of this assessment, and elements related to the ownership or control of the assessments. For Mitchell, the relationship to curriculum was perhaps the most important consideration. Authentic assessment is continuous with instruction: It complements and expands the curriculum, and preparation for the assessment should literally *be* the curriculum. It is contextualized, with respect to the educational system as a whole. A corollary of this view is that assessments should be developed by teachers themselves, rather than by professional test developers, and that the standards of achievement should be set by teachers, rather than by politicians or other external groups. The development of such assessments should be an enriching professional experience for the teachers. The content of such assessments should focus on complex forms of knowledge and critical thinking, and be close to what students normally do in the classroom. Authentic assessment should not deal with content that is memorizable and should not measure the same content as multiple-choice tests. As to methodological aspects, Mitchell's definition of authentic assessment required that it not be standardized, not timed, not bubbled-in, and not objective. It should consist of performance assessment. With respect to the uses and control of assessment, she was specific about authentic assessment not being used for accountability purposes, and not being "imposed" on teachers by others. Note that some of these definitional elements are traditional measurement concerns (e.g., standardization), but others are more consistent with social policy or values analysis.

In a view that echoes Mitchell's in many respects, Wiggins (1989) has defined authentic assessment as the performance of exemplary tasks that would be responsive to individual students and to school contexts, entail human judgment and dialogue, and not be norm-referenced. Again, it is possible to extract the measurement elements from these definitions and to respond to them. As is true of Mitchell's views, however, Wiggins' underlying value positions and inferences about dissatisfaction with current practice are the most pertinent concerns.

Geiger (1990) issued a brief statement on behalf of the National Education Association (NEA) calling for authentic assessment for students. He emphasized that assessment should consist of multiple measures of what students know, that these measures should deliver an aggregate picture of the student's knowledge, and that they should not be standardized. One could translate these criteria into measurement terms quite literally, but to do so would miss his main point: concern with assessment's power to oversimplify and to result in harm to students and teachers. Geiger's objection to "standardization" surely reflects this concern rather than a rejection of the measurement commonplace that test-takers be presented with equivalent tasks if they are to be compared.

Attitudes toward standardization are an especially revealing example of failed communication in this debate. As noted previously, an important element of many definitions of authentic assessment is that it is not standardized. In fact, standardization is fast becoming an undefined term, much like "bias" has become, with enormous potential to obscure debates and impede solution of important problems.

To measurement specialists, the meaning of standardization is quite clear:

It is the goal of providing identical conditions of test administration, or the "level playing field" notion that inferences about the comparability of individuals or groups can only be drawn when comparable tasks, under comparable conditions, have been undertaken. This is not what others mean by standardization. The measurement specialist's definition of standardization clearly pertains to a broad range of assessment methods, from multiple-choice to most kinds of constructed-response assessment. Wiggins' (1989) definition is more typical of the views of educational reformers in equating standardization with multiple-choice testing, and in characterizing it as mechanical or unreasoning assessment, concluding that "A standardized test of intellectual ability is a contradiction in terms" (p. 704).

Such diverse views, unless resolved by moving beyond the literal terms of this conversation, do not augur well for reaching a common understanding of the goals of using assessment to further educational reform. Once again, psychometricians may find their technical definitions being ignored or rejected and their innovations scorned.

One thing that is clear from these definitions of authentic assessment is that many educational reformers regard current testing practices as having had considerable negative impact on individuals and curricula. They are not satisfied that traditional tests accomplish any useful purpose, and do not accept measurement specialists' logical defenses of them. It is less clear how assessments should be designed to meet their concerns. A common measurement response to critics would be to isolate those concerns that are "properly" within the purview of measurement and to concentrate on devising new techniques that avoid the technical problems of existing ones. Another traditional response would be to avoid those reformist aspects foreign to the realm of measurement: questions of interpersonal power, values regarding accountability, and so on. Although such literal reactions might well result in interesting innovations in assessment construction and use, they would not be responsive to the underlying concerns and perceived needs of educational reformers, and would thus unnecessarily and unproductively prolong debates about ostensibly—but not actually—technical issues, while contributing little to the solution of important educational problems.

The very breadth of aspirations for authentic assessment reveals that it is a discussion of issues larger than simply the methods for evaluating teachers and students. It is a discussion of educational reform, beginning at a grassroots level, by seizing control of one of the primary instruments for that reform. It is an expression of profound dissatisfaction with the way that assessment is currently carried out in the schools, with its relationship to instruction, and with its practical and emotional impact on teachers and students. To what extent are these same aims and dissatisfactions significant in the drive of the measurement and educational research communities to develop innovative assessments in the form of "constructed-response" testing? What implications do these underlying issues have for the improvement of instruction and for the improvement of testing practice? At present, the call for authentic assessment relates more closely to modern measurement at the theoretical level than at the level of practice. Those asking for authentic assessment may have a clearer conception of the elements needing reform than does the measurement community, but the technical means for achieving this reform are still beyond their grasp. Measurement will be able to contribute solutions to these reform efforts only if we can come to understand measurement's place on the broader educational landscape.

Constructed Response Assessment

The existence of a book on construction versus choice in cognitive measurement illustrates the degree of attention that constructed-response assessment is receiving from the scientific community. The topics addressed demonstrate a diversity of interests and a variety of technical approaches. It is clear that this book is really as much about innovation in assessment as it is about constructed-response testing per se. We are part of a reform movement within our own field, but to become truly productive, we need to establish and maintain explicit connections to the larger reform movements of which we are a part.

One approach to understanding the current and proposed innovations in assessment has been to wrestle with definitional issues and to attempt to develop methodologically oriented taxonomies. This is recognizably "constructed response" work, in the literal sense, and is useful in clarifying complex discussions. For example, Bennett, Ward, Rock, and LaHart (1990; see also Bennett, this volume) have devised a categorization of constructed-response tasks. Their categorization is based on a continuum that involves the degree of constraint imposed on the examinee's response. The continuum is anchored at zero (multiple choice) and goes through six (presentation). Emmerich (personal communication, June 11, 1990), taking a somewhat broader view, has developed a matrix encompassing both content (knowledge, application, performance) and instrument or method characteristics. For the instrument characteristics axis (Fig. 12.1), Emmerich has included characteristics related to richness of context and degree of stimulus and response control; type of instrument; and scoring method. The cells of the matrix thus describe how constructed-response variables characteristically relate to the cognitive or skill content of interest.

Such analyses are helpful in comprehending and organizing the extremely complex array of measurement procedures now at our disposal, and in suggesting their strengths and limitations. They are part of the infrastructure of innovation in measurement, and operate from its traditional value system, but they do not aim to establish direct links with the goals of educa-

TEST SPECIFICATIONS

KNOWLEDGE ——⟶ APPLICATION ——⟶ PERFORMANCE

Method Characteristics	- - - - - - - -	- - - - - - - - -	- - - - - - - - -
Richness of Context	Minimal	Moderate	Extensive
Stimulus Control	Extensive	Moderate	Minimal
Response Control	Extensive	Moderate	Minimal
Type of Instrument	Paper & Pencil Test	Hybrid of Test & Simulation	Observations and/or Ratings
Stimulus Material	Written	Audio & Visual Skills	Classroom Environment
Response Mode	Writing	Speech & Writing	Speech, Writing, & Enactment
Response Format	Multiple Choice	Multiple yes/no; Constructed Response	Free Response
Scoring	Single Corect Answer;	Multiple Correct Answers;	Multiple Correct Answers;
	Objective	Mix of Objective Judgmental	Primarily Judgmental

FIG. 12.1. Content characteristics of various assessment methods. (Adapted from Walter Emmerich, personal communication, June 11, 1990. Used by permission.)

tional reform. Instead, they ask traditional measurement questions about non-traditional measurement techniques and applications.

Other work in measurement and educational research does aim to establish such direct links with educational reform. Shavelson, Carey, and Webb (1990), working within the context of science achievement, dealt with such broad reform themes as assessment's congruence with important curricular goals, and the importance of measuring complex cognitive processes by designing research instruments to address these goals. For example, they explicitly recognize the value placed by the general public on conceptual understanding and problem solving, and the prevailing reform theme that practitioners are best qualified to be the developers of assessments.

Another effort based in cognitively oriented educational research is the explication of a "systems approach" to testing by Frederiksen and Collins (1989). Briefly stated, Frederiksen and Collins' view is that an assessment that is systematically valid is one that is likely to lead to educational changes that bring about improvements in the cognitive skills that one is attempting to assess. In their view, a systemically valid test leads to good educational practice and worthwhile learning; a systemically invalid test leads to ineffective educational practice and irrelevant or suboptimal skills development. This characterization of the effects of assessment on education as an aspect of validity will be considered in more detail later, but it is important to note here its relationship to common themes in authentic assessment: the intertwining of curriculum and assessment, and the clear positioning of assessment as a tool in the service of curricular improvement, rather than as an end in itself. It should be recognized, although often it is not, that the validity question here concerns the validation of the entire educational system of which the assessment is a part, not just the validation of the assessment per se. It is at least theoretically possible that a negative outcome might imply that it is the instruction rather than the assessment that is in need of change.

Such work, although practiced by measurement specialists and educational researchers, is not primarily about measurement, as it has historically been defined; it is not so limited, being more closely connected with the broader educational reform debate. On a literal level, it is about constructed-response testing, but the underlying reform-oriented themes are far more important in this work than are the more narrow technical issues. Such research serves as a bridge between the architects of reform and educational and measurement practitioners, but it is not simply a matter of compromise or expediency: It has its roots in fundamental measurement change.

TECHNICAL ISSUES IN TEACHER ASSESSMENT AND RESEARCH

There are several technical issues in teacher assessment and research that are related to reform goals. These issues include changing perspectives on validation and the relationship of assessment to curriculum content (both at the theoretical and empirical levels). Recent shifts in the dominant educational research paradigm and growing technical accommodation to nonobjective measurement and research criteria have also had a significant impact on innovations in assessment practice.

Validation

The dominant technical view of validation has changed dramatically in recent years, shifting from a view that divided validity evidence into functionally and conceptually distinct "types," to a view that stresses the interrelatedness of such evidence under the conceptual umbrella of construct validity. One of the fundamental tenets of modern views of validity is the acceptance of data related to the context in which tests are used as well as data related to the tests themselves. Thus, the consequences of testing, intended and unintended, positive and negative, are important factors in judging the validity of assessments (Cronbach, 1971, 1980; Messick, 1989). Related to this view of validation as encompassing unintended consequences is the view that good assessment of teachers is consistent with the goals of the larger educational system, and that poor assessment has undesired consequences for the system of which it is a part. Messick asked not just "Is the test a good measure?" in the traditional technical sense, but "Should it be used?"—a values and ethical question. Such questions are clearly part of measurement now, and the social policy implications that flow from information about the test's consequences are clearly part of the validation network.

Another set of central validation questions plays a role in discussions of assessment's relevance to educational reform: How *well* does the innovative (or other) assessment represent the construct of interest? How *much* of the construct is represented by the assessment? Such questions are analogous to issues raised by calls for authentic assessment: Is what is measured some significant piece of our educational objectives? What is included and what is left out of the measurement? Both measurement specialists and educational reformers, for somewhat differing reasons, have an interest in the question of how much construct-irrelevant variance is introduced by the choice of assessment method. For the educational reformer, however, the question of accuracy, in the sense of reliability, plays a secondary role. Both in the educational reform efforts and in measurement theory, the critical referents are increasingly outside of the test itself; internal referents, such as reliability, are becoming secondary considerations. Coffman's view (1966, 1990) that a more direct but less reliable measure may often be a more valid measure of the educational construct of interest is still more characteristic of educational reformers than of measurement specialists, but this view flows inescapably from current validity theory.

Relationship of Assessment to Curriculum

The relationship of assessment to curriculum is a central one for both educational reformers and measurement specialists. A major reason for using constructed response assessment is increased validity (in Messick's, 1989, larger sense), especially the quality of the relationship between testing and instruction. This relationship needs to be considered in both its theoretical and empirical aspects. As noted earlier, current validity theory establishes a direct link between assessment and curriculum. The status of the empirical evidence showing the impact of innovative assessments on curriculum content, however, is far less clear. Cole (1988) suggested that a dominant problem in this area is that assessment is closely associated with two legitimate but different goals: the goal of measurement (and its associated accountability and policy goals), and the goal of instruction. Our understanding of the compatibility or incompatibility of these goals will thus be necessary to the resolution of some of our current theoretical and empirical difficulties.

Theoretical Relationships. In addition to broad theoretical views of the consequential basis for judgments about validity, other researchers have attempted to establish specific theoretical links between innovative forms of assessment and curricula. Frederiksen and Collins (1989) discussed systemic validity, with a somewhat stronger emphasis than Messick (1989) on the role of the assessment itself in the educational system, but in basic agreement with his underlying theoretical viewpoint. One area of contrast is that Messick's view relates to the integrity of the entire system (of which education is only one part), whereas Frederiksen and Collins focused on the power of the assessment to impact only instruction (positively or negatively).

In the context of writing assessment, Lucas (1988) asked us to consider "ecological validity," which she defined as ". . . the extent to which a test reflects (and hence reports results from) the whole writing environment of the learner, and the extent to which it impacts that environment in positive rather than negative ways" (p. 12). Again, such a view takes validity as a characteristic by which assessments are judged, rather than interrelationships that exist within entire educational systems.

These views of the theoretical relationship between curriculum and assessment are not new, having been set forth more broadly by Cronbach (1971, 1980) and Messick (1989), and echoed by Cole (1981, 1989) with particular reference to bias, and by Tittle (1989) with reference to models for the teaching and learning context. But work such as that of Lucas (1988) and Frederiksen and Collins (1989) deals very specifically with educational and assessment reform consequences. Their work is also illustrative of the power often attributed to assessment. Wiggins (1989) gave us another instance of this view, saying that "Reform begins, then, by recognizing that the test is central to instruction. Any tests and final exams *inevitably* [original emphasis] cast their shadows on all prior work. Thus they not only monitor standards, they also set them" (p. 704). The power of tests to influence curriculum is a widely held belief. Is there empirical support for it in teacher assessment?

Empirical Evidence. Given the assumptions that assessment can affect the curriculum, positively or negatively, and that data about this effect are legitimately part of judgments about the validity of inferences drawn from these assessments, it seems reasonable to ask what data exist. Unfortunately, empirical evidence is nearly totally absent from the discourse. A number of popular—and otherwise scholarly—treatments of this topic have tended to assume more than is actually known about the exact functioning of testing in education systems. Over and over, authors make assertions about the negative impact of multiple-choice assessment and the positive impact of constructed response on educational systems, but these assertions seldom move beyond rhetoric and anecdotes into the realm of qualitative or quantitative research. (An interesting recent exception to this is the work of Lorrie Shepard, 1990, on spurious test gains on student's multiple-choice tests.) We currently have very little empirical data on the differential impact of multiple-choice and other forms of testing on curriculum and other school- and learner-based variables, and, in addition, are far from clear about how to resolve related questions of causality and directionality. A great deal of research remains to be done in this area. Fowles, a leading authority on portfolio assessment in writing and other subject matters, responded to questions on the effect of constructed-response testing on curriculum or training (personal communication, June 25, 1990): "To my knowledge, the subject has never been systematically researched. In our assessment projects and programs [in writing] we see *the effects* [original emphasis], and teachers often pay tribute to the [constructed-response] approach anecdotally, but I don't know of anyone who has tried to research the effects."

In another view from the world of writing, where constructed-response testing has a very long history, Lucas (1988) said:

> What has been the effect of all this [constructed-response] testing on the curriculum? So far the tendency to teach to the test has worked in favor of bringing back composing in the public schools from the edge of extinction. Where a writing sample is included as part of proficiency tests or state skills tests, teachers clamor for training in composition as they scramble to include writing in the curriculum, many for the first time in their careers. (p. 2)

Lucas' remarks have the ring of experience and authenticity, but remain at the level of assertion rather than empirical research.

Madaus (1985) focused more on the limitations of multiple-choice testing than on the promise of constructed-response testing, and included such related topics as coaching and "cramming." He offered interesting anecdotal information from a variety of current and historical sources in the United States, Ireland, and Great Britain, but unearthed no empirical data. As noted earlier, Wiggins (1989) also linked authentic assessment to curricular improvement logically, but offered no empirical data.

Thus, we are left with the strong belief that constructed-response assessment has the ability to influence curriculum, and that it ought to be judged, at least in part, by its ability to do so positively. We can say virtually nothing, however, with the certainty of empirical data, about whether it does so, or to what extent, or under what circumstances. It is widely assumed that problems of poor teacher preparation are related to the use of multiple-choice assessment, and that alternative forms of assessment should thus have an ameliorating effect on teacher preparation, but however likely this seems, no conclusive data currently exist to support this view.

INNOVATION IN TEACHER ASSESSMENT PRACTICE

Despite the lack of empirical data on the impact of new forms of assessment on the educational system, there is a great deal of work currently underway on developing new forms of teacher assessment. A great deal of this innovation in current teacher testing practice could be categorized as constructed-response testing, but not all. Much of the change is directly responsive to national and state reform agendas, but not all of the changes relate to the form or methodology of the assessment instruments.

Important innovations are taking place at the national and state levels, although district-level innovation in teacher assessment is also occurring. Teacher assessment innovations can be viewed as differentiated according to the level of the teachers assessed (expert or novice) and the purpose of the assessment (licensing, voluntary or mandatory advanced certification, in-service education). Three kinds of innovation in teacher assessment are discussed: the work of the National Board of Professional Teaching Standards (NBPTS), state-sponsored assessments, and the work of Educational Testing Service (ETS) on new teacher assessments.

National Board for Professional Teaching Standards

The NBPTS, an independent organization started with private funding from foundations, has as its goal the development of assessments for the voluntary certification of expert teachers. Their first assessments are scheduled to become operational in 1993, and are expected to use a variety of constructed-response methods including assessment center exercises, interviews, observations, and portfolios. There is also the possibility that their assessments will include "strengthened" multiple-choice and essay components.

The constraints felt by the National Board reflect explicit connections to larger reform goals. They express these constraints succinctly: It is necessary for the National Board to design ". . . a set of assessment protocols that are professionally credible, publicly acceptable, legally defensible, administratively feasible, and economically affordable" (National Board for Professional Teaching Standards, 1989, p. 73). The Board's goal statements also reflect their deep concern with the nature of teaching expertise and its contribution to student learning.

The intention of the NBPTS is to complement, not replace, mandatory state systems for the licensing of beginning teachers. The National Board has spent considerable time reaching consensus about the basis for the content of their assessments, what teachers should know and be able to do. This consensus has been developed from their own large board of directors (numbering over 60, the majority of whom are practicing teachers), and through solicitation of suggestions from diverse groups and individuals, rather than through more formal mechanisms such as national surveys and job analyses.

The National Board has benefited from research directed toward developing prototype assessment techniques. Work done by Shulman under the aegis of the Teacher Assessment Project (TAP) at Stanford has been highly influential in the measurement community, as well as illustrating how assessments might eventually be handled by the National Board. The TAP measures are highly subject-matter specific and are designed for use within a classic assessment center format. These measures, although simulated in the sense that they do not take place within the classroom or with the teachers' own students, are highly interactive (between the teacher and the examiner) and are realistic recreations of situations that seem to be important for teachers. One of the main goals of this project was to demonstrate the possibilities for using such techniques to understand teachers' subject-matter knowledge and their ability to transform this subject matter for communicating with students. Another goal of this work was to show the importance of teachers' "craft knowledge" of their disciplines, and to demonstrate that assessment itself can be useful for operationalizing this knowledge base.

The TAP prototypes do indeed serve as clear examples of the power and variety of constructed-response assessment, and the acceptance of the assessment by the participants and others has been remarkable. The content of the TAP prototypes was derived from a common sense or face validity basis, rather than from an extensive research program, in keeping with the basic nature of the project as a prototyping activity.

The National Board's development efforts are still in their infancy, but the Board's commitment to innovative assessment and to teachers' control of the assessment process is evident. For the National Board, the issue of control is likely to remain clear-cut, largely because their assessments are voluntary. Teachers need to feel professional incentives to participate in a voluntary certification program such as this, and their profession's control over the substance and form of the assessment is a key element in creating such incentives. Although there has been skepticism from some quarters about teachers' ability to govern their own assessment affairs, there are actually few competing pressures for control. Unlike states' mandatory licensing processes, the work of the National Board to create voluntary assessments does not stress the function of accountability. Issues such as the nature of teaching expertise and its contribution to student learning are preeminent in their work.

State-Sponsored Teacher Assessment

State-sponsored activities in the development of innovative teacher assessment take many forms. The 1980s saw an explosive growth of assessment requirements for teacher licensing. These requirements are highly diverse, but 34 states now require some part of the NTE assessment battery as part of their licensing process, and all but a few of the remainder have developed or commissioned their own assessments. In state licensing of teachers, multiple-choice testing is not generally viewed as competing with constructed response. There is abundant criticism of multiple-choice teacher tests, and many states use performance-based teacher assessment, but the two forms of assessment typically coexist and are seen as serving different functions. In general, multiple-choice testing is better accepted for assessing prospective teachers' subject-matter knowledge than for assessing their pedagogical knowledge or skill. Conversely, performance assessments, which nearly always take the form of classroom observations, seldom purport to make direct judgments of the prospective teachers' subject-matter knowledge.

This methodological dichotomy is, however, weakening. Paper-and-pencil constructed-response assessment is now becoming part of subject-matter examinations in disciplines beyond writing (where it has long been taken for granted), but it is usually in conjunction with multiple-choice questions, and with the explicit recognition that the two methods are best used with different aspects of the subject-matter content. Constructed-response testing in these contexts is still largely restricted to use by a few states, and for a few subject-matter areas. The onus is still on the individual disciplines to make the argument that multiple-choice assessment is insufficient to measure some important part of the discipline, or some important cognitive skill such as interpretation or synthesis.

Today, 16 states (Connecticut, Florida, Hawaii, Indiana, Kentucky, Louisiana, Maine, Missouri, Mississippi, North Carolina, New Mexico, Oklahoma, Pennsylvania, Tennessee, Utah, and Virginia) have performance-based, state-mandated beginning teacher induction programs that are required for teacher licensure. Five others (Delaware, Georgia, South Carolina, Tennessee, and Texas) and the District of Columbia have programs that are similar in content and method, but are used for purposes other than licensure. Most programs began development in the early 1980s, but Georgia has been conducting observation-based assessments for teacher licensing since the late 1970s.

At the heart of these programs is live observation by trained evaluators in the teachers' own classrooms. These observations are usually supplemented by portfolios or interviews. The procedures and quality of these programs varies, but they have many common features. Until recently, one of these features has been a heavy reliance on the results of "process/product" research on teaching to define the tasks to be measured. This approach has, in recent years, been subject to two criticisms related to major reform themes: (a) that it may foster a sterile and fragmented view of teaching, with uncertain student performance outcomes; and (b) that it does not allow sufficient flexibility for evaluating teachers with innovative teaching styles because the process/product research is geared primarily to the direct instruction model. One recently developed performance assessment program (Louisiana) has responded to these concerns by focusing on teachers' interactions with students. Connecticut has also developed a more cognitively based component of its comprehensive teacher licensing program.

The question of accountability or control of the assessment process is a highly charged one in teacher licensing. The states are accountable for ensuring the basic qualifications of beginning teachers and thereby protecting the public from incompetent practitioners. Concern over equity and possible legal challenges also makes control of test use an important issue. Yet there is clearly a desire on the states' part to help professionalize teaching, assure a steady supply of teachers of all races, and promote educationally sound teacher induction processes.

One response by the states to these broader issues has been to establish formal beginning teacher induction programs, which have multiple purposes and forms. Some of these include summative assessment components, but many do not. Some beginning teacher programs are mentor programs, where beginning teachers are guided through their first year by a more experienced colleague. In many of these programs, assessment plays only a formative role, or may be absent altogether.

New Teacher Assessments: Educational Testing Service

As noted previously, the NTE assessments developed by ETS are used in 34 states for beginning teacher licensing. These tests are primarily multiple-choice, but with some limited paper-and-pencil constructed-response elements. ETS has recently develped new teacher assessments (The Praxis Series: Professional Assessments for Beginning Teachers™) to serve as a successor to the NTE beginning in 1992. These new assessments are explicitly designed to address some of the underlying educational reform goals, as well as to serve the traditional state beginning-teacher licensing function. Unlike the assessments being developed by the National Board of Professional Teaching Standards, ETS's Praxis Series is not intended to be used with expert teachers.

The Praxis Series is designed to be administered at critical milestones in the prospective teacher's career path. Although state-to-state variations are expected, basic enabling skills (reading, writing, mathematics) will be assessed early in college; subject-matter knowledge and general pedagogical principles will be assessed after formal undergraduate or graduate coursework is completed; and teaching performance will be assessed in the classroom during the prospective teacher's initial teaching experiences.

The development process for these new assessments has proceeded from a determination of the critical content to be measured for specific licensing decisions. These content determinations have been made through a series of national studies, using differing methodologies and soliciting the input of teachers, state teacher licensing officials, other educators and researchers, and the general public. Decisions about the appropriate methodology to be used were then made on the basis of what is to be measured.

In the case of enabling skills, the questions are computer-administered. Item types will include multiple-choice questions as well as various kinds of constructed responses, ranging from short answers to extended essays, with some computer-delivered item types involving spatial manipulation of text, such as locating or reorganizing information within a reading selection.

In the subject-matter assessments, the basic mode of administration is paper-and-pencil in a variety of formats that reflect the content characteristic of each subject-matter area. The assessments in each area are designed as a series of modules that can be selected by each state to conform as closely as possible to its own licensing requirements. Constructed-response modules form part of each subject area's offerings.

In the assessment of teaching skills, in addition to other content determination studies, it was especially important that the development of these new assessments begin with the articulation of a conception of teaching. The guiding conceptions of teaching for the performance assessments include recognition of the importance of the complexity of classroom interactions and the role of the teacher as a decision maker within this context (Dwyer & Villegas, 1992). Because the assessment of teaching skills covers both teacher tasks and student and subject-matter contextual variables (e.g., student individual differences, developmental level, and cultural background), these guiding conceptions can be incorporated to allow assessment of both thought and action in teaching. The assessments can thus draw on both the process/product research base and more recent cognitively based research on teaching. This part of the assessment is based on observation by trained evaluators in the teacher's own classroom, supplemented by two other methods integrated with the observations: interviews with the evaluators and written materials generated by the teacher. Specific criteria by which beginning teachers are to be assessed are drawn from a variety of cognitively and behaviorally oriented research and development sources. All of the teaching competencies to be evaluated are to be judged, taking into account the context of the individual teacher's students and the subject matter that she or he is teaching. Assessment thus requires direct interaction between the teacher and the evaluator, and significant professional judgment on the part of the evaluator.

These assessments, in form and content, are designed to be responsive to the underlying themes of educational reform. For example, concerns about the individual test-taker (prospective teacher) and the importance of aligning assessment with instruction in a constructive way have led to the incorporation of extensive instructional materials. In the enabling skills assessment, approximately 60–90 hours of computer-based instructional materials will be available to individuals for self-study in preparation for the assessments, or as a follow-up activity if additional help is needed. These instructional materials, which focus on the substance of reading, writing, and mathematics rather than on test-taking skills, are based on the model of "cognitive apprenticeship" as articulated by Collins, Brown, and Newman (1989). The major premise of this model is that cognitive and metacognitive strategies and processes are more central than either low-level subskills or abstract conceptual and factual knowledge. They are the organizing principles of expertise, particularly in such domains as reading, writing, and mathematics. These instructional materials are also aimed at concerns for ensuring a supply of capable teachers, especially minorities, who might otherwise be deflected from teaching through lack of guidance and instruction at this critical early stage. Another example of the integration of assessment and instruction in the Praxis Series is the instructional materials that form part of the assessment of teaching performance. Extensive evaluator training materials are part of these assessments, and can be adapted for staff development use with the prospective teachers who are being evaluated. These materials focus on the important elements of teaching that underlie the assessments, rather than on the assessment techniques themselves, and thus serve to establish a common understanding of the goals of teaching.

A second example of how these assessments are intended to respond to the themes of educational reform is the content of the assessment of teaching performance and the grounding of this assessment in classroom observation. These features respond to concerns about the value of directly measuring important complex skills in a manner that incorporates judgment, rather than relying on mechanistic rules or checklists that may be more reliable but do not allow the attention to context differences that may produce superior validity.

Third, an integral part of these assessments is the involvement of teachers throughout the development process. This is not a new phenomenon, as it is also characteristic of the current NTE tests, but it takes on new significance in the current climate of concern over the control of assessment and accountability.

A final consideration is the impact of these assessments on teacher preparation. As noted earlier, little empirical evidence is available about the links between assessment and learning, but there is a widespread feeling that the content of a national teacher licensing assessment, as well as the methods used to assess that content, will eventually become part of the teacher education curriculum. It should also eventually become part of states' and school districts' in-service curricula. All of these factors increase the burden of selecting the right content to be measured.

IMPLICATIONS FOR
THE FUTURE OF TEACHER ASSESSMENT

Innovation in teacher assessment presents a wide range of questions for practice and research. Despite the fact that not all of the constructed-response techniques in use or being developed today are new, they are being used in new ways, for new purposes. Inferences drawn from their use thus need systematic attention, as do policies and practices based on them.

Practice

It is clear that constructed-response assessments in whatever form will be a great deal more trouble for their developers and users than multiple-choice tests. They are considerable trouble to design, to score, to administer, and to interpret. Will this effort be judged worthwhile? Will teachers, states, and educational institutions continue to make the effort to use them? With reference to assessments of students, Mitchell (1989) cautioned us that although some teachers embrace authentic assessment enthusiastically, others resent the time it requires because they have not been trained to assume that level of responsibility, or they do not see information from such assessments as valuable. Only time and changes in the work force will alter teachers' views about what level of responsibility they have a right to—or a desire for—but the value of the information gained from assessments is at least partially under the control of measurement specialists.

Linn (1986) also raised the question of the practical difficulty in supplanting multiple-choice tests, pointing out that new measures must compete against multiple-choice's extraordinarily high efficiency and criterion-related validity. For better or for worse, the benefits of multiple-choice testing are tangible and can be communicated directly and simply; the benefits of alternative forms of assessment are largely long-term and intangible, and require a more sophisticated understanding. A great deal of potentially useful information can be generated, but important questions remain to be resolved about how this information can be synthesized and used as the basis for important decisions. This question of data aggregation is a central problem for areas other than constructed-response assessment. It was not completely resolved during the heyday of criterion-referenced testing, and is still part of the methodological struggles of qualitative research. Ironically, teacher assessment may be an area where progress can be made because, relative to students, teachers are few in number. At most levels in which decisions about teachers are to be made, the number of teachers affected remains low, and the problems of handling complex data about them may not be so overwhelming as they are for student testing.

In order for constructed-response assessment to meet the challenge of facing down more traditional modes of assessment, it needs to fulfill its promise of fuller integration with instruction. As a means of gathering *test* data alone, constructed-response assessment may not, in many cases, be worth the effort, even if it were to result in more precise measurement. As a means of improving instruction through the assessment and systematic study of important skills, however, constructed-response assessment probably *is* worth the effort. But these suppositions need to be demonstrated rigorously before they can be accepted as fact.

Another question to be addressed in the practice of innovative assessments is the control of assessments. As suggested in the earlier discussions of reform goals, this is a highly significant issue for teacher assessment, particularly in licensing applications. There seem to be two parts to the control question: who determines the content of the assessments (what is to be measured), and who determines the process (how it is to be measured). There is emerging consensus that teachers should control content. As is the case in other academic disciplines and professions, those *within* the specialty with a professional commitment to practice or theory in that area are in the best position to map the domains and indicate how they are operationalized in practice. We would not question the authority of the physician, the golf pro, or the barber to convey to the measurement specialist the essence of the knowledge base for assessment of these areas, yet we have done so regularly with teachers. The tide is rising against this practice, however, and will probably continue to do so with widespread support from teachers and others.

The question of control of the assessment process is less clear cut. Moral as well as legal authority to control the process varies with the uses of the assessment. States, for example, have a statutory obligation to regulate entry into teaching and other professions where the public cannot reasonably be expected to distinguish professional qualifications or standards. States must take into consideration their responsibility to protect the public and their obligation to treat potential practitioners equitably. Such decisions are difficult to disentangle from questions of appropriate content, and thus require sensitive negotiations with those who best understand the content.

Research

One of the main questions about the use of constructed-response or performance testing for teacher assessment is whether it fulfills its promise of increased validity. If one of the main points of using constructed response assessment is to increase the validity of assessment, at the presumed cost of some degree of control and reliability, then one needs to ask if the increased validity has actually been achieved. (It will be certain that the costs have been paid.) This is a general question, of course, and not one that is restricted to teacher assessment. In teacher assessment, as in other applications, this question can only be answered with reference to fundamental constructs. Content analyses of the assessment, or even criterion studies, do not give a full answer (Messick, 1989). In fact, in some cases, the new types of assessment are better "criterion" measures than any others in existence. Analyses of validity need to include attention to consequences: impact on teachers, students, and the entire system of which they are a part. The important issue of the impact of assessment on teacher education and other curricula needs systematic investigation. If this can be done, and if the answers are positive, then some of the reform goals proposed in the name of authentic assessment may be met.

A related validity issue is the question of fairness: Does the assessment innovation meet the hope of fairness, especially to minorities? At present, this is still an open question. Evaluation of fairness is plagued by differing views of fairness and the methods for achieving it. Is fairness demonstrated only through score-related data such as increased levels of achievement (higher scores) or reduced disparities between groups (smaller score differences)? Is consensus across subgroups on the appropriateness of the assessment domain a better strategy? How do affective and motivational factors enter into the evaluation of fairness? How do individual preferences for one mode of assessment over another affect performance? Our knowledge of these issues is still at a very rudimentary stage, but it is certain that inequality of educational opportunity will be revealed just as clearly through good constructed-response assessments as through multiple-choice, and that this news will result in much of the same unpleasantness that it does today. For some time, we as researchers will need to work at disentangling the effects of the assessment from the effects of disparate opportunities.

It is widely asserted that constructed-response assessment involves a higher degree of "subjectivity" than does multiple-choice testing. When subjectivity refers to human judgment in the process, this belief can be disputed. Multiple-choice testing also involves substantial human judgment about content. These judgments are, however, made before the administration of the test and are thus less easily observable. By contrast, constructed-response tests obviously require judgment at the scoring stage. This more public form of judgment can create the impression of a greater difference in the degree of judgment than is actually the case. Nevertheless, an important part of assessment reform is questioning the basis for making judgments about content and the acceptability of performances. As suggested earlier, constructed-response testing exposes the sources of judgment about performance. It becomes clear who is making specific judgments, and these judgments can then be called into question. Subjectivity is not synonymous with arbitrariness. It is usually used in a pejorative sense, but in fact "subjectivity" is that judgment that comes out of one's own cumulative experience and values; this is explicitly acknowledged when judgments are labeled "subjective." Today, research in many disciplines is questioning the meaning of purportedly "objective" methods and data, and education is no exception. Given emerging views of teaching as a complex and context-dependent activity, we need to come to terms methodologically with the use of professional judgment for evaluating its adequacy, and to question the simplistic view that such judgments are a contaminant in the measurement process.

This is not to say that judgments must be accepted without question. On the contrary, they must be questioned closely. Not all personal experience or personal values are acceptable for teacher assessments or other situations. Setting standards for evaluators (observers, readers, scorers, etc.) is a critical element in controlling the potential for bias and the overall quality of assessments. Thorough training is the primary vehicle for putting these standards into practice, and research on adherence to those standards is a continual obligation if the assessment system is to retain its integrity.

It is the unfortunate tendency, in education as well as in other complex systems, for bad practice to drive out good. This tendency means that for innovative as well as for traditional assessment systems, we must anticipate ways in which the system is likely to be debased. Safeguards against bad practice, to the extent that such practices can be reasonably anticipated, must be designed into the assessment system. Also implied is an obligation, as part of ongoing validation, to ensure the integrity of the system. We are currently better acquainted with the potential debasements of multiple-choice systems than of constructed-response ones. There are, however, numerous ways in which even a sophisticated and well-intentioned constructed-response assessment can be subverted through the introduction of irrelevant sources of variance. We do not yet know all of the ways in which such problems as superficial coaching, examinee dishonesty, evaluator "hidden agendas," or simply well-meaning attempts to streamline the process can corrupt performance systems, but we will surely face these problems for many years to come and a great deal of research on these issues remains to be done.

Another area in need of continued attention from research is the nature of teaching, and its implications for assessment. Current theory, as well as common sense, suggests that the context of the classroom and of the subject matter being taught should be important factors in teacher assessment. Can these beliefs be verified empirically? Is it possible for contextual factors to be included successfully in operational performance assessment systems? I expect that the answer to both these questions is yes, but additional data are surely needed.

CONCLUSIONS

Innovations and calls for the reform of teacher assessment demonstrate a larger truth: measurement must know its place. Measurement has enormous power to structure and illuminate important questions, but these questions themselves take precedence. The nature of teaching and the judgments that ought to be made about it are questions that arise from the field of teaching itself. The values of that field and its operating principles must be an integral part of teacher assessment if that assessment is to be judged useful in practice and successful in contributing to the solution of educational problems.

Traditional measurement values are sometimes in conflict with the dominant values of the discipline or system we seek to measure. In the case of teacher assessment, we are asked to sacrifice some control over sources of variation in order to take account of classroom context more intelligently. Classroom variability is thus not a contaminant in the measurement process, but an important part of what is measured. This conflict requires a reexamination of priorities and an openness to new ways of thinking about measurement. We have developed a formidable array of measurement and research tools that can be used in teacher assessment to improve education. But we can only be successful in the long term if we truly have the will to listen carefully to other voices, and to change.

REFERENCES

Bennett, R. E., Ward, W. C., Rock, D. A., & LaHart, C. (1990). *Toward a framework for constructed-response items* (RR-90-7). Princeton, NJ: Educational Testing Service.

California Commission on the Teaching Profession. (1985). *Who will teach our children? A strategy for improving California's schools.* Sacramento, CA: California Commission on the Teaching Profession.

Coffman, W. E. (1966). On the validity of essay tests of achievement. *Educational and Psychological Measurement, 3,* 151–156.

Coffman, W. E. (1990). Educational measurement in theoretical and political perspective [Review of *Educational measurement*]. *Educational Researcher, 19,* 36–38.

Cole, N. S. (1981). Bias in testing. *American Psychologist, 36,* 1067–1077.

Cole, N. S. (1988). A realist's appraisal of the prospects for unifying instruction and assessment. *Assessment in the service of learning: Proceedings of the ETS 1985 Invitational Conference* (pp. 103–117). Princeton, NJ: Educational Testing Service.

Cole, N. S., & Moss, P. A. (1989). Bias. In R. L. Linn (Ed.), *Educational measurement* (3rd ed., pp. 201–219). NY: Macmillan.

Collins, A., Brown, J. S., & Newman, S. E. (1989). Cognitive apprenticeship: Teaching the craft of reading, writing, and mathematics. In L. B. Resnick (Ed.), *Knowing, learning, and instruction* (pp. 453–494). Hillsdale, NJ: Lawrence Erlbaum Associates.

Cronbach, L. J. (1971). Test validation. In R. L. Thorndike (Ed.), *Educational measurement* (2nd ed., pp. 443–507). Washington, DC: American Council on Education.

Cronbach, L. J. (1980). Validity on parole: How can we go straight? In W. B. Schrader (Ed.), *New directions for testing and measurement No. 5. Measuring progress over a decade*. Proceedings of the 1979 ETS Invitational Conference (pp. 99–108). San Francisco: Jossey Bass.

Dwyer, C. A., & Villegas, A. M. (1992). *Guiding conceptions and assessment principles for The Praxis Series: Professional Assessments for Beginning Teachers™*. Princeton, NJ: Educational Testing Service.

Frederiksen, J. R., & Collins, A. (1989). A systems approach to educational testing. *Educational Researcher, 18*(9), 27–32.

Geiger, K. (1990). *NEA statement on authentic assessment*. Washington, DC: National Education Association.

Holmes Group. (1990). *Tomorrow's schools: Principles for the design of professional development schools*. E. Lansing, MI: Author.

Linn, R. L. (1986). Barriers to new test designs. *The redesign of testing for the 21st century: Proceedings of the ETS 1985 Invitational Conference* (pp. 69–79). Princeton, NJ: Educational Testing Service.

Lucas, C. K. (1988). Toward ecological evaluation. *Quarterly of the National Writing Project and the Center for the Study of Writing, 10*, 1–3, 12–17.

Madaus, G. F. (1985). Public policy and the teaching profession—you've never had it so good? *Educational Measurement: Issues & Practices, 4*(4), 5–11.

Messick, S. (1989). Validity. In R. L. Linn (Ed.), *Educational measurement* (3rd ed., pp. 13–103). NY: Macmillan.

Mitchell, R. (1989). Authentic assessment. *Basic Education: A Monthly Forum for Analysis & Comment, 33*(10), 6–9.

Mitchell, R. (1990, February 16). Open letter to B. Bidlingmaier, CTB/McGraw-Hill.

National Board for Professional Teaching Standards. (1989). *Toward high and rigorous standards for the teaching profession: Initial policies and perspectives of the National Board for Professional Teaching Standards*. Detroit, MI: Author.

National Commission on Excellence in Education. (1983). *A nation at risk: The imperative for educational reform*. Washington, DC: U.S. Government Printing Office.

Policy Information Center, Educational Testing Service. (1990). *The educational reform decade*. Princeton, NJ: Educational Testing Service.

Shavelson, R. J., Carey, N. B., & Webb, N. M. (1990). Indicators of science achievement: Options for a powerful policy instrument. *Phi Delta Kappan, 71*, 692–697.

Shepard, L. A. (1990). Inflated test score gains: Is the problem old norms or teaching the test? *Educational Measurement: Issues and Practice, 9*, 15–22.

Task Force on Teaching as a Profession. (1986). *A nation prepared: Teachers for the 21st century*. New York: Carnegie Forum on Education and the Economy.

Tittle, C. K. (1989). Validity: Whose construction is it in the teaching and learning context? *Educational Measurement: Issues and Practice, 8*, 5–13, 34.

Wiggins, G. (1989). A true test: Toward more authentic and equitable assessment. *Phi Delta Kappan, 70*(9), 703–713.

13

THE FEDERAL ROLE IN STANDARDIZED TESTING

Terry W. Hartle
Peter A. Battaglia
U. S. Senate Committee on Labor and Human Resources

Standardized testing, which usually means machine-scored multiple-choice tests, is a pervasive part of American education. The National Commission on Testing and Public Policy (1990; hereinafter referred to as National Commission on Testing) has estimated that each year elementary and secondary school students take 127 million separate tests. Some students may take as many as 12 tests a year. The National Center for Fair and Open Testing (Fair-Test) has calculated that roughly 100 million standardized tests were administered during the 1986–1987 school year (Medina & Neill, 1990). In fact, these estimates understate the amount of testing that takes place, because neither includes standardized testing done as part of the college admissions process or by institutions of higher education.

This much testing costs a lot of money. According to the National Commission on Testing (1990), purchasing and scoring these tests, plus the teacher time required to prepare students and administer the exams, costs between $725 and $915 million annually. It also involves a lot of time. The commission estimates that each year at least 20 million school days are spent taking standardized tests.

Despite the time and cost, the public generally likes the idea of standardized tests. The 1990 Gallup Poll of the Public Attitudes Toward the Public Schools asked whether children should be promoted from grade to grade only if they can pass an examination (Elam, 1990). Sixty-seven percent said yes, a figure that has changed only slightly since the question was first asked in 1978. The 1989 Gallup Poll asked whether or not the respondents favored or opposed the use of "standardized national testing programs to measure the academic achievement of students." Seventy-seven percent endorsed the use of such tests. Finally, the 1988 poll asked whether or not all high school students should be required to pass a "standardized nationwide examination" in order to get a high school diploma. Almost three quarters of the respondents (73%) approved such an exam—a substantial increase from the 50% that endorsed the idea when the question was first asked in 1958 (Elam, 1990).

The public's apparent enthusiasm is not, however, necessarily shared by education interest groups. The nation's largest teachers' union, the National Education Association, has historically been wary of standardized tests. The National Parent Teachers Association and the American Association of School Administrators have both taken positions in opposition to standardized tests. In addition, civil rights groups, noting the differential impact of such tests on minority groups, have also been reluctant to support standardized testing, and in some cases have opposed it.

The education community's unease over standardized testing was clearly apparent in the late 1970s when the Congress considered the desirability of a national graduation test. Despite widespread public support for the idea, education groups were hostile to the proposal and the plan died. Suggestions to revisit this proposal in the years since have not encountered any change in the view of the education community.

In the last 15 years, the public awareness of standardized testing has increased considerably. In part, the increase stems from the growing utilization of these tests and the widespread imposition of mandated exams—such as minimum competency tests—by state and local policymakers. At the same time, the number and intensity of complaints about standardized testing—especially about the multiple-choice format of tests—has grown. Critics charge that these tests are inaccurate, biased, expensive, time-consuming, and often poor indicators of what they purport to measure. Debates about the value and desirability of standardized tests have become an important part of education policy deliberation.

Because state governments are constitutionally responsible for education, it is not surprising that most of the action and debate is taking place at that level. However, the federal contribution to the development of standardized testing over the last century has been considerable and federal testing programs, mostly for employment, are extensive. In addition, there is widespread concern about the shortcomings of these tests by many congressional policymakers. This chapter explores the federal role in the development of standardized testing, reviews examples of the growing federal interest in standardized testing programs, and analyzes the major arguments for and against standardized testing most commonly heard by policymakers.

THE FEDERAL CONTRIBUTION
TO STANDARDIZED TESTING

The growth of standardized testing in the United States is the product of many factors. However, three early initiatives by the federal government—in civil service employment testing, military recruitment testing, and intelligence testing—had a profound impact on the development and expansion of testing in the United States. In addition to these major initiatives, the federal government has used standardized tests in other ways and contributed to their widespread usage.

Civil Service Employment Testing

The federal interest in standardized testing in the United States can be traced to the British civil service system. The success of this selection system in identifying high quality, efficient administrators for the British government led Senator Charles Sumner and Representative Thomas Jenckes to propose a U. S. civil service examination system in 1860. Eventually, following the assassination of President James A. Garfield by a disgruntled federal office seeker, the federal government adopted the Civil Service Act of 1883 (Wainer, 1990).

This legislation established the U. S. Civil Service Commission and authorized it to develop and administer examinations for federal jobs. The Commission was designed to replace the spoils system that had previously dominated federal employment with an objective examination that prospective federal employees would have to pass before being hired. Initially, only 10% of federal employees were required to take civil service examinations, but within a decade, the civil service selection system covered about 50% of all federal jobs (Haney, 1984).

The earliest federal civil service examination, which was used between 1883 and 1914, was an essay test. The second exam, a multiple-choice test of professional job knowledge, was administered between 1914 and 1947. From 1947 to 1955, the Civil Service Commission used the Junior Management Assistant (JMA) examination (U. S. Office of Personnel Management, 1990). In 1955, the exam was modified and renamed the Federal Service Entrance Examination (FSEE). In 1974, the FSEE was discontinued and replaced by the Professional and Administrative Career Examination (PACE).

The PACE exam was designed to help the Office of Personnel Management (OPM) in selecting the best qualified applicants for 118 entry-level professional and administrative occupations. PACE was taken annually by 150,000 to 200,000 graduating college seniors and others with equivalent experience (Downing, 1985). Those who passed with relatively high scores were certified to be hired. When a job opened, the agency was required to choose one of the three top scorers. PACE was not designed to test applicants' knowledge of specific job content, but as a general test of the mental abilities regarded as indispensable for many professional, administrative, and technical positions (Downing, 1985). These abilities were: capacity for deductive and inductive reasoning, judgment, numerical skills, and verbal comprehension. PACE was regarded as extremely difficult, and even at the height of government hiring, the vast majority of those who passed never got jobs (Havemann, 1987).

PACE was intended to ensure the competence of federal employees and to promote equal opportunity. However, civil rights groups regarded PACE as a barrier that restricted employment opportunities. Minorities, on the whole, scored lower than Whites and were denied access to entry-level professional jobs. Civil rights groups argued that attempts to measure mental abilities in the abstract were inappropriate and discriminatory in the selection process (Downing, 1985).

According to the Office of Personnel Management, only 0.7% of those who were certified to be hired were Black, although 11% of the PACE test takers were Black (Havemann, 1987). Moreover, in 1978 the Civil Service Commission noted that of all Whites who took the test, 13.2% attained total scores of 90 or above, whereas 0.7% of Blacks and 2.6% of Hispanics did so (Downing, 1985).

Because of the differential impact, civil rights groups filed a lawsuit, charging that the test discriminated against minorities. In response, the Carter Administration signed a consent decree to phase out PACE and to develop new tests that minorities would pass at a rate roughly proportionate to their numbers among test takers (Downing, 1985).

The decree, which took effect in November 1981, was designed to ensure the federal government's policy of a representative work force to include minorities in proportion to their populations in American society (Downing, 1985). The decree required OPM to make efforts to remove the negative effect of PACE or any subsequent test on minority groups. In 1981, the Reagan Administration abandoned the PACE exam entirely. Between 1981 and 1989, federal agencies were allowed to recruit and hire job applicants for entry-level positions without requiring them to take a standardized test. During that period, the Office of Personnel Management worked to develop an instrument that would not have a disproportionately negative impact on minorities.

The Administrative Careers With America (ACWA) examination, first administered in June 1990, consists of two components scored to produce a single composite. The first part is a Biodata Test (also known as an Individual Achievement Record). This is a questionnaire about experiences, skills, achievements in school, employment, and other activities (Havemann, 1990a). This section of the exam has removed all items dealing with conditions beyond the individual's control (e.g., questions that ask if an applicant's parents attended college).

The scoring for this portion of the exam is based on the successful job performance of 6,200 federal employees. The intention is to assess whether the applicant has the same or similar attributes as those currently holding the jobs. OPM claims that a test-taker performing well on this portion of the exam will have a high probability of succeeding as a federal employee.

The second portion of the ACWA exam is a multiple-choice test of the English language, verbal and numerical reasoning, and quantitative abilities; it assumes that the test-taker has college level reading and elementary algebra proficiency. Questions cover a wide range of difficulty, using words and concepts drawn from the everyday world of federal employees. This approach was taken to make the test more applicable and realistic than standardized tests that rely on abstract or hypothetical questions.

Although it is too early to make definitive judgments about the impact of the ACWA, as of November 1990, the initial pass rate by race and ethnicity was: Whites, 76%; Hispanics, 66%; and Blacks, 50%. The OPM believes that these results demonstrate that the ACWA exam does not adversely affect minorities and ethnic groups.

Currently, OPM is awaiting the plaintiff's comments (the same civil rights groups that filed the initial class action suit against OPM) on the preliminary results of the ACWA exam. If the Court rules that the test is nondiscriminatory, it will monitor the effects of the exam for the next 5 years to ensure that actual hiring is fair and demographically representative (Havemann, 1990b).

Military Recruitment Testing

The federal government has also relied heavily on standardized testing to meet its needs for military personnel. Given the large number of individuals to be tested, these testing programs have placed a heavy emphasis on low-level items that could be administered easily and scored quickly and cheaply. This emphasis has in turn shaped the use and nature of standardized testing in the United States.

Military testing of recruits began in World War I. At that time, psychologists under the leadership of Robert Yerkes developed an intelligence test that became known as the Army Alpha exam (Wainer, 1990). This testing program was used on 2 million men between 1917 and 1919. Two thirds of these received the Army Alpha; the remainder were tested with Army Beta, a nonverbal test devised for illiterate and non-English-speaking recruits. Together they represented the first large-scale use of intelligence testing (Wainer, 1990).

Military testing programs became much more extensive during World War II. In 1939, a Personnel Testing Service was established in the Office of the Adjutant General of the Army. This led to the Army General Classification Test (AGCT), which was an updated version of the Army Alpha (Wainer, 1990). The Navy used the Navy General Classification Test (NGCT), and both the Navy and Army Air Force used additional tests for other purposes. By the end of the war more than 9 million recruits had taken the AGCT in one form or another (Wiener & Steinberg, 1988).

In 1950, the Department of Defense initiated the Armed Forces Qualification Test (AFQT) as a screening instrument for all military services. This test was used from 1950 until the mid-1970s as a measure of military trainability (Wiener & Steinberg, 1988).

The AFQT consisted of 100 multiple-choice items and covered the following areas: vocabulary, arithmetic, spatial relations, and mechanical ability. There were five score categories; each service established its minimum standards for selection and used its own battery of aptitude tests for the initial assignment of recruits to technical schools or on-the-job training (Wiener & Steinberg, 1988).

On January 1, 1976, the Armed Services Vocational Aptitude Battery (ASVAB) was introduced as the sole Department of Defense (DOD) test to replace the various aptitude tests used by each service (Wainer, 1990). It is used both to determine eligibility for enlistment and to establish the individual's qualifications for assignments in specific military jobs.

The ASVAB measures vocational and aptitude skills of all prospective enlisted military personnel. There are two separate ASVAB programs: the Student Testing Program (STP), under which the military examines high school and postsecondary students; and the Enlistment Program (EP), which is administered to potential recruits at Military Entrance Processing Stations.

The ASVAB consists of 10 subtests. They are arithmetic reasoning, numerical operations, paragraph comprehension, word knowledge, coding speed, general science, mathematics knowledge, automotive and shop information, electronics information, and mechanical comprehension. The subtests are included in the battery because research has demonstrated that they are valid predictors of success in various military occupational specialties.

ASVAB results are reported as composites that are combinations of subtest scores. The most important combination is the Armed Forces Qualification Test (AFQT) score (to be distinguished from the test of the same name used from 1950 through the mid-1970s). The AFQT consists of four subtests (word knowledge, paragraph comprehension, arithmetic reasoning, and numerical operations). This score, supplemented by scores on various composites of aptitude subtests, is used in conjunction with educational, medical, and moral standards to determine the recruit's eligibility to enter the military (U. S. Department of Defense, 1982). Assignments to jobs are made on the basis of scores on other ASVAB composites, but there is a strong correlation between eligibility requirements for more complex jobs and AFQT scores. Using the AFQT and other indicators, the Armed Services annually screens about 750,000 applicants and subsequently enlists about 300,000 recruits (DOD, 1982).

In addition to the AFQT, a number of other composite scores are derived from the ASVAB. Military Service composite scores are used to identify, classify, and place applicants in areas in which applicants show the greatest aptitude. For example, the Army uses composite scores as a means to place applicants in combat, field artillery, electronics repair, food handlers, surveillance/communications, mechanical maintenance, general maintenance, clerical, skilled technical, and general technical positions. Each service is responsible for determining its own composite score criteria.

The ASVAB has not been trouble free. An error in the calibration of the exam in use from January 1976 through September 1980 resulted in inaccurate test scores for some recruits. The miscalibration inflated the AFQT scores of low-scoring enlistees. The problem was corrected with the introduction of the new test in October 1980. At the same time, the flawed scores from the 1976–1980 period were recomputed, using the corrected norms.

As a result of the miscalibration, the military accepted nearly 360,000 recruits (nearly one of every four recruits) who would have been disqualified for enlistment if the test has been properly calibrated. The problem was most acute in the Army where more than 200,000, or nearly one in three recruits, were erroneously enlisted. And, of those recruits who were accepted based on inflated test scores, many were enrolled in training programs for enlistees with high ASVAB scores, rather than in programs for those with lower scores (DOD, 1982).

The actual performance of these recruits, however, was much better than the ASVAB would have predicted. The on-the-job "failure rate" of enlistees whose low test scores should have kept them out of the military was not much higher than the failure rate for enlistees who scored above the cut-off. Analysts have suggested that this raises an important question about the value of a multiple-choice standardized pencil-and-paper test to allocate enlistment and training opportunities in the military. The experience also planted doubts in the minds of some policymakers about the extent to which standardized tests should be relied on by the Department of Defense as the primary criterion for enlistment (DOD, 1982).

Intelligence Testing of Immigrants

In the early 1900s, the federal government also experimented with standardized tests to assess the intellectual skills of immigrants. A common, and now discredited, view was that standardized tests provided a good way to judge the intellectual capabilities of immigrants and that the results of these tests were unlikely to change.

In 1923, Carl Brigham, who had helped develop the military tests, wrote *A Study of American Intelligence*. This book analyzed racial and ethnic differences in intelligence based on the Army data. He concluded that Alpine and Mediterranean peoples were intellectually inferior to members of the Nordic race. Black Americans scored below any White group Brigham studied. As a result, he warned against mixing the genes of various races (Brigham, 1923).

Brigham's science was shaky and easily attacked by other psychologists, and Brigham himself disavowed his interpretation in 1930. But the damage was done. As Tyack (1974) noted, Brigham's research appeared to give scientific validation to common social prejudice. As a result, it confirmed the alleged "inferiority" of some immigrants and gave powerful arguments to members of Congress who voted to discriminate against them in the immigration policy of the 1920s, most notably the Immigration Restriction Act of 1924. Eventually, of course, the federal government moved away from intelligence testing of immigrants, but the foray into this area is not a proud story for either testing or public policy (Tyack, 1974).

Foreign Service Exam

The federal government also uses a standardized test to screen applicants for the foreign service. The Foreign Service Exam (FSE) has been used since 1932 to assess applicant's knowledge of academic skills, American and world politics, and general information important to prospective foreign service officers. The current examination is administered by the Educational Testing Service on behalf of the Department of State, the United States Information Agency, and the Department of Commerce.

The FSE was exclusively an essay examination until the 1950s when a multiple-choice component was added. The FSE currently consists of a multiple-choice general background test that covers subjects basic to the functions of the foreign service and a three-part multiple-choice test of English expression. If an applicant passes the multiple-choice examination, he or she is eligible for a comprehensive assessment, which includes an oral examination, a written essay, a written summary exercise, a two-part group exercise, and a written "In-Basket" test. Job candidates who pass are given a thorough personal background investigation to determine eligibility for a security clearance and suitability for an appointment. In addition, the candidates are required to submit a 1,000-word autobiography and college transcripts (U. S. Department of State, 1990).

In October 1990, approximately 10,500 people took the FSE. Roughly 2,000 of them, or 20%, passed the multiple-choice portion of the examination and approximately 250 persons will eventually be appointed as Foreign Service Officer Career Candidates (U. S. Department of State, 1990).

Even though the Foreign Service participates in an affirmative action program aimed at hiring and promoting minorities and women, statistics show that the Service has not met a congressional mandate to develop a representative workforce. In January 1989, a class action suit was brought against the State Department by a civil rights group for failing to have a proportionate number of women in the Foreign Service. As a result, interim changes to the test were made in 1990 and final format changes to the FSE were expected in 1991. These changes are intended to reduce the adverse impact on minorities and women (U. S. Department of State, 1990).

National Assessment of Educational Progress

In the early 1960s, U. S. Commissioner of Education Francis Keppel began to seek a way to measure the educational effectiveness of our nation's schools. In July 1963, he asked Ralph Tyler to prepare a report outlining procedures for periodically gathering information to facilitate public debate and understanding of educational progress and issues (Wirtz & Lapointe, 1982).

Tyler's report led to the establishment of the National Assessment of Educational Progress (NAEP) in July 1969. A primary issue surrounding NAEP's establishment was whether or not it would lead to a national curriculum and therefore federal control of the schools. To address this concern, NAEP was initially prohibited from reporting scores except on a national and regional basis.

Since its inception in 1969, NAEP has measured the performance of millions of young Americans at ages 9, 13, and 17, in 11 instructional areas. Initially, NAEP was administered for the Department of Education by the Education Commission of the States based in Denver, Colorado. Since 1984, however, NAEP has been administered by the Educational Testing Service (ETS) in Princeton, New Jersey.

In May 1986, with America embarking on a multifaceted effort to improve the schools, Education Secretary William Bennett established a study group to examine the National Assessment of Educational Progress and to identify possible improvements. The study group, chaired by Tennessee Governor Lamar Alexander and Thomas James, released its report in January 1987.

The Alexander–James report noted that NAEP's data were useful only for the country as a whole and not for individual states or local communities and recommended that state and local data be collected and reported. In addition, the report proposed to increase the frequency of the assessments and the number of subjects assessed. The report estimated that the changes would increase the annual cost of NAEP from $3 million to roughly $26 million (Alexander & James, 1987).

The Congress considered proposals to expand NAEP as part of the Augustus Hawkins and Robert Stafford Elementary and Secondary Education Improvement Act of 1988 (PL 100-297). The Senate-adopted legislative provisions authored by Senators Edward Kennedy (D-MA) and Orrin Hatch (R-UT) expanded NAEP, but not as much as recommended by the Alexander–James report. The Senate-passed proposals were endorsed by the Reagan Administration, The National Education Association, the American Federation of Teachers, and the National Governors Association. They were opposed by the National Parent Teachers Association. Several other education associations, including the National School Boards Association and the American Association of School Administrators, expressed reservations about the proposed expansion.

The arguments against the expansion of the National Assessment included concerns that the state-by-state provisions would work to the disadvantage of low socioeconomic status states, harm minority children, cost too much money, and lead to a national curriculum. The arguments in favor of the expansion were that it would provide much more comprehensive and accurate data about educational achievement than was previously available and that the nation needed such data to improve the schools.

Eventually, as part of the House–Senate conference on the bill, the conferees authorized an expansion in the frequency of NAEP assessments and in the subjects assessed, and the collection and publication of state-level data on a pilot basis in the 1990 and 1992 assessments. In addition, the conferees agreed to establish a semiautonomous National Assessment Governing Board (NAGB) to oversee the expanded NAEP. The composition of the NAGB gave states and other constituencies a much greater policy making and oversight role than they had previously. In light of the concerns raised about the expansion of NAEP, the Congress mandated a thorough third-party review of the pilot state-level assessments and prohibited NAEP data from being used to compare individual schools or school districts.

The 1990 NAEP survey included a pilot state-level assessment in eighth-grade mathematics. The pilot assessment was to be expanded in 1992 to include fourth-grade mathematics and reading. Thirty-seven states signed up for the 1990 pilot—far more than the 25 that Congress expected when it approved the expansion.

In early 1990, the National Assessment Governing Board (NAGB) found itself in the middle of unexpected criticism after it adopted a resolution calling for further expansion of NAEP. The resolution, among other things, proposed that all states participate in a state-by-state comparison of student achievement, that the prohibition on the use of NAEP data at the district- and school-level be lifted, and that NAEP measure at least three subject areas each year. The NAGB proposals resulted in an "open letter" from a group of 75 education and civil rights groups urging policymakers to resist such steps. The NAGB proposals, which would require explicit congressional approval, were not endorsed by the Bush Administration or considered by the Congress.

THE GROWING FEDERAL INTEREST IN EDUCATIONAL TESTS

In addition to the major testing programs employed by the federal government, reliance on standardized tests by federal policymakers for educational purposes has increased recently. In some cases, the use of tests is a by-product of another goal, but the result is the same: The federal government is using or encouraging the use of more standardized tests.

In one case, the increased use of standardized tests is the result of an effort to ensure that disadvantaged students receiving federally funded compensatory education make academic progress. A provision added to the Chapter 1 program in 1988 required that states and local school districts adopt measures to evaluate the educational performance of students who participate in the program. Although precise estimates are hard to obtain, most school districts have responded to this requirement by increasing the use of standardized, multiple-choice tests.

A second example of the increased federal interest, this one at the postsecondary level, is a requirement that expanded the use of standardized tests for some students seeking federal student assistance to pay college bills. Under legislation enacted as part of the Omnibus Budget and Reconciliation Act of 1990 (PL 101-508), students who lack a high school diploma or its equivalent must take and pass an independently administered test approved by the Secretary of Education before receiving the financial assistance. This measure gives the Department of Education (ED) the authority to approve and set passing scores on postsecondary educational tests as a criterion for receiving a federal benefit. This new responsibility, which was designed to reduce the abuse of the "ability to benefit" eligibility criteria for student assistance by some schools, is a significant expansion of the Department of Education's statutory responsibilities that was little debated when it was enacted.

Still another example includes proposals for the development of a national (not necessarily federal) educational test. The President's Education Policy Advisory Committee (PEPAC) has proposed the development of multiple education tests (by multiple vendors) that could be given to students at several points in elementary and secondary school. States and local school districts would decide whether or not to participate in such testing programs and which test(s) to use.

A similar proposal has been advanced by Educate America, a group chaired by former New Jersey Governor Thomas Kean. They have recommended the development of a single test that could be given to all high school students before graduation.

It is too early to tell whether or not such tests will be developed, but the U. S. Secretary of Education already has the authority to "develop or designate" a national education test. This authority, which was provided in 1988, has never been used. However, Secretary of Education Lamar Alexander noted in his confirmation hearing before the Senate Committee on Labor and Human Resources in January 1990 that he favored the development of national education tests along the lines proposed by PEPAC. Both the House Education and Labor Committee and the Senate Committee on Labor and Human Resources conducted hearings on this issue in early 1990.

WHY POLICYMAKERS LIKE STANDARDIZED TESTS AND WHY THEY DO NOT

Federal and state policymakers use standardized tests for different reasons. At the federal level, some standardized tests are used to assess the employability of potential federal workers or military recruits. In addition, the federal government uses the National Assessment of Educational Progress (NAEP) to gather data about the quality of education in elementary and secondary schools.

Both types of examinations are important. The first, because the standardized tests are assumed to result in an effective and efficient allocation of employment opportunities that will produce a highly qualified workforce. The second is important because it represents the only independent, nationally representative source of data about the nation's educational achievement. Indeed, preserving the continuity and trend data provided by the National Assessment is always the first priority when changes to the NAEP are debated.

State policymakers have much more complicated reasons for using standardized tests. Perhaps the most important is that they must make informed choices about how to best spend taxpayer dollars on education. One of the easiest and most direct ways to justify the expenditures on education is by using tests to demonstrate what educators are providing in return for the money they are being given.

Testing is used at the state level for several other purposes. It is sometimes designed to identify which schools or districts have the lowest levels of educational achievement and need more help. In this fashion, testing is intended to enhance accountability or even, in the eyes of some advocates, to be an engine of reform that establishes standards schools are then expected to meet. Testing is also done to ensure that school personnel, especially teachers, meet minimum professional qualifications. Finally, testing is often used to measure the educational skills of individual students and to help diagnose areas where they need additional tutoring.

Statewide testing programs in each of these areas have become increasingly popular. In 1987, FairTest staff conducted a survey of education officials from all 50 states (Medina & Neill, 1990). This survey, compared to a 50-state survey conducted by *Education Week* in 1985, found that:

1. The number of states requiring students to pass a standardized test for high school graduation increased from 15 in 1985 to 24 in 1987.
2. The number of states employing standardized tests to determine whether students should be promoted to the next grade increased from 8 in 1985 to 12 in 1987.
3. The number of states using standardized tests as part of a state assessment program increased from 37 in 1985 to 42 in 1987.

There are, however, important differences in the purposes of these different testing programs. Tests that are designed to measure individual student achievement are not likely to be good for assessing the educational performance of an entire school district. Similarly, testing of school personnel provides little information about the overall educational quality of a school system or about student performance. Discussions of testing by policymakers often blur these important differences.

Regardless of the precise purpose, reliance on tests sends educators and the public an unwritten message that "We are serious about educational performance." Many state legislators—and the public, judging from the opinion polls cited earlier—believe testing provides a reasonable, simple, and efficient way to ensure educational quality and to maintain educational standards.

Although states have increased the number and types of tests that are administered in the schools, most policymakers are increasingly aware of the shortcomings and limitations of standardized tests. Among the allegations: tests are biased, inaccurate, expensive, time-consuming, and often poor measures of real-world skills that distort what is taught in the classroom. In some cases—such as the ASVAB miscalibration between 1976 and 1980—the tests can yield inaccurate and unreliable results. These arguments deserve further analysis.

Tests Are Inaccurate Measures of Real World Skills

Policymakers and the public are increasingly aware of what educators and testing specialists have known for a long time: Test scores are only an estimate of what someone actually knows or can accomplish. Extensive studies of college admissions have documented that standardized test scores by themselves are a weak predictor of classroom performance. According to the National Commission on Testing (1990), employment tests predict job performance even less accurately. Finally, as noted earlier, the calibration error in the Armed Services Vocational Aptitude Battery (ASVAB) showed that the test score was not, for many recruits, an accurate measure of future performance.

Testing Has an Excessive Influence on What is Taught in the Classroom

Critics argue that testing has a disproportionate influence on what is taught in the schools. The significance attached to test scores means that rote learning is often emphasized because that is what is measured by most standardized tests. The emphasis on rote learning may come at the expense of educational practices that would foster critical thinking and active learning. Among the troubling practices identified by the National Commission on Testing were: aligning instruction narrowly with test content, letting students practice on test questions, testing children with a test meant for those at a lower grade, and exempting low-achieving children from taking the tests.

A paper prepared for the National Commission on Testing by Haertel (1989) of Stanford University described the instructional shifts created by standardized testing:

> There has been a subtle shift, especially at the primary and upper elementary levels, toward instructional activities resembling objective test formats . . . Classroom discussion, simulations, and small-group activities, and extended writing opportunities will do less to improve test scores than will worksheets requiring students to answer brief, isolated questions by filling in blanks or selecting among fixed choices. (p. 36)

Some educators believe that the education reform movement has increased the pressure on schools to emphasize test score improvements. Walter Haney, an education professor and testing expert, recently told the *Wall Street Journal*, "There is incredible pressure on school systems and teachers to raise test scores. So efforts to beat the test are also on the rise" (Putka, 1990, p. A24).

Unfortunately, efforts to beat the test can include outright cheating. In one widely publicized case, a South Carolina high school teacher was fired after giving students the questions and answers to a state-mandated basic skills test. The teacher said she did this so that her disadvantaged children would do well on the test and have a better self-image. Cynics noted another possibility: Student scores on the test were used to determine teacher salary bonuses (Putka, 1990).

Standardized Tests Are Biased Against Minorities

There is a widespread perception that tests are unfair to minorities. Black Americans, Hispanics, American Indians, native Pacific Islanders, some Asian Americans, and other minorities have consistently scored much lower than their majority peers on standardized tests. These group differences can be seen on tests ranging from kindergarten entrance examinations to tests used in elementary and secondary schools, and from college and post-college admissions tests to vocational and employment tests (National Commission on Testing, 1990). There is no shortage of examples. On the Scholastic Aptitude Test, for example, Black Americans, on average, score about 100 points below their White counterparts. Although the difference has narrowed in recent years and is largely explained by socioeconomic status differences, it remains unacceptably large. Similar results are seen on the National Assessment of Educational Progress. The gap between reading and mathematics achievement for White and minority students narrowed in the last decade, but substantial disparities remain. A study by the Educational Testing Service concluded that test cut-off scores on the National Teachers Examination invariably resulted in a lower pass rate for Blacks and Hispanics than for Whites (DeMauro, 1989).

The National Commission on Testing (1990) suggested that there are two reasons for group differences in test performance. First, tests are culturally bound and almost always reflect the dominant or "national" culture in both format and content. Research shows that the orientation of the test—toward the topics and culture of one group as opposed to another—can significantly affect test scores. The second cause of differential group performance is economic and educational. Many ethnic, linguistic, and cultural minorities suffer economic disadvantages, such as lower educational attainment by parents, lower average incomes, higher rates of unemployment, and jobs with significantly lower occupational status than majority group members; these problems magnify the educational disadvantages (National Commission on Testing, 1990).

The low test scores of minorities and women are a particular problem for federal policymakers. Most federal education programs are designed to increase educational opportunities for disadvantaged groups. Evidence that most minorities consistently score lower than Whites on almost all testing programs makes policymakers somewhat suspicious of testing and reluctant to expand testing programs. On the other hand, it is also likely to increase interest in new assessment techniques that do not have a disproportionate racial impact.

Tests Harm Young Children

Many school systems now routinely administer some form of standardized screening or readiness tests for admittance to kindergarten or of standardized achievement tests for promotion to first grade. Pre-kindergarten tests are required in more than 16 states and widely used in seven more. Kindergarten exit or first grade entrance exams are used in five states. In some school districts up to 60% of the kindergartners are judged "unready" for first grade because of their scores on readiness tests. Achievement tests are required for first graders in nine states, for second graders in nine states, and for third graders in 27 states (National Commission on Testing, 1990).

Some assessment instruments for young children offer rational skill inventories with useful provisions for their administration and interpretation. However, not all such tests meet these high standards. The idea of widespread testing of very small children intuitively makes many people uncomfortable.

Three concerns in particular are often noted. First, the intellectual development of young children is volatile and sporadic, making rigid interpretation of such tests misleading at best. Thus, young children may be mislabeled and stigmatized by low scores even before they start school, and such a stigma may be hard to overcome. A second concern is that the options usually given to "unready" children are not especially desirable: either stay out of school for a year before starting kindergarten or enter a 2-year kindergarten track.

A third concern is that the "tests" given to small children do not always meet the highest technical standards. For example, the most commonly used readiness assessment was developed by the Gesell Institute of Human Development in New Haven. The assessment is meant to measure the overall behavioral readiness of children to adjust and adapt to appropriate age and grade expectations (Carmody, 1989). According to the *Ninth Mental Measurements Yearbook*, the *Gesell School Readiness Test* was normed on a sample of 640 children ranging from 2 to 6 years old, nearly all of whom were White and lived in Connecticut (Bradley, 1985). In addition, the *Yearbook* notes that makers of the test did not provide validity studies to demonstrate that the test measures what it purports to.

Use of the *Gesell School Readiness Test* as a means to place children in kindergarten was successfully challenged by a New York family. After taking the 15-minute long test, the plaintiff's daughter was deemed "unready" for regular kindergarten and placed in a "developmental" kindergarten. Upon investigation, the parents discovered that 61% of the children in the district were found to be unready for regular kindergarten ("Challenge to Gesell," 1988).

Tests Are Inaccurate and May Have a Bias Toward "Above Average" Scores—The Lake Wobegon Effect

Test results may be misleading or inaccurate. In 1987, physician John Cannell published a report documenting that all the states were, according to state data, scoring above average on nationally normed standardized tests (Phillips, 1990). Critics promptly dubbed this the "Lake Wobegon effect"— after Garrison Keillor's mythical town where "the women are strong, the men are good-looking, and all the children are above average" (Nitko, 1990). In 1988, the U. S. Department of Education (ED) sponsored a study to analyze

Cannell's findings. Even though the study criticized some aspects of Cannell's technical approach, the study confirmed Cannell's primary findings (Phillips, 1990).

ED's study identified five factors that contributed to the Lake Wobegon effect:

1. School districts may choose tests that are best aligned with their curricula, thus giving test users an advantage not shared by students in the norming sample.

2. Students in school districts using the tests may be more motivated to do well than students in the norming sample, for whom the test does not count.

3. School systems may have used the same test repeatedly, thus giving the schools more time to become familiar with the test content and format—an advantage not shared by the norming sample.

4. Higher achieving school districts may not participate in the norming process to the same degree as lower achieving ones. This may make districts that use the test look more adept than they would had they been compared to a sample more representative of the general population.

5. The segment of the school district being tested may differ from the norming sample. For example, the school system may exclude low achieving or limited English proficient students from the tested population while these students were included in the norming sample.

Equally significant is that there is a powerful incentive for school districts to convince taxpayers that the schools are doing a good job. There is no better way than to demonstrate that the schools are "above average" on achievement tests. It is much easier to attract support for bond issues if the taxpayers believe they are getting their money's worth.

CONCLUSION

The nation's drive for improved education is unlikely to end in the near future and testing is seen as a quick and easy way to get information about educational performance. Despite their flaws, standardized test results convey a clear impression of how students and schools are doing. These tests are here to stay.

By any yardstick, student testing expanded sharply in the last few years: 47 states had statewide testing programs in 1990, an increase from 37 five years earlier. Twenty-three states have gone beyond test scores and adopted an integrated set of indicators designed to enhance educational "accountability."

At the federal level, the Congress has approved, at least on a trial basis, an expansion of the National Assessment of Educational Progress. In addition, other federal actions have, somewhat unexpectedly, increased the use of standardized tests for students receiving Chapter 1 educational benefits and for those without a high school diploma seeking federal student aid. Interest in a national test or tests for elementary and secondary school students has never been higher.

But although standardized multiple-choice tests are popular, policymakers are increasingly aware of their shortcomings. The work of the National Commission on Testing and the emergence of organizations like FairTest will further call attention to the shortcomings of many current assessment methods. Some opinion polls suggest that support for testing, although still high, may be diminishing. The reservations about standardized testing are most pronounced among members of minority groups.

The dynamics that will shape public policy regarding tests and their use in the coming decade vary depending on the level of government involved. There will be differences between federal and state interest in the use of standardized testing because their roles in American education are distinctly different.

Most states already have testing programs and many others have accountability systems. It is unlikely that any state will abandon them. However, state policymakers will probably look skeptically at "high stakes" exams where a benefit is clearly linked to performance. Given the highly publicized shortcomings of standardized tests—especially cheating, teaching to the test, and race and gender score differences—many policymakers are wary of making a test score the sole criterion for allocating public benefits, such as scholarships or school rewards.

The federal role in education is supplemental. However, the federal government has played a major role in the development of standardized tests in the United States. It did this without a conscious plan, but the result of federal testing of military recruits, civil servants, and immigrants, and the development of the National Assessment of Educational Progress, have—for good and bad—shaped educational testing in America.

Educational testing makes widespread use of efficient, reliable tests based on multiple-choice items of low-level complexity. However, these characteristics have impeded the enhancement of testing to address higher level skills and improve student performance in specific academic subjects. The testing questions that plague educators and policymakers revolve around validity, equity, and the appropriateness of the tests. These are tough issues, and the debate about them will continue to be lively.

At the federal level, there will be extensive discussions about the national education goals and the best ways to measure progress toward them. A major debate over the necessity, desirability, and feasibility of a national education test (or tests) is likely. In addition, there is certain to be an extensive discussion about the National Assessment of Educational Progress. Three issues in particular will attract attention: the frequency of the NAEP tests, whether or not to continue reporting state level data, and whether or not to lift the prohibition on using NAEP data at the school district and individual school level.

It is also possible that the federal government will play a role in stimulating research about new forms of testing and assessment. Many educators and policymakers are interested in performance and portfolio assessments and computerized-adaptive testing. There is interest too in alternative employee-selection techniques such as trainability tests and work samples. The Educational Equity and Excellence Act of 1990, which failed to pass on the last day of 101st Congress, authorized research into "curriculum-referenced" testing. The federal government's historic support for education research makes this a logical area for federal involvement in the future.

Although promising, there are likely to be shortcomings to new assessment instruments that are similar to the concerns now expressed about multiple-choice standardized tests. For example, there is already evidence that teachers can teach to performance assessments, just as they can to existing standardized tests. In fact, some observers believe that performance assessments may actually narrow the curriculum more than existing tests. Moreover, performance tests will not necessarily result in better student performance, particularly for those who fared poorly in the past. For example, the 1988 writing assessment of the National Assessment of Educational Progress allowed students more time to complete the assignment, and score disparities between Whites and minorities actually increased on some performance tasks (Applebee, Langer, Jenkins, Mullis, & Foertsch, 1990). Finally, performance-based assessments are both expensive and time-consuming— much more so than standardized multiple-choice tests.

Because of the uncertainty over the validity of performance-based tests, the United States will not participate in the 1991 international assessment in mathematics and sciences. After concluding that the methodology of performance-based assessment was not sufficiently well-developed to implement on such a widespread and visible basis, the National Research Council (NRC) recommended against U. S. participation and the National Science Foundation accepted the NRC recommendation. The U. S. will take part in the multiple-choice portion of the assessment, however.

This is not, of course, to say that performance-based assessments are bad. On the contrary, these are promising assessment techniques that merit further attention and development. Nonetheless, performance-based assessments have potentially serious shortcomings that must be addressed if they are to represent a genuine improvement. In short, standardized testing will continue to be relied on by public policymakers for information about educational achievement. It will also continue to be a subject of vigorous debate.

REFERENCES

Alexander, L., & James, H. T. (1987). *The nation's report card: Improving the assessment of student achievement.* Boston, MA: The National Academy of Education, Harvard Graduate School of Education.

Applebee, A. N., Langer, J. A., Jenkins, L. B., Mullis, I. V. S., & Foertsch, M. A. (1990). *Learning to write in our nation's schools: Instruction and achievement in 1988 at grades 4, 8 and 12.* Princeton, NJ: Educational Testing Service.

Bradley, R. (1985). Review of Gesell School Readiness Test. In J. V. Michael, Jr. (Ed.), *Ninth mental measurements yearbook* (Vol. 1, pp. 609–610). Lincoln, NE: Buros Institute of Mental Measurements.

Brigham, C. C. (1923). *A study of American intelligence.* Princeton, NJ: Princeton University Press.

Carmody, D. (1989, May 11). Debate intensifying on screening tests before kindergarten. *The New York Times*, p. B1, 13.

Challenge to Gesell as kindergarten placement exam (1988, Fall). FairTest Examiner, p. 5–6.

DeMauro, G. E. (1989). *Passing the NTE: A classification of state requirements and passing rates, by ethnicity.* Princeton, NJ: Educational Testing Service.

Downing, P. M. (1985). *Elimination of the Professional and Administrative Career Examination (PACE): Suspension of testing for many federal positions.* Washington, DC: Library of Congress, Congressional Research Service.

Elam, S. M. (1990). *The 22nd annual Gallup poll of the public's attitudes toward the public schools. Phi Delta Kappan, 72*(1), 42–55.

Haertel, E. (1989). Student achievement tests as tools of education policy: Practices and consequences. In B. R. Gifford (Ed.), *Test policy and test performance: Education, language, and culture* (pp. 25–50). Boston: Kluwer Academic Publishers.

Haney, W. (1984). Test reasoning and reasoning about testing. *Review of Educational Research, 54*(4), 597–654.

Havemann, J. (1987, March 5). What next for choosing new workers? Court-ordered testing may face challenge. *The Washington Post*, p. A25.

Havemann, J. (1990a, July 20). In search of the perfect civil service exam. *The Washington Post*, p. A17.

Havemann, J. (1990b, April 30–May 6). Taking the guesswork out of hiring. *The Washington Post*, p. 31.

Medina, N., & Neill, D. M. (1990). *Fallout from the testing explosion: How 100 million standardized exams undermine equity and excellence in America's public schools* (3rd ed.). Boston: National Center for Fair and Open Testing.

National Commission on Testing and Public Policy (1990). *From gatekeeper to gateway: Transforming testing in America.* Chestnut Hill, MA: Boston College, National Commission on Testing and Public Policy.

Nitko, A. J. (1990). Lake Wobegon revisited. *Educational Measurement: Issues and Practice, 9*(3), 2.

Phillips, G. W. (1990). The Lake Wobegon effect. *Educational Measurement: Issues and Practice, 9*(3), 3, 14.

Putka, G. (1990, May 23). Study on school, job testing finds bias and misuse, urges special regulator. *The Wall Street Journal*, p. A24.

Tyack, D. (1974). *The one best system: A history of American urban education.* Cambridge, MA: Harvard University Press.

U. S. Department of Defense, Office of the Assistant Secretary of Defense. (1982). *Profile of American youth: 1980 nationwide administration of the Armed Services Vocational Aptitude Battery.* Washington, DC: Department of Defense.

U. S. Department of State. (1990). *History, development, and present structure of the Foreign Service Officer Selection Program.* Arlington, VA: Board of Examiners for the Foreign Service.

U. S. Office of Personnel Management. (1990). Interview with Magda Colberg, Chief of the Measurement, Research and Applications Division at OPM concerning the new civil service examination. Washington, DC: Office of Personnel Management.

Wainer, H. (1990). The first four millennia of mental testing: From ancient China to the computer age. *The Score*, 4–5, 11–13.

Wiener, S., & Steinberg, E. P. (1988). *Practice for the Armed Forces Test: ASVAB*. New York, NY: Simon & Schuster.

Wirtz, W., & Lapointe, A. (1982). *Measuring the quality of education, A report on assessing educational progress*. Washington, DC.

14

THE POLITICS OF MULTIPLE-CHOICE VERSUS FREE-RESPONSE ASSESSMENT

Sharon P. Robinson
National Education Association

> *In the United States a politician first tries to see what his own interest is and who has analogous interests which can be grouped around his own; he is next concerned to discover whether by chance there may not be somewhere in the world a doctrine or a principle that could conveniently be placed at the head of the new association to give it the right to put itself forward and circulate freely. It is like the royal imprimatur which our ancestors printed on the first page of their work and incorporated into the book even though it was not a part of it.*
> (Alexis de Tocqueville quoted in Gifford, 1989, p. 12.)

Numerous observers have noted the unrelenting growth of standardized testing in education and in the broader society (Corbett & Wilson, 1991; Rothman, 1990; Shepard, 1989). This chapter discusses the political dynamics fueling this growth, particularly with respect to tests characterized by multiple-choice and other "limited-response" items. It is argued that, whereas the need to reform schools is often the reason for policy mandates requiring testing, the intent of education reform will be frustrated by continued reliance upon limited-response tests. Given the needs of an information-based economy, the complexity of a democratic society, and the educational interests of students, this paper proposes that the assessment of school and student performance will be better served when educators, the public, and policymakers institute more appropriate forms of assessment.

LIMITED- VERSUS EXTENDED-RESPONSE ITEM TYPES

What is a limited-response test item? Item types described by Bennett, Ward, Rock, and LaHart (1990; see also Bennett, this volume) as multiple-choice, selection/identification, reordering/arrangement, substitution/correction, and completion are typical limited-response items in most current assessment. These formats require the test-taker to select the correct answer from the options provided, arrange given elements to form a correct answer, replace an incorrect formulation with a correct one, or, in the case of completion, to supply a word, number, or other short answer. Underlying these formats is the assumption that, at most, only a small set of the possible answers is correct, and that all possible correct answers can be recognized. Tests consisting of these items can be administered to large numbers of examinees simultaneously, and responses can be machine scored objectively and efficiently. Most limited-response items depend upon recall or recognition of isolated bits of information, rather than requiring the examinee to demonstrate the ability to use information for extended analysis or problem solving. As a result, these items provide little diagnostic information. Finally, multiple-choice items, in particular, are susceptible to guessing and coaching.

By contrast, extended-response items permit the examinee to develop an answer that illustrates the knowledge required for an acceptable response. For example, construction items (Bennett et al., 1990) require the examinee to develop an answer such as a graph, essay, or architectural drawing that is evaluated upon completion. Presentations, a second class of extended-response items, bring into play the process of constructing the response, as well as any associated product. Extended-response items are associated with more recent conceptions of intelligence and skill, specifically, those advanced by Gardner (1983, 1988) and Sternberg (1987), because they capture the different ways individuals express knowing, and because they emphasize that multiple ways of knowing can be developed, demonstrated, and accepted as creditable. Accomplishment is documented in a variety of products including written assignments, projects, and videotapes of performance. This portfolio of constructions and presentations can be viewed by education professionals, parents, the examinee, and others. Where the portfolio is maintained over the years, all interested parties can assess progress for content mastery, problem-solving skills, creativity, and other important factors not adequately represented in the more traditional limited-response data.

The same construction items can be administered concurrently to large numbers of test-takers, but machine scoring is not always possible. This greatly increases the cost of assessment. In the case of presentation items, it may not be possible to rate examinees on exactly the same content. Although both construction and presentation items provide rich information, they permit substantially more subjectivity in scoring than most limited-response items.

Confidence in evaluator objectivity is essential; the criteria by which a response is judged must be legitimate and universally applied to all responses. When using extended-response items, grader reliability is often enhanced through a jury approach, where multiple judges assess each examinee's responses. Although this technique increases cost, it permits various perspectives to influence the evaluation. In this sense, extended-response items graded by juries require the examinee and the examiner to perform "in public."

THE POLITICS OF ASSESSMENT

Interested Parties

The use of multiple-choice and other limited-response items is supported by a highly developed psychometrics; that is, standards for test construction and rules for data aggregation and interpretation. Technically, validity (the meaning that may be inferred from test scores) and reliability (the precision of scores) are honored hallmarks in the evaluation of a test. However, in the politics of assessment, validity means that what the test measures is important (and taught); reliability means that the test measures the same thing in all test-takers. The resultant score is an *objective* representation of the individual's accomplishment, capacity, and worth.

Those seeking to influence assessment policy are numerous; their interests are various, and sometimes conflicting. These interests constitute the politics of assessment. Numerous parties compete for influence regarding what is measured and how; who is assessed and for what purposes; who is responsible for conducting the assessment; and who has the authority to interpret the results to the education community and to the community at large. The following analysis illustrates just how complex this matter is.

Parents want evidence that their children are developing intellectually and progressing toward standards required for independent adult responsibilities. A 1990 Gallup Poll revealed that parents of children in public schools give their local schools higher grades than they would assign to public education generally (Elam, 1990). When grading public schools nationally, 69% of parents assigned grades from C to failing. When grading the school attended by their eldest child, 26% of the parents assigned grades from C to failing. These results continue a trend showing strong parental satisfaction with local schools.

Evidence from other quarters, however, suggests a need for concern. A recent report summarizing 20 years of National Assessment of Educational Progress (NAEP) findings (Mullis, Owen, & Phillips, 1990) concludes:

- A near majority of students assessed fail to demonstrate the capacity to use subject-related information for analytical purposes.
- Although progress has been made in basic skills, declines are noted in students' reasoning ability.
- Little attention is given to mathematics, science, history, and geography in elementary schools.
- Instructional techniques, especially for mathematics and science, do not conform with the active, student-centered techniques suggested by contemporary pedagogical research.
- Parents must encourage students to take more challenging courses and to spend more time on school work.

One wonders about the source of such strong parental satisfaction with the schools attended by their children, but dissatisfaction with public schools nationally. Parents may not have the information required to evaluate thoroughly their local schools relative to important learning outcomes. Possibly, the school's performance in district and statewide assessment programs is high enough on knowledge represented by such limited-response tests to divert attention from deficiencies in higher level skills.

Business leaders want evidence that schools are producing a literate workforce, as well as data that assist them in making reliable and efficient hiring decisions. Lately, these leaders have voiced expectations that workers be able to think independently, to work creatively and cooperatively, and to continue learning (Reich, 1988). Barton and Kirsch (1990) reported that illiteracy is not the problem facing employers and the nation. Virtually all young people can perform simple tasks requiring the interpretation of written and numerical material. The real literacy problem is that most young people are unable to process information required to accomplish the moderately complex tasks encountered in the workplace and in everyday life (Barton & Kirsch, 1990).

The six national goals for education that were jointly developed and formally adopted by President Bush and the National Governors Association establish the basis for uniform accountability. Whereas these goals embrace social issues, such as learner wellness and drug-free schools, much attention is focused on school performance (e.g., improved graduation rates) and student competence, especially in English, mathematics, science, history, and geography (National Governors Association, 1990). National debates regarding who should monitor achievement of the national goals and how, and debates regarding state-by-state comparisons, reflect a trend already apparent at the state level—policymakers are using testing (mostly employing limited-response items) as an instrument of reform (Coley & Goertz, 1990).

Education professionals contend they should be responsible for developing and using assessment strategies that accurately reflect what is taught, rather than implementing assessment that defines and constrains what is taught (Madaus, 1988). They argue for the authority and the opportunity to integrate pedagogy, curriculum, and assessment in a manner that permits all students to demonstrate success. This objective is the basis of several impressive efforts to restructure schools, including the National Education Association's *Mastery In Learning Consortium* (Livingston, Castle, & Nations, 1989), the NEA *Learning Laboratory Initiative*, Ted Sizer's *Coalition of Essential Schools*, the American Federation of Teachers' *Professional Development Schools*, and Philip Schlechty's *Center for Leadership in School Reform* (Schlechty, Ingwerson, & Brooks, 1988).

Reform by Comparison

Although educators, parents, business leaders, and policymakers bring different perspectives to issues regarding assessment and accountability, all parties share a concern for improved student learning, including learning by those whom the system has failed (National Center on Education and the Economy, 1990; Quality Education for Minorities Project, 1990). State policymakers have expressed a clear preference for deregulation of school operations, but with accountability for results (National Governors Association, 1990). Rather than mandate school operations, the governors advise that state policy should create an environment that encourages educators to enact changes designed to realize improved student performance (National Governors Association, 1990). Contemporary reform strategies have shifted from mandates requiring more time in school and more courses for graduation, to mandating the outcomes of schooling. Coley and Goertz (1990) reported that states are establishing minimum course content and learning outcomes for most grade levels, developing model curriculum guides, linking curriculum to assessment, and requiring more tests. Within the past 5 years, five states have initiated statewide student assessment programs, and nearly half the states have expanded existing programs to include more grades and subjects, and to assess higher order skills. Presently, 47 states either mandate statewide testing or require local districts to administer their own student testing programs. State and local policy seek to deregulate school districts and schools, then to challenge educators to restructure schools—to implement changes in school organization and teaching practice required to improve student learning—and finally, to be accountable for results. The dominant means to measure these results, however, is student testing characterized by multiple-choice and other limited-response assessment.

Corbett and Wilson (1991) used the term *reform by comparison* to characterize this trend. The key features of reform by comparison are: (a) increased accountability for student performance at the school building level;

(b) uniform indicators of school outcomes; and (c) the inherently political motives of policymakers who are rewarded with recognition upon the initiation of reform, but either are gone from office when results are announced, or blame failure on other parties. Corbett and Wilson reported that using mandated statewide student testing as an instrument of reform produces a crisis orientation/quick-fix response at the local level, which actually compromises serious reform efforts such as curriculum development, improved pedagogical practice, and school restructuring. Because the publicly reported test scores imply an assessment of educator as well as of student performance, educators are likely to focus on improving the test scores, even at the expense of carefully developed reform strategies that may be in progress. In other words, educators abandon reform and try to do what has always been done, but do it better: get more students to perform at higher levels on the assessment.

On its face, it is difficult to argue with this result. Even the most cynical must admit that at some level improved test performance can be taken to indicate improved learning. However, when student performance is defined by the scores achieved on statewide, multiple-choice tests, the test score is the objective of education reform, and other important considerations are subordinated. or not addressed at all. What the tests measure is what is taught—recall and recognition of isolated bits of information—not thinking, or extended problem solving, or writing, or cooperation, or creativity. The public hears that a majority of the students fail to identify correctly their home state on a map of the country; the public does not hear more consequential things students can (or can not) do; for example, that a multi-aged group of students developed a proposal for enhancing waste management in the community. Reports of these scores in local newspapers create winners and losers, even when differences among students, schools, and school districts may be insignificantly small.

The stakes are high for all concerned, but the certain losers are the students who perform below the standard and the schools they attend. As reported by the National Governors Association (1990), policymakers are determined that consequences for poor performance must follow. Historically, the consequences for poor performance on statewide tests have been pressure, stigmatization, and subtle withdrawal of support: a new principal is brought in to improve the test scores; teachers decline assignment to, or seek transfers from, low-scoring schools; and authority to implement different instructional strategies may be reduced in favor of teaching methods designed for efficient and immediate test score improvements.

Perhaps the most ironic consequence of reform by comparison is that the current rhetoric suggests policymakers, business leaders, and educators now understand it is possible to enhance learning significantly for all students. It is possible to design learning and assessment to guide and reflect genuine intellectual development without incurring losers. When assessment and instruction require constructing a response or writing an essay, for example, the student reveals command of content and more. Assessment requiring the student to demonstrate what he or she knows creates empowerment through personal efficacy and integrity. The suggestion here is that assessment must, at least in part, address each student's strengths by permitting the demonstration of knowledge and capacity through multiple assessment techniques, not just through multiple-choice items. This is not to say that weakness should be ignored. Rather, students should have the opportunity to build new knowledge based on a solid foundation of confidence that they can learn, and that what they have learned will be recognized.

The work in Connecticut, California, and Kentucky offers encouragement that state education agencies are attempting to employ performance assessment as a key aspect of statewide student testing programs. It remains to be seen if these performance assessments and the data they produce become perverted by the political needs of policymakers.

Testing and Opportunity Allocation

Bernard Gifford (1989) offered another analytical perspective to discuss the role and influence of testing. Gifford suggested that education is a primary means of allocating opportunities in a free and open "opportunity marketplace." Those who prepare themselves through education and training will be rewarded with greater status and economic well-being. Access to education also operates in an opportunity marketplace, where institutions must "identify, evaluate, and compare the relative merits of individuals competing for scarce, high-reward educational, training, and employment opportunities" (p. 12). These opportunities are limited and range in value. The problem of a democracy is to insure that all citizens have a chance to compete for opportunities based on individual merit.

Merit implies worthiness, as well as probability of success. When merit is determined by performance on multiple-choice assessment, those who score well typically get enhanced educational or training opportunities (i.e., computers with modems may be provided to access databases and communicate with others). Those who do not score well typically get less enhanced opportunities (i.e., computers with drill and practice courseware). Limited-response assessment limits the educational prospects of students who fail because, frequently, they are required to do more of the same. The test data provided rarely inform practice so that deficiencies can be addressed specifically and rationally.

Gifford raised a very important and troublesome question: What kind of opportunity must a democracy afford those who fail? Today, one might add: What kind of opportunity must be provided such students in an economy that needs more workers earning at higher wages? The National Center on Education and the Economy (1990) has proposed that both job training and academic educational opportunities be viewed as a system of options that students may select at various points. No single choice precludes a very different option at some later time. The Center has also proposed a system of credentials with benchmarks signifying skill and expertise levels. Theoretically, this is an open system rich in opportunities. Such a system succeeds only if all parties have sufficient and appropriate assessment information—drawn from a multitude of sources—to guide the selection of options. It would appear that educational, political, and economic interests would be served, as multiple-choice assessment would necessarily be but one aspect of a comprehensive assessment program.

Testing and Reform: An Historical Perspective

The politics of assessment and accountability in public education involve the individual aspirations of parents and students, the work-force requirements of a rapidly changing and unpredictable economy, the needs of political leaders to be responsive to the well-documented problems of schools, and the efforts of educators to bring about changes that meet all of these. This conundrum is not new.

The experiment of universal public education has severely challenged the skill of education professionals and the will of the public at large. A recent publication from the National Education Association (1990), *In Its Own Image: Business and the Reshaping of Public Education*, discusses the impact of rapid social and economic change on education—first during the age of industrialization, urbanization, and immigration at the beginning of the century, and now at the end of the century, defined by an emerging global economy, rapidly developing technology, and an increasingly diverse citizenry.

It is well to remember that the system requiring reform today is the result of an earlier education reform. Critics such as Joseph Mayer Rice, Frederic Burke, and Ella Lynch, writing from 1892 through 1912, observed that the schools were wasteful, unintelligent, and failing to meet the needs of society (NEA, 1990). More specifically, educators were criticized for using drill and practice and rote memorization techniques as the most prevalent pedagogy. The content of such exercises was denounced as outdated and more appropriate for scholars than for young people destined to enter the world of work. Significantly, schools were criticized as wasteful because the curriculum was directed to the brightest few, and not to the majority who were children of immigrants and working people. These children were failing, repeating grades, and dropping out in large numbers. They were neither literate nor prepared for the vocations of the day.

During this time, the principles of scientific management were developed to manage the large industrial organizations, structures that would provide the employment opportunities for the nation. These management principles were soon embraced by schools.

Among the industrialists of education were Edward Thorndike, who helped develop intelligence testing—the means to sort students according to "ability"—and Charles Judd, who helped inspire the differentiated curriculum. Thorndike and Judd shared hereditarian and racial determinist attitudes compatible with principles of scientific management and efficiency (Lagemann, 1989). Their thinking was that each student should receive the amount and kind of education appropriate to his or her role in life. The "scientific" and efficient approach to curriculum required the selection of content and learning activities that would prepare students for specific pursuits. Large-scale intelligence testing objectively sorted students according to these destinies. To state the point another way,

> Just as industry did not try to make tires out of leather or seat coverings out of rubber, schools were being advised not to try to make engineers out of factory workers. Moreover, just as the process for manufacturing leather goods was distinct from the process for manufacturing rubber goods, so the process of producing engineers was necessarily distinct from the process for producing factory workers. (NEA, 1990, p. 28)

This view was seen as undemocratic by reformers such as John Dewey and others in the Progressive Education Association. This Association's child-centered pedagogy was based on the premise that content and learning activities must be geared to the developmental readiness of the student. No standard practice was appropriate for all children; no standard measure predetermined the child's role in life. The school was not an agent to mirror or maintain the social order by sorting students according to class. Rather, the process of education could change the social order by preparing students to assume positions in the workforce other than those occupied by their parents.

The influence of concern for economic productivity on education imperatives is as apparent today as it was during the first three decades of the 20th century. The need to organize large numbers of diverse students for the purpose of an appropriate and high quality education is as urgent now as it was then. The performance outcomes for schools during the industrial age of the first three decades were literacy, reliability, and discipline. These skills were compatible with the standardized behavior of the assembly line where most students would find jobs. Research and development were invested in the technology, not in the workers. If the worker followed the rules, he or she would perform well in the workforce.

The criticism of education voiced during the early 20th century is familiar, but today's economic context is quite different. Although higher levels of literacy are needed, the precise skills required in the workforce of the future are unclear. Therefore, today's workers must first be able to learn. They must also have the confidence to accept responsibility for problem solving—on the assembly line as well as in the front office. They must be able to analyze and communicate potential solutions. These skills are not adequately assessed by multiple-choice items alone.

CONCLUSION

School deregulation and restructuring of curriculum and pedagogy are underway. The objective is to create schools that work for all students, but there is no one right answer. The challenge for the measurement professional is to create new systems of accountability that are substantively meaningful, extensive, and understandable. The research to develop extended-response, performance assessment is underway and the prospects are hopeful. Now is the time to begin carefully planned conversations with policymakers so that unworthy political ends do not interfere. For example, policymakers must learn that when an elementary school begins to implement child-centered, active science instruction, it is not appropriate to demand that the science scores on multiple-choice tests improve next year. In such a case, the school should be required to communicate information about student projects, appreciation of science, attendance (students and staff), and use of up-to-date scientific resources and information.

Accountability systems must begin to address factors in addition to narrow conceptions of student achievement. New assessment technologies permit the assessment of knowledge and skills well beyond those appropriately measured by limited-response assessment. We must exploit the power of that potential. The assessment community must provide ever more assertive leadership towards ending reform by comparison and creating the reality of reform by student empowerment. This is the case in which all students are validated by what they know, and that validation provides the foundation for future learning. As previously suggested, this is the case in which there are no losers.

But more to the interest of all, can we tolerate a system that fails no one? Can our economy and our personal efficacy survive without the competitive traditions embedded in reform by comparison and so conveniently operationalized through multiple-choice tests? These questions constitute the political test for educators and for the country. We cannot afford to fail.

REFERENCES

Barton, P. E., & Kirsch, I. S. (1990). *Workplace competencies: The need to improve literacy and employment readiness.* Washington, DC: United States Department of Education.

Bennett, R. E., Ward, W. C., Rock, D. A., & LaHart, C. (1990). *Toward a framework for constructed-response items* (RR-90-7). Princeton, NJ: Educational Testing Service.

Coley, R. J., & Goertz, M. E. (1990). *Educational standards in the 50 states: 1990* (RR-90-15). Princeton, NJ: Educational Testing Service.

Corbett, H. D., & Wilson, B. L. (1991). *Testing, reform and rebellion.* Norwood, NJ: Ablex.

Elam, S. M. (1990). The 22nd annual Gallup poll of the public's attitudes toward the public schools. *Phi Delta Kappan, 72*(1), 41–55.

Gardner, H. (1983). *Frames of mind: The theory of multiple intelligences.* New York: Basic Books.

Gardner, H. (1988). *Assessment in context: The alternative to standardized testing.* Unpublished manuscript, Harvard University, Cambridge, MA.

Gifford, B. R. (1989). The allocation of opportunities and the politics of testing: A policy analytic perspective. In B. Gifford (Ed.), *Test policy and the politics of opportunity allocation: The workplace and the law* (pp. 3–31). Boston, MA: Kluwer Academic Publishers.

Lagemann, E. C. (1989). The plural worlds of education research. *History of Education Quarterly, 29*(2), 184–214.

Livingston, C., Castle, S., & Nations, J. (1989). *Testing, curriculum, and the limits of empowerment.* Paper presented at the annual meeting of the American Educational Research Association, San Francisco.

Madaus, G. (1988). The influence of testing on the curriculum. In L. H. Tanner (Ed.), *Critical issues in curriculum* (87th Yearbook of the National Society for the Study of Education, pp. 83–121). Chicago, IL: University of Chicago Press.

Mullis, I., Owen, E. H., & Phillips, G. W. (1990). *America's challenge: Accelerating academic achievement. A summary of findings from 20 years of NAEP* (Report No. 19-OV-01). Princeton, NJ: Educational Testing Service.

National Center on Education and the Economy. (1990). *America's choice: High skills or low wages!* Report of the Commission on the Skills of the American Workforce. Rochester, NY: Author.

National Education Association. (1990). *In its own image: Business and the reshaping of public education.* Washington, DC: Author.

National Governors Association. (1990). *Educating America: State strategies for achieving the national goals* (Report of the Task Force on Education). Washington, DC: Author.

Quality Education for Minorities Project. (1990). *Education that works: An action plan for the education of minorities.* Washington, DC: Author.

Reich, R. B. (1988). *Education and the next economy.* Washington, DC: National Education Association.

Rothman, R. (1990). Survey shows expansion in programs to test students, teachers since 1985. *Education Week, 10*(5), 16.

Schlechty, P. C., Ingwerson, D. W., & Brooks, T. I. (1988). Inventing professional development schools. *Educational Leadership, 46*(3), 28–31.

Shepard, L. (1989). Why we need better assessments. *Educational Leadership, 46*(7), 4.

Sternberg, R. (1987). *A triarchic theory of human intelligence.* New York: Cambridge University Press.

AUTHOR INDEX

Page numbers in *italics* denotes complete bibliographical information.

325

Subject Index